Taxation, the State and Society

The Fiscal Sociology of Interventionist Democracy

P.I.E. Peter Lang

Bruxelles · Bern · Berlin · Frankfurt am Main · New York · Oxford · Wien

Marc Leroy

Taxation, the State and Society

The Fiscal Sociology of Interventionist Democracy

"Public Action" series
No.7

Original edition: *L'impôt, l'État et la société. La sociologie fiscale de la démocratie interventionniste*, Paris, Economica, 2010.

Translated from French: chapters 1, 3, 4 by Pierre Van Zyl; chapters 5, 6, 7, 8 by Kseniya Khovanova; Introduction, chapters 2, 9, 10, 11, 12, conclusion by Lussiana Beloshinova.

Translation reviewed by Pierre Van Zyl and by the author and partly financed by a grant of the CRDT Reims.

Éditions scientifiques internationales
Brussels, 2011
1 avenue Maurice, B-1050 Brussels, Belgique
www.peterlang.com ; info@peterlang.com

ISSN 1783-6077
ISBN 978-90-5201-697-9
D/2011/5678/32

Printed in Germany

Library of Congress Cataloging-in-Publication Data
Leroy, Marc, 1957- Taxation, the state, and society : the fiscal sociology of interventionist democracy / Marc Leroy.
p. cm. -- (Public action ; no. 7) Includes bibliographical references.
ISBN 978-90-5201-697-9 1. Taxation--Social aspects.
2. Fiscal policy. 3. Finance, Public. I. Title. II. Series.
HJ2305.L47 2011 336.2--dc22 2011005528

CIP also available from the British Library, GB.

"Die Deutsche Bibliothek" lists this publication in the "Deutsche Nationalbibliografie"; detailed bibliographic data is available at http://dnb.d-nb.de.

Contents

Contents

List of Tables, Boxes and Figures

Introduction

This book investigates the fundamental relationship between taxation, the State and society in our democracies, based on the development of a social science, fiscal sociology. Viewed as a political phenomenon, taxes have also been a field of study of economics for a long time. It is also a social process, of which the sociologist Tocqueville had an intuition in the context of the causes of the French Revolution or the tendency of the increase of public expenditure. Fiscal sociology is far-reaching in terms of its disciplines, general in terms of the set of problems it tackles, and empirical in terms of the diversity of the materials used. The importance of the fiscal State justifies the questioning of interventionist democracy as a real and ethical socio-political process.

1. The Importance of Multidisciplinary Fiscal Sociology

Being a result of financial sociology which appeared during the First World War, fiscal sociology constitutes an important approach to understanding the evolution of Western societies. The founders of the Austrian school of this meta-discipline have well perceived that the emergence of the modern State in Europe should be sought mainly in the establishment of a permanent tax system related to public action. Thus, ever since its formation, fiscal sociology has offered a major alternative to the Marxist interpretation of the State by discussing the evolution of capitalism. Without neglecting the economy, in particular currently through the effects of neo-liberal financial globalization, it sheds light on the importance of the socio-political development of fiscal State. In this respect, it also differentiates from Durkheim's analysis of the State as a functional response to the complexity produced by the division of labour. In addition, it relativizes the historical primacy of legal rational bureaucratization studied by Weber.

Goldscheid and Schumpeter create fiscal sociology as a result of their interest in the tax State crisis. They have conflicting approaches: Goldscheid is inspired by Marx, but upon revising his erroneous outlook on the State, predicts its collapse; Schumpeter, adhering to an ambiguous liberalism, rightly maintains that its financial failure is improbable in the developed countries. Historically related to the formation of the modern European State, this political issue of taxation has continued to play an essential role since the "crisis" of the interventionist State. The slump in the summer of 2008 gives a new vent to this problematic aspect as it led to public intervention at the end involving the taxpayers to bolster up the banking sector and stimulate the economy. Represented by Pareto, his followers and other authors in the financial science, the Italian school supports the Machiavellian tradition. From this point of view, public finance is considered as means for the elite to stay in power. The two schools have of course proposed other ideas for investigation. Mann, in particular, and some Italians, in their own way, introduced an approach based on the socio-political functions of taxation, an approach which has fallen into oblivion. Since then the literature refers more to the economic functions to the detriment of fruitful reflection on social regulation by the fiscal State.

After its creation by the founders, fiscal sociology experiences uneven development over different periods and in different countries. It tends to be divided into an economic approach and a socio-political approach which mobilize mainly Anglo-Saxon studies. Its scientific market depends on the attitude shown by the administration and individual societies towards overcoming the obstacles to the demand and the technical specialization of the supply of knowledge, devolved to lawyers and economists. The longitudinal approach suggests a relation, sometimes altered over time, with the evolution of the interventionist State. With the generalization of Keynesian and social politics, a consensus legitimates the tax State by the financing of its economic and social activity. A general reflection on financial public activity is substituted by the specialized study of taxpayers' behaviour, associated to the progress of social psychology. The underlying purpose is to reinforce tax compliance in order to finance Welfare State intervention. By focusing on the social attitudes, these studies ignore tax policy.

The economic crisis of the 1970s gives rise to a radical criticism of the interventionist State. The Public Choice school, based on the Rational Choice Theory, defends the doctrine of tax aversion, which completes that of the limitation of social expenses. The neo-Marxist analysis of the tax State's crisis also casts doubt on the legitimacy of taxation.

After the 1990's fiscal sociology is renewed. The context of economic globalization fuels the debate on the retrenchment of the State. The domination of utilitarianism (self-interest) is discussed on the basis of economic psychology whose success is explained by the recourse to the experimental method. It appears that taxpayers are (also) altruists when the fiscal State is legitimate. The enrichment of the studies in fiscal sociology is nourished by new domains, such as decentralization, developing countries, the former Soviet republics etc., and by several disciplines.

Fiscal sociology plays an essential role for researchers, citizens and decision-makers: as a matter of fact, the tax system is at the core of politics, constituting an original form of public action affecting society. Taxes are at the same time an instrument of the other public policies, benefiting enterprises, social categories, certain sectors etc., and an object of public policy through the tax redistribution of revenues, public program financing etc. It is a fundamental process of categorization, stratification and functionalization of society, and includes the relation with the market. It is therefore unfortunate that fiscal sociology has suffered the effects of the division of the financial science into specialized disciplines with a predominantly technicist vision. The diversification of public policies in developed countries and the specialization of scientific knowledge tend to create particularist models of knowledge, decisions and reforms. The interventionist State instrumentalizes the taxation to the detriment of the citizen-taxpayer. Beyond fiscal techniques, a global social science on taxes introduces a critical dialogue with the normative approaches of economics and law. Financial sociol ogy studies public budgets, while fiscal sociology focuses on research material proper to taxes.

By relying on a multidisciplinary approach, the purpose of fiscal sociology is to deal with fiscal phenomena in accordance with a general societal and political outlook. It focuses on the process of the intervention of public institutions in tax matters. It questions the legitimacy of the State for the citizen and proposes a reflection on social justice. It converts empirical data into models with wide-ranging influence. In this way fiscal sociology proposes a fundamental issues for public action and social sciences: tax reform is tied to social change; the administrative implementation of taxes leads to theories of bureaucratic regulation (in the business world in particular); the social acceptance of taxes refers to the legitimacy of public policies; tax burden is assessed in the real-life context of fiscal justice; tax evasion is explained by a sociology of deviance which studies the delegitimization of functional norms of public action; tax revolt, as a form of collective activity, reveals political dysfunction; taxpayer decision is a matter for a model of rationality subsuming the utilitarian model of interest: it validates the relevance of an altruist concept of the contribution-tax founded on political values and specific reasoning (cognitive rationality) etc.

Having a broad outlook due to its subject and sets of problems it deals with, this general social science is based on a hybridization of topics imported from several disciplines. Indeed taxation constitutes a "total social fact" as defined by Mauss: its study originates from several types of sociology.

Fiscal sociology is a political sociology because of its orientation towards the State, power and public action. Close to political science, it is different from it because of its sensitiveness to the societal dimension. Historically linked to the modern European State, the political dimension of taxation remains essential (marked by the crisis of the 1970's, by globalization etc.). The dialectic of taxation is that of an obligation to the sovereign authority and of a legitimately assented contribution to public policies. The tension between the constraint, like that of the globalized market, and the political choice of tax functions must be resolved in the framework of citizenship in democracy. It also has to do with the management of public decisions, with reforms, bureaucratic changes, the neo-liberal ideological impact etc.

Fiscal sociology is a legal sociology when it studies the connections between tax law and society. Its relation to technicist law is critical. For example, tax audit leads to questioning on the social mechanisms of the official qualification of fraud, on the strategic use of fiscal procedure, on national types of administrative regulation, on the determining factors of dispute etc.

Fiscal sociology is an economic sociology which goes beyond the limits of the rigid theory of rational choice (utilitarianism). It borrows the already old approach of social economics, but insists on the importance of the tax State. It shows a particular interest in the impact of economic globalization, in the "social contract" for the taxation of capital and labour, in the spreading of the guidelines of (the new) public management.

In the strict sense, the social science of taxation is a sociological discipline when the societal perspective leads to theorizing fiscal facts as being processes of society. Fiscal sociology does not however make a well-defined academic discipline. While there is extensive literature material concerning the Welfare State, it remains relatively less developed[1], despite its practical importance for individuals and public policies. In its theoretical models, fiscal sociology uses official data, its own materials, the results of fiscal psychology, of financial history, of economic psychology etc. It resorts to historical, cognitive and functional methods. Thus, the study of the genesis of royal taxation in the Middle Ages brings forward the typical ideal characteristics of the modern State. The logic of the knowledge of taxes explains the citizen's rational attitude towards this "obligation". The political, social, territorial and environmental functions of tax policies complete the economic and financial approach etc.

---

1 Sociologists do not show much interest in taxation (Leroy, 2002, p. 5; Morgan, Prasad, 2009, p. 1350). In addition, in certain countries like France, tax policy has been in a large extent ignored by public policy analysis.

2. The Fiscal State and Interventionist Democracy

This book has a double objective: on the one hand, it gives an integrated presentation of compartmentalized studies of taxation as a socio-political phenomenon; on the other hand, it explores the logic of interventionist democracy which is built around the fiscal State.

Regarding the first objective, it consists in constituting a corpus of data by uniting into one reflection studies and data dispersed in specialities that largely ignore each other. These studies usually divide the socio-political phenomenon of taxation into separate objects such as taxpayers, tax policies, revenue distribution etc. The particular approaches of each discipline often still struggle to go beyond technicist specializations. In the spirit of the fiscal sociology programme outlined above, our research uses, next to such dominant disciplines as fiscal law and taxation economics, the results of sociology, political science, management, and economic, experimental, cognitive and social psychology etc.

This effort is attested by the bibliography: a variety of publications from all disciplines has been quoted in order to reflect as best as possible the present state of knowledge. Certain choices are inevitable in order to ensure a delicate equilibrium between the precision and the clarity of the analyses. Some elaborations have therefore been excluded and others cut short with the intention to focus on the most interesting aspects. For example, by opting to go in depth into the unrecognized contribution of Tocqueville as pioneer in fiscal sociology, we have chosen not to quote a great deal of good authors. Purely legal accounts are summarized in order to emphasize their socio-political interpretation. The list of case studies, that includes numerous areas, could be extended even more etc. These choices will perhaps leave specialists in certain fields unsatisfied, while at the same time less informed or more hurried readers may regret the details and undertones provided. In spite of these limits due to the editorial format of a written work, the reader will find a big inventory of references, including public finance studies, especially on social expenses.

The second objective is to lay the bases of a democratic theory of political choices. A normative and ethical perspective is thus opened up, based on the results of studying the intervention of the fiscal State with regard to the civic society. Fiscal sociology sets the conditions of a civic idea of a "contribution-tax" to public action. Related to financing that support public policies, the execution of a social contract on interventionist democracy is then possible, even if there are numerous obstacles to the democratization of public action.

Without being concerned about maintaining a literary suspense less suited to scientific work, it is helpful to present the framework of our research, all the more so given the complex nature of the subject. The book consists of twelve chapters structured around the double prospect presented. Chapter 1 draws up a model of all the cumulative variables considered by Tocqueville in order to establish the law of the tendency of democratic State spending to increase. The discovery of this law, which is linked to subsequent studies of the economist Wagner, justifies the labeling of this founder of sociology as a pioneer of fiscal sociology. Drawing up a model of the study of the fiscal causes of French revolution set out in *L'Ancien Régime et la Révolution* completes this presentation. On a more normative level, one of the first foundations of the democratic theory of financial political choices is thus put forward, even though the intricacy of the evolution of the fiscal State requires other analyses.

Chapter 2 concentrates on the direct founders of fiscal sociology by looking at the Austrian and Italian schools. We have already mentioned the interest of the work produced by Goldscheid, Schumpeter and Mann. The Italian fiscal sociology is less well-known. It appears to be less homogeneous, even though it is influenced by the Machiavelli's thinking which separates the governing elite from those being governed. It is linked to the development of a science of finances, not in its purely economic aspect (marginalism), but in its (socio-political) aspect that concentrates on government. Current literature has retained Puviani's theory of fiscal illusion. On this basis, economists postulate the irrationality from taxpayers in their demand for public services, which is erroneous: for taxpayers, the idea (cognitive rationality) is that there are means for financing other than taxes, for example loans or the reallocation of expenses. In any case, the variety of the other contributions of the Italian school has been neglected.

Pareto deserves a separate place, he who, even though he taught in Lausanne, is linked to this Italian tradition by the influence he exercised on it notably through his followers. The ideas initiated in *Traité de sociologie générale* start by criticizing the financial science in order to prove that public finance depends on non-logical actions performed in the service of the ruling elite. In spite of his popularity as a classical figure in economics and sociology, Pareto's unfinished financial theory is known but to a few. It forms part of the complex research of a social equilibrium related to the circulation of elites. It accepts limited methodological "approximations" emphasizing the role of the economic cycle, ideology, clientelism and despoliation of certain social classes. This analysis, even if it is imperfect, provides an interesting counterpoint to the democratic theory of political choices. The tendency for public expenditure is denounced; but unlike Tocqueville or Wagner, the key factor of this "plutocracy" resides in the clientelism of the ruling elite.

Chapter 3 describes the path fiscal sociology has followed in its formation as a social science according to the approach presented above. It also includes a study of the sociology of knowledge which reveals the factors for its institutional recognition.

Chapter 4 contains a historical, intellectual and typological analysis of the fiscal State in Europe. The characteristics of the "modern" tax State are explained by the establishment of a royal taxation modifying the socio-political structures of feudalism. Permanent taxes become an attribute to the sovereign power of the national State. It fulfils financing functions, originally in times of war, functions that claim to be based on the general interest. This view differs from the Weberian model of bureaucratization and of the relation between domination and legitimacy. As the founders of fiscal sociology have understood it, it is precisely the search for the means of financing which has given shape to modern State: rationality, of a cognitive type, relates to the concrete justification of public action through taxes, by generalizing certain particular cases, such as feudal aid; this rationality is not formal and legal as it leaves a space for sheer moments of absolute domination (French monarchy), assigning at the same time a future role to tax consent. Through this turbulent historical and intellectual genesis, the fiscal State has asserted itself as a tension between the free consent of citizens, even if this political trait was not acknowledged by all, and the obligation of the sovereign who holds the power. The history of ideas, illustrated in this chapter by a brief presentation of the tax doctrines of Bodin, Bossuet, Smith, Montesquieu and Rousseau, confirms the importance of this tension between sovereignty and legitimacy. But for the democratic theory of political choices, it is finally the second pillar of public action that really matters. So the problem of the legitimacy of the State is posed by a typology which cross references the level of taxation and the level of intervention of public expenditure.

Chapter 5 presents another level of analysis, that of the public finance system. It confirms the reality of Western interventionist States whose effects on the economy and society are proven. The evolution of public expenditure, explained for the main part by social public activity, is characteristic for interventionist democracy. The extension of social rights, which would lead to the Keynesian Welfare State, despite some slight differences, forms part of the democratic theory of political choices. In fact, 19th century liberal ideas aiming to restrict the intervention of the State clash with the social issue which would be settled by the Welfare State. The socio-financial democratic contract extends social protection, public health care and education; as counterpart, it establishes mass taxation, according to different agreements.

This system is also that of rich countries. It contrasts with the system of developing countries where the fragility of tax revenue (including social security) is explained by the difficulties to institutionalize the fiscal State. Socio-economic differences should of course be taken into consideration when differentiating States living on rents from manna in the form of oil from States without natural resources, countries with an emerging economy from the rest, countries with a big informal sector from those with a more market-oriented economy etc. It appears here that the tax pressure (revenue) in developing countries is explained by the level of economic development. But the economic approach cannot on its own take into account the logic of the fiscal State which is political. This view supposes that one must define a relation to the democratization of working-class claims as a means of ensuring social services which are in a dramatic way deficient in these countries. It is also advisable not to eliminate specific kinds of social solidarity through an imitation (mimetism), constrained or voluntary, based on the Western "model".

Chapter 6 examines the relative influence of the causes of fiscal policy (including public expenditure) summarized in literature in a somewhat simplified list of ideas, institutions and interests. The influence of ideas is important for the conception of public finance. The transit from the neutrality of liberal ideas proper to the 19th century to the interventionist ideas of post-war social Keynesianism illustrates this observation. The effect of neo-liberalism appearing in the 1970s is specifically discussed in the symbolic case of anti-fiscal ideological clichés. The referential frame of budget performance, imposed at the end of the 1990s in many countries, is analyzed in its problematic relation with the political regulation of the choices of society. Institutions, shaping public policies, also find their place inspired by law in the classic sense, and by political science in the more modern sense. More specifically, the role played by the parliament, which varies in each country, is perceived as a challenge set by representative democracy. Other variables, such as the impact of veto points, are also examined. The influence of socio-economic groups is especially perceptible because of their access to institutions and the general validity of their arguments. The paramount importance of ideas can be found by not absolutizing the powerful pressure of interests, especially validated by studies of the American case. The left-right division affects expenditure especially during certain periods that appear more "ideologically charged". We also observe that programmes of political parties are rarely implemented in a radical way.

In conformity with the epistemology of this work, the level of analysis of the elemental factors of public policy is completed by the study of the causal biases of public action which are obstacles to democracy. Chapter 7, using empirical data, thus unmasks the ideology of constraints in its deterministic settings. In fact, the true causal variable is of cognitive nature. It is based on a reasoning centered on the fake necessities of crises (fiscal, military, economic, social etc.). In the same way, the weight of institutions appears exaggerated.[2] But it is especially the determinism of market constraints, that have become globalized, that is criticized. Since the 1990s the neo-liberal ideology of economic globalization has found a scientific echo in the theory of market efficiency. Nevertheless, as is demonstrated by the theory of compensation, the fiscal Welfare State shows firm resilience; it uses social expenditure to compensate for the negative effects of globalization. The complexity of converting interventionist fiscal policy into an instrument of action furthers this form of democratic alienation. The configuration of public action is distorted by the ideology of causal biases which conceals the reality of the choices of decision-makers. The political choices opened up by each context are denied. The fiscal State taxes the masses, while at the same time taking advantage of its power of exemption with respect to certain groups and tolerating a self-referential institutional game.

Fiscal democracy remains an ideal of public action to be achieved through a coherent fiscal policy. Chapter 8 deals with implementing fiscal policy within the framework of bureaucratic issues. It describes the administrative logic in the field of the history of French modernization and of the original organization of tax control. The bureaucratic regulation of tax evasion is questioned when compared with certain classical theories of bureaucracy. It is established depending on the model of performance which in many countries sets the basis of public management reforms. It is also confronted with the conception of new public management which validates, with unquestionable success, the cooperation with the business world. This conception is the subject of a critical deconstruction, starting from the case of re-invoicing goods or services provided within multinational corporations in the global market context (the case of transfer prices)

The logic of the individual with regard to taxes is the subject of chapter 9. The lessons of the complex history of tax revolts help to build

2 European Union legal criteria relative to limiting the deficit and debt of member states acquire a political overtone as is proven by the difficulties to impose sanctions on countries which failed to observe the Maastricht Treaty, as well as by the relaxation brought about by the Treaty of Amsterdam. The current extent of public expenditure on economic stimulation also questions the future effectiveness of this policy.

up the sociology of individual tax decisions. The level of analysis is that of the theory of rational choice that creates the individualist methodology of utilitarian interest. But the approach is broadened to the axiological rationality which goes back to the idea of the centrality of the political legitimacy of taxes, while at the same time settling the question of moral values. It also relies on cognitive rationality which examines the taxpayers' practical (concrete) reasoning, their way of processing information at hand. This third form of rationality allows one to clarify a certain number of enigmas (issues) like: the evaluation of the risk of tax audit (fiscal control), the relation experienced between taxes and public expenditure, the "painless" nature of indirect taxes such as the VAT etc. There again numerous empirical details are brought together. They show the limits of the utilitarian model whose scope is relativized. "Contribution-tax" is defined as citizen participation in general interest programmes. It reflects a credible sociological representation. It is opposed to taxes based on an "obligation" or "constraint" or a "tribute" that indicate the intensity of the fiscal burden, and to "exchange-tax" considered to be the price fiscally owed in exchange for services received by the individual.

The possibility of a "contribution-tax", on the more or less altruistic grounds of citizen consent, depends on the legitimacy of public action. This result constitutes another basis for the democratic theory of political choices. It justifies the criticism of the clichés of the anti-fiscal neo-liberal ideology, by supporting the following particular proposition, not very well-known: tax revenue (including social security) is not adverse to economic growth (cf. the Nordic countries) and does not necessarily foster fraud. Besides, from the point of view of procedural democracy, empirical evidence shows that participation in fiscal choices encourages the tax compliance. The problem of tax deviance is thus restated politically at the collective level of society. Chapter 10 deals with this question by firstly highlighting the state, difficult to assess, of the unofficial economy and of the tax evasion (fraud). The labeling of tax deviance is studied by means of a typology cross referencing decisions of public authorities with intentions of taxpayers to minimize taxes. This task is completed with a classification in socio-economic categories of the forms of tax minimization, which distinguishes between the large enterprises, the rest of the enterprises, the wage earners, those "excluded" and the economy of crimes. This is then followed by a reflection on the deviations of the socio-political regulation exercised by the tax State. The degradation of fiscal normativity is related to the axiological evolution of the interventionist role of public action with regard to the market. Under the impact of neo-liberal ideology, the norm of the minimization of corporate taxes is spread out. This leads to the international competition between States who offer attractive advantages for investments of the globalized market.

Chapter 11 pursues this reflection by studying the destabilization of the functions of the tax State. While also being wary of hyper-functionalism, it uses a renewed approach, based on financial, economic regulation, social, territorial, environmental and political functions of taxes. Taxation constitutes in general the principal revenue of public budgets. This function of financing public services is in competition with tax expenditure (advantages leading to the renouncing of revenue) and more and more with loans. While public debt increases as a result of the massive public interventions to curb the effects of the 2008 crisis, tax expenditure progressively fulfils microeconomic objectives. With the decline of Keynesian policies, the macro-regulation of the economy finds less usage. The policies of decreasing taxes (income and corporate taxes) have not always resulted in a reduction of tax revenue (including social security) because the tax basis was increased or other taxes were modified. The social function of taxation is evaluated with regard to the major challenge of the redistribution of income. This includes a study of the impact of social transfers (social redistribution). The results, although uneven depending on the country, show a failure to stop the escalation of inequalities in the era of economic and financial globalization.

Other social issues are concerned, such as the fiscal classification of families, the Workfare aimed for by the negative tax, the "vices" (taxation of gambling, spirits, tobacco etc.). The territorial function includes geographical sovereignty and the differentiated treatment of certain privileged territories (tax havens). It evolves towards difficult attempts to establish an ecology-oriented tax system in order to ensure sustainable development that shows consideration for the environment. The political function is at the core of the legitimacy of the fiscal State. The challenge consists in succeeding to establish the figure of the contribution-tax consented to democratically. Here one should not underestimate the neo-liberal movement calling into question the social-fiscal compromises of the Keynesian Welfare State, despite their resilience. It presents a tendency towards the axiological de-functionalization of the interventionist democracy of the "the Glorious Thirty" years by promoting market supremacy.

Chapter 12 treats the difficult issues concerning globalization and Europe directly. Durkheim's theory of anomie is used to analyze the neo liberal globalization of economics. They become more and more financial, accompanied by a succession of social injustices (deregulation, inequalities, employment crisis, destruction of the real economy etc.) and from this point of view that appears harmful. The loss of the social markers of economic globalization has become chronic in line with the Durkheimian model. But this is furthermore coupled with a perverse transformation of the regulation of the fiscal State which disrupts the social contract of the interventionist democracy. The absence of international regulation, based on the social logic of the human world, and not on a perverted ideology of the market, is at issue. As is illustrated by the tax competition between States or the growth of tax havens helping the globalization of profits, the soft law of international organizations is insufficient for the establishment of a social functionality. Tax Europe, in spite of certain achievements, is blocked in its normative conception of the market and in its institutional rules of unanimous decision-making. Its deficiencies in social matters are evident and its political legitimacy presents problems. No lessons have been learnt from the democratic theory of political choices in order to fight inequalities. In fact, the redistribution of income does not depend on a natural mechanism of cyclical stabilization, but on the vigour of the counterweight of democracy.

The conclusion therefore invites us to reflect on the elaboration of a new social contract of interventionist democracy on the basis of the fiscal State and with the ideal of an international political regulation.

CHAPTER 1

Tocqueville Pioneer of Fiscal Sociology

It is no wonder that Tocqueville was interested in public finance[1]: his political responsibilities, his interest for monarchic and democratic institutions could only lead him to these questions. It is therefore not surprising to find in the first *Democracy in America*, centered on institutions, a certain quantity of legal information.[2] The fiscal field is also used to illustrate or test different notions.[3] The second *Democracy* had hardly any observations on public finance.[4] In the same way, in his *Souvenirs*, Tocqueville several times referred to financial matters[5], but generally only in an anecdotic way. In spite of their importance for

1 This chapter contains parts of my article: cf. Leroy, 2010, *European Journal of Sociology* 51 (2). I thank the Editor of this Cambridge Journal for permission.

2 The tax and budgetary competence of the commune, the obligation to finance schools by taxes, the separation between tax assessors and tax collectors, the obligation of the commune to contribute to the State budget, the budgetary procedure and the power of the county to raise taxes etc.

3 The incidence of taxes on the freedom of trade, the salaries of civil servants employed by a democratic regime, the limitation of wars by the democratic control of public funds, the difficulty to tax alcohol, the impact of military expenditure, the financial relations between the States of the Federation…

4 Tocqueville mentions the taxation of the press, an obstacle which seems less important for him than the suppression of local freedoms. He quotes a letter of Madame de Sévigné relating, without emotion, the repression of a tax revolt to show that "real sympathies exist only between similar people" (2004, p. 656). He notes the tendency, widespread in Europe, to look for public employment "at the expense of the public treasury" (2004, p. 745). He recalls that, for centuries before the Revolution, individuals or independent bodies had raised taxes and that the sovereign, for a long time, "lived on the revenue from his land" (2004, p. 806). In modern times, "through borrowing the State thus attracts the money of the rich, and through saving institutions it gains the ability to do as it wishes with the pennies of the poor" (2004, p. 807).

5 Concerning the struggle that between 1789 and 1830 opposed the defenders of the *Ancien Régime* to the middle class, he points out that the latter lived nearly as much off the Treasury as off their own industry. Once more he denounces the inclination for public employment, the desire to live off taxes, that affects all political parties. Evoking the 1848 revolution in Paris, he refers to the abolition of the property (tax) qualification for the franchise, to the popular pressure to tax the rich, to the creation of new taxes, to the cost of the organization of working class celebrations in spite of the terrible state of public finances, and to the vote by the Assembly of a pension to the families of those that would succumb in order to defend the government against the June rioters.

erudition, these passages would not justify to retain Tocqueville except as a classical author in a fiscal anthology which lies outside our subject. The reason for this chapter comes from an unknown aspect of the thinking of the great sociologist that gives him the place of a pioneer in fiscal sociology. In fact Tocqueville was not satisfied only to describe the functioning of financial institutions included in his field of study. He placed public finance at the core of his analyses by exploring its relationship with society and the State within the framework of problem areas concerning the evolution of public expenditure in democratic societies, and the role of taxation and financial centralization in the Revolution.

Box 1: Public finance at the core of society and politics (Tocqueville)

Several times Tocqueville stressed the importance of public finance in order to understand society and politics, anticipating the conviction of the founders of fiscal sociology (cf. chapter 2). He looks closely at taxation in order to analyze the centralization brought about by the French monarchy of the Ancien Régime: "let us start with the right of taxation, which to some extent contains all other rights" (Tocqueville, 1998, p. 121). He puts forward the financial supervision of the central administration over towns and cities (1998, p. 128). He emphasizes that the confiscation of local liberties by the central administration did not prevent the financial difficulties of towns in the 18th century: "if only this strict submission by the towns had preserved their finances!" (p. 128) He considers the financial needs of the government to be at the origin of numerous institutions: "if you find some old establishment from the Middle Ages which continued to exist (…) or some pernicious innovation (…) you will find a financial expedient that turned into an institution" (1998, p. 167).

He also chooses taxes as a field of predilection of the privileges that contributed to provoke the Revolution in France: "Let us take the most hateful of all these privileges, that of tax exemption" (1998, p. 156). Tax inequality is considered by Tocqueville to be the most serious inequality, as is illustrated by the exemptions of the tallage in favour of the nobility, the clergy and certain bourgeois. Fiscal inequality is disastrous for the division of social classes, because "of all the ways to make distinctions between people and classes, inequality of taxation is the most pernicious and the most apt to add isolation to inequality" (1998, p. 157). Taxation, which becomes more moderate in its application, is also used to show the will of governments to ensure the well-being and prosperity of the country: "it is chiefly in the collection of taxes that one can best see the change which had occurred in the minds of those who governed" (1998, p. 219).

Tocqueville also appears as a pioneer of fiscal sociology when he uses taxation as an indicator, in the meaning of modern science, of a social phenomenon. Thus, within the framework of his analysis of social classes, he points out that "the peasant had not only ceased to be a serf, he had become a landowner" (1998, p. 112). In order to establish this socio-economic reality (property), he refers to the data of the documents establishing land taxes. In the same way, to prove another one of his governing ideas, namely that the French nobility deserted the French countryside in the 18th century, he referred to the capitation: that tax, collected at the domicile, comes in large part from the payments of the nobles in Paris (1998, p. 180). In another part of *L'Ancien Régime*, where he wanted to show that public prosperity had improved, he points out, amongst different indicators, the increase of consumption taxes (1998, p. 220).

1. Tocqueville and the Expenditures of Democracy

In chapter 5 of the second part of (the first) *Democracy in America*, Tocqueville examines "what influence democracy has on state finances" (Tocqueville, 2004, p. 239). To this essential question he gives an answer which in itself justifies his classification as a pioneer of financial sociology. In fact, using a complex analysis[6], he puts forward the general tendency towards the increase of public expenditures of democratic societies, which would be known after him as Wagner's law (Wagner was born in 1835, the year of the publication of the first *Democracy in America*). According to Tocqueville, in spite of objections which depend especially on method, the cumulative effect of the relative factors explains that public expenditures "tend to increase when the people govern" (p. 238).

a. Tocqueville's financial method

In the same way as modern financial analysis, Tocqueville points out that "one must determine, first, the wealth of the nation and, second, the portion of that wealth devoted to State expenses" (p. 246). The problem is that these data (measured today in relation to GDP) do not exist at that time. We also do not know "how much each citizen of the Union pays annually to underwrite society's expenditures" (p. 249). Tocqueville then retains as indicators which he calls "signs": apparent wealth, disposable income, the satisfaction of citizens, and the presence of capital for industry and of industrial opportunities for capital. From these indicators he deduces that "the American in the United States gives the State a much smaller part of his income than the Frenchman" (p. 250). But this result cannot be retained because France has, contrary to the United States, significant public expenditures linked to wars

6 The Tocqueville's analysis is short (about ten pages quoted here in the edition of 2004) but complex because of the number and the presentation of factors often quoted rapidly.

(debt, army)[7]: "there is simply no parallel between the finances of countries in such different situations" (p. 250).

In order to elaborate a comparative framework, which is methodologically pertinent, Tocqueville isolates the constituent expenditures of the democratic State. He excludes military expenditure, expenditure related to customs (liking for festivals, art etc.), cyclical expenditure in order to recruit civil servants on a labour market that favours private careers. He also distinguishes the items of expenditures (salaries, schools, maintenance etc.) in order to know the effects of the general tendencies of democratic budgets (effects which are sometimes in contradiction with one another). Anticipating Weber's notions of the ideal-type and of the scientific model of modern science, Tocqueville divides society ideally into three classes (p. 239), the wealthy, the well-to-do and the poor. He creates a special section for expenditure related to habits and customs (architectural ornaments, working class festivals), constituting what can be called the sociological factor of cultural values, because their effect is varied. For expenditure related to public agents, he draws a parallel (p. 244) between representative salaries in the United States and in France. He finally considers different factors that one can bring together, in order to systematize his analysis, in a model based on four causes according to their political, sociological, economic and cognitive nature.

b. The variables of democratic expenditure

Faithful to the liberal creed, Tocqueville's theory[8] firstly shows the superiority of the democratic State over despotism which "ruins men more by preventing them from producing than by depriving them of the fruits of production" while "liberty, by contrast, begets far more wealth" (p. 238). Public expenditures in free States are "considerably higher" but "the people's resources always increase faster than taxes" (p. 239).

Belonging to political causality (see table 1, cause 1), the first factor is institutional (noted 11 in table 1). It deals with the logic of the fiscal decision (No. 111) of the class in power. If the rich class governs, it economizes public money in a small way because "a tax imposed on a large fortune will subtract only from what is superfluous" (p. 239). The middle class in power is more economic because "nothing is as disas-

[7] The study of the impact of war expenditure will be taken up again notably by Peacock, Wiseman, 1967. In the second *Democracy in America* Tocqueville explains that in democracies "the martial passions will become rarer and less intense among civilized peoples as conditions become more equal" (2004, p. 761), but that the military push people toward war

[8] In order to better reconstruct the variables quoted by Tocqueville into a model, we do not follow the order of the presentation adopted in the analyzed passages.

trous as a heavy tax on a small fortune" (p. 239). When the poor class governs (No. 1111 in the table), taxes do not touch them because "only under a democratic government (…) can those who vote to impose taxes escape the obligation to pay them" (p. 240). Public expenditures, financed by the taxation of richer people, would always be high. Universal suffrage however "hands the government of society to the poor" (p. 240), that is to say to the majority of people who could not live without working. The government of the democratic majority cannot ignore the demands of its poor people who are numerous: it must be noted that this idea is still maintained today (Brown, Hunter, 1999, p. 780).

An ideological factor (No. 12) must be classified as a political cause. It concerns political and social progress (121), namely the improvement of the public expenditure of "well-being". The goal of "the improving spirit" is "to improve the lot of the poor man" (p. 241). Democratic government works for material prosperity firstly through a kind of electoralism (1211). It also wants, in a legitimate way according to Tocqueville[9], to improve the lot of deprived people (conception: 1212), which entails public expenditure: "in democracies, where the sovereign is needy, there is little likelihood of obtaining his benevolence without ameliorating his condition, which can seldom be done without money" (p. 242). It also generates public expenditure because of "a sort of permanent fever that turns to innovation of every kind" (p. 241).

The waste of public money by a democratic administration (13) constitutes the third political factor: "because the views of democracy change frequently (…) its undertakings are sometimes poorly managed or left unfinished" (p. 242). Administrative management (131) is defective (1311); it entails a waste of public money and thus pushes towards expenditure. Democratic governments "often lack perseverance in their designs (…), fail to maintain constant supervision of the men they employ (…), often spend the taxpayer's money to no purpose" (p. 251). The topicality of this analysis is in this case real as well, when we think of policies currently applied in most of the OECD countries in order to ensure the efficiency of public expenditures (Leroy, 2007). This willingness, periodically renewed in democratic history, to struggle against waste is well illustrated by budgets of results and objectives. In France,

---

[9] "These governments, faithful to their popular origins, make prodigious efforts to satisfy the needs of society's lower classes, to open up the avenues of power to them, and to sow prosperity and enlightenment among them. These governments care for the poor, distribute millions every year to the schools, pay for all services, and generously remunerate even the lowliest agents. This manner of governing strikes me as useful and reasonable; I am nevertheless forced to admit that it is also spendthrift" (p. 251).

budgetary performance is one of the bases of the reform instituted by the organic law (LOLF) relative to budget laws of the 1st August, 2001.

A social factor (21), classified as a sociological cause (2) in table 1, is related to the effects of education (211), and of civilization: "when the people begin to reflect upon their lot, they become aware of a host of needs they had not felt previously that cannot be satisfied without recourse to the resources of the State. That is why public expenditures generally seem to increase with civilization, and why taxes rise as enlightenment spreads" (p. 242). It must be noted that the analysis of the financial impact of the needs created (2111) by democracies is also made by Wagner (1967, p. 8): next to the impact of industrialization and of urbanization, which follows on that, he refers to the pressure for social progress in order to justify the law of increasing public expenditures. The values of each society (2211) that Tocqueville links to customs (221) form another cultural factor (22). Their impact on expenditures is, as we have indicated, different from one nation to another. Certain nations like public celebrations and "do not regret seeing millions go up in smoke" (p. 245); Americans prefer material advantages above ornaments in architecture.

In the passage relative to universal suffrage, Tocqueville adds that, fiscally speaking, "the extravagance of democracy" depends on the distribution of property, which thus acts as a structural cause (31). We will find this economic factor (3) in the socio-economic study of the classes of the Old Regime. It is referenced here as assessable matter (3111) relative to land patrimony (311). We must emphasize that the intervention of this variable has a general significance for financial sociology, even if its validity is proper to fiscal systems based on the taxation of property. In fact, it lays down the relation between the economic dimension (the characteristics of patrimony), the fiscal technique (based here on land tax) and the resources to finance public expenditures. In *Democracy in America* it is specified that when property is concentrated, as in England, taxes and thus expenditures are structurally assisted. If it is dispersed, as in France, and even more at that time in America ("where the vast majority of citizens own property" p. 241), the effect of this economic variable, defined by the distribution of this taxable matter, is the reverse.

Echoing the French debate of 1831 relative to public management in the United States, Tocqueville devotes a specific discussion to the salaries of civil servants of democracies. He refers to a cyclical economic reason (32), "that has nothing to do with the instincts of democracy in general" (p. 243), in order to explain that public agents can on the average be well remunerated; in fact, in the economic context of the American labour market (321), "the State would find no one to fill these lower public offices if it were not willing to pay its officials well" (p. 243). The cost of labour (3211) is a variable that explains the differences of remuneration of public agents. Its impact on the expenditure for the personnel of the State can vary from one country to another.

With this cyclical factor put aside, a factor of a cognitive sort (4), namely the preference (411) of the concrete (41) (Leroy, 2003, p. 236), is mobilized to formulate another structural tendency of the personnel expenditure in democracies.[10] Cognitive psychology has shown the importance of this factor for human reasoning.[11] To establish the salaries of public agents, the people "always think of their own needs, and this comparison enlightens them" (p. 243). It really concerns a cognitive factor, drawn from concrete information on the level of remuneration among his colleagues. The idea is that the social actor, the citizen, acts rather according to his own concrete situation (4111); "he will think of his simple home and of the modest fruits of his arduous labour" (p. 243). This cognitive rationality has a contrasted effect for the budget of democracies. It leads to paying less for high-level executives than in aristocracies, because for the poor "a sum that might seem modest to a wealthy man seems prodigious" (p. 243). One understands why, because of such an error of perspective, one sometimes thought that democracies were less extravagant. The same cognitive factor however explains that public agents in general, except the high officials, are rather well remunerated by the nation who decides in a democracy: "since they live quite comfortably themselves, it seems natural that their servants should share their comfort" (p. 243).

With regard to the fiscal logic of the working class, Tocqueville rejects the objection according to which the representative system curbs popular passions because "in the long run, however, one can be sure that the representatives will always reflect the spirit of the people who elect them" (p. 241). He firstly thinks "that if the people had a proper understanding of their own interest, they would spare the fortunes of the rich because they must soon feel the effects of any financial difficulties they create" (p. 240). We will not dwell here on refuting the idea, whose modern scientific caution comes from Laffer, that taxing the rich is bad (Leroy, 2003 p. 230; 2008). In fact, Tocqueville, while defending this

---

10 Tocqueville rejects the utilitarian factor (based on interest): that is true, but the fact is that "in democracies, high salaries are authorized by a very large number of people, few of whom will ever have the opportunity to receive such generous compensation" (Tocqueville, 2004, p. 242).

11 Cf. the notion of *concreteness* in Nisbett, Ross, 1980, p. 47. *concreteness* appears in general to be more typical, more representative, and more available for knowledge. On typicality, cf. for example, Lindsay and Norman, 1980, p. 404. Cf. also the bias (*Representativeness*, *availability*) in the work on subjective probabilities of Kahneman and Tversky (1972).

wrong concept, invokes (in a right way) the cognitive factor of the preference (411) of the short term (42) in order to explain the democratic budgetary logic: "is it not also in the interest of kings to make their subjects happy, and of nobles to know when to open their ranks? If long-run interests had always trumped the passions and needs of the moment, there would never have been tyrannical sovereigns or exclusive aristocracies" (p. 240). Democratic peoples, as regards taxation, follow here the natural tendency of man to choose an immediate gain (4112), especially since the risk of a negative effect is far off, and, we can add, uncertain. They tend to tax the other classes in order to facilitate the expenditures of the democratic State. In this context, cognitive variables tend to increase public expenditures.

c. *The tendency law of the growth of expenditures in democracies*

The systematization of Tocqueville's analysis stresses nine variables that are distributed in four dimensions (causes): political, sociological, economic, and cognitive. The model therefore has an interdisciplinary character which anticipates the thinking of the founders of financial sociology. All the political factors (11, 12, 13), the sociological factor of the education of the people (211), and the cognitive factors (41, 42) of human rationality come together to explain "why public expenditures inevitably tend to increase when the people govern" (p. 238).

We must of course exclude the economic factors whose effect is logically varied (31, 32) and the cultural factor (22) that is marginal for the budget. The tendency law of the growth of expenditures in democracies, linked to Wagner by economic history, has thus indeed been anticipated by the great liberal sociologist of democracy. From an ethical point of view, the liberalism of Tocqueville leads him to contrasted judgments: as we have seen, the improvement of the well-being of the people by expenditures of assistance, of instruction etc. is considered "as useful and reasonable" (p. 251), but taxation "would spare the fortunes of the rich" (p. 240).

We must of course exclude the economic factors whose effect is logically varied (31, 32) and the cultural factor (22) that is marginal for the budget. The tendency law of the growth of expenditures in democracies, linked to Wagner by economic history, has thus indeed been anticipated by the great liberal sociologist of democracy. From an ethical point of view, the liberalism of Tocqueville leads him to contrasted judgments: as we have seen, the improvement of the well-being of the people by expenditures of assistance, of instruction etc. is considered "as useful and reasonable" (p. 251), but taxation "would spare the fortunes of the rich" (p. 240).

Table 1: The expenditure factors of the democratic State according to Tocqueville

Cause/ domain	**Object**	**Variable**	**Financial effect in Democracy**	Example
1 Political **11** Institu-tional	**111** Decision	**1111** Class in power	Tax and expenditure increase	Taxation
12 Ideolo-gical	**121** Progress	**1211** Electoralism **1212** Conception	Effect > 0 by (rising) welfare expenditure	Assistance Instruction Services
13 Adminis-trative	**131** Manage-ment	**1311** Short-comings	Effect < 0: waste of public money (thus rising)	Works, Control of agents
2 Sociological **21** Social	**211** Education	**2111** Created needs	Collective expenditure	Roads
22 Cultural	**221** Customs	**2211** Society values	Varied: refusal of cer-tain expenditures (art, feasts, ornament…) but agreement for others (material gain)	Lucrative or pratical spirit
3 Economic **31** Structural	**311** Patrimony	**3111** Taxable base	Varied: concentration increases taxes, and vice versa.	Property
32 Cyclical	**321** Market	**3211** Labour cost	Varied effect on State personnel Expenditure	Salaries
4 Cognitive **41** Concrete	**411** Preference	**4111** Citizen's Situation	Weak for leaders, strong for others (thus increase)	Salaries
42 Short term	***411*** Preference	**4112** Immediate gain	Expenditure by taxing other classes	Taxation

The same analytical richness is applied to study the two phenomena of administrative centralization and political revolution which upset the institutional, political and social equilibrium of the Old Regime society.

2. Finance, Centralization and Revolution

In *L'Ancien Régime et la Révolution* Tocqueville wants to build up a model in the modern sense of the word. Even if historians find matter for reflection here, he specifically states that his book "is not a history of the French Revolution" (1998, p. 83). Here as well this study is a pioneer work in financial sociology through the generality of its questioning and the richness of the mobilized factors. It describes the permanence of certain institutions, such as centralization, or more specifically administrative supervision and justice that remain or reappear after the Revolution. It points out why the Revolution took place in France at the end of the 18th century. The demonstration is mainly based on the financial changes that contributed to destroy political freedom, to accentuate the divisions of classes, to delegitimize public action in a socio-economic context where cognitive and ideological factors have precipitated the movement.

a. Financial centralization

Tocqueville describes the bureaucratic continuity between the Old Regime and the regimes that came after the Revolution. Faithful to his "too strong a taste for freedom" (p. 86), he denounces the political misdeeds (*cf.* No. 1 in table 2) coming from the institutionalization (No. 11 in table 2) of administrative centralization (No. 111) by the monarchy. The 1789 revolution of 1789 is however welcomed by Tocqueville[12] as a tentative by the French to conciliate equality and liberty. The vote on taxes is quoted as one of "the conquests of '89" that will afterwards be betrayed by "silent and servile assemblies" (p. 86).

The authorities instituted to implement the concentration of powers are the *conseil du roi* or Royal Council, the controller-general, the *intendants* and their subordinates. Public finance constitutes the privileged domain of the centralization process[13], as is shown by the examination of the tax and budgetary competences of the quoted authorities (No. 1111 in table 2). The Royal Council administers the country. It is found "at the center of the kingdom, near the throne" and unites "all powers" (p. 119). It fixes and distributes taxes between the provinces in a discretionary way. It exercises supervision over expenditure, intervening even "for permission to spend 25 livres" (p. 131). Next to the Council, the controller-general is the central agent that executes and follows

12 "During the first stage of '89, when equality and liberty shared their devotion, when they wanted to create not only democratic institutions but free ones" (p. 85).

13 Centralization that Tocqueville has already described in the second *Democracy in America* (notably in chapter V) as a tendency of democratic peoples to demand everything from the State (thus anticipating the Welfare State).

all interior matters. "Gradually, he gained control of everything which has to do with money, i.e. almost the whole public administration" (p. 120), surveying the expenditure of "even a charity workshop located in the depths of a far-distant province" (p. 138).

These authorities are relayed in every province by intendants that are nominated and removable by the central authority. Tocqueville, quoting Law, points out that the kingdom is governed by thirty intendants on whom "the happiness or misfortune of those provinces" is based (p. 120). In the case of new taxes, the Council, the controller-general and the intendants decide on their own. In the case of old taxes, the old fiscal authorities have not been abolished; but, as in the case of the *taille*, it is the intendant who divides taxes between the parishes, directs the elected collectors, and decides on reprieves and discharges. The collector of the taille, often still elected, levies the taille under the direct order of the intendant. Tax litigation comes under the exclusive competence of the intendant and the Council. As regards expenditure, a few independent local bodies of the central authority remain, especially for public works, but here again the reality of the decision belongs to the intendant (assisted by the central body of the *ponts et chaussées*). As regards help for the poor, the Council decides on the part of the taxes destined to help the poor that the intendant is instructed to distribute. He regulates controls and follows all public affairs in detail, notably financial affairs, as is shown by the administrative supervision of towns. The administrative supervision is particularly visible in financial matters.

Administrative centralization places Paris as the most important town of the country: "it is neither the location, nor the grandeur, nor the wealth of a capital city which causes its political predominance over the rest of the empire, but the nature of the government" (p. 145). This preponderance is even reinforced by tax incentives (1112), because "the shackles of industry forged by the contemporary tax code were less heavy in Paris than anywhere else in the kingdom" (p. 148). The financial interventionism of the State is established (1113): "to this extent had the government already exchanged the role of a sovereign for that of a guardian" (p. 124). "Having thus replaced Providence, it was natural that everyone would invoke it in his own need" (p. 144). Help for the poor, already pointed out, indemnities for agriculture, help for industries etc. constitute illustrations of this change.

The establishment of a strong centralized State, notably through financial institutions, is explained by the will of the royal power, meeting the aspirations of the people, to weaken the nobility. By destroying the liberty (112) given to institutions representing a division of powers[14],

[14] Tocqueville brushes aside the objection of the opposition of parliaments to royal power because it meets "on political rather than administrative grounds" (p. 136). A

administrative centralization has encouraged the Revolution. Centralization has participated in the development of the democratic classes. It has also participated in the division of social classes (121) and the end of the liberties of intermediary institutions.

b. The destruction of political freedom by the financial power

The theme of political freedom is at the base of all Tocqueville's writings.[15] In *The Old Regime (L'Ancien Régime)*, he maintains that only political freedom can remedy "vices" secreted by the democratic tendency to the leveling out of conditions and to "a narrow individualism where all public virtues are smothered" (p. 87). In order to destroy all political freedom (112) susceptible to constitute a countervailing power, the isolation of classes (121) is encouraged by the royal power, notably in its struggle against the nobility, this "rival and dangerous class" (p. 165). The vices of the Old Regime come from "the art which most of our kings practiced, of dividing people in order to govern them more absolutely" (p. 191). Here again financial reasons intervene, in view of limiting the fiscal competences of intermediary institutions (1121); the monarchy wants to avoid submitting itself to an authorization of the Estates to levy taxes: "it was the desire to prevent the nation, from which money was asked, from demanding its freedom back, that made the government constantly alert to ensure that the classes (…) remained apart from each other, so that they could neither come together again nor join in a common resistance" (p. 170).

According to Tocqueville, the division of classes constitutes "the crime of the old monarchy, and later became its excuse; for once all those who made up the wealthy and enlightened portion of the nation could no longer agree with one another (…) it was necessary for a master to intervene" (p. 170). This effect, amply confirmed by the financial institutions, reinforces administrative centralization (111: above): "for a little cash one thus deprived oneself of the right to direct, to control, and to constrain one's own officials" (p. 168). The correction of financial abuses and privileges, that are the least tolerated, becomes impossible "it had been permitted to discuss them" (p. 169). These "new oppressions" would not occur, "if they had found rich and educated men alongside the peasants" (p. 187). The absence of political freedom is therefore harmful for all social classes, while "free institutions are not less necessary to the leading citizens, to teach them their dangers, than

---

new tax will lead to a reaction by parliaments (legislative power), but not to the real management of taxation, so sensitive for the people.

15 Political freedom, notably local institutions representing a division of powers (decentralization), has already been a strong idea in *Democracy in America*.

to the humblest, to assure them their rights" (p. 198). Social division is therefore one of the essential causes of the Revolution.

c. Political division of classes and financial privileges

Tocqueville defends political liberalism in order to counterbalance the excess of the levelling off of conditions which, for him, defines democracy. Paradoxically, this liberal thinker concentrates on an analysis of classes of the Old Regime, with certain formulations worthy of Marx: "Doubtless there were individuals who did not fit this description; I speak of classes, they alone ought to interest history" (p. 181). In table 2, the division of classes (121) refers to politics (1) because of the will of the central authority to divide the classes by playing on financial privileges. It is nevertheless classified in the table as a socio-political field (12) because it also describes the hierarchization and isolation of classes in society.

On the eve of the Revolution, the clergy has above all a political role (1211), the Church being a political institution (more than a religious institution). This analysis is supported by taxation because the clergy conserved annual assemblies deciding on their taxation. The moral powerlessness of the clergy is a factor of the division of social classes, and what we could call the decomposition of social links. The clergy is also a class on its own because of its financial privileges: "it occupied the strongest and most privileged place in the old society" (p. 97). Unlike the other superior classes, it maintains a presence in the countryside amongst the peasants. Through the priests in the countryside, the clergy would have become "the leader of the rural population" (p. 182), if its privileges that attached them to the political hierarchy did not give rise to the hate of the people.

The nobility (1212) is no longer an aristocracy useful for society.[16] It is isolated from other classes, having lost its action on the prince and on the people. It is politically deprived of its functions and its power. In fact, it does not govern the countryside anymore because, notably, it is not the lord of the manor, but government officials, that levy taxes. As is attested by the weight of the capitation or poll tax in Paris, the nobles prefer service of the king to administration of land in the countryside, whose ownership escapes them.

---

16 Tocqueville, coming from a noble family, shows his ambiguity here: he is caught between the acceptation of democracy and the Revolution of 1789 and his attachment to values favorable to aristocratic power over the people: cf. the preface of *The Old Regime*, where Tocqueville explains that despotism threatens societies where the aristocracy is destroyed because narrow individualism without public virtue is encouraged.

The nobility has become "a caste" (p. 156) through financial privileges.[17] Tax exemption has become "the most hateful of all these privileges" (p. 156). It shows the division of classes: "inequality of taxation is the most pernicious and the most apt to add isolation to inequality" (p. 157). Isolated from the peasant class that it does not govern any more, the nobility is also isolated from the bourgeoisie (1213), notably by its tax privileges: "every year, therefore, the inequality of taxation separated classes and isolated individuals more deeply than ever before" (p. 165). In the 18th century it is not bound any more by the feudal obligation in case of war, but disposes of an "immunity from taxation" (p. 150) still stronger. It does not supply "guaranteed" services any more in exchange of "its special rights" (p. 117). Taxation is thus the cause above all of these unjustified privileges that socially delegitimize the nobility. Inequality of taxation is felt much more on the eve of the Revolution (cf. further on) thus forming a structural factor for triggering it off: "when the nation (…) permitted the kings to establish a general tax without its consent, and when the nobility had the cowardice to allow the Third Estate to be taxed provided that the nobility itself was exempted (…) was planted the seed for almost all the vices and abuses which (…) caused its violent death" (p. 164). Finally it must be noted that Tocqueville considers that ennoblement does not solve the problem[18]; on the contrary, it increases "the hatred of the commoner for the noble" (p. 158).

Next to the separation between nobility and bourgeoisie there is also the isolation of the bourgeoisie (1213) with regard to the peasant class: "almost the entire middle class lived in towns during the old regime" (p. 158). Tax reasons play a very important role here as well, because "the bourgeoisie gathered in the towns has a thousand ways of lessening the burden of the taille, and often escaped it entirely" (p. 159). They escape from the big and perilous responsibility of the parish collector of the taille.[19] In general, they were not subject to the *octroi*, the tax on the circulation of merchandise. Pushed by the very French passion for

---

17 "Common object of hate and envy" because of tax exemptions and also rents that they levy on their domains.

18 Tocqueville did not therefore ignore ennoblement: "at no point of our history was nobility so easily acquired as in 1789" (p. 158). He argues that the newly ennobled people are rejected by the commoners because of their privileges and by the nobility of ancient origin, who "in their electoral colleges feel nothing of what bourgeoisie felt" (p. 158).

19 The collector of the taille, put under the authority of the intendant, was designated every year amongst the population of the parish and was accountable through his possessions and sometimes through his life for proper tax collection.

public posts[20], they were often occupants of positions that included fiscal exemptions that the monarchy sold in order to answer to its financial needs.

The peasant class (1214) found itself isolated from the superior class, without anybody present to explain to it: "there is no longer anyone but the central government which is interested in the village (...) in making a profit out of it" (p. 183). It is subject to the arbitrary character of the tax burden and of the old feudal rights. Using, as in all his work, the comparative method, Tocqueville emphasizes that in France it is the poor who support the fiscal burden, while in England it is the rich. In spite of some improvements, public action does not succeed in relegitimizing political power.

d. The delegitimizing of public action in financial matters

During the years preceding the Revolution, public action (13) marks a turning point, even if the erring ways caused by financial needs continue to undermine the foundations of the political system. The royal power has a fresh desire to fight against poverty and to ensure economic prosperity. The aim of the action of the government (131) is "to increase the public wealth" (p. 219). It is measured "the best" in the less strict application of fiscal law (1311): "the law was still as unequal, as arbitrary, and as harsh as in the past, but all its vices were tempered in execution" (p. 219). Less severe actions are taken against offences, and sanctions are more moderate. From now on the king takes into account public opinion and does not act in an arbitrary manner any more: "absolute by the letter of the laws, he was limited by their execution" (p. 221).

Political change is also manifested by the economic and social action of the State.[21] The expenditure linked to public intervention increases (1113). The dynamism of private individuals is encouraged by public action which modifies the role of the *intendant* whose missions become more diversified: roads, canals, agriculture, manufacturing, funds for charity workshops, indemnities for peasants who are wronged by hunting rights etc.

Public action also takes place in the area of institutional reform (1312). Nevertheless failures of reform attempts contribute to delegiti-

---

[20] According to Tocqueville, "the passion for public employment" started under the Old Regime. In chapter 20 of the second *Democracy*, he criticizes the tendency of modern democratic governments (in Europe) to encourage public employment: this tendency turns away from economic activities and legitimizes an excessive State interventionism that cannot however satisfy all the "new desires" (2004, p. 746).

[21] This public action must be compared to the spirit of improvement studied with the expenditure model of democracy, a factor which was then classified as government ideology.

mize the regime. Turgot has thus proposed important changes, particularly in the financial field. In 1776, his proposition to replace the *corvée* by a local tax failed. According to Tocqueville, the failure was assured because "the inequality was immediately transformed with it and went into the new tax" (p. 187). The Calonne's reform in 1787, that concerned the taille, by aiming for the reduction of the power of intendants to the advantage of the assemblées, again shakes the institutional base, while "the inequality of taxation" (p. 238) persists.

Tocqueville is finally interested in the financial needs of the monarchy, a factor which is often retained by analysts as the principal cause of the Revolution: The financial expedients of the monarchy are qualified as "monstrous fertility" (p. 166) or as "violent and dishonest practices". The vices of the Middle Ages that remain in vigor generally originate from "a financial expedient that turned into an institution" (p. 167). The retained examples show it well. Taxes on land transfers (or *franc-fief*) are constantly rising. The right to work is heavily taxed through corporations. The sale of municipal liberties (or offices), regularly abolished and then reinstated, constitutes a "shameful aspect of the Old Regime" (p. 125) that is a waste of town resources. The compulsory subscription to royal loans ruins numerous institutions (hospitals, towns....). The venality of public offices, for example numerous offices linked to courts, appears as "the need to disguise from the eyes of the French the taxes which no one dared reveal in their true light" (p. 169). The financial privileges of the occupants of a position, such as exemption from the *taille*, reinforce the sentiment of inequality. Arbitrariness is thus the rule: expropriations are not always compensated, or they are "arbitrarily and late" (p. 231). The abolishment of the *jurandes* and their reestablishment perturbs relations between masters and workers.

Tocqueville nevertheless does not give to the financial crisis the status of a direct cause of the collapse of the Old Regime. Financial needs are covered by the described expedients in order to prevent the meeting of the General Estates and the opposition of the nobility to taxes and to the abolition of their privileges. As we have seen, this policy participates in "the crime of the old monarchy" (p. 170) constituted by class division and by the stifling of political freedom that results from it. This point is important for fiscal sociology because numerous authors place, wrongly as we will see, the crisis as the univocal and determining variable of the social change (cf. chapter 7). The venality of the offices does not concern the intendants indispensible for the centralization of power which is a determining process in the eyes of the author. Its effect is complex: on the one hand, it undermines the legitimacy of institutions that are degraded and sold off cheaply according to financial needs; on the other hand, it also maintains a formal counterpower to administrative centralization[22] and it keeps up a spirit of independence.

Public action, even if it improves the general prosperity and the conditions of the people, paradoxically leads to an acceleration of the revolutionary process by provoking cognitive mechanisms of relative frustration (see below). Its incapacity to succeed in institutional reform produces *a fortiori* the same effect. In short, the venality of public functions and the diverse financial expedients used by the authorities reinforce this cumulative process of delegitimizing, by pointing out the arbitrariness and fragility of the system. In this context, the improvement of France's socio-economic situation does not act in favour of the stability of the regime.

e. The levelling off of socio-economic conditions

Socio-economic variables (2) are at stake in order to understand the stratification of society (21) at the end of the 18th century. A democratic process of levelling off of conditions (211) of social classes is taking place. On an economic level, the condition of classes comes closer together. Here one must take into consideration the factor, important according to Tocqueville, of the redistribution of landed property (2111). In France, as is confirmed by land tax documents of that time, property is from then on well apportioned. The importance of small properties is favourable for democracy: "the peasant had not only ceased to be a serf, he had become a landowner" (p. 112). This inequality does not exist anymore and one must look for the impact of inequality on the Revolution in the existence of unjustified inequalities between classes. The advent of property amongst ordinary people is one of the principal causes of the "hatred so fierce" (p. 116) of feudal rights that persist. Here the fiscal factor is still very important, because the peasant landowner is sensitive to the often unjust burdens of ownership (*dîme* or tithe, ground rents etc.). The other cause, already mentioned, is the end of the political role of the nobility that disposed of unjustified privileges, notably in the tax field.

Next to property, Tocqueville indicates that the inequality of wealth between classes is smaller (2112) in the 18th century. The division of the classes, the educated bourgeois elite (2113), enriched but moved aside from power, the jealousies of positions within the nobility[23], the discontent of the intellectuals, the burdens weighing on small property owners characterized by an independent spirit, left the whole nation to adhere to

[22] "Its greed had counterbalanced its ambition" (p. 171).

[23] Nobles wearing swords and those wearing gowns, nobles of the king's court and those of the villages, ancient nobles and recent nobles etc.

the idea of equality. Thus through equality, the France of the end of the Old Regime comes closer to modern France. It is already closer because for Tocqueville democracy means this process of the leveling out of conditions. This contradiction, when speaking like Marx, between factual equality (or at least the diminution of inequalities) and legal inequality explains why the privileges of the nobles appeared from then on to be intolerable: the privileges of the nobles coming from the feudal system were not justified anymore by their political role; feudality ceasing to be "a political institution" useful for society became "a civil institution" of privileges that were badly viewed in spite of their real impact.

Concerning the economic situation (22), public prosperity (221) improved on the eve of the Revolution. Tocqueville bases his argumentation on the improvement of the indicators of the standard of living (2211), of economic activities (2212), of population size (2213). He also gives the tax indicator of the rise of excise duties (2214). Public action expresses a change (see above) with the purpose of improving the economic and social situation of the people by implementing a policy of a more just taxation and of intervention expenditure. In comparison to other countries, the fiscal privileges which were drawn from the ancient feudal rights at the end of the 18th century "were much heavier" (p. 116) in the rest of Europe. The objective weight of taxes is less heavy in France than in England.[24] By taking account of fiscal repercussion, that leads in particular to make the nobles subject to taxes through farm rents, inequality is "more apparent than real" (p. 156). Cognitive factors become involved in the social discontent.

f. The cognitive factors

The cognitive reading of Tocqueville's work is rich with lessons, even if, as is often the case with our thinker, it cannot be based on an explicit theory but only on punctual observations. In any case, the analysis is connected, not with a simple psychology of man, but with a sociological study (of social science) of cognitive rationality. The general traits of human reasoning are every time linked to the social or historical context that puts them into operation and gives them their sociological meaning; the reasons, even objectively wrong, are studied from the point of view of the actor in order to search for the logic in the context. For example, the imitation principle is invoked as the cognitive basis of ideological theories (see below). As a pioneer in financial

24 "In eighteenth-century England, it was the poor man who enjoyed tax privileges; in France, it was the rich" (p. 164). This observation of Tocqueville is confirmed by historians: Mathias, O'Brien, 1976, p. 604; Chaunu 1977, p. 47; Tilly, 1986, p. 292; Bonney, 1996, p. XXXI. See also: Mann, 1947, p. 339 (chapter 2).

sociology, Tocqueville regularly uses cognitive determiners (No. 3 in table 2).

The well-known theory of relative frustration (No. 31 in table 2) that underlies several passages of his work can be linked to the cognitive approach. The effects of relative frustration and of concrete injustice increase the sentiment of illegitimacy that the authorities stir up by their behavior. Popular discontent then tends towards violent rupture. The theory of relative frustration accounts for the following paradox: while the situation improves, the discontent increases (311). This helps to explain why the Revolution takes place at the end of the 18th century, and not at another moment: "it is not always in going from bad to worse that one falls into revolution (...) The regime that a revolution destroys is almost always better than the one that immediately preceded it" (p. 222). The Tocqueville's masterly demonstration is based almost entirely on the relation between taxation and the sentiment of social injustice.

Discontent increases however. The felt tax inequality (3111) appears to be bigger, less supportable and is furthermore more visible in France than in other countries. "But in this matter the visible inequality was more galling than the inequality that one actually felt" (p. 156). The real fiscal impact is not visible and it appears to the people that the exonerations of the nobility have increased with the increase of levies such as the *taille*. The application of tax law is certainly more just (cf. 1311), but its residual vices appear to be more insupportable: "the evil has decreased it is true, but the sensivity to it is greater" (p. 222). The improvement in the financial administration made its vices "more sensitive" (p. 224). The arbitrariness of decisions, the secret of the procedure, the insecurity of financial relations, more and more numerous with the intervention of the State (lenders, traders, manufacturers, small investors etc.) precipitate the Revolution in order to reform the financial system.

The relative frustration of the people leads to a questioning of the institutions of the Old Regime. It accentuates the aggravation of the sentiment of injustice linked to the perception notably of tax inequalities (cf. 1211 to 1213). This theory is also pertinent to explain the geography of the Revolution. The Generality of the *Île-de-France*, where taxes have become more just, more equal (the *taille* still serves as an indicator of improvements), is thus the principal source of the Revolution. It is in fact in the regions where "progress was most apparent" (p. 222) that the discontent is the biggest. The same logic accounts for the resistance of the Old Regime in the regions that appear to be lagging (Bretagne, Poitou, Charente...). The theory of relative frustration rejects any determinism of economic and/or financial variables. Its pertinence is that of a brilliant application of the cognitive approach of the relation between the concrete context and the sentiment of tax injustice.

We also find the cognitive principle of concretization (32), according to which man prefers (321) concrete knowledge of the situation in order to determine himself. This factor, that Tocqueville does not name, is combined with the effects of relative frustration. It intervenes to explain the end of the political role of the nobles and the judgement of privileges. The nobility has lost its political influence so much so that it does not intervene anymore in the affairs of the State that provide a real contact with the people and concern their interests, such as the establishing of taxes. The division of classes, already questioned by the relative frustration, has become illegitimate because of the concrete vision of financial privileges (despite the leveling off of class conditions: cf. 2111 to 2113)). Money privileges are more dangerous than those linked to power because they are measured in a concrete way. Feudal burdens that strike people in their everyday life appear to be injust, because "the political part had disappeared; the financial portion alone remained, and sometimes had greatly increased" (p. 115). In the context of the end of the 18th century, cognitive factors are added to the blunders of the royal power so as to destroy its legitimacy. They participate in the diffusion of revolutionary ideology. The failure of the attempts to reform the system and the practice of financial expedients (see above) convince people in a concrete way that institutions are inadapted. "The government itself had long worked to make several ideas, since called revolutionary (…). The king was the first to show with what contempt one could treat the oldest and apparently most established institutions" (p. 230).

g. *The particular influence of ideology*

One finds in the Tocqueville's work the architecture of an interesting theory of ideology, although he does not use the word directly. In *L'Ancien Régime et la Révolution* he studies how general theories such as the existence of rules or universal truths applicable to human societies, or the necessity of equality and liberty appear and are diffused. The richness of the analysis of revolutionary ideology (4) stands in the way of its classification in a unique category (while in the model of the expenditure of democracy it clearly falls under politics). In table 2, it is classified as a distinct cause, with the indication of its links to the other fields (cf. 11 and 12). Ideology falls under the political field (41) because it concerns the big political problems put into question by the theories of equality and liberty. It implies cognitive factors (42) as a rational mode of knowledge applicable in the concrete context of the reception of the theories (421), in this case those of the Age of Enlightenment. It is also sociological (43), for example with the diffusion and then post-revolutionary rejection of anti-clericalism, and especially by taking into account certain social relations (431).

The general theory of equality (4111) spreads easily considering the injustice of privileges and the political division of classes (see above). The absence of political freedom (see above), illustrated by the loss of influence in institutional places of debate such as the General Estates and the local assemblies, stands in the way of the confrontation of theories to practice. Faced notably with fiscal privileges, the conviction spreads in the whole nation that equality, and thus political democracy, is legitimate: "there was no taxpayer hurt by the unequal distribution of the *tailles* who did not feel warmed by the ideas that all men ought to be equal" (p. 198).

At the end of the Old Regime, the "spirit of liberty" was still present, according to Tocqueville, in spite of centralization by the royal power and the destruction of political freedom. It had a "more general, more systematic, more democratic character". Political freedom (4112), by nature democratic, is from now on conceived as a right to have an independent life from other equal individuals. The political division of classes, that destroys real freedom, maintains a spirit of independence initiated by the defense of the privileges of every class. The sale of public offices also maintains the desire for political freedom. Finally, the diffusion of private property takes place in a context of class isolation that leads to the experience of independence thwarted by tax burdens that weigh on property.

Delegitimization also comes from the denunciation by the government of the abuses of the system for which it is responsible. Political criticism becomes a kind of official doctrine (4113), a new ideology, for all public authorities. Considering that "the people (…) listened without understanding" (p. 227), taxation flaws are particularly questioned by authorities in public documents. Tax laws that harm peasants are censured. The organization of work in corporations is described as "the result of the kings' fiscal greed" (p. 227). The *taille* is critized, in particular by those who are exempted from it, as a vexatious process weighing on "the poorest portion". Inquiries are launched by several provincial assemblies in order to know the detail of fiscal abuses and privileges that "have disastrous consequences for the farmer" (p. 229).

Encountering the cognitive rationality of classes (42), ideology proposes convincing general solutions (4211) for concrete problems (realism) of society and politics. The delegitimization of royal power in the years preceding the Revolution also comes from the destabilization of institutions by public action in the fields of institutional reforms, which fail, and of finance, where expedients reign (see above). The demonstration is made by the monarchy that its institutions can change. In another field, that of religion, anticlerical ideology does not encounter the same success because the clergy are hated, not for their moral doctrine, but for their privileges (experienced in a concrete way): "the war on religions was only an incident", once the levelling off of conditions were realized by democracy.

The development of international exchanges (4311) reduces the credibility of the particular values and principles of every country[25] that was previously isolated in feudal Europe.[26] Within this precise context, the cognitive principle of imitation explains the success of the idea that a common rule, which is neither national nor foreign, can be applied in all ages for all men. France proposes a convincing way of knowing and interpreting the world with regard to the real context of flaws of the political regime and of the organization of society. Revolutionary ideas are spread out in all countries, because of their universal character.

The principles of human reasoning are well contextualized in order to indicate their meaning when in action. In this way the elaboration of the ideas of Enlightenment and of the physiocrats at the origin of the Revolution is attributed to their social position. The social class of intellectuals (4312), cut off from the political world, lacks in experience and political realism. It is thus inclined to radical criticism and abstract general theories. In the public opinion it becomes "a political power" (p. 200) taking the place left by other classes. On the eve of the Revolution, the field is free for the reception of ideas of the Enlightenment philosophers and the physiocrats. The idea of the need for a radical change is more and more convincing (cognitive), the situation becomes revolutionary. A strategic dimension (4313) is present: every class upholds the ideology of equality in order to justify its struggle against the particular idea of privilege that certain social groups in its midst or other classes put up against it. These factors are combined to form a complex model of financial sociology.

h. The financial model of the revolution

The financial sociology model of the Revolution, that we have tried to follow step by step, is complicated to draw up for several reasons. The form is agreeable by its clear and literary style, but it does not follow a linear path in the thematic statement that is recurrent while implicating various facts and arguments each time. The factors are cumulating through their effects and are retroactive between them. The analysis mixes the "long-term and general facts" and "the particular and

[25] Tarde (1895) has very much stressed the importance of imitation, but he was wrong in making it a universal foundation of societies.

[26] Cf. Tocqueville "*État social et politique de la France avant 1789.*"

more recent facts" (p. 195). The short-term causes are linked to the cognitive factors of relative frustration, to the diffusion of the revolutionary ideology and the public action of government, and to the improvement of the economic situation at the end of the 18th century. The direction of the demonstration, the coming of the Revolution, is well determined by the listed factors which are selected, as we have seen at the beginning of this section, to form "a study", a model. The difficulty is especially to schematize the relations between the intermediary variables, which we did in the column "effect" of table 2. Certain general causes implying several variables become in turn singular variables of other general causes. The model is really based on essentially cumulative effects. It combines political, socio-economic, cognitive and ideological "causes" that are declined in 9 domains (institutional, socio-political, public action, stratification, economic situation, relative frustration, "concrete", and political that has the role of a general cause in 1 and a particular cause in 41). Variables are then linked to these domains through the concerned object.

Table 2: The financial factors of the French Revolution

Cause/domain	Object	Variable	Effect
1 Political **11** Institutional	**111** Administrative centralization (Long-term)	**1111** Financial power: Royal Council, controller-general, intendants **1112** Preponderance of Paris through (inter alia) tax incentives **1113** Expenditures of State intervention	Same effects of the 3 variables:Weakening of the nobility Effect on 112: end of politicalfreedom (end of local liberties): Effect on 121: political isolationof the classes and on 32 and 42
	112 Destruction of political liberty (Long-term)	*111* (cf. above) Centralization *121* (cf. below) Division of classes **1121** End of tax competences of intermediary institutions (except clergy)	Same effects of the 3 variables: Monarchy without counterpower, no brakes on abuses, no practice against general theories (effect on 32 and 42), individualism etc.
12 Socio-political	**121** Political division and Isolation of classes (Long-term)	**1211** Clergy: political role (tax assemblies, tax privileges)	Loss of its moral role (in spite of presence in the countryside)

		1212 Nobility: loss of its financial attributions, tax privileges	Caste without political role, attracted by Paris, rejected by the people
		1213 Bourgeoisie: tax avoidance and exemptions (linked to offices), refuses rural charge of tax collector	Spirit of independence, rejected by the nobles and the people, flee from the countryside to go to towns, also has its privileges
		1214 Peasantry: submitted to the arbitrariness of tax burdens (old feudal rights), no elite to guide it	Dissatisfaction with other classes and inequality (delegiti-mized) Isolation facing the central authority
-------------------	------------------	-----------------------	----------------------------
13 Public action	**131** Govern-ment action (Short-term)	**1311** Softer application of tax law	Bigger frustration (cf. 311), Effect on 221: prosperity of the country
		1113 Increase of social expenditure 1312 Institutional reforms	Idem + interventionism increases Failure, Delegiti-mization of authority
		1313 Financial expedients: taxation of corporations and of property muta-tions, loans, venality (sale) of offices	Illegitimacy (effect on 312) of institutions, privileges with offices: cf. 1213, but centraliza-tion counterweight 111 and taste of independ-ence
2 Socio-economic **21** Stratification	**211** Levelling off of class conditions (Long-term)	**2111** Property: acquisition of land by peasants, numerous owners	Dissatisfaction with property taxes and privileges (cf. 1211 to 1213)
		2112 Wealth: better shared, few big fortunes	Spirit of independence of people. Bigger frustration (cf. 311)
		2113 Education: brings nobles and bourgeois together	Frustration of bourgeois with regard to nobles (cf. 311)

22 Economic situation	**221** Economic prosperity (Short-term)	**2211** Living standards (indicator) **2212** Economic activity (idem) **2213** Population size (idem) **2214** Consumption taxes (idem)	The 4 variables have the same effect: bigger frustration (cf. 311)
3 Cognitive **31** Relative Frustration	**311** Increased dissatisfaction (Short-term)	**3111** Felt tax inequality ***1311 and 1113, 2211 to 2214*** (cf. above): improved situation *1121* (cf. above): end of political freedom	These variables are united in their effect: dissatisfaction with residual abuses (tax inequality) Questioning of political institutions: effect on 121
32 Concrete	**321** Permanent preference	***1211 to 1213*** (cf. above): classes ***1121, 1211 to 1214, 2111 to 2113*** (cf. above) (Long-term)	Dissatisfaction with financial privileges. Effect on 121
4 Ideological **41** Political	***11* and *12*** Institutions and liberty (Short-term)	**4111** Political equality: including equality before taxes	Effect on 111 and 112: Criticize centralization
		4112 Political freedom	Criticize absence of political liberty
	7	**4113** Official criticism of the system	Basis of revolutionary ideology
42 Cognitive	**421** Reception of theories	*32* The concrete as knowledge **4211** Convincing general solution	Vision of the problems (1312 and 1313), diffusion of ideology 41
43 Sociological	**431** Social relations (Long or short-term)	**4311** Exchanges between societies: Long-term	Tendency to general criticism
		4312 Intellectuals (Short-term)	Comparison and imitation
		4313 Class strategies (Short-term)	Criticize political inequality 121

Conclusion

Tocqueville's fiscal sociology is remarkable for its methodology (even if it is not very explicit) and for its results, if we take the trouble to arrange and classify the described variables. Understanding the scientific importance of financial phenomena, he turns to the modern method of models to study the democratic State and the Revolution. In the financial field he stresses all the cumulative factors so as to explain two essential social changes for democratic societies, namely the causes of the French Revolution and the future of the democratic State. His political liberalism, that leads him to the denunciation of the centralized financial State and of institutionally unjustified fiscal inequalities, does not deviate from the scientific quality of his modeling. The ethical horizon of political freedom, which aims at notably preserving intermediary institutions, can certainly be discussed. The shortcomings of contemporary French decentralization (cf. chapter 6) thus illustrate well the difficulty of finding a good institutional answer to the erosion of the political system. It is nevertheless so that the discovery of the law of the tendency of public expenditure to increase, attributed to Wagner, anticipates well the growth of the democratic interventionist State. In the same way, the coherence and clarity of the analysis of the causes of the French Revolution must be welcomed.

Tocqueville's pioneering work is not referred to by the founders of fiscal sociology, not even by current research (Leroy, 2007). And yet the Austrian school, with Goldscheid and Schumpeter, also adopts an historical approach to study the crisis of the fiscal State. Mann is interested as well in the role of public finance in revolutions, while at the same time orientating his reflection towards a functional socio-political approach. The Italian school around Pareto uses, as in the case of the approach of Tocqueville, a synthetic methodology combining several factors. But it is focused on the theme of the elite who want to remain in power by using public finance. Furthermore, the disciples of Pareto aim to construct not naturally selective models, but a general theory of social equilibrium.

Chapter 2

The Founders of Fiscal Sociology

Fiscal sociology originates from two intellectual movements, made up of an Austrian and an Italian School. In Austria, Rudolf Goldscheid proposes the term *Finanzsoziologie* in his book *Staatssozialismus oder Staatskapitalismus*, published in 1917. In *Die Krise des Steuersstaats* (1918), Joseph Alois Schumpeter welcomes and discusses this new approach[1] to the budget, defined as "the skeleton of the State once stripped of its deceitful ideologies". The reflection of the two authors focuses on the crisis affecting the tax State. Following a historical approach, it paves the way for the new social science of finance, which Fritz Karl Mann enriches by emphasizing the socio-political functions of taxation.

The Italian founders of fiscal sociology adhere to the development of a finance science including the study of its economic, political and sociological dimensions.[2] Pareto, one of the important thinkers of the Italian School, taught in Lausanne, but his influence on fiscal sociology made itself felt mainly in Italy through his disciples Borgatta, Griziotti, Murray, Sensini and, more distantly, through Scotto. Three other authors, not directly linked to Pareto, stand out: Conigliani, Puviani and Montemartini. The economic approach refers to pure economics, to marginalism, to "hedonism"[3], whereas the socio-political approach, which founds the Italian fiscal sociology, supports the questioning of the elite from Machiavelli. The economic approach also proposes original reflections on public goods, the nature of the State, the tax illusion etc. The Italian School is not homogeneous, even though the distinction between the governing and the governed occupies a central position. Differences show up in particular with respect to the role of the State and of coercion. Pareto should be given a place apart, with regard to his

1 "The scientific significance of this highly intelligent book lies in the fundamental idea of a fiscal sociology" (Schumpeter, 1954, p. 6).

2 In the financial science, the economic approach, which is not directly part of sociology, is based on the voluntary exchange in reference to marginalism, in particular with Pantaleoni, De Viti de Marco, Mazzola.

3 Hedonism designates an economic conception of public finance aiming to satisfy collective needs and therefore to calculate the cost (taxation) to finance the expenses corresponding to those needs.

followers and other thinkers of the Italian School, particularly because of the importance of his sociology of "non-logical" financial actions.

1. The Austrian Founders

The work of the Austrian founders of fiscal sociology appears rich in ideas to rebuild a genuine social science of public finance. Goldscheid's Marxist questioning is again taken up several times in the literature (O'Connor, 1973; Habermas, 1978). Non-Marxist writers also refer to the crisis (military, economic, financial etc.) in order to explain the change in tax policy (Peacock and Wiseman, 1967; Rosanvallon, 1981, Campbell, 1993, Streeck, 2007). These crisis theories quite justly emphasize the importance of the legitimation of the tax State. As Schumpeter has shown, they are however more dubious as to the structural fragility of the State in the developed countries. Nowadays this analysis is confirmed by the State's resilience crises as diverse as those concerning the financing of social policies (economic crises, impact of globalization) and the recent collapse of banks sector and stock markets. In another perspective, Mann, who is member of the Austrian school, shows the interest of considering the socio-political functions of the interventionist tax system.

a. Goldscheid's financial Marxism

A sociologist renowned in his lifetime who was also interested in economics, Goldscheid (1870-1931) has more particularly founded with Max Weber the German Society for Sociology. His book *Staatssozialismus oder Staatskapitalismus* (Goldscheid, 1917) establishes financial sociology: "it alone can show up the part played by the origin and composition of public revenue in the development of society as a whole and thereby in the destiny of nations and individuals alike" (p. 206).[4] Public finance thus becomes the field of prediliction, since "every social problem and indeed every economic problem is in the last resort a financial problem" (p. 212).

Goldscheid's financial sociology is characterized by his historical approach under Marxist influence which gives a central place to the crisis of the tax State. The functional relationship between revenue and expenditure is called into question. The finances of antique, feudal and capitalist States are compared within the framework of the evolution of public property (domain). The Marxist outlook involves an analysis of social classes and of dialectical contradictions: "enrichment of some classes at the expense of others has always been the purpose of contributory systems" (p. 203). Much more than that, tax exploitation is consid-

4 I refer to the text: Goldscheid, 1967.

ered, for the same reason as a whole slavery completely apart, as the most ancient form of class struggle: "nearly all class privileges were tax privileges, the classes were largely tax classes" (p. 204).

Nevertheless, Goldscheid reproaches Marx for not having drawn the conclusions from his analysis of public debt as a lever for the accumulation of capital. He considers more generally that Marx "so completely neglected the State in his conclusion" (p. 208), ignoring the phenomenon of its expropriation by the private sector. There is a "contradiction between social and economic structure and its juridical and financial superstructure" (p. 206). This contradiction is not, as Marx and Engels thought, "the separation of worker and means of production", but "the separation of State and means of production" (p. 209). The State has become poor because it is dispossessed of public property.

The fiscal State is thus at the core of Goldscheid's ideas. Its origin is linked to the military and financial needs of the political power which leads to the establishment of taxation. There is a link between the appearance of capitalism[5] and the tax system: "in all these original forms of exploitation and early forms of capitalism, public finance and tax system played a decisive part" (p. 204). Finances are of fundamental importance in the evolution of the State and society.[6] From a historical point of view, the State owned significant properties in the Antiquity and the Middle Ages in the form of personal possessions of the prince. It was natural for the State, including the pure Absolutist State, to be rich. This situation constituted an advantage despite the abuses in expenditure and the lack of control by the people.[7] But the State was dispossessed of its properties (domain) in relation to the "advanced capitalism which became the creator of the poor State" (p. 204). The imprudent recourse to loans, the alienation of State domain, the incapacity to manage the economy well, the princely waste impoverished the State: it became dependent on private creditors to whom it appealed in order to meet its needs. As a result of this evolution, modern democracy consisted for the poor in acquiring, not a rich State, but a poor State: "the poor State can calmly be allowed to fall into the hands of the people, which thereby acquire nothing but empty coffers" (p. 205).

---

5 "We can trace this development in the oldest forms of exploitation which were war and slave economy, as also in the oldest forms of capitalism, the capitalism of the princes, nobility, and guilds, as well as of the Church" (p. 204).

6 Goldscheid mentions the example of the establishment of parliamentarism in relation to the control of public finance and of "censal" suffrage (voting system based on poll tax).

7 Nevertheless, Goldscheid (p. 206) notes: "it is perfectly possible to praise the virtues of the feudal State or absolute monarchy or the capitalist economy; but it is absurd to believe in the possibility of just taxation within these social systems."

Here Goldscheid, who witnessed the financial difficulties of the Austrian State, adopts a structural conception of the crisis of the tax State which persists in different forms up to present times. Not having at its disposal the revenues from its properties any more, the modern State is obliged to resort to taxation, which becomes its main source of revenue for financing its needs. But it cannot tax the economic profits of the bourgeois class which fights to preserve its tax privileges and prefers to maintain its position as a State creditor. "The rising bourgeois classes wanted a poor State (...) because these classes knew their own power to depend upon what the State did or did not have money for" (p. 205). The State is therefore in a structural crisis because it has big needs notably on account of war financing and social programmes. A poor State does not sufficiently dispose of choices as for its revenues; it is forced to maintain indirect taxes; it "is fated to fall more and more into debt" (p. 210). Modern capitalism uses the (poor) State in order to exploit it financially through the mechanism of debt interests[8] and through economic policy (inflation and deflation notably to its own benefit).

To resolve the social question, the solution consists in creating "State capitalism" which allows to accumulate public capital and to create sustainable public investment goods within the framework of what is today called the mixed economy. Only a rich State is in a position to be a fair State which assumes its function of changing in society. The financial system inherited from the past must therefore be modified in order to reach "a State which gradually needs to take less en less and yet can give more and more" (p. 213).

In a way that one can certainly discuss, Goldscheid thus deserves credit for proposing a general "theory of public property" (p. 213) both as a key explanation and a normative horizon. For him, science must inquire into the causes which "are fully determined by the given social structure" (p. 206). Financial sociology must take into account the vital needs of society through the study of "the finances of the people" (p. 210). On the basis of his State theory, Goldscheid criticizes the classical liberal conception, but also socialist doctrines to which he is nevertheless close.[9] His method consists in searching for the historic law of the tax State. By indicating the sense of the moral and political evolution of the State in the modern capitalist regime, this thesis offers an

---

8 "Fiscal exploitation is an indispensable adjunct of exploitation by private enterprise: it constitutes the legal foundation of capitalism and an element of its fulfilment" (p. 211).

9 "In this respect, the socialist theory of society and economy fails no less than the bourgeois theory, because in the last analysis both are equally hostile to the State" (p. 207).

ethical point of view and an epistemological positioning to financial sociology. It arouses reserves however, as Schumpeter shows.

b. Schumpeter's ambiguous liberalism

Schumpeter (1870-1950) uses Goldscheid's study as basis for the exposition of his conception of the crisis of the tax State.[10] He develops an interesting essay[11], but difficult because of the factors considered and the nuances presented. In the presence of the financial crisis, he adopts an ambiguous liberal position, or if one prefers a moderate position, in order to defend the tax State, whose action completes that of the market. The problematic is still part of the historical sociology of public finance.[12] Incidentally, the limits of the history of law are indicated.[13] Sociology is emphasized because, like economics, it disposes of concepts applicable to many periods in order to scientifically settle the debate initiated on account of the crisis of public finance. In the context of the First World War, this debate questions the modern tax State and the liberal economy.[14]

The essay starts with a review of the crisis in feudal society which saw the emergence of the modern tax State at the end of the Middle Ages. Germany and Austria illustrate the analysis. The modern State is distinguished from antique tax State, then from feudal system which Schumpeter refuses to characterize as the medieval State since the

---

10 R.A. Musgrave (1992, p. 100) proposes an economic interpretation of Schumpeter's thesis in relation to his other written works, while at the same time acknowledging that there is a sort of epistemological gap in his thinking: "The young Schumpeter's idealized end-state view of socialism as liberation from scarcity (1918) had nothing to do with his later thinking (1940)". More recently, other economists considered Schumpeter's financial sociology as a sub-discipline of his economic thinking: by linking his work to other important writers of that period (cf. Backhaus, 2004), or by interpreting his sociology of the tax State on the basis of the theory of entrepreneurial innovation (Ebner, 2006). My choice is different and consists in only taking into account the "young" Schumpeter's essay on financial sociology, published in 1918, while at the same time privileging the socio-political conception, which is of fundamental here.

11 I refer to the American translation from german by Stolper and Musgrave: Schumpeter, 1954 (1918).

12 "The fiscal history of a people is above all an essential part of its general history" (p. 6).

13 With regard to the history of law, a note specifies that "juridical concepts as such are not suitable for the interpretation of historical series, especially not for the comparative characterization" (p. 8).

14 "Everyone endeavours to proclaim the fulfilment of his own wishes to be a necessary consequence of the war. Some foresee that high capitalism (...) must now collapse; others look forward to more perfect economic freedom (...) others expect an administered economy" (p. 5).

separation between public law and private law did not exist.[15] In the feudal system, the prince had to finance his expenses himself, notably the war expenses, "at least unless he had a right to the necessary contributions by virtue of particular titles" (p. 11) (from his vassals). The revenues from his properties (domain) and the contributions of his subjects[16] formed the main resources of the prince. Except for the towns, the legal possibility to levy taxes did not really exist. The financial crisis that puts an end to this period is explained by three factors: the bad management of the properties which is a contingent factor[17] of no sociological interest; the "courtly waste" (p. 13) which is a determining form of financial power because "the prince wanted to gain ground (…) when the ties of the vassal relationship began to loosen" by transforming "a recalcitrant country nobility into a pliable court-, official-, and military nobility" (p. 13); the war expenditure which necessitates recourse to an army of mercenaries. This last factor is the most important because it refers to a major social change, that of the heredity (in fact) of the fiefs. "The vassals began to feel as independent lords of their soil" (p. 14) and wished less and less to participate in war.[18] They devoted themselves more and more to their private economic activity, sanctioning the birth of a private sphere distinct from the public sphere which would be that of the tax State. In this way Schumpeter shows that the revenues of the princes were insufficient to finance wars: "The prince did what he could: he got into debt" (p. 14).

This analysis leads Schumpeter to identify a real crisis of the feudal financial system which is defined as "obvious, ineluctable, continuous failure due to unalterable social change" (p. 14). This crisis is that of the state property economy (based on domain); it explains the appearance of the modern tax State at the end of the Middle Ages. The tax obligation at the beginning concerned only the people who had given their consent; then it followed the rule of the majority to become a general obligation. The State progressed in all the fields, but "the fiscal element was frequently the driving element (…). This led to the growth of an estate tax system (…) which reached its peak during the second half of the 16th century (…). The newly born state acquired a solid framework,

---

15 "As long as the state does not exist as a separate and real power, the distinction of public and private law has simply no meaning (…) The organizational forms of that time combined both what we nowadays call the public and private sphere in one essentially different unity" (p. 11).

16 Generally the contributions had been paid in money since the 13th century.

17 "So long as the cause is accidental, i.e., so long as it does not follow from the inner logic of the system and so long as remedies can be found within the system (in this case more efficient management)" (p. 13).

18 Apart from the fact that the insufficient number of vassals had already justified the recourse to mercenaries.

created its own organs, became a separate power" (p. 15). This is a general phenomenon in Europe. It leads to the development of a State bureaucracy. Taxes no longer served only the purposes set by the princes but also, for example, education or culture. But Schumpeter specifies that the development of tax State, based on the struggle between the princes and different corps and corporations, did not have the general interest as its goal. It constituted especially "a policy of a class" (p. 16) which exploited the peasants in particular.

Reinforced with this conception of the tax State, Schumpeter then studies the crisis of public finance linked to the First World War. His response, which parts from that of Goldscheid[19], is clear: "in this, the only essential meaning, there is no crisis of the tax state" (p. 37). This statement refers to the case of Austria[20], but since this country was in the worst situation, it is applicable to every country in Europe. In a general way, the collapse of the tax State of developed societies does not fall within his logic: "the point is that the system of the tax state has so far met all challenges, and whenever it has failed to do in particular cases, causes can be found which are not inherent in its nature" (p. 25).

Regarding the recovery of the economy, Schumpeter militates in favour of a complementary action of the tax State and liberal economic mechanisms[21] focused on the activities of entrepreneurs and capitalists. The war economy, by favouring the production of instant goods, has not renewed the production equipment by means of investments. If Schumpeter thinks that the intervention of the tax State is necessary in order to

19 Acknowledging the perils threatening Austria, he emphasizes in a note that "it is no accident that the voices which speak of the insufficiency of the tax state come almost all from Austria, and particularly that R. Goldscheid is an Austrian" (p. 26). He quotes different countries that would succeed in preserving the tax State.

20 In the case of Austria, Schumpeter distinguishes the problem of covering the war costs from that of economic recovery. The recovery of the economy "is not, or at least not in the last resort, a question of raising *money* but a question of securing *goods*" (p. 27): this is not a problem depending directly on the tax State. Hence the tax State is only concerned by the question of war costs. Here Schumpeter demonstrates that "the problem is soluble" (p. 27) by putting forth a type of economic theory on financial choices. Initially, Austria had several options to finance the war and should have rather used taxes (like England) and avoid the "uninhibited paper money economy" (p. 28). After the war, there were two solutions consisting in either reducing the money supply (in order to reduce inflation), or introducing a wealth tax (which would allow the State to tax the indebted State creditors). The problem is rather political: as for the taxing of wealth, he notes that "only a strong government on the broadest political base (…) could dare to attempt the task of overcoming all resistance" (p. 30).

21 "It suffices to insist that the organizational form of the competitive economy can reconstruct the economy after the war exactly as it has created the modern economy in its essence and that therefore its public counterpart, the tax state, has an effective method of reconstruction and will not come to grief on *this* task" (p. 36).

repair war disorders, he does not follow Goldscheid concerning the thesis on the necessity of recapitalization of the economy by the State (becoming capitalist through its properties). This task falls on the liberal economy because the reconstitution of the production equipment requires "beside entrepreneurial activity, something which can do without private motives as little today as it could in the youth of capitalism"[22] (p. 36).

This important crisis theory is completed with a reflection about the nature of the tax State whose evolution is linked to the economy and social change. The historical sociology of public finance shows that the choice of State taxation, in order to respond to financial needs, is explained by the transformation of the medieval socio-economic system with the appearance of a private sphere distinct from the public action sphere: "without financial need the immediate cause for the creation of the modern state would have been absent. In its turn, the appearance of this need and its satisfaction precisely by the method of tax demands is explained by the process of disintegration of medieval forms of live. This process itself may very well be traced through all intermediate causes to changes in the very foundations of the economy; its ends up in the free economy of the individual family" (p. 16). By studying the relations between State and taxation, tax sociology is thus essential in order to understand social changes in their relations with socio-economic structures: "this process itself may very well be traced through all intermediate causes to changes" (p. 16). The tax institution is constitutive of the creation of the State, its form, its evolution and its impact on society and the economy.[23]

Schumpeter then isolates the historical specificity of the modern State in distinguishing it from the primitive horde, the socialist State (which in principle is not a force separated from the economy) and the feudal system which, as we have seen, does not accept a legitimate public sphere. Drawing the conclusion of the emergence of a private sphere linked to the heredity of fiefs, he connects the possibility of the modern State to the establishment of what we can call social individual-

---

22 Here we find again the entrepreneur which is central in Schumpeter's thinking.

23 "Taxes not only helped to create the state. They helped to form it. The tax system was the organ the development of which entailed the other organs. Tax bill in hand, the state penetrated the private economies and won increasing domination over them. The tax brings money and calculating spirit into corners in which they do not dwell as yet, and thus becomes a formative factor in the very organism which has developed it. The kind and level of taxes are determined by the social structure, but once taxes exist they become a handle, as it were, which social powers can grip in order to change this structure" (p. 16-17).

ism.[24] He defends the idea, important for political sociology, of an autonomous State machinery which is constructed, parallel to the establishment of this private sphere adapted to society. The objective of the modern State is functional. It aims at social goals, such as financing war at its genesis: "the state can never be its own end but only a machine for these common purposes (...) Only then is it a separate, distinguishable social entity" (p. 18). Nevertheless, Schumpeter prefers an intermediate conception between the Marxist vision of a State as "the ruling classes' means of exploitation" and that, of lawyers for example, who consider it as "something above all parties and classes" (p. 19).

The essay continues with explanations, today not so original[25], of the limits of the tax State.[26] The economic analysis of the incidence of taxes thus anticipates Laffer's curve. It has to be pointed out that unlike Pareto, the potentially harmless nature of indirect taxes, which makes the increase of the tax pressure possible, is not taken into account.

Finally an interesting economic psychology[27] is outlined. Thus, the notion of "Patrimonialization of the personality" (p. 14) designates the process of creation of a private sphere at the end of the Middle Ages; this is at the same time, as we have seen, an economic process (linked to the fief as a private patrimony) and a modification of the representation of the relations between society and politics (the prince, then the State). In another even shorter paragraph, he refers to the notion "habit of thought" (p. 19-20) to explain the modification of the social representation with regard to the State, from then on considered as "something impersonal, a machine manned only by serving, not by dominating spirits" (p. 19). A third manifestation (also very short) of Schumpeter's economic psychology is found in the analysis of the limits of the tax State: these limits must be linked to the nature of tax State, as illustrated in the case of the bourgeois tax State: "though the state may be felt everywhere (...) it remains something peripheral, something alien to the proper purpose of the private economy, even something hostile, in any case something derived" (p. 20). A relation between the tax State and the utilitarian rationality of the modern individualist economy is also

24 "Only where individual life carries its own centre of gravity within itself, where its meaning lies in the individual and his personal sphere, where the fulfilment of the personality is its own end, only there can the state exist as a real phenomenon" (p. 18).

25 On the other hand, the difference, rapidly noted (p. 20), between the "entrepreneurial states", with "new, active and growing wealth", and the "rentier states", with "old wealth" is interesting because it finds a prolongation in another form in the shortcomings of the tax State in developing countries (cf. chapter 4).

26 "There is a limit to the taxation of entrepreneurial profit beyond which tax pressure cannot go without damaging and then destroying the tax object" (p. 22).

27 Or, if one prefers, elements for psychological bases of an economic sociology.

suggested, though its content is not clear, except to consider in a very strict sense that this is a reason for the limitation of the tax State (which must respect citizens' interests). Schumpeter's economic psychology finds a last expression, discreet in this essay but significant in the rest of his work, in the figure of the entrepreneur whose virtues are exalted.

Schumpeter's economic psychology remains orientated by his preference, better postulated here than demonstrated, in favour of the liberal economy. This independent thinker[28] of course often restrains this ideological tendency, notably because of his fascination for Marxist analysis[29] (of Marx himself and of Goldscheid). Despite his careful remarks[30], he sometimes forces his conclusions[31], as in the case of the social representation of the role of the State: "everyone works and saves for himself (…). The driving force is individual interest – understood in a very wide sense and by no means synonymous with hedonistic individual egotism. In this world the state lives as an economic parasite" (p. 20). This classical conception of the finances of the liberal State became however a subject of criticism from notably the socialist movement that Schumpeter knew so well.

Schumpeter's contribution is therefore important because of his historical methodology which follows the way opened up by Goldscheid, and before them by Tocqueville. His sociology of the crisis as social change, his sociology of the State as differentiation between public and private spheres, and his economic psychology open a useful reflection. The conception of the fiscal crisis, in particular, puts forward a theory of financial choices which does not support the dominant conceptions of

28 For example, he defends "the capital levy (…) not only compatible with a free economy (…) (but) appropriate to the principle of economic freedom" (p. 31).

29 "With private enterprise the hour also belongs to the tax state (…) By and by private enterprise will lose its social meaning through the development of the economy and the consequent expansion of the sphere of social sympathy" (p. 38).

30 For example: "our argument applies (…) only to the particular historical moment in which we live. It is not intended as an apotheosis of the free economy, as the last word of wisdom" (p. 37).

31 Here are a few examples of these more ideological moments: concerning the economic system of free competition, already transformed by the "attempts at state tutelage" (p. 5), he notes: "yet whatever drive and success it had were due to such elements of free competition as remained in spite of everything" (p. 5). Likewise, he affirms that "the historian is often inclined to overestimate the influence of the state on the formation of the economy. At no time have economy and budget formed a really uniform 'state economy', never has the state been able to create something lasting which the free economy would not have created" (p. 7). Or furthermore, against the controlled war economy, he points out: "the enormous industrial achievement of switching the economy over the exigencies of war was due for at least 90% to the automatism of the free economy and to the play of self-interest (…) the worker does not owe his livelihood to any government measures" (p. 35).

the deterministic constraint. This theory is based on economic analysis in order to justifiably reject the false inexorability of the financial failure of the tax State. Nevertheless, it does not propose a real study of politics which is found discarded in a simplistic theory of constraint. This asymmetry between the economic theory of public finances and the pessimistic exhortation to political courage, in order to impose the economically necessary reforms, expresses a gap which remains one of the constants of the analysis of the financial State up to now. From this point of view, Mann's studies appear to be more pertinent.

c. Mann's functional analysis

We refer here to the Mann's essays published in the United States which prolong the work of the founders of the Austrian school. In 1943, Mann (1883-1978) publishes in *The Review of Politics* an article[32] which justifies the functional approach to taxes from the socio-political point of view (Mann, 1943), whereas today most of the studies on public finance follow Musgrave's analysis of the three economic functions of taxation. Like Goldscheid and Schumpeter, he recalls that tax, exceptional at the beginning because revenues came notably from State property, has become permanent: "current taxation is the inseparable twin of the modern State" (p. 225). But Mann underlines the importance of another change that took place in his time, namely that the financial function of taxation has been combined with "a function of social control" (p. 226). He then analyzes three forms of social control through tax: the correction of undesired kinds of behaviour, the readjustment of economic power between social groups, the fight against the social abuses of capitalism and the transition towards another economic order.

Concerning the orientation of behaviour, he firstly takes as an example the tax policy concerning the family. He underlines that this policy, which is motivated by demographic reasons, is very old, dating back to the Roman Empire at least. It is present in many countries, notably in France, and has known a particular application in totalitarian regimes which surtaxed unmarried people. Mann cites other examples, such as that of the suffrage regime reserving the right to vote to the taxpayers who pay property tax, or such as that of taxation on "laziness" (p. 227) targeting the voluntarily unemployed people. Taxation educates citizens to comply with government policies, to eliminate vices[33] etc. The func-

32 Before his departure for the United States, Mann had published in German a series of studies on financial sociology in *Finanzwissenschaftliche Forschungen*, Jena, G. Fischer, 1930-1935.

33 Examples: Soviet Russia that doubles the taxes for farmers which do not respect the instructions of the plan; legislation on coal also surcharging producers who do not

tion of social control often prevails in these domains over the financial function. With regard to the power between the social classes, Mann points out that "in all periods of history, the ruling class has made use of the taxing power to increase its own welfare and to strengthen its economic position" (p. 229). Taxes can however be used in two opposite ways: either in order to accentuate the inequalities in wealth, as in the case of the taxation of the Third Estate in France and Germany in the 18th century; or in order to reduce the economic gap between the classes through progressive taxes. He takes as examples the redistribution of social spending for the benefit of the poorest, financed by taxes on the richest, the difference of taxation depending on professional categories, and the taxation of non-proletarian classes or of farmers refusing the kolkhozes in Soviet Russia. Regarding the economic organization, he points out the "regulatory function" of business, for example, in the 1930s, expressed by the "punitive taxation" (p. 233) of big American enterprises in order to avoid the formation of monopolies. He also mentions the possibility for taxing wealth by means of a "confiscatory tax" (p. 234) or, in an intermediary way between liberalism and socialism, by means of a tax on wealth that is inherited and not gained.

In an article published in 1947 in the same journal (Mann, 1947), Mann is interested in the financial dimension of revolutions. In a way also used by the Italian founders of fiscal sociology, he starts from the historical division between the ruling class and the class of the ruled: he notes that taxation has often permitted both to manage the State and to strengthen the position of the group in power. He emphasizes however that public finance constitute on the whole forces acting sometimes in the sense of maintaining order and other times in the sense of revolution.

On the conservative side, the rulers of democracies have certainly ensured the financing of public assistance and of several public services, but they have also granted benefits to members of their social group.[34] Besides, corruption is a widespread phenomenon. Mann also shows that taxation preserves "the existing social", when tax is conceived as the price to pay in exchange for the benefit received from a public service. So within the conception of the exchange-tax, the taxpayer's economic situation is the same before and after tax: the social structure therefore

---

comply with the code on coal. As for the "vice", Mann mentions the taxation on drugs, gambling, and alcohol.

34 "As long as any government represents the class or party in power, neither government regulation nor parliament control will suffice to prevent the channelling of fiscal funds into the pockets of the leading group" (p. 332). Here, without explicitly mentioning Machiavelli or Pareto, Mann refers to the "lions" to describe this behaviour.

remains identical. On a more general level, this observation is valid for all taxation techniques inspired by the principle of tax neutrality.

On the revolutionary side, Mann studies several situations of change through taxes. He criticizes Goldscheid for having overrated the place of fiscal sociology in the whole field of sociology. He evokes the historical case of an "oppressive" tax pressure (p. 336) characterized by the squandering of public funds, tax privileges, the reduction of the public domain leading to budget deficits. He estimates that public finance rarely constitutes sufficient a factor to explain revolutions. The Fronde of the Parliament in 1648 was also explained by the rejection of political centralization. Before the French Revolution, the situation had improved at the end of the *Ancien Régime*, despite public debt and taxation. Bankers, merchants, lawyers, bourgeois proprietors belonging to "the middle class" carved out for themselves a "lion's share" from the national wealth (p. 339) and desired to adjust their political power to their economic importance. The American Revolution of 1689 is also explained by the "political and religious motivation" (p. 340) against the English authority. For Mann, financial factors especially play the role of psychological incentives, of a "starter" in the revolutionary process (p. 342).

In a third article, Mann (1949) proposes a reorientation of financial theory. Within the context of the Keynesian New Deal, a major change has taken place: the government assumes more and more functions by means of public expenses (growth of the public sector); taxes fulfil from then on a "social function" (p. 119) apart from its classical financing function; public debt has a beneficial effect on the economy at certain stages of the economic cycle.[35] He distinguishes "fiscal theory" from "public finance", the two approaches differing "in their ends rather than in their means" (p. 122). Public finance is concerned by the financing of the government, the efficiency of revenues in comparison to the expenses; fiscal theory is about the regulation of the social sector or of the economy through the finances. Drawing conclusions from Keynes's theory, he proposes that fiscal theory studies the size and the structure of tax revenue, public investment, the role of debt. He especially defends "a broader concept of taxation covering both its regulatory and its redistributional function" (p. 128), in addition to the traditional financial function. The political and ethical aspects must therefore be taken into account.

So, beyond the outdated debate on vocabulary, Mann was one of the first to conceive the necessity for a functional fiscal sociology. This direction remained little explored afterwards, insofar as economists have

[35] Mann (p. 120-121) observes that precursors have ever since the 18th century defended the usefulness of public loans.

refocused and hence reduced the functional analysis to its economic dimension. It is however a promising direction in order to widen and renew the economic approach in taxation through its socio-political functions. By basing itself on other premises, the Italian school proposes, with notably Pareto, another structuring of the economic and social dimensions of public finance.

2. Pareto's Fiscal Sociology

Pareto is a complex writer, considered at the same time as a classic in economics and in sociology. He did not present a complete theory of public finance, but opened up serious tracks to be followed while at the same time encouraging his students to invest in this field in a sociological way. The *Trattato di Sociologia generale* (*The Mind and Society: A Treatise on General Sociology*[36]) begins with a criticism of the financial science in order to show that the finances constitute non-logical actions in the service of the ruling elite. The economic dimension cannot thus be considered in either an autonomous or normative way, but depends on this socio-political reality where the idea is to think by means of successive approximations.

a. Criticism of financial science (and of pure economics)

On several occasions Pareto criticized the public finance science of his time.[37] In this sense he legitimates financial sociology as a socio-political approach. In *The Mind and Society* (*Traité de sociologie générale*), he introduces the "two kinds of derivations"[38] intrinsic to this domain (Pareto, 1968, § 2273): those "that aim at drawing inferences from certain ethical or sentimental principles and which may go far wide of realities"; those that "aim at giving a theoretical tinge to results which have been arrived at in an entirely different manner."

Pareto justifies his financial sociology with criticism of the economics of "needs".[39] After having highlighted a first group of derivations in

---

36 The study comprises advances in public finance. In the quotations we refer to the paragraph number in Pareto, 1983.

37 As noted by Fasiani, 1949, p. 267; Boccacio, De Bonis, 2003, p. 89; McLure, 2006, p. 523.

38 The derivations are systems of justifications where interests and passions are hidden, pseudo-scientific constructions. It is not useful to develop the general presentation of Pareto's thought which is the subject of numerous studies.

39 He takes the example of the defense budget (§ 2272): let there be country G which has sovereignty over province A whose inhabitants want to unite with country F. G charges a tax, also levied on A, in order to finance armament to be used against F. G pretends that it is a collective need of the whole country (including A). The collective need thus covers according to Pareto the need of all the members of the community,

the political field, where people prefer "ethical derivations" (§ 2262) to logical-experimental arguments, he refutes the analysis of needs made by pure economics and, in its wake, by the science of finances: "noteworthy among such derivations is a pseudo-scientific variety obtained by extending the notions of pure economics to the social 'needs' of a people" (§ 2271). Now, according to Pareto, the science of finances (of that time) based on marginal utility does not provide any help[40] since "the concept of 'public needs' is used to eliminate artificially the difficulties". Public finance where "non-logical actions figure very largely" forms part of a socio-political approach. They are not a subject for pure economics which, in a "first approximation" studies the logical actions in procuring economic property. They generate numerous derivations among which that relative to collective needs; but reality is placed in the objectives of the rulers: "such persons may be fooled by a well-conceived derivation. A government is never short of such sophistries, and theorists are always available to provide new ones. It should not be forgotten, however, that the derivations are consequences of the government's policies, never the political consequences of the derivations" (§ 2273).

Methodological considerations occupy an important place in the *Treaty*. By referring to the pseudo-scientific notion (derivation) of need[41], the simple budgetary analysis of the revenue (taxes) and expenditure is not suitable for obtaining a "conception of the economic

of certain members, of most of the community, or of the elite. Normally, financial science deals with the needs of the first type.

40 Which provokes his criticism of the hedonistic approach to utility: "it is assumed that such 'needs' are satisfied by the 'state'; then by consideration of marginal utilities, one derives the norms of a certain equilibrium between 'needs' and the 'sacrifices' required for satisfying them. So one gets theories that may conform to formal logic in certain cases but which are so far removed from realities as at times to have nothing in common with them (...) The concept of 'needs' is in no way definable (...) All that could have a meaning, as applied to a community, only if the community could be considered as a single person" (§ 2271).

41 "After the cost of the government plant has been determined (...), its product has to be computed. That is a very difficult problem (...) Approximate solutions have had to be adopted, therefore. One such is (...) that the government provides for 'public needs', and does so by levying taxes. That is a way of balancing the two sheets in the socio-economic ledger of the state (...) Then, to satisfy the need for logical developments, a series of derivatives are put forward to show the 'need' and to justify the apportionment that 'ought' – so it is preached – to be made, according to the sentimental principles of one or another of the many social moralities current. In that way one gets the solution most compatible with the sentiment of the author of the theory (...), but not the solution that the best pictures the facts as they are" (§ 2269 and 2270).

results of the various types of government"[42] (§ 2269). One should therefore discard the biased arguments of the strictly economic approach, which indeed specifies the idea that public finance corresponds to non-logical actions. It is also a question of distinguishing ethics from social utility, even if "it is better" (§ 2274) for those who benefit from it that the people concerned by a certain measure confuse the two.

In order to solve this difficult problem, we must consider "the complexity of the situation" (§ 2274) by studying its constituent elements such as the relation to prosperity, to the stimulation of the economy, to social prosperity[43] and to "class-circulation" (*elite*). As approximation, we should consider the interdependence between the political domain, through the (logical) types of government, and the economic domain, through the cycles of economic prosperity.

b. Finance as an instrument of the ruling elite

Pareto's financial sociology is then anchored in his theory of elites which is in line with the Machiavellian tradition carried on also by Mosca and Michels. Apart from the already noted denunciation of the ideology of needs, it is based on the study of the instruments of government. Regardless of the form of political regime, the government is always that of a category of people, the governing class or the ruling elite: "A governing class is present everywhere, even where there is a despot, but the forms under which it appears are widely variable" (§ 2253). It governs by using two principal instruments – force and ruse: "Consent and force appear in all the course of history as instruments of governing" (§ 2251).[44] Democratic regimes tend to use ruse (like a fox) rather than force (like a lion), by creating loyal clientele and, as we have seen, by using derivations: "Evolution towards 'democracy' seems to stand in strict correlation with the increased use of that instrument of governing which involves resort to artifice and to the 'machine' (*clien-*

42 "As regards expenditures (…) for account has to be taken of the costs of economic and political favouritism, of the wastage resulting from so-called social legislation" (§ 2269).

43 Social prosperity aims at defence, public security, the quality of justice, public works, and the other governmental functions which for Pareto must nevertheless remain limited: cf. below.

44 An assertion which Pareto repeats on several occasions, for example: "for purposes of maintaining its power the governing class uses individuals from the subject class, who may be grouped in two divisions corresponding to the two principal instruments for holding power secure. The one group uses force (…) the other uses skill (*ruse*)" (§ 2257). "The governing class sees to appropriating other people's property not only for its own use, but also to share with such members of the subject class as defend it and safe-guards its rule, whether by force or by fraud (*ruse*) – the support the client lends to the patron" (§ 2267).

tela), as against the instrument of force" (§ 2259).[45] The clientele can be satisfied by different instruments drawn for example from economic policy (protectionism, corruption: § 2257), but public finance plays an important role because "money has to be spent to secure the support both of armed force and of political machines" (§ 2258).

The theory of public finance must take into account the true nature of government. The government tries to tax taxpayers as much as possible except when their resistance is too strong: "Governments try to get all they can out of the public and are never embarrassed by lack of 'needs' to satisfy. Their one check is resistance on the part of the taxpayers" (§ 2273). Taxes serve to finance expenditures that interest the classes who support the government: There are "ways of estimating the forces prompting expenditures and originating in individuals who are to profit by them, and the forces running counter to new taxes and originating in individuals who will be damaged by them" (§ 2273). Here Pareto's analysis is particularly severe for democracies "tending more and more to become demagogic plutocracies" (§ 2257) by using ruse and clientelism, and public expenditures, in order to convert this regime into "a sort of feudalism that is primarily economic" (§ 2259).

In this way the scientific study of public finance as government instruments is part of the particular problematic of the expenditures of democracies which Pareto links to clientelism. He refers to the general theory of "residues"[46] to describe the two main types of government in this field.[47] Governments using force have a ruling class where "Class II residues predominate" (a tendency to the "persistence of aggregates"). They are "not expensive governments", but "fail to stimulate economic production" since "they are conservative by temperament"; the coming to power of economically more dynamic elites is difficult because the "class-circulation is generally slow" (§ 2274). Democratic governments use ruse to act upon interests, without neglecting feelings.[48] The ruling

45 "One extreme is marked by the Rome of the praetorians, where the chief *de facto* instrument of governing (…) was armed force. The other extreme is represented by the United States of America, where the chief actual instrument of governing (…) is the political machine" (§ 2257).

46 Residues are studied in chapter VI of the *Treaty* and aim at the roots of social phenomena (just like linguists search into the roots of words. § 879) which are then often disguised under diverse justifications (the derivations). It retains 6 classes of residues (the name is arbitrary according to Pareto: § 868) which only an inductive method can show.

47 Pareto does not exclude other, less widespread, types of government and emphasizes that there are in reality variable combinations between these two major types of government (§ 2277).

class possesses "combination instincts in high degree" (§ 2276) (with Class I residues) to cover up its particular goals by general justifications. These governments are "expensive (...), but they produce actively", which can create an excess of revenue (in a broad sense) over expenditure if the economic context is favorable.

c. *The economic dimension*

The economic dimension of finance is analyzed through the oscillations of prosperity and stagnation, and through the distribution of wealth. With regard to economic prosperity, Pareto is interested in the relevant quantitative indicators and considers various factors that influence economic prosperity. As usual, he relies on numerous historical examples (conquests, precious metals, discoveries, technical innovations etc.). As for the modern period (since the 19th century), he emphasizes the "preponderance of economic over other interests" and "a greatly accelerated circulation between classes (*elite*)" (§ 2300). From a methodological point of view, it is a question of a "first approximation" of the phenomenon, knowing that the general objective aims at the comprehension "of the elements upon which the social equilibrium depends", which are in a situation of "interdependence" (*mutual dependence*) (§ 2203).[49] From that point onwards, according to Pareto, economic interests prevail in foreign policy (§ 2300). In addition, "class-circulation at the present time, therefore, raises to membership in the ruling class large numbers of persons who destroy wealth, but even larger numbers who produce wealth" (§ 2301).[50] The growth in the economic prosperity in the 19th century stands as a proof.

---

48 Even though history has known other cases, these characteristics concern "the very important type of government flourishing in our day – government by speculators" (§ 2275). One overlooks, going along with Pareto's thinking, the ("disappeared") governments that use ruse to act on feelings.

49 In fact, in order to compensate for the impossibility of a mathematical consideration of all the elements and interdependencies according to quantitative methods based on equations and indicators, Pareto retains only the most important factors which he combines by successive approximations. The 4 possible combinations are those between the 4 factors formed by the residues, the interests, the derivations and the circulation of the elites (heterogeneity and social circulation) (§ 2205 and 2206). For the societies "of the civilized peoples of the West from the beginning of the nineteenth century down to the present time" (§ 2299), combinations II and IV bring to the forefront the interests and the circulation of the elites.

50 "Nowadays almost anybody who possesses a good supply of Class I residues (combination-instincts) and knows how to use his talents in industry, agriculture, commerce, and the arts; in organizing financial enterprises, honest or dishonest (...) is certain (...) not only to amass wealth but (...) to become, in a word, a member of the ruling class" (§ 2300).

This analysis[51] leads to establishing, by using empirical examples, the relation of the government with the economic situation which facilitates its action: "since modern governments are keeping in power less and less by resort to force and more and more by a very expensive art of government, they have a very urgent need of economic prosperity" (§ 2305). On a directly budgetary level, the recourse to loans[52] is "convenient" (§ 2306) in order to finance these expenses which are in a way constraint by the necessity to remain in power. Pareto also mentions special or extraordinary budgeting processes that conceal the reality of public finance.

As long as economic prosperity is present, this mode of action remains possible, but in case of economic stagnation, the government can no longer use public expenses to satisfy its partisans and the "selfish interests" (§ 2309). Thus, the periods of growth are favourable for those whom Pareto calls the "speculators" (*S*) "who grow rich and win places in the governing class" (§ 2310). Growth put the "rentiers" (*R*) at a disadvantage, with the opposite occurring in periods of stagnation.[53] Social heterogeneity actually depends largely on the proportion of the two categories in the governing class, proportion which corresponds to various "types of civilization" (§ 2236). "In modern democratic countries industrial protection increases the proportion of *S*'s in the governing class" (§ 2236).

The conception of history and society put forward by Pareto is based on the theory of oscillations by discarding "the narrow ethical ground" (§ 2316). The periods of economic stagnation when savings rise prepare the periods of prosperity when savings drop "and so on indefinitely" (§ 2318). These oscillations are superimposed by a longer oscillation (generally lasting centuries), resulting from the struggle for power

---

51 It must be pointed out that Pareto, whose study concerns reality and not norms or ethics, refuses to see whether economic prosperity would have been attained by saving on the expenses of "financial, political, and other parasites" (§ 2301).

52 "In arranging for the combinations that are indispensable to their existence, modern governments commonly spend in a given period more than their revenues would allow, covering the difference by contracting overt or secret debts" (§ 2306).

53 Speculators (§ 2232 to 2235) possess a strong instinct for combinations, "indispensable to success in enterprise" (§ 2232), they love movement, adventure and understand "individuals whose incomes are essentially variable and depend upon the person's wideawakeness in discovering sources of gain" (§ 2233), whereas rentiers are provided with residues ("persistence of aggregates "or 'conservative' residues of Class II: § 2232) and are more timorous, depending on their savings, on their properties, in short, on any non-speculative income. These categories therefore depend on residues, and even though there may be points of contact, these are not the categories of innovators, revolutionaries, conservatives etc. Rentiers are easy to despoil; speculators are quick to engage in economic ventures (§ 2313). We must also note that a capitalist can be a speculator or a rentier.

between the rentiers and the speculators. The speculators, with their corporate activity, are not sensitive to business taxes which they pass on (economic incidence) to consumers (§ 2231), while the rentiers, possessors of savings, are despoiled among other things by taxes (§ 2316). In this way economic crises, here the despoliation of savers, are not exceptional phenomena.[54] Actually, a crisis constitutes an example (oscillation) "as regular, as normal, as any other development in human society". The difference does not lie in the content, as history is made up of these more or less important oscillations, but in the form, with the advent of ruse "in view of the gradual elimination of the more brutal procedures". It will thus be a methodological error to think that the despoliation, the recurrent attacks on private property, the periodicity of crises[55] and the historic persistence of (real) inequalities in conditions could be modified. In fact, this type of attempt is an error "namely, of using a qualitative instead of a quantitative analysis" based on the respective number of speculators and rentiers. On a more general level, this approach consists in neglecting the interdependence of the social phenomena that form part of the "conditions determining the social equilibrium."

Concerning the distribution of wealth, the method is based on tax data (tax returns) in order to question the theory of distribution. Pareto aims to position himself against State intervention strongly recommended by the socialist programme in tax matters. He has explained his method and his conclusions in several written works, notably in the *Course in political economy* (Pareto, 1964). According to him, the distribution of incomes is not the effect of chance. It does not depend on economic organization: "the form of this curve seems to depend only slightly on the different economic conditions of the countries considered" (Pareto, 1964, § 960). It has the form of "an arrow whose point is very sharp and base very wide", and not the form of a (social) pyramid (Pareto, 1965, p. 16). According to Pareto, the conclusion is emphatic: changing the situation of the poor depends only on wealth.[56] It consti-

54 This idea is developed in the course book on political economy, in volume 2 chapter IV.

55 The usual theories of economic crises are wrong; they are derivations on social prosperity, since "the term 'crisis' designating nothing but the descending period in an oscillation" (§ 2335). This analysis had been developed in the *Course in political economy*: "one must therefore not imagine a crisis as an accident that comes to interrupt the normal state of things. On the contrary, that which is normal is the wave motion; economic prosperity bringing depression, and depression leading back to prosperity" (§ 926 of the *Course*).

56 Pareto admits that beneficiaries may change by reason of mutually dependent elements, notably the circulation of the elites (social mobility) and the economic situation. But the reality of the law of social inequality depends neither on the economic

tutes a problem of production and not of distribution: "it is imperative, so that the reduction of income inequality takes place in a regular, average, permanent way, that the sum total of incomes increases in comparison to the population" (Pareto, 1964, § 965). The socialist programme aimed at reducing inequalities is doomed to failure: "the first effect of the efforts made by State socialism to artificially change this distribution is a destruction of wealth. So the goal they achieve is exactly opposite to the goal they had in mind: that is, they worsen the conditions of the poor class instead of improving them" (Pareto, 1965, p. 17).

For the sociology of public finance, this economic perspective thus presents less interest than the financial theory which is in the *Treaty*. In fact, Pareto's "law" neglects the lowest, non-taxable incomes and the high incomes which escape tax. Pareto's political conclusion concerning the immutable character of inequality is unsubstantiated: as is underlined by Piketty (2001, p. 528), if a limited number of parameters certainly account for the distribution of wealth, these parameters may vary considerably. We must add that Pareto's reticence to any State intervention precludes him from proposing a real link with the general sociology of social heterogeneity and of the circulation of elites explained in the *Treaty*. He thus only proposes the economic solution for the improvement of prosperity, but the mutual dependence method is then denied. The objective of the universal "law" of the distribution of income, first published in 1896, is above all ideological. It concerns the history of economic thought but also shows the limits of the Paretan system.

d. The contribution and the limits of the Paretan theory

The financial theory presented by Pareto in the *Treaty* is methodologically elaborate. It is basically coherent with the general context of its analysis and with its basic concepts. Of course, Pareto did not develop a complete theory of public finance. He is satisfied to touch on the problem ("let us barely touch upon it": § 2274) which gets numerous interdependent elements to intervene, elements which he wanted to involve in the conditions of the general social equilibrium. Although incomplete in its general intention, this theory provides interesting ideas but already contains certain limits. The method of non-logical actions and of derivations (ideologies, wrong scientific theories) opens perspectives for financial (fiscal) sociology, on the conditions of not retaining a skeptical conception of rationality. As we will see (chapter 9), the approach through cognitive rationality leads to transcending the all too rigid separation between the logical action, which one can assimilate to the utilitarian methodology (rational choice theory) in a restricted meaning,

---

organization nor on improvement of the education nor on the establishing of a socialist regime.

and the non-logical action, which has to be viewed from the actor's viewpoint in his context. The methodology of interdependance is also important. It emphasizes the complexity of the financial phenomenon as well as the political dimension which, according to Pareto, is to be sought in the activity of the ruling classes. It calls upon a synthetic approach (§ 2258) to the various topics of financial public action (after the analytic approach of each topic). It supposes that one must not separate the economy from politics, while at the same time authorizing by approximation the particular study of the interdependence of the economic situation and the circulation of the elites.[57]

This methodology nevertheless remains guided by determinism, a subtle one undoubtedly[58], but marked by a profound historical pessimism. The intrinsic limit of Pareto's financial sociology basically resides in the failure to link three levels of analysis: the commitment against State intervention, the wave conception of history, and the synthetic methodology. This positioning of the problem[59] leads him to focus on the flaws of the science of finances of his time and on the denunciation of the real functioning of democracies.[60] Rekindling an idea expressed by Tocqueville, he notes: "there is a tendency in our societies to have taxes voted by the great majority that does not pay them, and to lay the burden on a small minority" (§ 2553). But unlike Tocqueville in his financial sociology, his liberalism leads him to a scientific impasse.

57 For a reflection on the hegemony of economics as a mirror image of politics: cf. M. Tucci, 2007. For a study on the historical influence of the elite conflict in the cases of early modern Spain, France, the Netherlands and Britain: cf. Lachmann, 2009 and chapter 4.

58 Comparing "the Imperial authority in the days of the decline" with "the democratic plutocracy ruling", he concludes: "We are very apparently moving along a curve such as Roman society traversed in its day after the founding of the Empire and showing a period of prosperity and then, as it was prolonged, a period of decline. History does not repeat itself. Unless one chooses to believe in some 'yellow peril' there is little likelihood that the next period of prosperity that is to come will originate in another Barbarian invasion" (§ 2553).

59 A position which is explained, on the one hand, by his project to create a general sociological framework, valid for all particular sociologies and, on the other hand, by his deep conviction of the evils of State intervention, which he had observed in Italy in particular with the adoption of a customs tariff in 1886.

60 While Pareto vilifies the diverse forms of ethics which he invites to be distinguished from reality, he has written much in defense of free trade. On this point he distinguishes himself from Walras, his predecessor in the university chair in Lausanne, who, despite having demonstrated in pure economics the importance of the competitive market model, considered that in applied economics total laissez-faire would not be suitable.

Pareto uses a polemic tone to denounce all forms of public interventionism: exploited people's money goes to "a demagogic plutocrat" (§ 2553) who defends his "comforts and pleasures". He denounces the waste that results from it.[61] He also criticizes the increase of corruption by the interventionist State.[62] He vilifies the surcharging of the rich.[63] These critiques are in coherence with the conception of the clientelism of the ruling elite in modern democracies, who governs using ruse by buying social peace and by favouring the "speculators". But they do not fit in well with the idea of the inexorability of the succession of historic (and economic) waves due to the circulation of the elites between the lions and foxes (and speculators and rentiers): there is no point in denouncing the interventionist State if its wretched manifestations are inherent to the general shape of society and to the heterogeneity of class relations. Above all, this position contradicts Pareto's methodological postulate which consists in excluding all ethical bias in favour of science, notably because of the primacy of the study of the general social equilibrium.[64] This postulate is put forward (§ 2316) in order to show the uselessness of any reform meant to fight against the attacks on property and against despoiling and social inequalities. By condemning State intervention, the master from Lausanne contradicts his own methodology. In his system of thought, public action would actually be perceived as a clientelist ruse of elitist democracy whose relations to the general social equilibrium must be examined. Pareto thus fails to explore the link between his ethical horizon and his sociological analysis, unlike Tocqueville when he analyses the French Revolution (cf. chapter 1).

---

61 For example, in the passage following the analysis of expenses as means of power or of clientele, he criticizes the construction of a courthouse in Rome in 1913 meant "to give employment to (…) labourers who were so faithful and so inactive" (§ 2259, note 1).

62 "Uses and abuses of power will be greater, the more extensive the government's interference in private business. As raw material increases, the amount that can be earned from it increases" (§ 2267).

63 "To escape unbearable burdens, taxpayers are sending their funds to other countries, and the governments under which they live grow indignant and try to reach them in various ways. And so agreements of mutual aid have been reached – and they may well be called conspiracies between exploiters – between the governments of the democratic plutocracies" (§ 2553).

64 "From an ethical standpoint a measure may be judged apart from all other social phenomena, but from the standpoint of social utility that cannot be done; the effects of the measure on the equilibrium as a whole have to be considered. A measure that is reprehensible from the ethical standpoint may be altogether commendable from the standpoint of social utility; and, *vice versa* (…). But in that connexion it is better for the subject portion of the population to believe that there is an exact identity between the ethical value of a measure and its social utility" (§ 2274).

Without dwelling on this hiatus[65], we should also consider his model of financial democracy. This model is more restricted (method of approximations) than the general theorization of the relations to the social equilibrium. Two levels ("elements") are treated explicitly: the political level with the four variables of ideology (the derivations targeting the "feelings"), clientelism, despoiling (targeting the "interests") and the circulation of the elites; the economic level with the two variables of economic waves (prosperity/stagnation) and the circulation of the elites (already present at a political level). This model, though created by Pareto as a methodological principle, remains below the complexity of the phenomenon of financial democracy. It is less elaborate than Tocqueville's model, which considers, apart from the political and economic dimensions, the sociological level of the effects of education and of social values, and the cognitive level of the preference for the concrete[66] and for the short-term benefits.

If the theory of public finance introduced by Pareto is taken as a particular sociology of the general sociology of social equilibrium, appreciating it is more complicated. The complex determinism of the general form of society which aims at taking into account the structural forces of history[67] remains very abstract[68] in order to examine its value in the field of interventionist democracy. Unlike Tocqueville's tendential (or conditional) laws, the laws of history and of society are seen as immutable, even if the problem of the dynamics of social change is taken into account beyond the precarious (static) social equilibriums achieved. A very concise proposition of this theory is that history is that of elites struggling for power, while helping themselves from expenditures and growing rich at the cost of others. To the fundamental question to know whether modern democracy is in its essence spendthrift (interventionist), Pareto's response is affirmative, like Tocqueville and Wagner, in consideration of the strong clientelism. Pareto insists on this especially for

---

65 Another example is given by Pareto's denouncing of the elites who do not defend their power.

66 Pareto was however on the track with this cognitive factor, which he classifies as "derivation": "among the derivations which they use to show that their rule is to the advantage of a country, interesting is the assertion that the public is better qualified to pass on general questions than on special ones. The fact, in reality, is the precise opposite. One has to talk only for a very brief time with an uneducated person to see that he grasps special questions, which are usually concrete, much more clearly than general questions, which as a rule are abstract" (§ 2253).

67 In other words: "the fact that history shows certain groups of simultaneous ties functioning in every age proves that those ties are interdependent (real movements) not only among each other but also with other conditions determining the social equilibrium" (§ 2316).

68 Combining at the general level residues, interests, derivations, heterogeneity (stratification) and circulation of the elites (mobility).

the modern democracies where "the practical financial science of a minister of state (...) comes down altogether to finding ways and means for overcoming the taxpayer's resistance, for plucking the goose without causing too much honking" (§ 2273).

His response, however, is not so clear and cannot be considered as describing a definite tendency. In fact, his historical determinism and his pessimism concerning the permanence of the oligarchic structure of society, even if the elites in power seemingly circulate, do not allow him to formulate such a categorical theory of democratic finance. The "synthetic" methodology of the interdependence of the elements turns out to be in this case an obstacle for the exploration, even by "approximation", of a tendential analytical law, proper to the democratic society. This deficiency is reinforced by Pareto's ideological preference against any State interventionism. In this way, the ruling elite can mislead the masses (ideology of "feelings"); it is dependent on the economic cycle and the structural modification of the social stratification (and of the residues) which modifies the circulation of the elites and the social equilibrium etc. But the main lesson remains that State interventionism is harmful, however that may be.

Finally Pareto, despite the richness of his fiscal sociology, remains trapped in a theory of financial constraints which conceals the real possibility of choices in a democratic society (cf. chapter 7). In spite of the complex political sociology which surrounds it, the economic situation remains apprehended as a simple determinism for the clientelism of the ruling class. Furthermore, Pareto, who saw the birth of the idea of the Welfare State, does not try to anticipate the compromises which will be found in this field by democracy (cf. chapter 11). Influenced by an ethical bias, not very compatible with his methodological vocation, he condemns in advance the *Welfare State* which leads to the destruction of all individual initiative, to the annihilation of all human dignity, and degrades man to the level of sheep (*Course in political economy*, § 998). Rejecting all form of redistribution of wealth through tax or through expenditure, he presents a strong theory of constraint to the detriment of the democratic theory of political choices, while relying upon a conception of power which characterizes the Italian school.

3. The Italian School (*stricto sensu*)

All the Italian authors in the science of finance are acquainted with Pareto's financial sociology, whether they accept it or not. Four names however stand out among the writers influenced by the master from

Lausanne[69]: Guido Sensini and Gino Borgatta, Roberto Murray, Benvenuto Griziotti. We do not consider here the approach based on voluntary exchange with reference to marginalism[70], in order to retain on three authors representative of the political approach (not Paretan): Carlo Angelo Conigliani, Amilcare Puviani, Giovanni Montemartini.

a. *Guido Sensini*

Guido Sensini, a student of Pareto, tried to treat the problem of public finance in relation to the social equilibrium.[71] He summarized his position in a text published in 1929, "Cenni di finanza teorica" in the *Giornale degli economisti* that is used here in its recent English translation. For this writer public finance contains two problems: the determination of revenue and expenditure, their effect on the social equilibrium (Sensini, 2007, p. 249). He starts by classifying human actions into three types and introduces the category of "mixed actions" (p. 21) as a complement to Pareto's binary classification, which distinguished between logical and non-logical actions. He specifies in a note that actions combining logical and non-logical actions are the most important ones.[72]

He then states the importance of the relation government/governed, while specifying that the government does not only include the official holders of government positions, but also those whose interests are taken into consideration (note 5). In Paretan vein he then rejects the reality of governments acting in strict logic, taking up here (note 10) again the criticism of the notion of needs from the *Treaty* which we have already presented: real governments act in accordance with "the possibility of remaining in power" (p. 252). Still following his master, he points out that "the class that supports a government" tries to draw "the greatest advantage possible from this situation" (p. 253). Nonetheless,

69 We refer to the passages quoted in the English translation of the article reproduced in the book by McLure, 2007. It neglects Aldo Scotto's attempt, more restraint and more distant from Pareto's thinking, on the notion of financial decentralization.

70 Notably Pantaleoni, De Viti de Marco, Mazzola. Buchanan (1960) presented the Italian tradition of public finance from a predominantly economic point of view which does not concern fiscal sociology directly. The authors of the Italian financial science have sometims taken into account socio-political elements in their economic approach (Boggeri, Sundelson, 1938, p. 252). For example, Pantaleoni (1967, p. 27) points out that the parliament's attitude is a political factor to assess a country's level of tolerance to taxation.

71 We leave aside Sensini's work on the Ricardian equivalence between an extraordinary tax and a loan, in relation to the economic and social equilibrium, since, according to McLure's study (2005, p. 620), the author came to the conclusion that it is impossible to find a solution to this problem with regard to available knowledge.

72 The minimum of the "non-logical" is found in economic actions, so that in a first approximation pure economics may rightly neglect this part, and the maximum of the "non-logical" is linked to religion.

the government can also use ideal motives when responding to the feelings of the masses in order to better establish its domination, and thus satisfy these demands with expenditure financed by taxes.[73] The goal of the ruling class is to maintain the tax pressure as low as possible, while at the same time obtaining advantages through public expenditure. Fiscal policy thus varies in accordance with the composition of the dominant class to be favoured and with class conflicts in the sense of Pareto.

In this way, Sensini's analysis answers the question about the determination of revenue and expenditure by following Pareto's theoretical scheme, but by putting mixed actions, combining logical and non-logical, at the centre of financial sociology. The relation to the social equilibrium is then treated, starting by the economic effects, which is in compliance with the Paretan methodology of equilibrium. For that he distinguishes the individual effects from the collective effects both of taxes and expenditure. At the individual level, or at the level of a class of individuals such as the entrepreneurs, "the principal aim of pure fiscal theory" is to produce within a process of pure economics "the mathematical theory" of the phenomena of repercussion or incidence[74] (Sensini, 2007, p. 255). At a collective level, the effects of the revenue should be examined in accordance with the type of tax (for example, direct or indirect), with the rates and procedures of taxation (proportional, progressive or regressive tax), with a similar procedure for the expenditure. Here Sensini (p. 256-257) emphasizes, following Pareto, that "economic prosperity increases" when public finance favours a transfer of wealth "from those who are the less able to those who are more able in economic operations", that is by favouring the "speculators". But, by introducing elements of the pure science of finance (incidence…), he disagrees with his master who considered that only the sociology of non-logical action had to be applied to the study of public finance. He also gives a place to the budgetary technique which he calls "the fiscal effects" (p. 257). He studies the budgetary impact (for the State) of the characteristics of taxes, for example a wide tax base, and of expenditure, for example the impact of social legislation.

Sensini finishes his analysis of the social equilibrium with the study of the "political effects" which concern the phenomena which link

---

73 He quotes Pareto's passage in the *Treaty* (§ 2273: cf. before) on the practical science of a minister consisting in overcoming the taxpayer's resistance (cf. before).

74 Sensini (2007, p. 256) underlines the difficulty of the operation. For example, an alcoholic, faced with the increase of excise taxes on alcoholic drinks, may diminish his consumption, or may continue drinking as much and save on other expenses. In order to establish the equations of economic equilibrium, economists brush aside these questions.

"revenue and expenditure" (...) and the various types of government (...), (and) the circulation of the *élites* (p. 257). He recalls that whatever the form of budget and the type of government, the aim of expenditure will be that the "government can stay in power". Quoting *The Treaty* of Pareto once again, he notes that the expenditure necessary for force and for clientelism, which corresponds "to the level of the taxation burden imposed on the nation" is related to "the quantity of wealth the nation can produce", and hence to the "periods of economic prosperity" (p. 257). These questions, according to Sensini, fall in the field of sociology. His concludes that the factors thus analyzed are the principal elements for a scientific theory of public finance, even if other factors (psychological, demographic, moral etc.) might intervene.

b. Gino Borgatta

Gino Borgatta, another one of Pareto's followers[75], also criticizes the dominant approach of the science of finance, in particular in a text published in 1920, as always in the *Giornale degli economisti*, entitled "Lo studio scientifico dei fenomeni finanziari" (Borgatta, 2007, p. 203-204). Following Pareto's thinking, he considers that one must treat the sociological problems as well as the economic problems. The financial phenomenon cannot be studied only from the point of view of pure economics or as a pure system of logical actions. Nevertheless, he gives a certain place to economic analysis because, contrary to Pareto, he admits that finance comprises a part of "logical" actions: "it is evident that the study of the effects and of the laws of fiscal facts would not be possible if we did not have the strictly economic knowledge provided by the science of economics. The fact that the activities and the functions carried out by the governing groups have a cost (...) implies in itself a series of logical economic actions in the groups that were hit and in the groups that were favoured. The fiscal phenomenon contributes to change and to determine the economic equilibrium of each aggregate" (p. 237). He then gives a list of problems depending on the pure economic approach and on logical action: the incidence of taxes, public monopolies, public loans etc. He calls for a dynamic approach that considers the impact of these measures as a "variation", "new conditions" of a "static economic equilibrium" (p. 238).

But the analysis must above all focus on the sociological dimension of financial phenomena. Quoting Pareto, Borgatta (p. 108) takes up again the criticism of the State conceived as responding to collective needs by levying taxes in order to finance expenditure. The sociological dimension of the financial phenomenon is given by his scientific defini-

---

[75] On the relations between Borgatta and Pareto, cf. McLure, 2006.

tion as "a transfer of wealth from certain individuals and groups to certain other individuals or groups that does not happen on the basis of economic acts and exchanges. Sociological finance must establish the forces and laws because of which these movements of wealth actually happen" (p. 211). Like Pareto, Borgatta specifies that "the governing class must find the means to secure the necessary or desired profits for itself and for the groups that support it and share its interests" (p. 217). He considers in a more original manner, in a line of thought which Mann explored for the Austrian school, that public expenditure fulfils "political-social functions" p. 217 (defence, justice, administrative organization, police etc.) that taxes must finance. But, like Pareto, he emphasizes the importance of relating these elements to the social equilibrium, considering that "societies are governed by a minority that is never confined to one individual" (p. 218).

The manner in which Borgatta specifies in the field of public finance the Paretan analysis is interesting.[76] Treating the economic equilibrium, which participates in the social equilibrium, he privileges the interdependence of the speculators and the rentiers: "the classes described as speculators' classes are those that generally have the greatest opportunities of evading taxes (...) because their incomes are either formally exempt from tax (realization of capital gains) or far harder to ascertain" (p. 221). The consumption tax affects only slightly the commercial profits of speculators. The rentiers who live on fixed incomes escape taxes less and put up with the measures of conversion of public debt (which they finance) to a lower level, monetary devaluations etc. Wars, which were not directly wanted by the speculators, benefit them since they adapt to the war economy (p. 223). The characteristics of the tax advantages consecrated to this class vary from one State to the other, but in modern times this is a common phenomenon (cf. chapter 11 of this book): "in all the great modern nations, the fiscal phenomenon, with all the transfers of wealth that the political fact brings about, has powerfully contributed to the formation of the high economic classes from the end of the eighteenth century to the Great War" (p. 221).

Even more than Pareto, Borgatta insists on the positive role of these classes in the economy. The destruction of wealth linked to the financial advantages granted to these classes has to a large extent been compensated by the favourable factors for the general prosperity that resulted from it. In fact, the aptitudes of the groups enriched by public finances lead to favourable initiatives for the economy, even if it was specified that it is not a question of moral or political justification (p. 233).

---

76 Even if Borgatta's presentation, in the way of the master from Lausanne, does not clearly draw the conclusions that he brings up in relation to the numerous interdependent factors taken into account.

This analysis diverges from Pareto's theoretical base by the positive role attributed (with precaution[77]) to public expenditure in modern societies: expenditure has a positive function for what would be called social well-being. The starting point is roughly the same: "the movement of increase in public expenditure in the last 150 years" (p. 227) is to be linked to the economic prosperity which has released revenue encouraging "the political groups to expand expenditure" (p. 228). But Borgatta then establishes a link between public expenditure and economic growth. Public expenditure creates a favourable environment in the form of "public services and functions" (p. 234) useful to the economy.[78] He mentions the security of revenues and goods provided by the police, the guarantee of contract enforcement by the legal system, the personal security due to military defense, but also the roads and other methods of communication created by public works. This economic function of public expenditure is all the more useful because its cost is, as Borgatta reiterates, lower than the tax revenue provided by economic growth. One must not either forget the "reasons that do not allow the taxation systems to hit the elements that gradually contribute to the increase of average private income", the speculators widely escaping taxes.

Finally, as a complement to the development of the Paretan method of synthetic study of the interdependent factors, Borgatta proposes several original analytical conclusions. So he considers that the economic functions of public expenditure are not the same in "a poor economy" and "a rich and complex economy" (p. 227). He emphasizes the importance of the augmentation of the middle class for the tax system, especially when it is composed of "rentiers": "income taxes essentially weigh on middle rentier classes and leave out high classes, especially the speculators' classes." (p. 226). He points out the importance of indirect taxes as a technical process of taxation favoured because of its painless character, even if he comes up against the explanation of the phenomenon.[79] He maintains that "democratic" policies prevail "in

[77] Since, in order not to contradict the phenomenon of the oscillations between periods of economic prosperity and stagnation, he adds after this conclusion that "the relationships between movements of private wealth and movements of public expenses cannot be precisely defined in a single and reliable formula" (p. 234).

[78] "When the political-judicial organisation has reached a certain degree of development (…) without the need for a proportional increase in (public) expenses: the pre-existing organisation automatically creates the environment in which the advancing economic activity can grow and intensify" (p. 234). He mentions the security of revenues and goods provided by the police, the guarantee of contract enforcement by the legal system, the personal security due to military defense, but also the roads and other methods of communication created by public works.

[79] The approach using the taxpayer's cognitive rationality explains the painless character of the consumption tax better than "economic ignorance" (p. 225).

historical periods and in places in which wealth and population are more developed" (p. 229). In fact, these factors, also associated with industrialization and urbanization, favour the formation of big pressure groups which the new power elite (speculators) must satisfy through public expenditure. In another passage, he links parliamentarism to the bureaucracy which the elite engenders in order to provide work to many unemployed, but which afterwards does not manage any more "to simplify and reduce the bureaucratic body" (p. 223). Lastly, he explains the predominance of the economic approach, especially in the science of finance, with business profile of the ruling elite, an observation which is of interest to the sociology of knowledge (cf. chapter 3).

c. Roberto Murray

We will focus on Roberto Murray's text "*La scienza delle finanze, il diritto finanziario e la nozione di stato*" published in 1915 since the question of the State is at the heart of the problematic.[80] He considers that public finance constitutes an activity of the State, and not of individuals (Murray, in McLure, 2007, p. 180). He gives the example of a special tax to finance a war: the adoption of this tax is only possible within the framework of the constitutional law of the State. It does not express the mere will of individuals or, in this case, of the ruling class. Another example is given (p. 181) in the case where a taxpayer pays a tax for public services whose use he ignores, a situation illustrating the coercive nature of the State. As we see, Murray diverges here from Pareto when considering the tax State. Yet he follows Pareto's methodology by asserting that the financial science must look for general regularities[81], but does not hesitate to include public needs in his analysis, a notion whose criticism we have seen in *The Treaty*. Public needs, constituting financial activity (p. 181), are defined as those that are satisfied by public institutions.

Murray distinguishes the economic approach and the political approach in financial phenomena by referring to Pareto's method of approximations in order to study each dimension separately. He insists on the importance of the political dimension, for example in the wake of

---

80 The question is "whether or not it is necessary to define the notion of State before the treatment of fiscal phenomena for what concerns the science of public finance and fiscal law" (Murray, 2007 (1915), p. 179).

81 For Murray (2007, p. 180) it is a question at this level of generality to study the transfer of wealth from public institutions to private individuals. The method is that of Pareto, as he specifies in the *Lessons in Political Economy* (Murray, 1920), where he refers to the search for uniformities (laws), to the relations of mutual dependence, and to the necessary approximations. But he adds that laws are always tendential due to the complexity of reality. In his book on political economy, Murray also refers to (chapter 8 of his *Lessons*) Pareto's theory of crises (as a normal oscillation etc.).

Puviani's fiscal illusion (cf. below). For him, the notion of the State and of public needs is necessary in order to carry out the synthesis between the two approaches (p. 183). The State determines and satisfies public needs, two functions which depend on pure economics[82] and on pure political science (as approximations for the study of public finance). Two notes specify, contrary to Pareto, that public finance is logical actions where the State has an autonomous activity, even if the class struggle to obtain advantages plays a role. Political Science is concerned by the study of the State methods of coercion, and economics by the economic methods to achieve a political equilibrium of the financial satisfaction of public needs.

d. Benvenuto Griziotti

Concerning Benvenuto Griziotti, we will not dwell on the study of Ricardo's equivalence principle relative to the comparison between a extraordinary tax and a loan. This economic question is not central for our subject, even though this Pareto's student invites us to take into account political and economic contexts.[83] In spite of a starting point close to his thinking, Pareto considered that the problem was badly presented insofar as the relation to the social (and firstly economic) equilibrium was not specified (McLure, 2005, p. 614). It is especially interesting to emphasize that Griziotti's financial sociology has evolved, as McLure reports (2005, p. 624), towards a multidisciplinary functional approach presented in *La studio funzionale dei fatti finanziari*, published in 1940.

In the article "Alla scuola di Vilfredo Pareto e Maffeo Pantaloni", published in 1949 in the *Giornale degli economisti*, Griziotti explains himself on Pareto's legacy[84] and puts forward the importance of the State "which is a political entity *par excellence*" (Griziotti, 2007, p. 261). Faced with "the predominance of political factors" (p. 260) which does "not exclude other (socio-economic) influences", he conceives public finance as a "political choice" by studying the functions of each element: here the political function, or the analysis of the "ends (be they public or collective or individual)", is central, next to the economic function and to the legal function which questions "the interrelationship of fiscal laws with social laws" (p. 260).

---

82 Spending satisfying public needs. Taxes obtained by State coercion allowing the financing of spending.

83 Griziotti discusses the Ricardian equivalence principle using its renewed presentation by De Viti de Marco, another name in the science of finance in Italy: cf. for a discussion, Buchanan, 1960, p. 51-55.

84 Which he especially claims as a scientific method based on real facts.

Public finance refers to the State so that "revenues cover public expenditure" (p. 260); it constitutes the "instrument of economic policy", and concerns the State and the society by means of the "interaction with social phenomena" (p. 260). These three domains determine three "disciplines": the science of finance for the first one, economic and fiscal politics for the second and financial sociology for the last. Financial sociology can question the social laws to which public finance is subjected, in particular "the dynamic of the dominant classes who wield political power" (p. 260); but it must especially study, and this is the essential input of this author, the tax State which is a "moral, political, patrimonial and juridical" (p. 263) reality, and not a metaphysical entity (a derivation) denounced by Pareto. But other Italian authors have used a socio-political approach without referring to Pareto directly.

e. *The other Italian authors*

Using as basis the study of Boccacio and De Bonis (2003) related to the Italian political approach from the end of the 19th to the beginning of the 20th century, three authors are retained: Carlo Angelo Conigliani, Amilcare Puviani, Giovanni Montemartini.

Conigliani criticizes the economic conception based on the needs of the State using trade and production to satisfy them. The economic personality of the State is a fiction (Boccacio, De Bonis, 2003, p. 83). It could not be considered (in the line of hedonism) that the individual needs of citizens are expressed as collective needs of social well-being which would be satisfied by goods. It is not a matter either of satisfying needs for which the private sector cannot take charge. The object of public finance is therefore not the citizens but the government: the rulers follow their own interest and handle constraint, coercion. There is no link with the theory of the value because the only law is political: it consists in seeking the power that the government exercises over the dominated classes through taxation, which is the only aspect of public finance that, in Conigliani's opinion, must be taken into consideration.

Puviani also considers that taxes weigh on the masses who do not receive State benefits in exchange (Boccacio, De Bonis, 2003, p. 84). He refutes the "exchange tax" theory (paid in exchange for benefits obtained). But to explain taxation, he refers rather to class conflicts, in a kind of historical materialism, than to the elite theory. The State defends the interests of the rich classes who hold the economic power to the detriment of the other classes of society. And yet, this element does not suffice to explain financial phenomena as Puviani maintains by proposing the theory of fiscal illusion which will enjoy a good future. This theory is based on the idea that taxpayers underestimate the amount of taxes compared with the (overestimated) value of the benefits expected from the public spending. As we see, the theory of the (objective) value is not rejected, but is modified in the subjective sense of the individual's feeling when facing taxes. The way opened up by Puviani will be followed by numerous studies on the attitude of taxpayers as regards the financing of public services by taxes. Nevertheless, the postulate of the citizens' unrealism (or irrationality) which will try to impose itself on the basis of this type of theory appears erroneous. We will see in chapter 9 that the link between revenue and expenditure is logical in the sense that it responds to a cognitive rationality which leads citizens to underestimate the taxes necessary for public spending, when they think that there are other methods of financing (loans, reallocation of expenses, reduction of waste etc.). In the theory of fiscal illusion, Puviani also considers that it is the government who tries, to use Pareto's vocabulary, to mislead taxpayers by ruse[85]: this point moreover supports the criticism of the modern theory of the lack of financial realism of citizens, because it is logical to be sensitive to the advantages of a public good or of a service if the costs are minimized or hidden.

For Montemartini, the essence of the economic activity of the State is coercion, but the analysis remains strictly economic (Boccacio, De Bonis, 2003, p. 86) and has less interest for financial (fiscal) sociology. His writings, for example on savings and of course on public finance, concern pure economics.[86] The State is seen as an entrepreneur whose distinctive feature is to use coercion to obtain (from the weakest) revenue useful for its own benefit. Theoretically, the entrepreneur may be a person, a class, the entire community, but it is the second case that is found in reality. This perspective therefore excludes the idea of a State guaranteeing liberty, or ensuring a harmonious coordination of interests, or still motivated by the production of collective goods.

Conclusion

Through its Austrian and Italian founders, fiscal sociology has at its disposal a pertinent corpus of analyses. Their reflection aimed at the elaboration of a global social science, even though the Italian school was at times divided on the question of the respective place of normative economics. This lesson is important, in particular for a sociology conceived as a general questioning in the field of taxation, of relations

[85] Buchanan (1960, p. 60 et s.) emphasizes the importance of the fiscal illusion for example by the praising of public expenditure, the use of indirect tax, the taxation of amusement (revenue from gambling), by the putting forward of the gravity of the situation etc.

[86] Cf. Montemartini G., *Il risparmio nell'economia pura*, *Milano*, Hoepli, 1896; "Le base fondamentali di una scienza finanziaria pura", *Giornale degli economisti*, 1900, 2, p. 535-576.

between the State and society in a multidisciplinary perspective (cf. chapter 3). Even though their problematics sometimes intersect, the two founding schools differ distinctly. The Austrian school privileges above all the historical study of the crisis of the tax State. The Italian school, while at the same time presenting different analyses, is interested in the domination of the ruling elite. It must finally be pointed out that the two schools have rather neglected the interest of redistribution in order to focus on production, even if Mann[87] and some Italians set the base for a functional theory of taxation. Finally, the contribution of the founders is to put the question of the interventionist democracy. Their response varies, going notably from the necessity of a State capitalism (Goldscheid) to the refusal of all interventionism (Pareto), passing by the complementary role of the State and the market (Schumpeter).

[87] Who lived long enough to witness the triumph of the interventionist State.

CHAPTER 3

Fiscal Sociology as a Social Science

Fiscal sociology was created by the reflection of Goldscheid and Schumpeter on the financial crisis of the State and by the establishment of an Italian school of thought interested in the means of the elite in power. After this founding period, fiscal sociology had an irregular development according to the period and the country. The factors explaining the institutional recognition of an academic discipline are numerous, as is illustrated by the case of the establishment of fiscal sociology in France. The scientific market of the demand and supply of this knowledge depends on the ability of the administration and of every society to go beyond the technicity of this field dominated by jurists and economists. The longitudinal approach shows the relation between fiscal sociology and the interventionist State. The epistemological process tries to set forth theoretically the levels of analysis of the problems within a general socio-political theory. It aims to establish a hybrid social science whose definition is rather large in order to maintain a specific relationship with the variety of disciplines that are interested in its field of research.

1. The Factors of Institutional Recognition

The institutional recognition of fiscal sociology has to be considered both in a diachronic and a synchronic way. The longitudinal point of view puts forward the impact of the interventionist State on the historical diffusion of this approach founded at the time of the First World War. The synchronic view is based on a sociological model of knowledge that brings together several variables, specified according to the French case, namely: the position of the administration, the particularity of social issues, the technical nature of the matter, the domination of law and the economy.

a. The relation to the interventionist State

The longitudinal analysis of the historical and social context shows that fiscal sociology has a link with the interventionist State, even if it does not exactly reproduce its historical intricacies and even if other factors intervene (cf. below). The Austrian founders studied State intervention in a war context by raising the question of the tax crisis (see chapter 2). The Italian school was interested in public finance as a means for the elite to keep political power. The two schools tried to create a social science that takes into account the economic and socio-political aspects of financial phenomena, while also criticizing at times quite strongly the narrow normative point of view of economists. The balance between the two perspectives was modified with the generalization of Keynesian policies and the Welfare State in Europe. A socio-political consensus legitimizes the tax State by the financing of its economic and social interventions, which leads authors like Mann, Borgatta, Murray and Griziotti to propose a functional approach.

After the period of the founders and until the effects of the economic crisis of the 1970s[1], researchers were less interested in the study of the legitimacy of the tax State. This led to the decline of fiscal sociology as a study of all the socio-political phenomena relating to taxation. Instead of the tax State, studies concentrated on the behavior of taxpayers by using (socio-) psychological surveys.[2] A factor proper to the field of scientific supply also intervenes, namely the increasing specialization of social sciences that has seen the growth of social psychology in this period. The historical context is that of the comprehension of the taxpayer with the aim of strengthening his sense of fiscal compliance in order to finance the interventionist State. These studies are based on social attitudes. They neglect fiscal policies and the administrative regulation in tax management.

The following period was a logic continuation of the economic crisis of the 1970s. The radical criticism of the interventionist State by the public choice school, based on the rational choice theory applied to democracy (Buchanan, Tullock, 1962), encountered a real academic and social success. Starting from the strictly economic hypotheses of utilitarian rationality (self-interest), this movement had an interdisciplinary impact which cannot be ignored by fiscal sociology. Simply put, public choice theory develops a utilitarian conception of public decisions where politicians, public agents and voters maximize their interest on the political market. Politicians try to be reelected, which creates an

---

1 The periodisation of the evolution of knowledge often differs in several aspects from the evolution of the historical context, because of the plurality of the factors of the supply and demand of knowledge and also because of the difficulty to modify paradigms and objects of research.

2 The first essay on the psychology of public finance was published in Germany by Schmölders (1932). In France, a short study by Raynaud (1947) and an essay by Laufenburger (1956) were made. But it was really during the 1960-1980 period that studies on the taxpayer's psychology were conducted: in England (Lewis, 1982; Furnham, 1984), in France (Dubergé, 1961), in Germany (Schmölders, 1970), in Israel (Dornstein, 1976), in Sweden (Vogel, 1974), in the United States (Spicer, Lundstedt, 1976; Keenan, Dean, 1980; Grasmick, Scott, 1982).

electoral cycle of expenditure, higher just before elections than the following year. In a democratic system, public policies of expenditure financed by taxes are those wanted by the median voter, especially in the case of two dominating parties (Tullock, 2006). Bureaucrats tend to maximize their budget (Brennan, Buchanan, 1977). Citizens have a general aversion for taxation (Downs, 1957). Therefore, as discipline of the tax State centered on the study of deviances of taxpayers, financial sociology is called into question by the impact of public choice.

The O'Connor's neo-Marxian analysis (1973) on crises of the fiscal State constitutes another socio-political answer to the question of the legitimacy of taxation. According to this author, the capitalist State intervenes more and more by public expenditure to support the economy and finds itself in deficit because it cannot legitimize increases in taxation. The impact of crises is also put forward by the economic theory of Peacock and Wiseman (1967) with regard to the role of the two World Wars. In peaceful periods public intervention through expenditure is limited by the reticence of citizens to taxes, while wars increase fiscal tolerance. Without anticipating the discussion of these theories of fiscal crises (cf. chapter 7), it must be noted that crisis periods seem favorable to fiscal sociology.

The abovementioned studies generally neglect the lessons of the construction of modern State in Europe. Historically linked to this construction, the political dimension of taxation remains essential in view of the crisis of the interventionist State. One should consider the dialectic arguments concerning taxation seen as an obligation to the sovereign and also as a contribution, legitimately agreed upon, to public policies. The second element of the dialectic, which foreshadows the tax-contribution or the tax-citizen, will definitely be established in the nineteenth century in the form of a Parliamentary authorization to levy taxes (and to spend them) within the framework of the traditional finances of industrialized countries. The Austrian founders certainly understood quite well the interest for a sociological approach to base itself on the history of the State in Europe. But, in the context of war in which they create this public finance sociology, it is especially crisis periods that are of interest to them. This characteristic of the beginning remains true. It explains the focalization on crises, as is shown by the analysis of tax revolts (cf. chapter 9) that give rise to numerous studies.[3] This relationship, proper to the history of the European tax State, explains why fiscal sociology has, until very recently, rather ignored developing countries.

---

[3] Cf. Hoffmann, 1956; Buchanan, 1979; Musgrave, 1979; Bercé, 1980 and 1991; Lowery et Sigelmann, 1981; Crush, 1985; Cox, Lowery, 1990; Jinno, Dewit, 1998; Caron, 2002; Burg, 2004.

Financial history is a traditional field with well established credentials. It proposes data and an analysis of socio-political processes which could be useful for fiscal sociology. But the demand for a sociological approach to the history of public finance emerges with Goldscheid and then Schumpeter at the time of the First World War. Initiated by its founders, historical fiscal sociology continues to develop, particularly with sociologists like Ardant (in France) and Wildavsky (in the United States).[4] Ardant adopts a fiscal theory of economic nature which makes free trade the essential factor of the historical evolution of tax systems in the world. Wildavsky is situated on the socio-political side of the discipline with his cultural theory of the growth of public expenses and deficits, and also his theory of political incrementalism that expresses the weight of the past in the continuation of expenditures (cf. chapter 7).

Since the 1990's tax sociology has been renewed, while historical studies of a sociological character were continued (Witt, 1987; Daunton, 2001; Piketty, 2001; Caron, 2002; Peukert, 2006; Lachmann, 2009; Morgan, Prasad, 2009). Here again, a relationship, certainly not deterministic nor exclusive of other factors, can be established with the call into question of the State in the context of economic globalization. The domination of the utilitarian paradigm of rational choice founded on self-interest is being discussed. New empirical studies allow one to answer to popularized conclusions due to the persistent ideological influence of the public choice school: they show that the taxpayer is not only motivated by the rationality of self-interest, but that he is (potentially) altruistic if the fiscal State is legitimate. Recent years have also been characterized by the diversity and the enrichment of studies. Campbell (1993), in a survey article, consistently considers a crisis as the key variable of tax policy changes, with interest groups in the middle, but he points out other issues. In France, the studies of Leroy on fiscal bureaucracy (1993, 1996, 2002, 2010) and taxpayer rationality indicate the ambition to theorize on empirical data in a dialogue with economics and law (1992, 2003, 2008).

New socio-political problem areas and/or unknown fields are explored in relationship with: the foundering of the Soviet bloc (Hanousek, Palda, 2003; Appell, 2006, Gërxhani, 2007; Miller, 2007), the ground swell of decentralization and federalism (Garman *et al.*, 2001; Roden, 2002), developing countries (Moore, 2004), and of course with regard to globalization (cf. chapter 12). On the scientific supply side the devel-

4 Cf. for the history: Webber, Wildavsky, 1986; the incrementalism: Wildavsky, 1964; the cultural theory of public budgets: Wildavsky, 1985. According to Ardant (1971), if trade is not sufficiently developed, taxes payable in the form of money becomes more difficult to levy. For example, trade declarations in 17th century Europe (lower imports of precious metals) explain tax revolts.

opment of economic experimental psychology has revived on other epistemological and empirical bases the debate of the 1970's relative to the respect of the fiscal obligation. Studies on individual and social values of taxpayers justify a reflection on fiscal democracy (cf. chapter 9). The issue of bureaucracy has evolved towards the new problem area of the regulation of multinational companies (Leroy, 2008).

b. The attitude of the administration (the case of France)

The first institutional obstacle relates to the attitude of the tax administration. In France, since its creation in 1948[5], it has shown itself to be defiant to any interference in its autonomy. It hesitates to authorize an independent study of its functioning, preferring to develop an official communication policy.

On an organizational level, the centralizing, authoritarian and formalistic tradition of the tax administration is often put forward to explain the culture of distrust of the French financial administration (Leroy, 2003). Traditionally, the administration positions itself in the mission of sovereignty to levy taxes and as the authority responsible for applying the tax law. It is therefore not inclined to encourage the sociological analysis of public policy, bureaucratic change and taxpayer behavior. The real functioning of the administration differs however from this reiteration of a French administrative tradition supposed to be immutable (Leroy, 1993). The administration has of course encountered difficulties to "modernize" itself[6], but it has shown a big management capacity and an original way of organizing fiscal control (cf. chapter 8) in view of perpetuating the tax return system and implementing fiscal reforms (Leroy, 2008). All this is therefore not really based on structural reasoning, but on a well established institutional logic.

On the level of administrative rationality, the attitude of the persons in charge of the French administration can be explained especially by their concern to avoid any questioning of their power. The permanency, even indecisive, of anti-tax reactions fuels the reticence of the administration to show transparency. The history of tax revolts, especially the successive vicissitudes of the movements of Poujade and Nicoud, remains a sensitive issue. The presence of recurrent anti-tax statements reinforces this withdrawal tendency (Leroy, 2009). The control of information, theorized by the French school of the sociology of organi-

[5] Decree of 16 April 1948 on the creation of the *Direction Générale des impôts* (cf. chapter 8).

[6] It took more than twenty years, from 1948 to 1970, to merge the old financial administrations. In the same way, the process of change initiated in 1990 had difficulty to conciliate the points of view of the public, the State and the personnel (Leroy, 1994, p. 828).

zations, therefore has a specific nature. The logic of tax records, consisting of collecting data on the position of taxpayers in order to confirm tax returns, is complemented by a logic of secrecy which aims not to yield to criticism. Secrecy is not only part of the finance ministry, but here it is well established.

This institutional positioning is coupled with a valorization of administrative communication. In France, a general service for relations with the public was created in 1977 with the aim of improving the relation of taxpayers to taxes, while the creation of the Tax Council in 1971 and of approved administrative centers in 1975 had already entered into this logic of dedramatisation. The creation in 1991 of a service of communication followed upon unrest shown by striking agents in 1989. Internal communication was therefore emphasized and external communication is carefully controlled. This point complicates the task of tax sociology. Communication policy has a decided technical character. Taxation in France is rarely envisaged as a global socio-political problem.

c. *The fragmentation of the social issues of taxation*

The second obstacle to the institutionalization of tax sociology is social. Taxation does not appear to be a social problem at certain times or for certain countries, especially during calm periods. Taxation becomes an instrument serving heterogeneous sectorial objectives where the question of equity is not put in a global way (Leroy, 2003, p. 257). Modern finance remains interventionist in developed countries but the diversity of policies muddles up the important economic and social functions of taxes (cf. chapter 8). The logic is that of fragmentation because of the complex usage of taxes as instruments. The issues are very much dispersed and concern economic, social, cultural and territorial particularisms. The comprehensive change of the fiscal system, notably in view of social justice, is rarely part of the agenda. The absence of a big social movement does not encourage a social demand for the analysis of the sociological phenomenon of taxes. The partial knowledge obtained from ad hoc opinion polls is sufficient for the authorities involved in the elaboration and negotiation of tax specificities. This does not facilitate the social demand for a comprehensive analysis of taxes. This factor is certainly not necessary for scientific development, but it is useful (many examples exist) for the institutionalization of research teams in step with pressing social questions.

The relation between social demand, even socially urgent, and research is however more complex. In this field, while the movements of tax revolt have given rise to social science studies[7], this relation has not

---

7 For example, about a hundred articles were published between 1978 and 1980 on what happened after Proposition 13 of California (Lowery, Sigelman, 1981, p. 963).

been decisive in the French case. It seems that the "modern" context of fiscal dissatisfaction encourages non-protesting strategies, that is to say individual and corporate strategies to avoid taxes (fraud, evasion, lobbying for tax advantages) rather than collective action. There is however an evolution of social demand with notably debates on capital taxes within the context of economic globalization (cf. chapter 12) and on the (neo-liberal) economic ideology of anti-tax language (Leroy, 2009). The market of fiscal research can also be approached from the side of the specialization of the supply of knowledge.

d. The technical nature of taxation

Taxation is complex especially as an instrument of public interventionism that the law crystallizes into arcane expressions discouraging non-insiders.[8] This discipline attracts few people with a vocation for research, including amongst jurists, who in general prefer to enter into the lucrative market of tax counseling by developing technical and specialized competences. It can be noted that the attraction of legal positivism explains the reserves of certain jurists concerning the other approaches of social sciences with a general vocation. The problem is accentuated by the very much applied character of fiscal teaching. For the sociology of knowledge, but also in order to anticipate the future of tax sociology, it is important to ask whether it is possible to establish a general knowledge, without mastering its technical aspects. The answer is certainly positive but merits being refined according to the relation between the legal techniques and the scientific knowledge of the subject of taxation. Taxation constitutes of course, beyond its technical nature, an essential social and political process and therefore accessible on this ground, in a theoretical as well as a methodological way, to sociologists.[9] The knowledge of fiscal techniques, in addition to the comprehension of a particular legal, economic and financial language, allows one to go deeply into certain research questions (Leroy, 2003). For example, the complex formalism of tax law blurs the legitimacy of the

---

8 This is well pointed out by the example (amongst others) of fiscal territoriality. In order to know the place of imposition and therefore determine the applicable national tax law, one has to examine the complex criteria of the fiscal domiciliation of natural and legal persons, in internal law, with regard to international conventions, without forgetting European community law.

9 Taxation is a difficult subject because of its technical nature, but this should not discourage the scientific community who does research in fields a priori as difficult as taxation. To give only two examples, it is obvious that the sociology of the "hard sciences" or of the health sciences doe not require one to have a Nobel prize in physics or medicine, even when the Sokal case questioned the relevance of results based on the deficient mastery of the processes of a discipline (which does not invalidate a sociology of scientific production).

fiscal obligation for the citizen-taxpayer (cf. chapter 9); it encourages the administrative logic of the negotiation of the output of fiscal controls (cf. chapter 6). The technical knowledge of tax law, without constituting a necessary prerequisite to every sociological study of taxes, is therefore indispensable in order to treat questions relevant (notably) to legal sociology.

It is certainly possible to account for taxes sociologically without being interested in fiscal techniques that remain a black box in that case. For example, the reflection on the rationality of the taxpayer or the sentiment of fiscal justice progresses even in the absence of technical considerations. But the knowledge of legal techniques also sheds quite an original light on the way that law structures action: examples are given by the sociology of tax litigation (Leroy, 2008), of family taxation (Leroy, 2009), of the bureaucratic methods of fiscal control (Leroy, 1994), of the adaptation of legal logic to the context of a developing country (Leroy, 2002, p. 42-49) etc. Sociological reflection on the realism of law cannot easily give up on techniques. The multi-disciplinarity of researchers or research teams finds another justification here, on the condition of escaping from the disciplinary domination of law and of economics.

e. *The paradigmatic hegemony of economics and of law*

Technical instrument of State intervention, taxation is apprehended in a hegemonic way by law and by economics. It is considered as a subject of study whose hard core depends on the paradigms of economics and of law. The epistemological lecture of the status of taxation in the scientific field shows that it is still too often defined as a field of expertise rather than a subject of social sciences. The scientific offer is focalized on an instrumental knowledge of taxation. It nevertheless produces some general propositions (sociologically fragile) in order to maintain the power of its model of paradigmatic hegemony, in the Kuhn' s meaning.

Fiscal knowledge is especially applied knowledge. Technical expertise is emphasized to the detriment of the socio-political dimension of the phenomenon of taxation. Amongst jurists, with the exception of a few generalist academics, one finds first and foremost specialists of doctrine and of the wheels of government. Former civil servants in the field of taxation and /or students with specialized graduate degrees are experts sought after by enterprises, consultancy firms and big taxpayers. The characteristics of tax law orientate and maintain this market for expert practitioners. Tax planning and, more prosaically, tax avoidance require adapted technicist competences. Amongst economists, taxation is one of the tools of economic policy and dresses itself up in the mathematical rigor of this discipline in order to legitimize its recommendations to the Prince.[10] Finally, the (rather restricted) community of tax experts carries on, more or less, the applied profession of consultancy in all its forms. Therefore, even if there are sometimes reflections of a philosophical nature, the most wide-spread knowledge of taxation is of a practical nature.

Without the existence of theoretical propositions of a universal nature, the hegemony of economics and of law over fiscal phenomena will however be limited. Jurists and economists (those who do not only stick to applied techniques) want to cover the three big problem areas of tax policy, of taxpayers and of fiscal justice. They use, each one in their own discipline, a universal conception of taxes which has the vocation of modeling every social representation of fiscal facts. But the obligation-tax of jurists and the exchange-tax of economists[11], while having a certain sociological relevance, do not however account for all the sociological figures of taxes. Next to the painless tax which indicates the absence of social representation, the contribution-tax aims for the political form of consent to the tax and is based on the possibility of an altruist taxpayer (cf. chapter 9). There are also social forms of "constraint-tax" and of "tribute-tax" which express the tax burden felt by individuals. The lack of sociological realism of the dominant theories is based on an epistemological manipulation that consists of presenting specific normative hypotheses as general positive results.

One remembers the criticism formulated by the Italian founders against pure normativity. "The fiscal phenomenon is not seen as a collection of facts and of systems of relations" whose "general regularities" must be searched for, for reasons linked to the "practical necessities" of teaching in "the faculties of law or of commerce" (Borgatta, 2007, p. 205). Examples of this normative drift are varied (Leroy, 2003, p. 266). For example, single tax theories depend on a fiscal myth and/or on an overgeneralization of a particular situation or of a specific constraint.[12]

---

[10] The mathematics here uses simulations of the collection of taxes, of the impact of a measure, of the interest in lowering a tax etc.

[11] A tax is defined by jurists as a unilateral act of a sovereignty nature implying a financial levy by a public authority, definitive and without counterpart; for economists (at least for the utilitarians), a tax is the price to pay by an individual for the benefits (services) that he receives from the community.

[12] The single tax, by neglecting (by definition) certain revenue sources or a part of taxable matter, and therefore by overtaxing a particular element of the system, always finishes by appearing to be socially unjust, even if certain specialists maintain the contrary.

A symbolic case is given by the brilliant plea of M. Allais (1989, p. 36-41) in favour of a capital tax. In spite of its formal rigor, this theory is remembered for its sociologically doubtful hierarchy of the objectives of a good fiscal system: "the taxes paid (...) can be considered as the remuneration of all kinds of services that the State renders (...) Taxation must not aim to distort individual choices (...). The impersonality principal leads one to prefer analytical taxes (...) and is an answer to the profound wishes of citizens of Western democracies (...). The concern for efficiency links up here with the concern for justice. Equality before taxes is in short the neutrality of taxes (...). Taxation must strike those incomes that cannot be considered as legitimate". The conception of an exchange-tax, to which we will come back, is however not unique. The preference for analytical taxes is not appropriate these days. The assimilation of equality before taxes and the neutrality of taxes conceals the real variety of the conceptions of fiscal equality. In short, it is a question of a universal conception in its normativity (sometimes ideological), but particularly in its epistemological and sociological pertinence.

The propensity of economists is thus to slip from a normative discourse to a positive discourse, from particular results to universal recommendations. It is obvious that these studies, seen as economic models, are technically serious as is attested by the justified renown of this discipline. As we will see in detail concerning the utilitarian rationality of the taxpayer, these conceptions, which are general because of their hegemonic pretentions, make it difficult to elaborate a real social science of fiscal phenomena.

For jurists, the diagnosis is more qualified. There is a real tendency to cover the whole fiscal field by globalizing analyses where the distinction between normative data and factual data is not always clear. But the majority of the scientific studies are specialized and technical, to the detriment of the theorization of taxes as a multidisciplinary social science. Here we can take the example of handbooks concerning the tax procedure. Academic tax lawyers however, while remaining close to legal positivism[13], sometimes show a certain open-mindedness to other non normative social sciences.[14]

---

[13] In France, the National University Council (of public law) gives privilege to traditional theses in constitutional law and administrative law, which contributes to nourish a certain withdrawing attitude of the discipline.

[14] Cf. for example the review of international law of Claudio Sachetto: *Diritto E Pratica Tributaria Internazionale*. The appeal for a return to a multidisciplinary fiscal science can be understood in this way. But a certain number of fiscal jurists remain attached to a technical specialization going beyond the rhetorical incantation for a fiscal science.

f. A formal model of the diffusion of fiscal sociology

Even when retaining a wide definition of fiscal sociology, and thus when including other disciplinary approaches of public finance, it appears that its institutional recognition in France (Leroy, 2003), and in a certain number of countries, is sometimes difficult. The state of knowledge is not questioned because fiscal (and financial) sociology disposes of an important body of knowledge (Leroy, 2003, p. 249-251). The answer to this question of the sociology of knowledge is found in the characteristics of the market for fiscal research. The formal model of the diffusion of fiscal sociology allows for the intervention of several variables: the public demand for knowledge (noted D afterwards), the supply of scientific research (S), the general (G) or particular (P) characteristics of a country, the socio-institutional (I) or epistemological (E) logic.

In the case of France, the recognition of this approach came up, as we have seen, against the following factors classified according to the model given below: the administrative reticence (D, P, I), the fragmentation of the social questioning on public policies (D, G, I), the evolution of the social movement (D, P, I), the technical character (S, G, E), the hegemony of the economy (S, G, E), the status of law (S, P, E), the orientations of sociology (S, P, E). This analysis is well situated within the general outline of the epistemology of the paradigm and of the research program while at the same time insisting, over and above the technical characteristic of the fiscal discipline[15], on the importance of the socio-institutional context. All this explains the slow development of tax sociology in France. Fiscal sociology finds a field to develop itself when the administration encourages research, or when a social movement of revolt against taxes gives rise to questioning, or when the evolution of the scientific field opens up opportunities etc. In France the described difficulties are progressively absorbed, even if their permanence is not certain (Leroy, 2002; 2007).

The formal variables put together in this model allow us to understand the variety of the situations according to time and country, even if specialized studies by country[16] would be necessary. For example, the

---

15 The logic of normative appraisal used by the fiscal discipline leads one to answer the enigmas of taxpayers and of the government, without considering the general problems of taxes in their relation to the State and to society.

16 McLure (2007) considers that the decline since the 1930's of the Italian school of fiscal sociology, created at the end of the 19th century under the inspiration of Pareto, is due to epistemological criticism by Italian academics who chose an economic approach.

encouragement of the administration[17], the appearance of anti-tax social movements, familiarity with theories and quantitave economic methods, the debate around the narrow theory of rational choices, the modification of scientific supply as is illustrated by the mounting interest for economic psychology and the boom of experimental studies are all favorable factors. Other factors like the general hegemony of law and of economics appear more difficult to surmount. In the same way, the diffusion of studies in fiscal sociology is bound to overcome the last reticences of the administration and of the scientific community. Finally, the context of State intervention has to be taken into account. In Austria, the founding of financial sociology and its interest for the crisis of the fiscal State are linked to the encouragement of cameralistic sciences that are by nature disciplines of studying the State. In Italy, the development of financial sociology has found a favorable factor in the tradition of the reflection on the elite applied to the science of finances.[18]

The effect of this paradigmatic hegemony of the strictly normative approaches is particularly efficient when sociology neglects the study of social phenomena constituted by the taxation process. The combination of a technical hard core and wide-ranging theories ensures the monopoly of economics and law in this scientific field. The empirical way, within the spirit of the social psychology of taxes, has constituted a less risky solution with regard to the dominant legal-economic paradigm. It puts forward useful descriptive data without pretending to theorize on taxation facts in a sociological way. Its critical range remains peripheral with regard to (in the words of Lakatos) the hard core of the taxation program of the legal-economic block. It is however the way of theorization in a refounded social science that seems to be the most promising.

2. Fiscal Sociology Viewed as a Social Science

The epistemological positioning of fiscal sociology is that of a general social science. It is a question of theorizing, using empirical bases, on fiscal problems within a comprehensive socio-political logic, while at the same time aiming for the correct structuring of the levels of analysis. The normative dimension of the analysis is not refused, as long as it does not contradict the sociological realism.

---

17 This is the case of countries, like the USA, who put data of tax returns at the disposition of researchers.

18 Of which Borgatta (2007, p. 224) underlines the link for the economic approach with the "speculator" profile of the elite in power: "the autonomous development of the science of public finance that takes place during the last century is due to the development of the economic characteristics of the governing classes in relation with the general progress of wealth and with the prevalence of activities relating more to economic goals than to other goals of modern society."

a. A general questioning and a wide definition

The vocation of tax sociology is to treat fiscal phenomena according to a general social and political questioning. It does not aim, without excluding it, to produce a technical expertise or a body of knowledge limited to specialists in the matter. It wants to shed light on the relations between taxation, the State and society. It is centered on the process of the constitution and intervention of public institutions concerning taxes. It questions the legitimacy of the tax State for the taxpayer-citizen. It proposes a reflection on social justice, notably in the field of revenue redistribution. Beyond its relation with economics and law, it aims to reflect (in a coherent way) on the social and political process of taxation, the characteristics and the pertinence of the global and sectorial modeling (classification) of society by taxes.

Fiscal sociology theorizes on empirical data using wide-ranging models. It treats concerned social phenomena within the framework of the general problematic in social sciences. Tax reform is thus linked to social change. The administrative implementation of taxes leads to the theory of bureaucracy. The social acceptation of taxes refers to the legitimacy of public action. Tax levies are appraised within the real-life context of social justice. Tax fraud is linked to deviance sociology. A tax revolt is understood as a form of collective action. The decision of the taxpayer enters in a large model of rationality etc.

While taxation represents a total social fact according to the meaning of Mauss (1923), its study calls attention to several types of sociology. Fiscal sociology studies society by modeling notably the decision of the taxpayer and the functions of taxes with regard to general variables (social groups, values, inequalities etc.). It has recourse to a cognitive approach that consists of finding a real knowledge of the actors in a social or historical context in order to understand the appraisal of the subjective weight of a tax, the diffusion of fiscal myths, the logic of fiscal deviance etc. The approach consists of reuniting in the same rigorous process the empirical pole and the theoretical pole of the study of fiscal processes, within the framework of a general sociological posture. A wide definition of fiscal sociology is thus retained because of the disciplines that are involved. This social science is alternately political, legal and economic (and linked to management) (cf. 3).

This process has not up to now formed a trend of sociology clearly identified in an institutional way, even by including here the work in political science or, for example, certain positive studies in economics and in law. The promising contribution of tax sociology in the classical fields of bureaucracy, of deviance, of the State… remains to be established in a durable and international way. It is true that, since the work of the founders, significant contributions have been available. But this corpus does not cover the whole field of fiscal sociology, as is illustrated by the rarity of work on developing countries. Finally, a lot of work concerns a wide approach of fiscal sociology by the connecting disciplines, while they prefer to be linked to a hyper-empirical concept that neglects the search for general models.

b. The empirical material

On an empirical level, the data come from several sources: historical data, surveys by questionnaires, meetings or scenarios, experiences in laboratories, documents and official statistics, opinion polls, referendums on taxes etc. Here it is important to underline that there are methodological limits. For example, relative to fiscal deviance, it is impossible on a macro level to know the exact scope of fraud whose measure varies according to calculation methods. On a micro level, empirical techniques used by researchers, in spite of their scientific rigor, do not always allow them to make pertinent generalizations.[19] They leave a margin of incertitude about the reality of deviance behavior. Official data (statistics, administrative data) are not always accessible and rarely respond to research problematics. Opinion poll data depend on the contingent logic of the sponsors. The solution is of course to seek confirmation of the data by intersecting the different kinds of material enumerated above and to get the missing data.

Another empirical difficulty comes from the complexity of taxation (cf. chapter 7) that separates law and facts with difficulty: concerning deviance for instance, the border between what is legally allowed and what is forbidden is thus difficult to determine, which tends to blur the difference between legally admitted tax avoidance and fraud or tax evasion. All the involved variables and the different possible modellings cannot always round off the empirical verification of a hypothesis. As is shown by the case of fiscal deviance, empirical data are nevertheless sufficiently sound to allow a sociological theorization, if not exhaustive, at least sufficiently pertinent as model. As a social science, fiscal sociology constructs general models integrating multidisciplinary data by privileging the empirical verification of hypotheses. But it does not refuse to make propositions simply congruent with available data. This epistemological posture is justified by the necessarily partial knowledge, on the level of a strict and complete empirical verification, of the socio-political complexity of fiscal phenomena. Linking up again, on this point, with the original project of financial science, the sociological approach does not deny the other dimensions of taxation as object of economic, legal, historical, psychological etc. research. It wants to

[19] Cf. notably the problem of the generalization of laboratory experiences in real cases.

articulate (to bring together) them in socio-political models of a general scope.

c. *The selection and articulation of levels of analysis*

Particular attention must be given to the levels of analysis and their articulation. This epistemological question has become very important for several complementary reasons. Firstly, management logic becomes more and more indispensable as benchmark of public action (Leroy, 2007, p. 45). It tends to substitute political choices by putting forward the performance of public policies measured by the indicators of results appearing in the budgets of objectives.[20] By concealing the reality of political choices, this change of logic constitutes a breach of the democratic pact whose consequence must be considered on an epistemological level. The result consists of privileging, in the decisional sphere, one single level of analysis, namely that of management performance. The "total" character, in the meaning of Mauss, of socio-political phenomena relative to taxation is denied. By updating the vocabulary of Marcuse (1964) to the present period, we note a "recuperation" of the wealth of the stakes by the "uni-dimensional" epistemology of the performance of public management.[21]

The second reason is found in the context of globalization. Globalization has several dimensions (at least economic, political and cultural). A real analysis of social science must therefore determine the pertinent level of analysis and correctly articulate the concerned dimensions. It is not an easy task. The field of social justice constitutes a good example. Suppose that the need to struggle against income inequalities is admitted (which is not always the case). The question is to know for example whether a taxation policy of the richest (or of capital) would not lead to economically detrimental delocalizations. Or furthermore, must a country encourage the attractivity of its territories (national, regional or local) by fiscal measures that risk accentuating international tax competition and impoverishing other countries? Without anticipating the solution of these questions treated in other chapters, we see the importance of the levels of analysis.

The third question has already been taken up. The sociology of knowledge shows that the failure of the big systems of thinking opened the way for theories of moderate scope (Merton, 1949). This movement

---

20 Management centered on results within the logic of budgets of objectives (Leroy, 2007) becomes widespread under influence of the OECD who classifies the best performance practices inspired by the new public management. In France the adaptation of this new reference was put into concrete form by the Organic Law relative to the Budget (Finance) Laws (LOLF).

21 This is also an ideology and a social process.

is also represented by a bigger and bigger specialization of disciplines that elaborate specific models. Without denying the contribution of in-depth studies, whose empirical solidity is often a quality, it is time to reverse the tendency. It is a question of rebuilding social sciences with big domains or general objectives. A dialogue and even a certain hybridization of disciplines are necessary in order to integrate specialized data in a general research problem.

The success of this program implies the development of an epistemology of "contextualized problems".[22] This is particularly true for the analyses of public action where the notion of public problems has a distinct meaning.[23] The question is really to know how a social problem becomes a political problem or why a social problem is treated (or not) by an authority. For example, one may think that tax evasion is not a real social problem considering the weakness of its moral disapprobation (cf. chapter 9). Its political handling thus gives an important place to administrative regulation (cf. chapter 8). Another example treated in this chapter is given by periods (of crisis, of public interventionism) to explain the development of fiscal sociology. We have to study the positioning of the problem. For example, the difficult refutation of the paradigm applies well to the predominance of the theory of rational interest concerning the decision of the taxpayer. In the opposite meaning, the mobilization of the empirical material is a means of taking into account the criterion of the refutability of Popper. Fiscal sociology must insist on the construction of a unified epistemology of the problem as an articulation of the levels of analysis. It aims to subsume the traditional questions of object and method, and of relations between what is empirical and what is theoretical, and between what is respectively normative, moral or ethical. In the case of the taxpayer, fiscal democracy must therefore theorize on the basis of the historical lessons of the construction of the modern State in Europe and on that of the empirical data of fiscal deviance. The renewed analysis of the functions of taxation for society takes into account the institutional complexity of financial systems (cf. chapter 5). The notion of congruence between the theoretical hypotheses and the data is also a way to elaborate a general social science that takes the normative road.

---

22 Post-modernism or cosmopolitanism are endeavours with regard to this issue.

23 In the Jones's traditional guidance (Jones, 1970), the problem was especially linked to the first stage of the analysis of public policies (that also comprises solution formulation, decision, implementation, evaluation, termination): that of its inscription on the agenda of a public authority. The public problem has presently become an important object of analysis of public action.

d. The normative dimension

The normative dimension rounds off the theorization of the fiscal fact on empirical grounds from an ethical point of view.[24] For example, the reflection on thc contents of a fiscal democracy is conducted with reference to the studies and empirical data on the decision of the taxpayer-citizen. This leads one to hold up the possibility of a voluntary and even altruistic contribution to the financing of socially useful public policies (cf. chapters 9 and 11).

The epistemological articulation of the levels of analysis within general theories opens up a normative[25] perspective. This conception is that of the classical authors in social sciences and of the founders of financial sociology. In fact, the classical sociologists were preoccupied with the effects of the French Revolution and of the industrial revolution (Nisbet, 1966). They were aware of the importance of the levels of analysis. There are many examples: it suffices to think of the already mentioned notion of total social fact of Mauss, of the wish of Durkheim to define the research object objectively, of the well-known distinction of Weber between the scholar and the politician etc. The conception defended here can cut across certain authors or certain research trends. It is however far from constituting the usual approach of social sciences. One must for example refer to the efforts of hybridization of sociology and economics[26], the attempts of rebuilding a financial sociology of economic (Backhaus, 2002) or socio-political (Campbell, 1993; Leroy, 1991, 2002, 2007) inspiration, the use of the notion of "*decommodification*"[27] to classify the types of welfare States (Esping-Andersen, 1990) etc.

Current social sciences do not ignore what is at stake, notably through the interplay of paradigms, the construction of the research problem area, or by the choice of a macro- or micro- or even intermediary (meso-) approach etc. The accentuation of specialization nevertheless encourages disciplinary withdrawal. The rare interdisciplinary paradigms, such as the rational choice paradigm, either takes up a conservative position in order to avoid any scientific revolution (Kuhn),

---

24 Or deontological or moral according to the vocabulary proper to the context and/or the scientific discipline. One must of course distinguish vocabulary in a precise way, but it is more urgent to open up a normative horizon of social sciences by conserving the essentially empirical achievements of the specialization.

25 The necessity to bring together the multi-levels of analysis.

26 Cf. the "new" economic sociology

27 The theory of "social-democracy" evaluates social policies according to the degree of liberation of workers constrained or not to sell their labour force ("*decommodification*"), while social rights allow citizens not to be reduced to the status of merchandise.

or adapt themselves to a peripheral place by preserving the hard core of the positioning of the problem (Lakatos).

3. The Relation of Fiscal Sociology to other Disciplines

Fiscal sociology originates from the study of public finance. It is constructed as a certain hybridization of several disciplines (Dogan, Pahre, 1991). It is situated in a relation of reference to general sociology and political science. It dialogues with law and with economics. It uses the data of history and of (ordinary, social, economic) psychology and does not exclude opening up to other disciplines.

a. The relation to public finance

Since its creation, the theory of public finance has not always been constructed around one single approach.[28] It constituted however a unique discipline where the eventual schools of thought dialogued between each other or opposed each other. Fiscal (tax) sociology put up with the effects of the splitting up of the science of public finance into autonomous and specialized disciplines. The tax domain is now a subject existing on its own that is separate from the budgetary domain. Economists and jurists develop distinct approaches of fiscal and budgetary phenomena by ignoring the others to a large extent. The studies are more and more technical, notably in the cases of econometrics and legal positivism. Fiscal sociology, without being spared from this decline of the financial science, is subject to its own factors of evolution. It can already be divided into two largely independent schools of thought, with on the one hand the economic approach and on the other hand the socio-political approach. The picture is nevertheless more complex because a discipline is not only defined by its approaches but also by its object: the link between the approach and the object is made by the positioning of the questioning, and therefore also by its objectives. The methodology is important, even if the methods of social sciences generally offer adapted tools which do not require the invention of specific techniques.

Tax sociology as a specific field supposes the autonomization of taxation with regard to the budgetary subject. In fact, the sociology of public finance is a sociology of public budgets distinguishing revenue and expenditure while at the same time looking at their relationship. In its current form (Leroy, 2007), it proposes a sociological analysis of public finance, a financial reading of public action and a field of questioning theories of social sciences. Fiscal sociology focuses on taxes in their relation to the State and to society within the framework of its own corpus of studies. Financial sociology is interested in public expenditure

28 Cf. Buchanan (1960); Musgrave, Peacock, 1967; Boccacio, De Bonis, 2003.

policies, but also in loans, deficits, privatization, financial partnerships etc. The bridge between these two subjects is situated in the study of the link between revenue and expenditure. It is especially created by the analysis of the functions of taxation that constitutes the principal budgetary source of developed democratic societies. The relation to political science is thus involved.

b. The relation to political science

Fiscal sociology is a political sociology that is part of political science[29] which is a science of the State and of power, but also a science of public action (and policies). It is distinguished from political science by its attention given to social (even non-political) facts. But, considering the origin of taxation based on sovereignty and its interventionist character, fiscal sociology must privilege the problematic of public action as a political choice. In relation to the process of change opened up by the "crisis" of globalization and recently by the financial market, it questions the fiscal intervention of the State both as a form of power and as a form of democracy.

The political sociology of taxes is that of obligation, constraint and fiscal citizenship in democracy. Historically, the political dimension of taxation is established in relation to the construction of the State, of the Western constitutional regime, and of an administrative centralization (Ardant, 1965, p. 7; Schumpeter, 1954, p. 249; Bercé, 1980, p. 17). It is anchored, and we will come back to that in detail, to the decisive moments in the evolution of the fiscal State (chapter 4). Taxation, since its origins based on sovereignty, is at the heart of the legitimacy of government. It gives rise to fiscal revolts that mobilize political movements (Ardant, 1971, p. 400; Campbell, 1993, p. 175; Leroy, 2003, p. 220). The political nature of taxes moreover takes shape in the recurrent debate on the crisis of the fiscal State. Fiscal sociology also asks questions about factors involved in the public decision, reform and bureaucratic change (Leroy, 1993 and chapter 8). For example, the case of income taxes (Leroy, 1996) shows that the classical determining factors[30] do not suffice to take account of this policy that is analyzed by

[29] Our intention is not to enter into the recurrent debates on the possibility of a real political sociology and on its status with regard to political science (seen as singular or plural). In the same way, we can admit that a fact of society, a social phenomenon, has nearly always a political impregnation, but that this impregnation is more or less strong, while political science concentrates on facts with strong political dimensions. The frontiers between the disciplines depend on questions of epistemology but also on social questions when looking at positions of power, knowing that innovation finds a fertile source in the recomposition and rapprochement of disciplines whose frontiers, titles and contents vary.

[30] Namely the left-right divide, the economic and legal constraints, the crisis situations.

proceeding from the social function of the welfare State. The sociology of taxation links up here with that of the interventionist State (Mann, 1943). It questions the policies of limiting the tax State (Cox, Lowery, 1990) impulsed by the neo-liberal movement of the 1970s. It studies the questioning of the social function of taxation by the economic-financial globalization which is faced with the weakness of legal regulation.

c. The relation to law

Tax sociology is also a legal sociology when it is interested in the reciprocal relations between fiscal law and society, that part of society which is in law and that part of law which is in society. It is distinguished from the pure technique of specialized legal positivism without reference to a general problematic.

From this point of view, a whole field of research is opened up. For the sociology of law, the control of the respect of fiscal obligations notably puts forward the question of the social mechanisms of the qualification of fraud by public authorities (cf. chapter 8). The dialectic of fiscal procedure, variable from one country to another (Leroy, 2008), opposes the powers of the administration to the rights of the taxpayer (Leroy, 2007, p. 22). Social factors (income in particular), determining whether a case is referred to the court, and the national differences of the administrative regulation of the business world (cf. chapter 10) have to be taken into account. The legal sociology of taxes underlines the contradiction between interventionist fiscal law and the law of fiscal control which, in practice, aims to question advantages accorded by legislation. It is particularly interested in administrative applications in order to determine the opportunities given by fiscal law (degree of constraint, of clarity etc.) to the business world.

d. The relation to economics

Fiscal sociology is an economic sociology. It is part of the critical dialogue with notably the theory of rational choice applied to the decision of the individual faced with taxes. It must be noted that, in spite of its success, the new economic sociology still remains discrete in this field[31], while social economics disposes of much older studies.[32] In any case, the economic dimension of taxation is obvious as has been showed

[31] Which however concerns public sociology: Economic sociology privileges the study of the welfare State (Huber, Stephans, 2005, p. 552-569; Block, 2005, p. 512-516) over that of taxation.

[32] Etzioni (1998), who militates in favour of a moral paradigm of social economics, has thus retained taxes as an object of research (Etzioni, 1986). See the studies in the *Socio-Economic Review* and chapter 5.

by academics like Keynes, Smith, Ricardo, Schumpeter, Pareto, Weber etc.

The economic sociology of taxes is interested in the pertinence of the utilitarian model of rationality (cf. chapter 9), in the relation between economic globalization and taxes (Leroy, 2008), in the impact of neo-liberal ideology, in criticism of determinist theories of economic constraint (cf. chapter 7), in types of "social contracts" concerning the respective taxation of enterprises (capital) and wage-earners (labour), in the economic foundations of the anti-fiscal discourse (cf. chapter 6), in the mounting power of the business referential of performance etc. These questions are treated on the basis of empirical material produced notably by psychology and history.

e. The relation to psychological and historical data

Fiscal sociology uses the work of psychology, of the social psychology of taxes, and of history. In fact, these disciplines are in a position to supply empirical data that sociology tends to integrate in theoretical models with a general scope. History is one of the best approaches to be used by fiscal sociology (chapter 4), as the Austrian founders have already understood (Schumpeter, 1954): in this sense one must also refer to the enterprise of Gabriel Ardant (1971) who proposes an interpretation of the whole history of taxes in accordance with the development of economic exchanges. To give another illustration, the historic context intervenes to categorize fiscal justice. For example, in the context of feudalism, it may appear fair to give a fiscal privilege to those that defend the country. In the context of Western democracies, an evolutionary relation has been established between fiscal justice and fiscal equality, until the appearance of the idea, consubstantial with the Welfare State, of the redistribution of taxes (Leroy, 2002, p. 86-100).

With regard to psychology and the social psychology of taxation, the position of sociology is identical. It finds precious empirical data in these studies. The opinion polls, using questionnaires, conducted in the years 1960-1980, thus supply data on the attitudes of taxpayers (Dubergé, 1961; Schmölders, 1973; Vogel, 1974; Dornstein, 1976; Lewis, 1982; Spicer, Lundstedt, 1976; Keenan, Dean, 1980; Grasmick, Scott, 1982). The results are interesting for a sociologist on the condition of integrating them into a theory (Leroy, 2003). In fact, these studies generally neglect the problematic of the analysis of public policies and avoid the theorization of fiscal facts.[33] They rightly insist on the necessi-

[33] Certain notions of the (social) psychology of taxes appear to be doubtful such as those of a "characterological profile" proposed by Dubergé, or of a "fiscal mentality of nations" defended by Schmölders. This observation does not remove at all the empirical interest of the studies concerned.

ty to consider attitudes between the economic stimulus and the answer (decision) of the taxpayer (Lewis, 1982). They are interested in subjective fiscal pressure (Vogel, 1974, p. 50), in the sentiment of fiscal justice, in ethical attitudes of good fiscal citizenship (Reckers *et al.*, 1994, p. 827).

In this field, the critical dialogue with economists, based on the data of opinion polls, appears to be fertile.[34] It was renewed by the studies in economic psychology (cf. chapter 9) that systematically use the technique of experimentation to test the results of economics by strictly controlling the variables. A mass of empirical data is thus available on the behavior of taxpayers. A theorization that goes beyond the strict framework of the rational choice (self-interest) school is justified. For example, recent studies experimentally explore the advantages of participative democracy for good fiscal citizenship (Alm *et al.*, 1999; Feld, Tyran, 2002; Torgler, 2004).

Fiscal sociology can of course mobilize other disciplines, even if they do not propose a systematic study from this angle. For example, anthropology disposes of data useful for knowing the foundations of "compulsory levies" in traditional societies. The relation with the symbolic and social characteristics of gifts and with the appearance of the redistribution of an economic surplus offer directions of research that are rarely exploited. The history of religions also disposes of material in order to understand the passage from religious offerings to taxes. Linguistics allows one to understand the social functions of taxation by studying fiscal vocabulary.

Conclusion

The institutional characteristics of the market of fiscal sociology explain its unequal development. The situation of socio-political change created by the successive crises of the interventionist State, that of the 1970s and then that linked to economic globalization, opens up new perspectives. In spite of the renewal of fiscal sociology in the 1990s the ways and means of a social science based on the ambitious epistemology of social problems remains to be developed. The difficulties of the economic-financial globalization of capitalism form a favorable context for going beyond the resistances to this hybrid discipline. Finally, fiscal sociology aims to study, in its socio-political dimension, the relation between the taxpayer-citizen and the interventionist fiscal State within

34 For example, Clotfleter (1983) pretends to validate empirically that individuals situated in the upper brackets of the tax scale have a weaker fiscal citizenship than others. Another example: it appears that the tendency to avoid taxes is correlated with the number of evaders known personally.

the general framework of science linked to society. It uses its own empirical data or those of specific disciplines according to the adopted normative horizon.

CHAPTER 4

The Political Logic of the Evolution of the Tax State

One of the contributions of the founders of fiscal sociology is to have clarified the importance of the appearance and the evolution of the tax State. Historically, the genesis of the modern State in Western Europe is closely linked, from the Middle Ages onwards, with the creation of a royal taxation. This process, which comes in more or less pure forms according to the countries involved, is hard to analyze. The difficulty is to select and to treat on a hierarchical basis the criteria which characterize the modern State and to distinguish the relevant levels of analysis, whereas the approaches, the theories and the modelling are not always reconcilable. The economic approach is interested in the evolution of feudalism towards capitalism, by including in particular the Marxist analysis of the modes of production. But here the ternary periodization of Marxism in three stages, the antique, feudal and capitalist societies, does not correspond to that of French historians who distinguish the feudal Middle Ages from the "modern" monarchical epoch. The causes of the appearance of the modern State are also the subject of different interpretations. We have seen that Schumpeter considers that the change of the feudal regime is explained much more by changes of a social nature than by the crisis of its economic model.[1] The theory of Max Weber, who insists on the monopoly of the legitimate violence of the modern State and on the process of bureaucratization, neglects the impact of public finance. Historians, in spite of the diversity of the proposed criteria[2], stress however that the possibility of perceiving

1 The recourse to mercenaries replacing the war duty of noblemen was accompanied by a heredity in fact of fiefs and by the constitution of a private sphere distinct from the public sphere (cf. chapter 2).

2 Certain historians (Chevalier, in Genet, 1990, p. 9) stress the abstract character, the internal political (and not religious) legitimacy, the monopoly of public authority over citizens with rights and duties involving a professionalization of the State apparatus (excluding a religious, aristocratic or plutocratic authority). Other historians (Bérenger, Tollet, in Genet, 1990, p. 44) retain royal sovereignty over all individuals, an administration at the local or regional level, the absence of private armies, and directly include the financial dimension as criterion of the modern State.

financial resources[3] by means of regular taxation constitutes an essential element of this genesis.

Thus the idea of a certain political autonomy of the modern State in which taxes play a central role, at the beginning in relation with the financing of wars, is generally allowed.[4] This position does not exclude the study of its economic, sociological and ideological bases with notably: the role of merchants and the creditors of the State; the link and/or the struggle with certain social groups (the noble, the town bourgeois); the work of legists to establish the authority of the sovereign by modifying the scope of feudal law when borrowing from canon law or Roman law. Certain moments and certain reigns were thus decisive, for example the reigns of Philippe le Bel[5] in France and of Pierre le Cérémonieux in Catalonia. Wars provided pretexts to create taxation by changing the scope of feudal assistance. The idea that the king must "live off his own", by limiting himself to income from his estate (domain), is replaced by the justification of a State taxation. In addition to the recognition of the idea and reality of the State, the "feeling of unity" was a prelude to the national sentiment (Le Mené, in CNRS, 1987, p. 241): the birth of the nation State seems to accompany that of the modern tax State. The study of the political logic of the tax State starts from its historical genesis of the modern State in the Middle Ages, and is then interested in its conceptualization in a few selected parts of 16th to 18th century philosophical works, before proposing a typological analysis that insists on the pregnance of the interventionist State of developed countries.

1. The Tax Genesis of the Modern State in Western Europe

The genesis of the modern State in Europe forms a complex process difficult to interpret. Historians question the operational character of the concept of a modern State (Genet, 1990). In particular, they want to know whether it was created in the Middle Ages or if it belongs to the 16th and 17th centuries (Follain, Larguier, in CHEEF, 2005, p. 19) and if it forms a general model. Without trying to settle this dispute definitely, the fiscal sociologist can learn some general lessons. It is thus accepted

3 Other than the *domaine* and the *regalia* (mines, customs, tolls, currency).

4 Even if certain Marxists reduce the State to a simple superstructure determined by the economic infrastructure.

5 "It is quite evident that the reign of Philippe le Bel constitutes an important turning point and that it is at the same time a real starting point. A time of the State with jurists conceiving its architecture, a time of territorial rebuilding and of often difficult military operations, this reign also becomes the necessary time of taxes" (Rigaudière, 2003, p. 524).

that royal taxation played an essential role. Through the tension of a sovereign authority torn between domination and negotiation, it encouraged the emergence of the principle of consent which is at the basis of democratic parliamentarianism. The transformation of the feudal system led to the specificity of the European tax State.

a. Processes of institutionalization of a royal taxation

The institution of a centralized taxation takes part in the genesis of the modern State in Western Europe as of the Middle Ages (Genet, 1990, Bonney, 1999). The modern State is a particular form of political organization generated from the progressive transformation of the feudal system as from the 12th century. A tax was attributed to the Monarchy to build up the State and maintain itself in power. Several processes made it possible historically to justify and ensure the rise of royal taxation. The link with wars, which is constant in medieval Europe, is of primary importance. Other processes, like the legal and ideological work of legists[6] in France, the action of certain monarchs, the extension of the scope of the system of feudal assistance, the institutionalization of financial expedients etc. explain this transformation.

The licit war "becomes a specific function of the State" (Genet, 1990, p. 263) whose financing by taxes marks a change of logic compared to seigneurial levies. In France, the Monarchy devotes "50%, on average, and much more in times of war, for an army" within the framework of "the State of finance" (Chaunu, 1977, p. 17 and 48). The relation of the taxation to war is also highlighted in the case of England, in particular at the time of the wars of the 13th and 14th centuries (Prestwich, in CNRS, 1987). In England, revolt does not aim at the principle of royal taxation, especially when the war justifies the needs: in the countryside, it concerns the exaction and the corruption of royal collectors or the seigneurial takings; in the towns, it often blames the urban elite's privileges (Hilton, in CNRS, 1987, p. 171). The financial needs relating to war require and justify the levy of taxes. As Schumpeter indicated concerning the recourse to the mercenaries (cf. chapter 2), the buy-out of the feudal obligation of military service opened the way to taxes.

War is used as an argument to make the traditional system of feudal assistance evolve into the establishment of taxation. In the beginning, only the vassal owes a financial assistance to his suzerain in the four cases of the dubbing of the eldest son, the marriage of the eldest daughter, the payment of a ransom to release the king, a crusade. According to

6 The legists had in particular drawn from the feudal law of the fiefs the maxim "*le roi est souverain fieffeux*" to constitute a doctrine allowing the king to extend feudal assistance.

feudal law, military aid had to be accomplished by the vassals of the king in person (the *ban*). The vassals of the king could mobilize their own vassals (the *arrière-ban*) and their ordinary men (the *manants*). The evolution consisted in justifying the rule according to which the seigneury of the king is that of the whole kingdom and thus that its defense falls on all the subjects and not on vassals only. In France, the reign of Philippe le Bel (1285-1314) is decisive (Vuitry, 1883, p. 142; Favier, 1978, p. 173; Rigaudière, 2003, p. 533).This king had sought to extend or modify feudal assistance into a wealth tax by replacing military service, and established a tax on the sale of goods and a direct tax equal to a hundredth or a fiftieth of the goods. The feudal military obligation is at first replaced by the sending of sergeants financed by the families (the *feux*); then the choice is proposed between serving in person or paying a tax; finally the justification of the defence of the kingdom takes place by paying a tax to the State (*pro republica*) and not to the king or the seigneurs. In 14th century Catalonia, a similar process takes place under Pierre le Cérémonieux.[7]

The extension of the scope of feudal assistance had thus brought the legitimization of taxes by "separating the rights of public sovereignty from those of private property" (Vuitry, 1883, vol. 2, p. 4). In England, the traditional services relating to the law of justice, consequence of the feudal rights of sovereignty, evolve into a true tax system of penalties, fines and taxes for the benefit of the Anglo-Norman State (Wagner, 1913, p. 264). In the same way, direct taxes translate as of the Middle Ages (in advance on the continent) rather good uniformity, by restricting the privileges of the exempted orders. But other processes are used. In France, the gabelle is in the beginning (1315) a system of regulation of the trade of salt. This economic police force aims at fighting against price speculation and at ensuring the provisioning of the population in periods of shortages (Rigaudière, 2003, p. 566). This situation justifies the constitution of a royal monopoly on salt[8], involving the establishment of an administration whose functioning is ensured by a royal duty which becomes a permanent tax. In the case of the monopoly on salt[9] (whose methods of organization are varied), "the tax was created from the exercise of a prerogative expected from a Welfare State" (Hocquet, in Genet, 1990, p. 119). Another case of justification of the tax State is the use of some financial expedients of the Monarchy. The control of

7 Even if there are certain details, the invocation of *Princeps namque* is transformed into a tax paid by everybody: cf. Sanchez Martinez, in CHEEF, 2005.

8 Salt was a very useful food product, used in particular for the conservation of food.

9 The organization, scope and effects of the monopoly of salt varied in Europe. In France, salt was not regarded as State property, but as a good provided by private merchants and deposited in the royal storehouses.

French exports (Rigaudière, 2003, p. 569) was thus justified for economic or military reasons. It was a question of not depriving the country of food products in periods of food shortages (cereals etc.) and of not providing other countries with products useful for prosperity or defence (gold, horses, weapons etc.). These prohibitions were accompanied by special exit permits obtained through payment. The licences granted under Philippe le Bel "create at the same time monopolies in fact and a tax resource" (Favier, 1978, p. 187) for certain merchants. A bureaucracy is constituted to manage the regulations of foreign trade. Regular indirect taxation[10] is thus justified by the granting of exemptions. As this case shows, an element of the acceptance of the tax State was the granting of advantages to the nobility and the cities on the collected sums.

b. Consent to taxation

The problem of the acceptance of taxes is a crucial question for sociology. The anthropological roots of this question are to be sought in the sharing of surpluses appearing in societies and the passage of gifts to taxes. The historical point of view also makes it possible to update the figures of the establishment of taxes. The transformation of the corvée into a monetary levy constitutes an important step. As we have seen, the evolution of feudal assistance and military obligations is constitutive of the modern tax State in Europe. The dime and various levies of a religious kind also prepared the way for the monarchical tax (Biget, 2002, p. 650).[11] The dime was justified at the beginning by the services rendered by the bishop and the clerks and was also used to tariff alms for the poor.

The idea of accepted taxation came across various misadventures as is illustrated by the history of tax revolts (cf. chapter 9). At the creation of the modern State, the relations of rivalry, dialogue and association between the king, seigneurs and towns constituted a big part of the political reality of the construction of the tax State.[12] The collected

---

[10] A decree of 1305 prohibits in particular the export of many kinds of goods: it involves the establishment of an administration (ports, customs offices, various kinds of controllers...) which grants exemptions. The duties paid to export will gradually be transformed into two indirect taxes, the duty of *Haut passage* and the duty of *Rêve*.

[11] "The dime, a universal levy the most precociously instituted in the rural milieu, has without doubt formed, together with seignorial taxation and urban taxation, the matrix of monarchical taxes (...) The levies given to God prepare so much better the taxes reserved for the prince, since the peace of the prince participates in the peace of God."

[12] "The income of the king, in the Middle Ages, is only seignorial royalties which do not have the character of true public impositions, and royal taxes come from feudal assistance. But this transition only comes after a long struggle that the monarchy, which was at the same time the highest suzerainty, will be obliged to engage with the

money also benefits groups with the capacity to oppose the king's claims. Schumpeter (1954, p. 13) speaks of "courtly waste" to qualify this general phenomenon of transformation of the seigneurs into courtiers of the court (cf. chapter 2). The "prestige expenditure" of the court society studied by the sociologist Elias (1974) also explains this logic of power. In France, the granting of pay, employment and pensions to the nobility (Genet, 1990, p. 266) illustrates this process. As Tocqueville showed, it is also an element which will lead to administrative centralization, the nobility preferring service to the king above the administration of land in the countryside (cf. chapter 1). It must also be remembered that tax exemptions made it most of the time possible for these classes not to support the new taxation. Philippe le Bel, whose action was decisive for the monarchical taxation, forgoes a part of the tax of the fiftieth or hundredth in favour of the seigneurs (Vuitry, 1883, p. 147; Favier, 1978, p. 176). In the case of Castille at the end of the Middle Ages, "the structure of the tax system was discriminatory in favour of the dominating categories, which facilitated its acceptance" (Menjot, in CHEEF, 2002, p. 204). Concerning the gabelle, the system also benefited the nobility who moreover was exempted from this indirect tax imposed on the people (especially in the countryside).[13]

In addition to the nobility, the towns and the Church[14] were able to benefit from the new taxation. Resistance to taxes, strong at certain periods, was thus overcome. Negotiation with the urban elite is made possible because the taxation of the State is superimposed on that of the towns. In the 14th century, the set of alliances and rivalries between monarchy and the big towns is attested in France. The king asks for war subsidies by the play of feudal assistance, the towns claim *octrois* (royal authorization for the towns to levy taxes) for their expenditure. It is finally necessary to underline the relation between royal taxation and the

---

suzerains of a lower order and their vassals, and furthermore with the commoners and the bourgeois, the commoners depending directly on each one of these seigneurs and indirectly on the king, the bourgeois organized in communes. This struggle which will continue, for more than a century, through all the disasters of the Hundred Years War, will reveal the need for requiring and obtaining the vote for public subsidies" (Vuitry, 1883, p. 420).

13 The gabelle is entrusted by the king to the farmers-general, to the detriment of the constitution of an autonomous administration (re-feudalisation). The tenant farmer (or the holder of the office) paid the amount requested in advance and paid himself out of the tax collection. The high-level nobility bought the rights created by the leasing or the offices or they granted against remuneration the funds necessary for the advance payments. "Until the end of the *Ancien Régime* and merging with it, important persons were the main beneficiaries of the salt tax" (Hocquet, in CNRS, 1987, p. 215).

14 On the role of the Church in the genesis of the modern State, cf Genet, Vincent, 1986.

merchant economy. We saw that exemptions from the prohibition to export favoured certain commercial companies, for example those held by bankers (private) that lent money to the king, thus becoming financiers (public). Under the *Ancien Régime*, the titulars of tax farms were often merchants who granted loans (advances) to the king on the proceeds of taxes that they then raised to refund themselves. These "merchant-bankers" (Bouvier, Germain-Martin, 1969, p. 58) form an influential elite. In France, they are often titulars of a public office (receiver) thus becoming powerful and enterprising financiers in the 18th century (Chaussinand-Nogaret, 1993).

Notwithstanding historical variations, the modern tax State is founded on the legitimacy of taxes which is required in the consent of taxpayers. "The first structural change concerns the legitimacy of taxes (…). Taxes (…) come from subjects to meet a need (…) of a transcendent recipient who is none other than the State (…)" (Genet, in CNRS, 1987, p. 5). In England the consent to taxes puts forward the Parliament, in Spain the Cortes (where towns play a significant role) and in France the States General. England is the prototype of the institution of parliamentarianism based on the consent to taxes. After the defeat of Bouvines (1214), King Jean sans Terre sought to reconstitute resources by instituting new taxes. Facing a revolt of the barons, he conceded the Great Charter of 1215 (*Magna Carta*) which required the authorization of the Great Council of the Kingdom for the levy of taxes. The conflicts between the King, who sought to retract the Great Charter, and the barons, anxious to control taxes, resulted in attributing a real power to the Parliament (enlarged to other classes than the nobles and the prelates). In 1628, the Parliament proclaims the *Petition of Rights* which reaffirms the principle of tax consent. But the English history of parliamentary consent to taxes is eventful. In fact the monarchy, for example under Charles I (1649), regularly tried to govern without the Parliament and thus to raise taxes without authorization. The first English revolution, marked by the execution of Charles I, resulted in reaffirming the principle of consent to taxes. Finally the Bill of Rights of 1688 established in a definite way the tax power of the Parliament at the origin of modern budgetary law.[15]

French history is different because parliamentary law did not get the recognition found in England. The establishment of the States General finds its origin in the feudal tradition of consultation of the seigneurs (Hervieu, 1879). As everywhere, war justifies taxes, but feudal assis

15 The historical relation between parliamentarianism and the implementation of the budgetary law is found, though in a more approximate way, in the case of France where parliamentarianism finds its true effectivity under the Restoration from 1814 to 1830.

tance was asked within the framework of consultative assemblies. In the beginning it is difficult to distinguish the specificity of the States General compared to traditional feudal consultative assemblies. In both cases, it is a question of a royal will to widen the council for advice. Besides, the Church had a system of representation with synods, councils and episcopal elections which seems to have been used as an example. The turning point came under Philippe le Bel, in 1302, with the first meeting in Paris of an enlarged assembly[16] which can be regarded as the first meeting of the States General. In the 13th century, the enlargement of the assemblies of barons and prelates with town representatives constitutes a change.[17] In the tax field, the enlarged councils of 1303 and 1314 grant subsidies for war. The assembly of 1314 tries to create a precedent for the consent to taxes. It is only in 1355 that the States General meet for the first time with elected delegates from the three orders. In 1484, elections are generalized to all the baillages. But the rivalry between the monarchy and the seigneurs did not have the same outcome as in England. The authority of the king is strengthened. In 1343, King Philippe VI obtains from the States General the levy of a tax in a period of truce. François I or Henri II never get them to meet, preferring to resort to noble and urban assemblies. The States General are not convened for long periods, for example during the first half the 16th century (from 1506 to 1558) and not any more after 1614 (minority of Louis XIII) up to 1789. Consent to taxes, in germ in French history since the Middle Ages, will find a dedication in article 14 of the declaration of human rights. It constitutes a principle of the modern tax State.

c. *The characteristics of the modern tax State*

A radical change in the politico-social system of feudality takes place by establishing a State taxation. This taxation has certain original characteristics compared to the feudal levy. It became permanent, centralized and relates, not simply to the domain of the suzerain any more, but to the territory of the kingdom (national). The tax is from now on based on a legal and political conceptualization of the sovereignty of the State.[18] Its legitimization is sought after in the consent of taxpayers to the financing of needs of general interest. A last feature concerns its development. The modern State is based on a tax system of a certain

---

16 To obtain support in the conflict which opposed him to Boniface VIII (defeat of Courtrai).

17 For the crusade, Philippe Auguste had brought together a few bourgeois of Paris. In 1262, for the revision of weights and measures, Saint Louis convenes bourgeois from Paris, Provins, Orléans, Sens, Laon.

18 Concept that one finds formulated in philosophy (cf. below).

level[19], in the beginning to finance wars, then to fulfil other functions. It also supposes a tax system with a structure of diversified levies in order to attain various sources of economic and social income.

It thus appears that the role of finance in the constitution of the modern State tallies badly with the Weberian analysis of the State (Weber, 1971). The differences concern the important process of explanation, the approach to the role of the State, and also certain of its characteristics. The role of taxation was underlined in the genesis of the modern State in the Middle Ages. As underlined by the founders of fiscal sociology, the search for financial means (for wars in particular) is the first criterion with regard to those of the Weberian model. The historical establishment of a State taxation by the monarchy shaped the processes of domination, administrative organization and the elaboration of a law leading to the monopoly of public violence. The historical analysis validates the relevance of a functional approach to the modern State[20], that of its functions (in particular fiscal) in the social and political system. The approach to the State as an organization, which refers to bureaucratization in conformity with the tendency of rationalization in the West, seems to be a consequence of the establishment of a functional State. Its rational legitimization through the development of an abstract formal law is conditioned by the necessity to find a justification, in an ideological way and/or based on general interest, for its functions which are largely determined by tax levies and their utilisation.

Even by disregarding the question of the principal factor and the causal historical sequence of the components of the modern State, certain characteristics distance themselves from the Weberian ideal-type. The discussion is delicate because, as Weber underlined, a model does not reproduce reality. One can thus for this reason admit that the monopoly of legitimate violence is indeed a characteristic. Nevertheless,

---

19 In France, even if the reconstitution of amounts remains approximate because of the sources, the calculations of Clamageran (1867, p. XXIV) show that the level of taxation progressed: 1439, 1.7 million pounds, 7.4 in 1547, 89 million in 1645, 155.55 in 1715 and 880 million in 1786. This progression does not exclude periods of pause or a small retreat, but remains true even when taking into account the incidence of the value of the currency and the progression of economic wealth (Chaunu, 1977, p. 47): the tax State progresses at the beginning of the 14th century, in the middle of the 15th century and in the 17th century. It remains nearly stable in the 16th century and recedes in the 18th century (compared to the previous century). Examining the revenue of France, England and Spain between 1250 and 1500, Ormrod (in Bonney, 1996, p. 150) speaks of a "tax revolution" to indicate the role of taxation in Europe at the end of the Middle Ages in "the evolution of a more coherent concept distinct from the State."

20 In this meaning the Marxist approach is also relevant, and the debate then concerns the nature of the State functions, the possibility of its autonomy with regard to capitalism and the scope of the class struggle.

the assertion, certainly difficult and often imperfect, of consent to taxes establishes a sociology which is not exactly that of Weber. In the Weber's pair, consisting of domination and legitimacy, the rationality of the modern State is formal and legal. In the same pair of the modern tax State, the justification is concrete in relation, at the beginning, with the extension of feudal assistance and with the financing of offensive or defensive wars. It represents a generalization of the specific and not the reverse. It is based on the rationality of circumstances (cognitive) and depends on relations with the nobility (and with towns). At other times, the domination is brutal, as in the case of the French absolute monarchy which gives up justifying itself and does not let the States General meet any more. It is the force of power and not the legitimacy of the State which is essential. The fact is proven concerning the development of a bureaucracy, even if it is rather like a rational process of the functional State. Nevertheless its rationality is more debatable, even if the epistemological flexibility of the ideal-type makes it possible to defend this characteristic better by retaining only that what tends towards a State civil service, built up in a hierarchical way, guided by general rules etc. In any case, the French example attests the big distance separating reality from the model.[21]

Another aspect must be underlined with regard to the characteristics of the modern tax State. The search for a fair tax distribution does not exist at the beginning of the modern State as the case of France of the Old Regime (*Ancien Régime*) shows where there is a high tax inequality linked to privileges granted. In the same way in the establishment of consent to taxes in France, the representation of taxpayers follows the unjust stratification in three orders. However, as Clamageran (1867, p. XXXVI) underlines, "a distribution far too iniquitous decreases the yield of it". In addition, the case of England, where the burden of taxes is less (Tocqueville, 1998; Mathias, O' Brien, 1976, p. 604; Tilly, 1986, p. 292; Chaunu 1977, p. 47; Bonney, 1996, p. XXXI), better divided and consented to on more representative bases, suggests a lesson: that of the relation between fiscal justice and the "democratization" of control (here parliamentary) of public finance.

The modern tax State is distinguished from the feudal financial system in so far as constituting a legitimate powerful public sphere, distinct

21 In France the administration does not always comply with the criteria of Weber's model of the modern State. Certain taxes such as the gabelle generated a certain re-feudalization as we have seen; the system of leasing of taxes shaped the institutions in a way that was not always favourable to the tax State (exactions, less output, weight of the financial creditors ensuring the advance on receipts to be perceived). The distinction of public offices remains badly ensured compared to the functions and offices whose venality ensures State receipts.

from the private sphere.[22] Let us recall that for Schumpeter, the distinction between public law and private law was meaningless in the medieval situation (cf. chapter 2). Feudal finances are not unaware of taxes but they fall under the political, legal, economic and social system of the domain. The seigneurial levy does not distinguish the rights of sovereignty and property. The king, like any seigneur, must live off his property, the income of his domain.[23] In spite of the extension of the royal domain, this system had entered in a crisis and was not enough any more to face up to expenditure. This crisis was not simply economic and started from a modification of the political and social relations of the feudality based on the fief. Beyond some resistance, the establishment of the tax State was facilitated by the profit-sharing of the dominant classes in the new royal taxation in the form of exemptions, sharing of receipts and appropriation of a part of the expenditure. In accordance with the theses of the Italian founders of fiscal sociology, domination and coercion are not negligible. The permanence of the tax State is nevertheless based on its legitimacy as a sovereign authority and as an institution with a social purpose of general interest. By the affirmation of the consent to taxes, the modern State is distinguished from the oppressive State and the coercive State, even if it can take the way of "legitimate violence" (Weber) to let the legitimately determined tax obligation be carried out. The historical appearance of royal taxation illustrates a form of domination, but coercion can only be exerted if the social contract is legitimate (cf. chapter 11).

The modern State is not reduced either to a predator seeking to maximize its income. The theory of the Leviathan of Brennan and Buchanan[24], what a tax constitution must limit, does not correspond to

---

22 J.C. Waquet nevertheless made out of the public/private distinction the criterion of the financial system and not only that of the modern tax State in an historical meaning (this distinction aims at "the prior recognition of an abstracted, incorporeal entity, distinct from individual economies, founded by a superior need", 1990, p. 176).

23 As the historians Omrod and Barta (in Bonney, 1996, p. 66) underline: "the true flow of State construction and the real beginning of 'contemporary' public finance can be only discerned during the time when feudal private laws were sub-ordained to the public authority of the State and where more economic activities were subjected to government taxes."

24 Brennan and Buchanan (1977) consider that the tax State is a Leviathan which seeks to maximize its receipts while being not very constrained politically or electorally: "Our discussion is, however, phrased largely in terms of 'monopoly' government in which returns maximization arises from the maximization of the partially unconstrained politician-bureaucrat rather than from the democratic political process itself" (p. 258). The taxing power is based on coercion, independently from the supply of public goods: "Taxes are coercive instruments that allow governments to lay burdens upon persons without any corresponding individualized expression of current willingness to pay." Democracy implies only the maximum of transfers from the minority towards the majority. They propose to think of a tax constitution to limit the power

this situation. The tax decision-making process takes account of political forces. Conflicts and the search for legitimacy constrain the authority to negotiate with the privileged groups. The consent without being permanent (France) is renewed periodically. In England it is constitutive of parliamentary control. The level of taxation is certainly significant, but there are refluxes, for example in France.[25] Illegitimate taxes cause tax revolts.

In medieval Europe, the model of the modern State does not take the same form everywhere and is delayed in certain countries. In Spain, the model is specific (Rucquoi, in Genet, 1990). The royal power is strong because it is invested with the sacred mission of the reconquest of the territory. It is the result of the union of two models, Castilian (centralizing) and Aragonese (not centralizing). Starting in the 14th century, feudalization comes late. The cities are influential and widely recognized. In Eastern Europe, at the end of the Middle Ages, Bohemia, Hungary, Poland and Austria do not have the characteristics of the modern State (Berenger, Tollet, in Genet, 1990). The tax State therefore has several faces. In the Roman Empire, it draws its resources from the tribute of the defeated, the other resources coming essentially from the imperial domain, the confiscation of goods and the variations of the currency value. Taxation is geographically unequal (the town of Rome and Italy being imposed little) as well as socially unequal.[26] The weakness of the interior taxation, made possible by the tribute, the wealth of the domain and the system of slavery, corresponds with the image of a predatory State. This image of predation in the form of tributes to the advantage of certain groups or populations in position of domination is recurrent in history[27], but is opposed to the idea of the modern State as is underlined by philosophical views.

---

of the tax Leviathan (it deduces the rules of taxation from this constitution). In the contractual tradition, they admit that taxpayers are under a veil of ignorance because of the effect of taxes and expenditure and that the agreement must be unanimous. A tax system is fair from the moment it complies with the rules of the constitution (procedural or deontological justice) and not according to its results (teleological). This model is not historical. It is close to the theory of extension of bureaucracy of Niskanen (1971), but is distinguished from the models of very powerful government, of the government of the democratic majority (reflecting the preferences of the median-voter), or of the benevolent and informed government.

25 "What prevents the taxation of the 15th century from finding, before the end of the reign of Louis XI, the 14th century levels, is a demographic trough, war destruction, economic collapse. The State goes forward; it will not be caught up any more. According to its own dynamics" (Chaunu, 1977, p. 145).

26 Exemptions of certain social groups like legionaries and veterans in particular.

27 At the end of the Middle Ages, one finds it for example in the practice of the "*appatis*", a kind of taxation of badly controlled areas, "where there is neither a natural assent to taxes, nor a sufficiently stable law and order" (Contamine, in CHEEF, 2002,

2. The Modern Tax State in the History of Ideas (An Outline)

Without excluding the arbitrary aspects of the choice of authors[28], financial works of Bodin, Bossuet, Smith, Montesquieu, and Rousseau confirm the historical importance of the tension between sovereignty and legitimacy. They are connected with three centuries of institutionalization of the modern tax State (from the 16th to the 18th century) whose roots go back to the Middle Ages. They contain original contributions to fiscal sociology, thus suggesting the interest to reread the history of ideas from this angle. They are representative of the diversity of approaches to financial phenomena, according to whether the point of view is legal-political (Bodin, Bossuet), economic (Smith) or plural (Montesquieu, Rousseau).

a. Sovereignty and consent to taxes according to Bodin

Jean Bodin (1530-1596) is the first philosopher to make sovereignty the principle of the State. This concept marks a watershed in political thought[29]: it opens the way to the definition of the modern State. In *Les six livres de la République*, he devotes an important development to finance and begins chapter II of book VI by this formula: "finance is the nerve of the Republic" (Bodin, 1986, p. 35). It is thus interesting to give a place to his financial doctrine by confronting it with the theory of sovereignty.

Sovereignty is perpetual, absolute and indivisible. This power is an attribute of the State and not of the government which is distinguished from it. The sovereign does not merge with the governed people who are subjected to him. He is subjected to divine laws, but in the image of God, who is at the origin of the divine natural law, his power cannot be disputed.[30] The first attribute of sovereignty is expressed in the estab-

---

p. 11). The *appatis* taxes indicate an agreement concluded between the warring people and the population which is spared or protected by means of a contribution in kind, through services or in currency.

28 For example, Vauban, well-known French author of *La dîme royale* at the end of the 17th century, has not been retained in spite of his interest for economic analysis and fiscal techniques. On the tax theories of the Middle Ages and the Renaissance, cf. Isenmann, 1996 and on that of the 17th and 18th centuries: cf. Bonney, 1996. On the contribution of the cameralist philosopher Justi (18th century): cf.Peukert, 2006.

29 Historically, as we have seen, the construction of the State in France finds its origin in the Middle Ages, in particular with the reign of Philippe le Bel (1285-1350) and the action of the legists.

30 "Because there is nobody bigger on Earth after God, than the sovereign Princes, and because they are established by him as his lieutenants, to command other men, it is necessary to take care of their quality, in order to respect and revere their majesty in every obedient way, to feel and speak about them in every honourable way: because

lishment of general laws without seeking consent[31]: "the first distinction of the sovereign prince, is the power to lay down the law to all in general, and each one in particular: but this is not enough, because he must adjust, without the consent of those bigger, not the same, nor less than him" (book I, chapter 10, p. 306). In this part devoted to the attributes of sovereignty, the power to tax is included in the enumeration of what is called the sovereignty rights: "under this same power to give and break the law, all the other rights and distinctions of sovereignty are included: (...) to impose on or exempt subjects from responsibilities and subsidies" (book I, chapter 10, p. 309). A little further he confirms this analysis in connection with the *taille*: "as for the right to burden subjects with *tailles* and taxes, or to exempt some of them from taxes, that also depends on the power to create law and privileges" (book 1, chapter 10, p. 334).

In book VI where finances are specifically treated, the financial doctrines of Bodin appear however more moderate, even in contradiction, compared to the theory of absolute tax sovereignty. He indeed preaches explicitly the need for consent to taxes, which does not tally with the theory established in book I relating to the content of the power to levy taxes: "that there was no Prince who had the power of raising taxes on subjects, nor prescribing this duty if not with their consent" (p. 71). In the historical context of this analysis, the necessary consent is that of the States General. But Bodin also introduces the notion of general interest concerning notably the *taille*, presented however in book I as an attribute of tax sovereignty (that is not limited). The testament of Saint Louis is quoted in order to support the argumentation: "don't take *tailles*, nor assistance from your subjects, if urgent necessity and obvious utility don't make you to do it, and for a just cause, and not voluntarily: if you do it differently, you will not be considered as a King, but as a tyrant" (p. 7). The financial theory of Bodin marks an evolution in the way of looking at the role of taxation. The formal assertion of the absolute tax sovereignty of the State (of the sovereign in the language of Bodin) is more attenuated in the study of the objectives of taxes. The finance of the State must be healthy, "built on and secured by an unquestionable and durable base" (p. 36).

A measure preliminary to any choice of source of income is to ensure a census by "the Censure" of the assets and incomes of each person. The first chapter of book VI details its advantages, but does not refer

---

he who despises his sovereign Prince, despises God, of whom he is the image on Earth" (book I, chapter 10, p. 295).

31 Customs could not limit the sovereignty of the State, even if Bodin sometimes quotes them in examples: "laws can break customs, and customs could not fail to comply with laws" (book I, chapter 10, p. 308).

directly to sovereignty to justify its institution or its re-establishment. The same prudence is found in the chapter relating to finance, which among the "seven means of raising funds for the finances" (p. 37) refers firstly to the domain[32]: "the domain is the surest means to raise funds (...) the most honest" (p. 36-37). Taxes are mentioned as the last means of financing[33]: "the seventh means is on the subjects, to which one should never come, unless all the other means lose strength, and necessity presses to provide for the Republic" (p. 67). Pre-empting the Godscheid's thoughts (cf. chapter 2), the Austrian founder of fiscal sociology, he underlines the harmful effect of wasting the public domain.[34] Nevertheless, the abolition of taxes is not categorically defended: "because there are no changes, seditions and ruins of Republics more frequent, than in the case of excessive burdens and taxes. And the only way to prevent these disadvantages, is to remove extraordinary subsidies and burdens, ceasing the cause for which one put them up: but one must not also run from one extremity to the other, and abolish all taxes, assistance and *tailles*, as several endeavoured to do, having neither funds, nor domains to support the state of the Republic" (p. 73).

The political conception of finance that Bodin defends is heterogeneous. It reflects the contradictions of the historical struggle between the royal power and feudality. It also shows the tension between a representation of taxes as an obligation towards a sovereign authority and as a legitimately authorized contribution to expenditure of general interest. It again takes up the traditional domanial theory according to which the king must "live off his own assets", establishes the absolute sovereignty of the tax law of the State, and finally admits the need for consent. It is concerned with the functions of taxation, pre-empting in particular the studies of Mann, of the Austrian school of tax sociology, on the social control exerted by taxes (cf. chapter 2). The Censure thus performs the social functions of the control of customs and social justice: "One thus sees, that there was hardly any well-ordened Republic, that did not use Censors and censure" (book VI, chapter I, p. 10). The Censure is a useful instrument to count people, to estimate their assets, to control

32 Knowing that "the public domain and the patrimony of the Prince (are) different: it is therefore not licit for sovereign Princes to misuse the fruit, and income of the domain, now that the Republic is in good peace, and free towards all" (p. 42).

33 The other sources of income to be used before taxes are tribute-money levied on the defeated, gifts, contributions of allies, lucrative activities of the prince (the "*traffique*" (p. 60) like trade in products of the prince), duties levied on the transport of merchandise.

34 "And so that Princes were not constrained to levy taxes on their subjects, or search for means of confiscating their assets, all the peoples and Monarchs have held as a general and indubitable law, that the public domain must be saintly, sacred and inalienable" (p. 39).

certain kinds of behaviour (banishment of vagrants). It is also a question of "rendering burdens and taxes equal according to the assets of everyone" (p. 15) because "by the fault of Censure, the poor are fleeced, and the rich always escape" (p. 18). This functional conception of public finance is also illustrated by the recommendations put forward. The institution of real and not personal *tailles* aims at relieving the poor. The tax on luxury expenditure[35] is justified because nobody is obliged to consume what is superfluous. A symbolic angle will also be developed by the sociological analysis of conspicuous consumption (Veblen, *The Theory of the Leisure Class*). In the same way the expenditure for the poor is considered as necessary.

This functional conception also provides (by reading between the lines) an indication of the way in which the tax State built its legitimacy. Bodin in fact lingers on the distinction between ordinary taxes, extraordinary taxes and "accidental funds" (p. 69) "which resembles one another". This point is interesting. It shows how work on the contents and especially the frontiers of the juridical-political categories took part in this major change consisting of the institution of the modern tax State.[36] The financial theory resulting from the conception of sovereignty as a power tries to go beyond that by extending the domanial conception of property proper to feudality. The relation between those who govern and those who are governed, and its possible shortcomings, which will be at the heart of the elitist theories of the Italian founders of fiscal sociology, is already theorized by Bodin. Later on, as we saw with the Tocqueville's sociology on revolution (chapter 1), the problem will move towards the question of the equality of the fiscal burden. In the 17th century, however, the conception of Bodin is still present in the writings of Bossuet.

---

35 "But if one asks for the means to raise taxes which are to the honour of God, to the benefit of the Republic, according to the wish of good people, in relief of the poor, it is to put them on things, which are of no use if not to spoil and corrupt the subjects, as is done by all the delicacies, and all kinds of small jewellery, perfumes, cloths of gold and silver, silk, crêpe, cloth lined with brass, braiding, fabrics" (p. 81). Bodin notes incidentally that this taxation won't slow down consumption "because the nature of men is such that they do not find anything softer nor more beautiful, than that which is strictly forbidden for them."

36 On this question, cf. the first part, and also on the ambiguity of the domanial theory, cf. Scordia, in CHEFF, 2002. On the case of an ambiguous tax (imposition on travelling shows), cf. Lassalmonie, in CHEFF, 2002. On the mixed nature of certain feudal duties like the duty on the exploitation of the patrimony because of the power of sovereignty: cf. the example of the *banalité*.

b. The need for and moderation of taxes according to Bossuet

The text of Jacques-Benign Bossuet *Politique tirée des propres paroles de l'Écriture sainte* was written in the 17th century, but the preserved editions came out later on.[37] The need for taxes is put forward in article 2 of book 6: "one owes the tribute to the prince" (third proposal, Bossuet, 1967, p. 194). One must allow the Prince to defend the State and individuals "so that, to tell the truth, the tribute is nothing but a small part of his assets that one pays to the prince, in order to give him the means to save everything" (p. 196). The conception of taxes of Bossuet remains close to that of Bodin. Sociologically it pre-empts the representation of taxes as an obligation, namely as "recognition of the supreme authority" (p. 195), of sovereignty. As with Bodin, taxes could not constitute the principal public resource. It comes in the fourth position after trade and navigation (the first source), the domain (the second) and tributes imposed on the defeated (the third). Bossuet recommends, if not to seek consent as proposed by Bodin, to see to it that levies are moderate: "the prince must moderate taxes, and not overwhelm the people" (p. 386). He refers to the rules of Solomon: "he who presses the udder too much in order to draw milk from it, by heating it and tormenting it, draws butter; he who blows his nose too hard, makes blood to come out; he who presses men too much, excites revolts and seditions" (p. 386). In the 18th century, the question of taxes is taken up again on different bases, in particular by the founder of liberal economics, Adam Smith.

c. Going from economic maxims to a moral horizon according to Smith

Considered as one of the founders of economic liberalism, Adam Smith, in his book *An Enquiry into the Nature and Causes of the Wealth of Nations* printed in 1776, proposes maxims on taxes (Smith, 1979). The first maxim justifies the principle of taxes with reference to the interest of taxpayers: the subjects of a State must contribute to support the government. They are in the position of joint owners of a big domain, who are all obliged to contribute to these costs in proportion to the interest that they respectively have in this domain. The following two maxims concern fiscal technique which must avoid arbitrariness (by posing clear and precise rules[38]) and hinder taxpayers as little as possi-

---

[37] One refers here to the decisive edition with introduction and notes of Jacques Le Brun, Geneva, Droz, 1967.

[38] According to Smith the "tax or portion of tax which each individual is held to pay must be certain, and not arbitrary. The time of payment, the mode of the payment, the quantity to be paid, all that must be clear and precise".

ble.[39] The last maxim is more directly economic: any tax must be conceived so that it causes the less possible money to leave the hands of the people less possible money and that it does not remain out of the hands of the people before entering this Treasury. Here, Smith specifies his thoughts by describing four possible shortcomings: the recourse to intermediaries in order to raise taxes unnecessarily increases the costs weighing on the people; taxes can have a demotivating character for economic activity; too heavy penalties on badly founded taxes destroy activities useful for society and sources of tax payment; vexations must be avoided.

These common sense maxims are followed by the discussion of the compared methods of imposition of rents, profits and wages which belongs essentially to fiscal technique. One will retain that the requirement of clarity and simplicity remains an ideal which modern tax systems are far from having reached. The question is rather to know the extent of the intervention of the State to be financed by taxes. Smith admits public intervention for national defence, the protection of assets and people (justice), certain big public works of collective interest[40], public and religious education for the poor.[41] But he tends towards a limitation of the State and does not outline any proposal towards an unspecified form of social State or redistribution of income in the modern sense. As also put forward by Pareto later on (cf. chapter 2), the increase in the wealth of the country is considered necessary to improve the condition of the poor through better wages on the labour market. Many passages of *An Enquiry*, in particular those against the obstacles to the freedom of trade, thus justify a liberal reading of the superiority of the market over the State.[42]

This interpretation nevertheless supposes the creation of an epistemological gap in the moral philosophy that Smith (2001) intended to build up starting notably from *The Theory of Moral Sentiments*, printed in 1759. Whatever it may be with regard to the continuity and the coherence of the Smithian system[43], it should be stressed that the horizon of

39 He writes that "any tax must be perceived at a time and according to a mode that, one can suppose, hinder taxpayers the least" (p. 457).

40 Communication arteries useful for trade (roads, bridges, channels…) or the fortification of foreign counters in dangerous countries.

41 Smith writes that "the expenditure of institutions for public education and religious instruction is likewise undoubtedly an expenditure which benefits the whole society, and which consequently can well, without injustice, be defrayed by a general contribution".

42 Reading that starts from the neo-classical economists and is based on the idea of "laissez-faire, laissez-aller."

43 *The Wealth of Nations* is generally regarded as the founding book of an autonomous economic science centered on the utilitarian interest. This interpretation is based in

the impartial spectator constitutes a criterion to gauge public action. This concept, whose thorough discussion goes beyond our object, opens up an interesting approach for fiscal sociology. Points of view in fact emerge that can explain public opinion by means of a spectator, not impartial, but equitable (Boudon, 2001). For example, an empirical study of public opinion concerning the minimum income in France (Forsé, Parodi, 2004) establishes that, in the position of an impartial spectator[44], an individual tends to choose an increase in this social security benefit without a constraining counterpart.[45] This result, which probably goes beyond the Smithian theory inscribed in the history of economic thought, offers an important methodology for moral sociology and the ethical study of the financing of public intervention. Moral philosophy remains a source of inspiration for fiscal sociology, as is also illustrated by the case of Montesquieu.

d. Political freedom and the context according to Montesquieu

L'Esprit des Lois of Montesquieu (1689-1755) gives rise to diverse readings by philosophers, historians, sociologists and legal and political scholars.[46] Book XIII is devoted to taxes. Its starting point is not sovereignty but property. A tax is a levy on property that is given to guarantee the conservation of one's assets: "State revenues are a portion which each citizen gives of his assets in order to have the guarantee of his remaining assets, or to enjoy them agreeably" (XIII, 1).[47] But beyond

---

particular on the following famous quotation: "it is not from the benevolence of the butcher, the brewer or the baker that we expect our dinner, but from the attention which they pay to their own interest. We address ourselves not to their humanity, but to their love of themselves; and we never speak to them about our own needs but about their advantage". However, the political economics of Smith can also be linked to his ethical analysis of sentiments and behaviours (Sen, 1991). It can be read as an element of his system of moral philosophy which grants an important place to the principle of sympathy (Biziou, 2003). The application of the rules of justice to the principles of government is studied (cf. *An Enquiry into the Nature and Causes of the Wealth of Nations*) for defence, the police and income.

44 The equitable spectator is distinguished from the impartial spectator of Smith (or the judicious spectator of Hume) because "contrary to the latter ones, we do not need to make an anthropological assumption on the sympathy of individuals. We avoid the problems of utilitarianism which result from it and which suppose a weighting between selfishness and sympathy" (Forsé, Parodi, 2004, p. 42).

45 "That leads it to a solidaristic opinion, not because of compassion or cynicism, but because of arguments sufficiently flexible to be acceptable for anybody else" (Forsé, Parodi, 2004, p. 87).

46 Cf. for example: R. Aron, 1967, p. 25-76, who makes Montesquieu a sociologist; C. Larrère, 2002, p. 124 who insists on the political dimension of taxes.

47 Montesquieu (Charles-Louis de Secondat), *Œuvres complètes*, Paris, Seuil, 1964. It should be recalled that in the 18th century the guarantee applied to an asset means the

this conception of insurance tax (concerning property), the Montesquieu's tax theory is interesting because of the diversity of the selected plans of analysis.

A place of choice is granted to political freedom[48], as the title of book XIII reveals it.[49] A relation between the amount of a tax and the nature of the government is put forward according to the following "general rule": the freer a country is politically, the higher is the tax (and vice versa): "one can raise higher tributes, in proportion to the freedom of the subjects; and one is forced to moderate them, as the constraint increases (…). There is, in moderate States, a compensation for the weight of tributes; that is freedom. There is, in despotic States, an equivalent for freedom; it is the modicity of tributes". The moderation of the government authorizes higher taxes, on the condition of not misusing them.[50] Here the legal-political analysis of the tax State is linked, without many precise details, to the constitutional object of the types of regime which is central in *L'Esprit des Lois*.

This analysis is prolonged by economic considerations. The amount of the taxes is thus linked to the economic wealth of the country, which leads Montesquieu to criticize the idea that the increase of taxes is favourable to the economy.[51] In the same way, an economic limit to taxes is specified for the taxation of goods where "it is necessary that there is some relationship between the goods and the tax" (book XIII, chapter VIII). We also know, in the meaning of this economic dimen-

---

assurance to be able to preserve the assets and their fruits (the enjoyment of an asset meaning the fact of being owner).

48 For Montesquieu, "political freedom does not consist at all in doing what one wants. In a State, i.e. in a society where there are laws (…) freedom is the right to do everything that the laws allow" (XI, 3).

49 Book XIII is entitled: "Relations that the levy of tributes and the size of public income have with freedom."

50 "Because moderate government produced admirable effects, they left this moderation; because they drew big tributes, they wanted to draw excessive tributes, and, ignoring the hand of freedom that gave this present, they addressed themselves to the servitude that refuses everything" (XIII, 15).

51 Cf. XIII, 2: "How bad is it not to reason when saying that the size of tributes is good in itself". Montesquieu (as Hume) discusses this idea (which comes from mercantilism) that taxes create wealth. He anticipates incidentally the modern concept of fiscal disincentives: "but if an arbitrary power removes the rewards of nature, one takes up again the dislike for work" (*ibid.*). This analysis is also that of David Hume in the chapter on taxes in his *Essais moraux, politiques et littéraires et autres essais.* On the historical level, he also criticizes the increase of taxes justified by the needs of the princes in Europe: "the edicts of the princes (…) always speak about their needs and never about ours" (XIII, 15). He again refers to this criticism in connection with "the perpetual increase in tributes" (XIII, 17) related to the increase in the number of troops.

sion, that Montesquieu develops elsewhere the virtues of agreeable trade.[52]

The important question of the social acceptance of taxes is finally raised. With this sociological question in mind, the mechanism of the painless tax paid by the salesman on the goods is described as follows: "the taxes on goods are those that the people feel the less (…). For that, it is of great consequence that it is he who sells the goods who pays the tax. He knows well that he does not pay on behalf of himself; and the purchaser, who in substance pays, confuses it with the price" (XIII, 7). Another aspect of tax sociology is brought up in connection with the discussion of the respective merits of the systems of management of taxes by the farmers-general or directly by the State: the importance of the concrete relation to taxes (chapter 9). This relation structures the feeling of justice of the citizen: "through State management, the prince is the master to press or delay the levy of tributes, according to either his needs or those of the people. Through State management, he spares the State the enormous profits of the farmers-general, who impoverish it in an infinite number of ways. Through State management, he spares the people the spectacle of sudden fortunes that afflict them" (XIII, 19,).

In sociology, the approach of Montesquieu based on the relation of taxes to freedom will be followed by Tocqueville (cf. chapter 1). Considered sometimes as the 19th century Montesquieu, he analyzes, within his own framework of study, the role of freedom in his fiscal sociology of revolution and democracy. In the 20th century, the historical sociology of Ardant will study taxes as a technique of the liberal economy, i.e. made possible (and legitimated) by the development of economic exchanges (without obstacles). One will finally see that the mechanism of tax incidence, according to the modern economic vocabulary (repercussion of taxes in the prices) brings into play a social logic which is explained by the cognitive rationality of taxpayers who associate taxes to consumption prices (chapter 9). As of the 18th century, Rousseau will discuss the ideas of Montesquieu.

c. *The correction of social inequalities according to Rousseau*

Jean-Jacques Rousseau (1712 1768) devotes a study to taxes in *Discours sur l'économie politique.*[53] He considers that taxes collides with the right of ownership, "more important in certain ways than freedom even" (p. 263). Indeed, "it should be remembered here that the base of

52 "Trade cures destroying prejudices; and it is almost a general rule, that everywhere where there are agreeable manners, there is trade; and that everywhere where there is trade, there are agreeable manners" (XX, 1).

53 The references are drawn from Rousseau, *OEuvres complètes*, Gallimard, La Pléiade, 1959.

the social pact is property". He recommends, like Bodin to whom he refers, to resort to the income of the public domain. Furthermore, as for "the annoying resource of taxes and subsidies" (p. 269) he defends, always with reference to Bodin, consent to taxes, "not because of a particular will (…) but of a general will, with a plurality of voices, and based on proportional tariffs which do not leave anything arbitrary in the imposition" (p. 270).

Like Montesquieu, his analysis is also at the crossroads of economics and politics (from where the title of political economics comes). The first duty of the legislator is to conform the laws to general will, so "that the administration is in conformity with the laws"[54] (p. 250). But that is not enough; it is also necessary, and that is the second rule of public economics, that virtue reigns: "nothing cannot compensate for manners in order to maintain the government" (p. 252). He thus discusses the merits of real taxes and personal taxes and foresees, like Montesquieu whom he quotes, the problem of economic incidence. He shows however that in certain cases (producer of corn) taxes cannot be passed on. Contrary to Montesquieu, he gives a positive opinion on personal taxes which "are exactly proportional to the means of private individuals (…), more suitable to free men" (p. 270-271).

Rousseau is distinguished by the virulence of his criticism of the privileges of the rich[55] and the attention he gives to social inequalities that taxes must correct. Sensitive to the shortcomings of governments in the absence of public virtue[56], he recommends, next to love for the fatherland and public education, the equalization of wealth: "the law that one misuses is used at the same time by the powerful as an offensive weapon, and as a shield against the weak, and the pretext of public property is always the most dangerous plague for the people. What is most necessary, and perhaps most difficult in government, is a severe integrity to render justice to all, and especially to protect the poor

54 Rousseau specifies that it is not necessary to convene the nation for all public decisions, "because the leaders know well enough that the general will is always for the party the most favourable to the public interest, i.e. the most equitable; so that one should only be just in order to be sure to follow the general will" (p. 251).

55 "Aren't all the advantages in society for the powerful and the rich? Isn't all lucrative employment filled by them only? Aren't all the favours, all the exemptions reserved for them? And isn't the whole public authority in their favour?" (p. 271).

56 That he analyzes in passages which precede the development on taxes: "soon the price of virtue becomes that of brigandage" (p. 253). "It is then that to the voice of duty which does not speak in the hearts any more, the leaders are forced to substitute the cry of terror or the lure of an apparent interest (…). All that remains of vigour in the government is employed by its members to lose their way and supplant one another, while the affairs remain abandoned, or are executed only in as much as personal interest requires it, and according to whether it directs them" (p. 253).

against the tyranny of the rich (…) It is thus one of the most important concerns of government to prevent the extreme inequality of fortunes" (p. 258). On the subject of taxes, he argues in favour of the quest for the consent of citizens to taxes on income and on necessary goods. Like Bodin, he particularly recommends taxation on luxury goods, while stressing that express consent is not necessary "in the case of things whose use one can give up" (p. 278).

It should finally be noted that Rousseau goes beyond the framework of analysis of taxes as infringements (to be justified) to the right of ownership by denouncing the defects of taxation in non-virtuous governments. The legitimacy of the tax State requires the virtue of the leaders: "the people on their side, who perceive the greed of leaders and their insane expenditure, rather than public needs, murmur when they see themselves stripped of the necessary in order to provide for the superfluous of others; and (…) the most honest administration would succeed in restoring confidence. Even if the contributions are voluntary, they do not produce anything; if they are forced, they are illegitimate, and it is in this cruel alternative to let the State perish or to tackle the sacred right of ownership" (p. 264). One finds in the case of Rousseau another anticipation of the reflexion of the founders of the Italian fiscal sociology related to the tax State in its relation to the satisfaction of the dominant classes. Political legitimacy is difficult to construct; it is at the base of the tax State which is justified in the amount of the receipts taken compared to its interventions.

3. Typological Approach of the Tax State

Starting from the problem of the relation between receipts and expenditure, the typology crosses the level of taxation and the level of intervention of the State in order to define four forms of the tax State, among whom the interventional State emerges.

Table 3: Typology of the tax State

Level of intervention→ Level of taxation	Low	High
Low	Liberal State	Crisis of the tax State
High	Wasteful State	Interventionist State

a. The liberal tax State

A level of low taxation associated with a low level of public interventions characterizes the conception of *the liberal State*. This ideal-type models notably the liberal State of the 19th century in France. At the time of the classical or liberal finances, the intention is to limit the role of the State for reasons of political doctrine and economic theory. It is an apology for the State limited to its sovereignty functions (diplomacy, security etc.), it is the reign of economic competition, of the invisible hand of the Market supposed to ensure prosperity. The tax State is limited by the prohibition of economic and social interventions, but it must also remain neutral with regard to the behaviour of economic agents. Taxes have a strictly financial role consisting in covering the limited public expenditure. This conception is that of the English school (Smith, Ricardo and their disciples).

The neo-liberal ideology has spread the conception of a minimum State. As we will see in chapter 6, the reception of the anti-tax discourse and of the criticism of the Welfare state is explained by several factors (Leroy, 2009). It depends on the capacity of its system of argumentation to mobilize economic knowledge to create social commonplaces. The anti-tax discourse, while being based on the results of utilitarian economics, becomes, because of the social context, more convincing for all the social groups, and not only for those who have big incomes. Economics has become the social science of reference for the government of modern societies in the post-war period. Public choices are not any more discussed as political choices of the society, but as managerial constraints of economic efficiency. Budgetary performance can then serve as a pretext for the withdrawal of the State basing itself on the intention of avoiding waste.

b. The wasteful State

A high level of taxation associated with a low level with intervention represents a wasting that can be explained by corruption, inefficiency, oppression etc. This form of *the wasteful State* is not theoretical. In many countries, the annual reports of the Court of Auditors swarm with examples of the waste of public resources related to badly controlled expenditure. The case of the corruption of the State, more serious, can be defined as the systematic organization by the governing classes of the misappropriation of public money. For example, in the context of the enrichment of the oligarchs in the Russia of Boris Eltsine, the lack of confidence expressed by the citizens in the corrupted State explains the decline of tax morality.[57] This situation is normally unthinkable in

[57] Based on data of European and world surveys on values, that include a question on tax morality, Alm *et al.* (2005) show that the lack of confidence of citizens with regard to the State, which is seen as corrupt and incompetent vis-à-vis tax evasion and the Mafia, explains the decline of tax morality between 1991 and 1995 in Russia. Thereafter, the improvement of confidence in the State improved, according to data of 1999, tax morality.

democratic countries where financial controls are exerted correctly, even if current news regularly reveals indelicacies of some politicians. A study measuring the legitimacy of the State in 72 countries[58] shows that established democracies like France or New Zealand are badly classified. This study nevertheless confirms that in general the countries of Western Europe and the Anglo-American countries, followed by the countries of Asia are well placed.

The relation between corruption, democracy and the economy is complex. The majority of specialists regard corruption as negative. Based on data of a 100 countries from 1982 to 1997, Drury *et al.* (2006) conclude that corruption does not have a significant effect on the economic growth of democracies, because democracy attenuates the negative impact of corruption on economic growth. On the other hand, it has an effect on the economic performance of nondemocratic countries. Pellegrini and Gerlagh (2008) show with data from 107 countries that the opening of the market (globalization), measured by imports and exports, has no effect on corruption. On the other hand, corruption is negatively correlated with the duration of democracy, while political instability, measured by the number of veto players, is associated with added corruption. Gerring *et al.* (2005) define democracy as a political stock of capital. Exploiting long-term data on the 20th century, they confirm the widespread idea that the democracy does not have a statistical effect on economic growth if the comparison relates to the levels of democracy of the countries. It only has an indirect effect by constituting an institutional environment favourable to investments. But measured as a stock of capital, democracy is correlated positively with economic performance. A study on enterprises in Uganda (Fisman, Svensson, 2007) highlights the strongly negative effect of corruption for enterprises (micro-level of analysis): an increase of 1% in the rate of "bribes" is associated with a reduction of the growth of enterprises of more than 3 points, an effect which is 3 times bigger than the effect of taxation. Lastly, Rothstein and Uslaner (2005, p. 48) underline, on the basis of another empirical study, that inequality is linked with the lack of general confidence, even if confidence does not have a direct effect on inequality (measured by the Gini index). The virtuous circle of the State combines a low level of inequality, a high level of confidence, an honest government and universal social policies (p. 67). In any case, it appears clearly that democracy tends to diminish corruption, as is notably shown

58 The study uses 3 indicators. The first relates to the expectations of citizens with regard to legal norms ("views of legality"). It shows that the State exerts political power in a way that is consistent with these expectations. The second ("views of justifications") is based on the conformity of the shared principles, ideas and values. The third ("acts of consent") relates to the concrete acts of assent and includes good fiscal citizenship.

by the study on bureaucratic corruption in 49 developing countries from 1982 to 1990 by Halim (2008).[59]

Corruption has especially an effect on the output of certain types of taxes, namely those that require frequent interactions between taxpayers and agents of the administration. A study of 17 developing countries shows that the covering of customs duties, of import and export levies and of excise duties is affected negatively. The amount of the other taxes is not much affected. On the other hand, no statistically significant correlation is highlighted between the total of the tax incomes and corruption (Iman, Jacobs, 2007, p. 19).

It is nevertheless clear that a wasteful or corrupt State has in general neither the financial means, nor legitimacy to finance public programs. In these contexts, social interventionism is also badly accepted because of the low level of social confidence. As the Italian founders of fiscal sociology maintained, it is also advisable to take into account clientelism which leads governments to grant advantages to social classes or groups which support them, and thus to seek tax resources. Nevertheless, clientelism and similar forms of distribution of financial resources do not directly qualify the wasteful State under consideration in the relationship between resources and expenditure. In fact, it supposes a sufficient level of resources in order to be efficient and is more appropriate for the interventionist type of tax State. The question of the legitimacy of clientelism does not enter into the typology proposed here, and refers to the question of tax functions (cf. chapter 11).

Thus, while liberal doctrines and waste are not phenomena to be neglected, the two types discussed here, the liberal State and the wasteful State, do not correspond to the current situation of developed countries who have high levels of tax revenue (including social security) and public expenditure.

c. *The crisis of the tax State*

A (too) low level of taxation associated with a high level of interventions raises the question of a tax crisis. This idea is like the one we saw at the heart of the work of Goldscheid (1967, p. 202). According to this Marxist author, the capitalist State has a structurally poor financial system, contrary to the old societies where the prince draws big incomes from his properties. For Goldscheid, the State must extend its public domain[60] in order to escape from the tax crisis and meet the needs of

59 More precisely, parliamentary democracy is associated with the reduction of corruption of the administration. The quality of the judicial system is also a significant factor.

60 The nationalization of enterprizes is a way which corresponds with the conception of Goldscheid.

society. The neo-Marxist theory of O' Connor (1973)[61] raises the question differently: the "capitalist" State intervening more and more through public expenditure to support the economy finds itself with a budgetary deficit, without being able to legitimize an increase of taxes (which in this sense are too weak). The interest of these theses is especially to insist on the importance of the legitimization of the tax State. As one saw with Schumpeter, the intrinsic fragility of the tax State of developed countries is not verified.[62] In the case of developing countries the question is especially to create a real tax State (cf. chapter 5).

The increase of tax revenue (including social security) and the existence of unpopular financial decisions[63] also contradict the inexorability of the crisis of the tax State. Even in a period of economic crisis, there are several possibilities to finance expenditure (taxation, loans, budgetary cuts, privatization etc.).[64] The relation between taxation and State expenditure is not mechanical, nor deterministic. It especially concerns a political choice. The problems of the crisis of the tax State are also mentioned by Campbell (1993), in addition to the economic, geopolitical, crisis to explain tax reforms. In the case of Germany, it is explored by Streeck (2007) from the institutionalist point of view to analyze the political constraints and opportunities which structure finance public. Peacock and Wiseman (1967) consider that war increases the tolerance towards taxation in order to finance expenditure, but that afterwards one does not go back (a ratchet effect) and that public expenditure (and taxes that finance them) are thus regularly increasing. In opposition to this theory of irreversibility, it should be mentioned that under the influence of neo-liberal ideas public expenditure was reduced in certain countries. In the same way, the relation between war and the development of the

61 Cf. also the link established by Habermas (1978) between the financial crisis and the crisis of legitimization of the State: the social compromise with the working classes is undermined by the lack of financial means of the State.

62 "The system of the tax State has so far met all challenges, and whenever it has failed, to do so in particular cases, special causes can be found which are not inherent in its nature" (Schumpeter, 1954, p. 25).

63 Cf.: in France the rigour imposed by the leftwing government in 1983, the reform of the retirement system initiated by the rightwing government; in the United States, successive increases in income tax from 1916 to 1986; the stimulation policies in Europe and in the United States to support the banking system following the crisis of August 2008 etc.

64 As Gold (1995) points outs in a study of 6 American States, budgetary expedients and financial innovation are strategies which open choices. King and Gurr (1988) show that political decision-makers thus choose to maintain (1972 to 1982) a high level of subsidies to local governments in order to ensure public services in crisis periods. In the 1980's in Ghana, and in the 1990's in Peru, reforms led to a reduction of the budget deficit and a rapid increase of public expenditure (Toye, 2000, p. 41).

tax State[65], which was lead to increase taxes in order to finance war expenditure, is not universal. In the case of 19th century Latin America, "wars did not make the state" (Centeno, 1997, p. 1598).

The cognitive theory of taxes (Leroy, 1996, p. 41 and 2002, p. 16) shows that crises are used as a cognitive argument to justify changes in tax or budgetary policy. A crisis is a process and not given information. The presentation of arguments directs the representation of a situation as is shown by empirical data concerning the American debate of 1998-1999 on social security (Jerit, Barabas, 2006). Incorrect information leads one to overestimate the gravity of the social protection crisis and to (wrongly) forecast the bankruptcy of the American system. This argumentation is developed in chapter 7.

d. The social interventionist State

The interventionist State, defined here by a high level of taxation and intervention, corresponds, on a variable scale, to the current situation of developed countries. Thus, since 1914, the modern finances of the Welfare State and then of the Keynesian State are interventionist. Taxes are not any more as at the time of liberalism the provider of the Treasury. In addition to the traditional financial function, the functions of intervention and redistribution (Musgrave, 1959) become apparent. According to Mann (1943, p. 225), taxation gradually passed from the sphere of public finance (financial function) to the sphere of sociology (social lever function). In spite of the attempts of neo-liberalism to limit resulting tax levies (Cox, Lowery, 1990), the evolution of the functions of taxation did not cause State interventionism to move back (cf. chapter 11). In Europe, in particular, the rate of tax revenue (including social security) (38.3% of GDP in 2006) remains high.

It should be recalled that the Welfare State represents a form of public interventionism in the name of a certain conception of social justice which emerges in the 19th century as a criticism of the excesses of the industrial society. The golden age of the Welfare State corresponds to the period of continuous post-war growth and also shows the generalization of the Keynesian policies (economic action through expenditure). The economic crisis of the 1970's is also that of the Welfare State and the Keynesian State whose financing is called into question. And yet, as we have seen with tax crises, solutions exist to politically desired social public actions. It is a question of democratic choice, even if the political decision afterwards refers to the problem of good public management.

---

65 Cf. the theory (Peacock and Wiseman, 1967) relative to the peaks of expenditure in periods of war, linked with the increased tolerance towards taxes.

The level of social protection desired by each country determines the form of Welfare State which can be classified in one of the Esping-Andersen's categories (Esping-Andersen, 1990).[66] The European and world surveys on values indicate that, in spite of differences between countries, Europeans remain attached to the Welfare State. Public opinion is in particular in favour of the minimum wage in the case of a high level of unemployment (correlation indicated by Pfeifer, 2009, base on the Eurobarometer). Forsé and Parodi (2002, 2004) show the empirical reality of the moral citizen, the "equitable spectator" not guided by his egoistic interest, to approve social policies. The study of Lynch and Myrskylä (2009) of 11 European countries in 1992 and 2001 confirms this result: the beneficiaries of public pensions are not motivated by a selfish egoism when forming their opinion on social expenditure in this field. Even the American public opinion appears to be favourable to social programs targeted on the poor within the framework of a humanitarian ethos (Feldman, Stennbergen, 2001). A study of 14 democracies in the OECD from 1980 to 2000 (Brooks, Manza, 2006) shows that the political preferences of the masses are important for the maintenance of the Welfare State (and thus of the financing of social interventions). Leaders are in fact obliged to take account of public opinion in particular in the Welfare State of the liberal type.

These results are confirmed by a study of the OECD countries which shows the attachment of citizens to the traditional institutions of the Welfare state, in spite of the high rates of imposition (Bay, Pedersen, 2006, p. 421). The success of Nordic countries, that combine a social protection of quality with a high level of imposition, illustrates this reality. A high level of social protection is therefore not necessarily contradictory with economic efficiency (Headey *et al.*, 2000; Steinmo, 2002). In accordance with Sen (1999), we can maintain that social services in the broad sense (education, health etc.) participate in the well-being of society and contribute to economic growth. The stimulation policies in Europe and in the United States to support the world banking structure following the crisis of August 2008 mark once again the interventionist character of the tax State. Once we admit the relevance of the interventionist State, the reflection must be about the type of financial social contract which characterizes the tax revenue (including social security) of a democracy (cf. chapter 11).

---

66 Cf. table 3 in chapter 5. The recent reforms of social protection tend however to build mixed models, as in France with the introduction of "social" taxes (CSG) and the universal health covering (CMU).

Conclusion

By its historical and intellectual genesis the modern tax State is proper to Europe. The agitated history of taxes is one of the bases of the Western liberal democracies. The right relation to freedom and to the consent of citizens constitutes the procedural counterweight to the obligation that levies establish to the benefit of the State. The legitimacy of the tax State is basically that of interventionist public action such as it is conditioned and shaped by taxes to finance social policies in particular. The difficulty, even more salient for developing countries, lies in rendering the State permanently legitimate. The categories of thought of the neo-liberal globalization are not favourable to taxes nor to expenditure which is regarded as opposite to the efficiency of the market. The Welfare State however, as we will see, sometimes resists quite well to the economic globalisation. The crisis of the tax State is always that of politics, even if economic circumstances play a role. Certain countries, like those of the old Soviet block, have the opportunity of defining new tax systems by avoiding the institutional complexity which characterizes the old systems of the developed countries. Other countries try to reform their tax system. Everywhere, the stake is to go beyond simple economic aims so as to make tax revenue (including social security) part of a political project whose finality is social.

CHAPTER 5

The Public Finance System

The financial system is defined as the whole system of public revenue and expenditure. In developed countries, taxation occupies a central place that prolongs, at least for Europe, the historic legacy of the development of the modern State. Since the First World War and the crisis of 1929, the financial system of industrial countries has been modified under the influence of the politics of intervention. After the Second World War, the Keynesian Welfare State expanded rapidly. Despite the crisis of the 1970s and the decline of Keynesianism, financial intervention through taxation and public expenditure was maintained while the level of tax revenue remained high. The impact of the crisis of the summer of 2008 reestablished public action through expenditure in order to support the banking sector and the economy: the reduction of tax revenue is thus not on the agenda of the majority of the countries entailed in the globalization of the American crisis.

Systemic analysis[1] allows one to reflect on the interrelations that structure the different components of public finance and its economic, legal and social environment. From this point of view, it appears that the financial system is from now on divided between the finances of the State, those of local authorities, and those of State associations (federal-

1 Systemic analysis insists on the system as a set of interrelated units. It emphasizes the feedback effects and the essential dimension of complexity. Qualities emerge from the interrelations to form a holistic totality non-reducible to its parts. A system is understood by studying at its organization based on its structural and functional aspects. This is an example of Parsons' theory of society. The construction of typologies is a means to account for the variety of configurations in a system. In general the systems in societies are open to their environment, which may induce certain evolutions. The founders of systems analysis are: Norbert Wiener, mathematician at the origin of cybernetics, inventor of an automatic system for air canons which underlined notably the notion of feedback; Warren McCulloch, neurophysiologist working on the brain who is at the origin of bionics (prosthetics) and of connectionism in the cognitive sciences; Karl Ludwig von Bertalanfy who is the author of *General System Theory*, Jay W. Forrester, electronics engineer who, among other things, influenced the Club of Rome on diminishing economic growth. The Macy conferences of New York (1946-1953) allowed the meeting of researchers from several disciplines including the social sciences. Authors such as Edgar Morin, J.L. Le Moigne and H.A. Simon emphasized necessity to study the complexity of systems. The political system is the subject of the classical analysis of Easton.

ism, the European Union etc.). Taxation is a central element of public finance, but it also constitutes a largely autonomous system which justifies a study of public action proper to this domain (cf. chapter 6). The adoption of a systemic level (macro) of analysis thus sheds light on certain general tendencies, but cannot account for either the variety of social phenomena implicated by taxes and public spending (cf. the other chapters). The choice retained here consists of presenting the system of tax revenue in relation with expenditure, within the comparing framework of OECD countries, before studying the particular case of developing countries.

1. The Systemic Analysis of Tax Revenue

Without trying to study the interrelations of public finance with the whole of the environment exhaustively, the relations of tax revenue with budgetary and tax law, with the economy and with the growth of public expenditure are schematically presented (cf. Figure 1).

Figure 1: The system of tax revenue

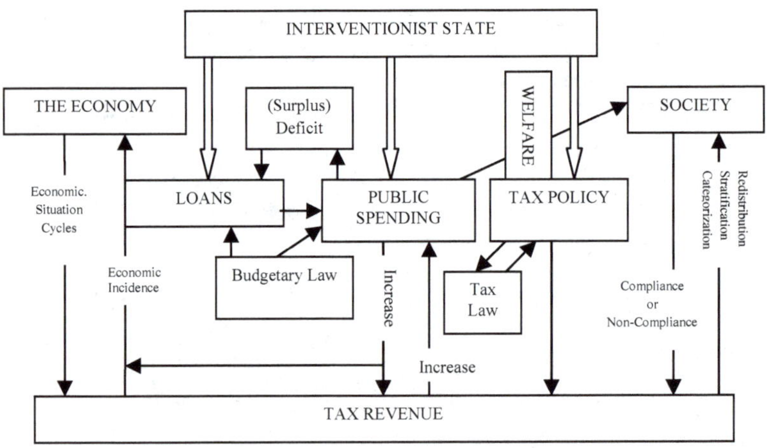

a. The interdependence with law

Legally, the financial system is apprehended through budgetary law and the rules of public accounting on the one hand, and the provisions of tax law on the other hand. We must remember that the development of budgetary principles and the obligation of consent to taxes (cf. chapter 4) served as a foundation for parliamentary democracy. In this way, in addition to the vote on taxes, the rules of annualisation (the duration of authorization and execution is one year), unity (a single document for the whole budget), universality (no allocation or compensation between revenue and expenditure), and speciality (giving the detail of expenditure) are the legal instruments for the political control of the parliament over the government. The division of the financial system leads one also to consider in a separate way national, local and, in Europe, community finance. For example the rules established by the Maastricht and Amsterdam treaties[2] on the control of public debt, which must be contained within the limit of 60% of GDP, and of public deficit (limited to 3% of GDP) aim to weigh on the management of the public finance of the member states in the European Union. Nevertheless, the effectiveness of this legal constraint largely depends on the political process that controls the decisions of the member States (cf. chapter 8).

By setting up the rules for the taxation of taxpayers, tax law, which is modified according to policy, has an impact on tax revenue. The sources of tax law are formed by the tax provisions of the constitution, international treaties, laws and rules of the executive. The constitution and the texts and principles of constitutional value that belong to the constitutionality block contain provisions that are legally the basis of certain important elements of the tax system, notably: the distribution of powers[3] between parliament and government and between the different administrative levels of the country, and various principles. The principle of equality in front of taxes is generally recognized, but its scope, specified by constitutional jurisprudence, varies from country to country. At the world level, in spite of the recommendations and reports of international organizations such as the OECD, the tax sovereignty of the States remains the rule (Leroy, 2006). The national particularisms of tax law (Leroy, 2007) are found in the divergences of the tax revenue of every country. The importance of derogatory taxation (cf. chapter 7) also shows the limitations for the tax revenue output. In the same way the evasion of tax revenue (fraud) and the legal avoidance of taxes depend on the rules for the taxation and for the audit.

The struggle against tax evasion must therefore take into account the accentuation of tax globalization which results from the economic and financial globalization. Tax law tries to find an equilibrium between the powers of the administration and the rights (guarantees) of taxpayers in the case of tax control. In many countries, the means of control of the

2 The Maastricht treaty instituted "convergence criteria" for establishing the Euro as the single European currency. The main criteria reaffirmed by the treaty of Amsterdam are related to public debt and deficit (i.e. State administrations, local authorities and social security financed by tax revenue).

3 For example, in the case of fiscal federalism in Germany, the Bund and the *Länder* share legislative power with preponderance for the Bund: cf. Preisser, in Leroy, 2005. As for the Italian case, Constitution amendment of 2001 reinforced power of regions (Succio, in Leroy, 2005).

tax administrations were reinforced in order to face up to international tax evasion. A comparative study (10 countries) of the relations between the administration and citizens (Leroy, 2008) shows a certain degree of convergence between legal regimes, in spite of certain particularisms. The extent of the obligations and rights of taxpayers[4], the rules of litigation and the control powers of tax inspectors constitute legal stakes. But the scope of these stakes differs more or less according to the countries. We will also see that sociologically the implementation of tax control law depends on the administrative regulation that prevails in the organizational functioning (chapter 7). New legal questions[5] also arise with the development of electronic procedures and databases (files) and with the use of the Internet in the relations between the tax administration and taxpayers (the E-administration: Sacchetto, in Leroy, 2008).

As for international treaties, we must first mention the conventions aiming to avoid double taxation which are numerous. These conventions are, apart from a few exceptions, bilateral. The OECD developed a standard model (Succio, in Leroy, 2006) which more or less inspires the States, knowing that the particular content of every convention depends on the negotiation between the two signatory States. The standard model of the OECD also proposes an amicable procedure for solving disputes. In general, conventions deal with at least the taxation of individuals and of enterprise profits, including notably the notion of permanent establishment taxable within a country. The influence of treaties applicable to associations of States constitutes another domain of interrelations with national tax systems.

For instance, community law influences the tax revenues of the member states in the European Union, modifying the national tax systems. The legal instrument used for the harmonization of tax systems is the directive: once transposed into the national legal system, the directive modifies the tax law in a sense of conformity with the prescriptions of community law. Customs duties were eliminated. The Single European Act of 1985 completely abolished the internal borders of the Union. The harmonization of tax law in Europe particularly concerned the VAT (article 99 of the Treaty of Rome, becoming article 93 of the treaty of the European Communities). Being less advanced for the other forms of taxation[6], the European tax system is nevertheless constructed

---

4 Obligation to hand in tax returns, to collaborate, to give information etc. and right to get information, to have an adversarial procedure, to get assistance from a taxlawyer, to have recourses etc.

5 Problems of signature authentification, of secrecy, of privacy protection, of the opening up of networks to users etc.

6 The goal is to avoid discriminations, notably in the case of the regime of the merger of enterprises or of the determination of the profit of enterprises in several member

through the jurisprudence of the European Court of Justice (ECJ).[7] The tax sovereignty of every member state constitutes a difficult obstacle to overcome, especially since the rule of unanimity is required for every decision in this domain.

The contribution of the OECD, in addition to the above mentioned standard-model conventions, concerns harmful tax practices. Tax competition between countries is not called into question in its principles: it is not about condemning the efforts of countries to make their tax systems more attractive to investors. It is about putting an end to anticompetitive practices of a harmful nature. This soft law has an impact on tax revenue by trying to propose legal regulation. The OECD, where experts and representatives of member states and associated countries negotiate, thus sets "norms"[8] based on criteria to decide if a preferential regime has a harmful character. The reports are not devoid of effects since most of the countries abolish or modify the tax systems aimed at in order to take into account the observations of the OECD. Competition nevertheless remains the key notion, while offshore zones offer derogatory legal measures in order to escape from taxes. The effective scope of the attempts to regulate tax havens depends on the will of every State which can anchor itself to the principle of the tax sovereignty of every country in order to refuse international pressures. The attacks of 11 September 2001 (the financing of terrorism) in the United States and the crisis of financial capitalism of 2008 show the acuteness of the problem of "tax havens" which escape from taxation. Economic factors must therefore also be considered.

b. *The relation to the economy*

The financial system is not the same according to the type of economy. Until the fall of Berlin Wall, a distinction was made between the public finance of industrial countries, developing countries and planned-economy countries. Since the collapse of the USSR, even if subdivisions have been made with regard to the level of advancement, we have distinguished between the financial systems in developed countries, in

states or furthermore in the case of tax on the income of the citizen of another member state.

7 The Court even seems (Maîtrot de la Motte, in Leroy, 2006) to substitute for the decision-making authorities of the Community (Council, Commission, and Parliament). Without neglecting the reversals of jurisprudence, it appears that the ECJ covers up the timidity of the progress made in the harmonization of taxes in Europe (Leroy, 1995) which is the subject of a limited number of directives.

8 Cf. OECD "Harmful Tax Competition: An Emerging Global Issue", Report 1998; and the different intermediary reports and their updating relative to "The OECD's Project on Harmful Tax Practices". In 2000, the report was titled "Towards Global Tax Cooperation."

countries in transition towards the market economy (former member countries of the USSR) and in developing countries. The interdependence between the financial system and the economy emerges in a number of ways. As Figure 1 shows, the level of tax revenue depends on three main factors: tax policy, public expenditure, and public borrowing. Firstly, the economic situation has an impact on the level of tax revenue. In the case of economic recession, "automatic stabilizers" intervene: tax revenues decline and social security spending increases in the absence of reaction of the interventionist State (in particular the spending compensating for unemployment). In the case of economic growth, the increase of tax revenue facilitates new spending (or spending on debt repayment). Economic cycles of growth and of recession therefore do have an influence. In France, a study by the *Caisse d'Epargne* in 2003 (*Les finances locales à l'horizon 2007*) shows on the one hand a correlation (for the period from 1995 to 2002) between the economic cycle measured by the GDP indicator and the evolution of the bases of the four main local taxes. On the other hand, tax rates, which are decided by local authorities, appear to be less sensitive to economic trends. A correlation is also established between the economic cycle and the cycle of local investment (period from 1982 to 2002).

Reciprocally, tax revenue does have an economic incidence[9], raising the problem of passing the tax burden by the tax legal debtor. An enterprise can, in particular in the case of a monopoly, in certain cases to pass on all or part of the tax to its prices. The reality of the incidence is difficult to measure and varies according to the situations. It depends on the economic sensitivity of the demand to the variations in the price of the good (elasticity of demand). The VAT is characterized by its neutrality to economic channels, since every enterprise retrieves the VAT paid on its purchases by deducting it from the VAT collected from its customers. The real taxpayer is then the consumer who bears the VAT included in the price. In the context of economic globalization of the 1990s, a certain number of countries, notably the new member states of the EU, adopted the "flat tax" in order to increase the yield of tax revenue. Nevertheless, this strategy consisting of providing for a low unique rate of imposition concerning taxes on the revenue of natural persons and on the profits of enterprises do not appear to be efficient (Keen *et al.*, 2008) in countries in transition to a free-market economy (cf. chapter 12).

9 We have seen that Pareto (but not all of his students) rejected this type of calculation as not corresponding to the reality of policies on which the financial system is built. This position, however excessive it may be, invites one not to neglect the socio-political characteristics of public decisions and not to over-generalize the model of rational choice based on actors' self-interest in the economy.

Concerning public spending, investment expenditure, certain operating expenses (purchases) and certain transfer expenditures, by stimulating the economy, generate a surplus of tax revenue. We can recall in particular that public spending financed by tax revenue also benefits enterprises in the form of procurement contracts, different kinds of public grants (controlled nevertheless by the OECD or the EU), and consumption of goods and services by public administrations etc. Public spending aims to improve the environment of enterprises: creation and maintenance of infrastructures in transport, telecommunication networks, training of the workforce etc.

Loans are not part of tax revenue[10] but they occupy an important place in the public resources of many countries. They imply expenditure, financed by taxes, on interest and on the repayment of capital for a number of years. The impact of the crisis of 2008 of the American property market on banks, then on stock markets, then on the "real" economy led governments to put into place measures of support to the banking sector and plans to reflate the economy. The public spending involved is financed for a good part by loans. The growth of public debt will have to be repaid from the return on investment (if they are profitable) and from taxation. For the European Union, the plans to reflate the economy put into place should reach the amount of 200 billion euros (of which 30 billion in the european budget), that is to say 1.54% of the european GDP.[11] The decline in taxes and the additional public spending are estimated (Saha, von Weizsäcker, 2008) at 0.87% of the GDP for the European Union, at 2% for the United States, and at 7.1% for China. According to the estimation of the European Commission (Jamet and Lirzin, 2009), the GDP dropped in 2009 by 1.8% in the European Union, by 2.2% in the United States and by 2.6% in Japan. The situation is nevertheless variable from country to country. Public debt will reach very high levels between 2008 and 2010 going for the EU of 27 on average from 58% of GDP to 71%. In the United States, the plan of 790 billion dollars of February 2009 will lead, according to the forecasts of the Office of Management and Budget to a deficit of about 12% of GDP.[12] The debt should thus represent about 85% of GDP in 2010.

10 Without being classified in tax revenue, the tariffing of certain public services also offers an additional source of public revenue, although of lesser importance.

11 Source: European Commission (COM, 2008, No 800) of 26 November 2008, a European plan for economic stimulus; the European Council, December 2008.

12 Between 1980 and 1988 (the R. Reagan presidency), the maximum deficit was about 6% of GDP. Between 1988 and 1992 (the G. Bush presidency) it was 5% maximum. Between 1992 and 1996 (the B. Clinton presidency), a surplus was generated from 1998. Between 2000 and 2004 (the G. W. Bush presidency), the deficit reached a maximum of 3%.

c. The growth of public expenditure in developed countries

The phenomenon of the growth of public expenditure corresponds to what one should call from now on the Tocqueville and Wagner' law.[13] As is illustrated by the box, various explanations were proposed by economists in order to explain the growth of public administration. They establish a relation between the financial system and the level and especially the type of economic development. We have also noticed (chapter 4) the particular role of warfare for the European countries in the constitution of a State tax system. This phenomenon is also observed with the two World Wars which had a significant impact on the financial system of the 20th century (Peacock, Wiseman, 1967). The example given here of spending in the United States shows that the impact of social public action is essential for explaining the growth of the spending with the interventionist State and thus the growth of tax revenue.

Box 2: A few classic economic approaches to public spending

Wagner (1835-1917) attributes the continuous growth of public spending to industrialization and to the resulting urbanization. The State intervenes more and more by spending on general administration, police, education, social action, and infrastructure. For the Austrian economist this historic law is rather positive since it also resulted from pressure for social progress (Wagner, 1967, p. 8). Economic growth leads to spending by the revenue which it generates stimulating the demand for public goods. Empirically, the case of developing countries (cf. below) shows a relation between the GDP/person and fiscal pressure, but the relation between economic growth and public spending does not always go in the direction indicated by Wagner. A study of nine industrialized countries (1953-1992) (Koren, Stiassny, 1998) concludes: for Germany, the United Kingdom, the Netherlands and the United States, the priority given to revenue is verified, in conformity with Wagner's theory; but the priority of spending over revenue is verified for Austria, France and Italy, knowing that for Sweden and Switzerland no tendency exists. Another study (Midtbo, 1999) covering one century shows that in the three Scandinavian countries retained (small, open and corporatist) the relation between revenue and expenditure goes in the direction of Wagner's law: the improvement of economic growth is accompanied by an increase in public spending, when in three Anglo-Saxon countries the relation is rather of a Keynesian type, that is to say public spending is used to stimulate growth. A study (Falch, Rattso, 1997) on expenditure for education in Norway from 1880 to 1990 verifies the importance of this factor raised by Wagner with regard to the increase of salaries and of the number of teachers. As for France, the determinist relation between industrialization and the

13 To render justice to the pioneering Tocqueville's work who anticipated, as we have seen, Wagner's law.

increase of spending remains uncertain (Delorme, André, 1983, p. 105). Sociologically, this approach is not very well adapted to the post-industrial society, but it clearly indicates the historical tendency to the increase of spending, while at the same time being interested (following the example of the Durkheim of *The division of social labour*) in the socio-economic differentiation and in the appearance of new social needs.

According to Baumol's law, the sectors with low productivity (education, health etc.) require State intervention in order to respond to demand, which generates growth in these public expenditures less profitable for private activities.

According to Marxist theory, the State spends more and more to compensate for the decline in capital profitability, which is debatable: social expenditures admittedly alleviate the cost of the workforce for capitalists, but this spending also depends on social movements; administrative spending ensures the functioning of the capitalist society; spending on warfare is not economic, even if wars serve the interests of capital.

Peacock and Wiseman (1967) notably emphasize the role of the two World Wars. In periods of peace, public intervention is limited by reticence to taxes, while war increases the tolerance to fiscal pressure. Resources for warfare are then spent for the satisfaction of social needs (irreversibility or the ratchet effect of public spending), such as those described by Wagner. The recent decline in public spending in certain countries contradicts to the ratchet effect. Sociologically, the conception of taxpayers being naturally recalcitrant to taxes is false. Furthermore, the relation between war and the development of the tax State is not universal: this is the case of the Latin America of the 19th century which did not finance its war expenses by taxes (Centeno, 1997, p. 1589). The acceptance of taxes (Leroy, 2003) depends on the political legitimacy of State interventions and on the socially structured reasoning on its role (cognitive rationality): crisis has the status, not of a strict determinant, but of an argument justifying taxation and State intervention.

The school of Public Choice proposes a certain number of theories on the growth of public spending. Niskanen (1971) explains the growth of public spending by the bureaucratic drift of the managers of public services who tend to maximize their budgets. Without even discussing here the limits of the use, by the school of public choice, of the model of the rational maximization of utilitarian interest (Leroy, 2007, p. 18), we can note that empirical studies do not confirm this theory. For instance, a study (Ryu *et al.*, 2007) using the answers of 1175 American administrative executives shows that if the bureaucrats' preferences are statistically well correlated with budget projects, the Executive's influence (the governors) and the Congress also matters (correlation with credit projects). Furthermore, the bureaucrats' preferences are not always oriented towards the maximum increase: 26% of the demands for credits for 1998 are smaller or unchanged with regard to the previous year and the essential part (86%) among the 74% of demands for higher budgets is for a moderate amount. We must finally note that the real cost of the management of administrative services is better known with spreading of reforms concerning objectives (or results, or performance) budgets.

The school of Public Choice also maintains that public spending increases under the influence of pressure groups which try to have public services they use financed by the (unorganized) taxpayers/voters as a whole. The influence of these groups is reinforced by the fact that they are sometimes simultaneously users and employees of the public services in question (Stigler, 1972). This last point is empirically confirmed in a certain way, for example, in the field of education and health in Great Britain (McNutt, 2002, p. 114). In the same way, the Danish survey by Winter, Mouritzen, (2001, p. 132) shows that the users and the providers of public services demand public spending more than others and oppose spending cuts more than others. But the impact of pressure groups must be relativized according to their access, variable in different countries, time periods and sectors, to decision-making institutions and according to other variables (cf. chapter 6).

A "new" theory of public growth (Meltzer, Richard, 1981) considers redistribution based on the model of the rationality of the median voter. It affirms that inequalities explain the growth of public budgets, where the growth of inequalities implies a demand for redistribution which governments take into account. This theory is however not verified empirically (cf. chapter 6).

At a more general level, two major theories subsume particular explanations, according to whether the relation to the interventionist State is linked to capitalism or to democracy. The capitalist theory of the interventionist State is represented by Wagner who analyzes the increase of public spending linked to the needs of industrialization and urbanization. For him the point of departure is constituted by the output of tax revenue, where economic growth creates revenue in order to finance needs. The democratic theory of public finance can refer to the pioneering work of Tocqueville who, as we have seen, considers the cumulative effect of the political, sociological, economic and cognitive factors. Two points are important: firstly, both authors share the conviction that this evolution constitutes a progress[14]; secondly, they differ more by the field of explanation (capitalism vs. democracy), and less by the approach because a variety of factors is studied by these two pioneers.

14 "Faithful to its popular origins, it (the democratic government) makes prodigious efforts to satisfy the needs of the lower classes of society, to open up for them the road to power, and to spread out well-being and enlightenment in their midst. It supports the poor, distributes millions to schools every year, pays for all the services and remunerates generously its low-rung agents. If such a way of governing seems useful and reasonable to me, I have to recognize that it is expensive" (Tocqueville, 2004).

The evolution of public spending and of tax revenue is linked to the reinforcement of interventionist democracy which has taken charge of poverty, education, health, unemployment, retirement and families. This fact justifies the democratic theory of political choices opposing the theory of the market efficiency and the theory of the constraints for public action (cf. chapter 7). For the moment, let us note with Lindert (2004, p. 12) that, in spite of national specificities, the social expenditure of OECD countries was insignificant before 1880, then progressed slowly until the Second World War, and grew considerably until the 1980s, before stabilizing or declining slightly as a result of the neo-liberal questioning of the Welfare State.

Table 4: Evolution of public spending (in % of GDP)

	1880	1913	1920	1960	1974	1987	1995	2004
Sweden	n.d.	10.4	10.9	31	48.1	59.4	66.8	57.3
France	11.2	17%	27.6	34.6	39.3	50.9	54.4	50.6
Italy	n.d.	11.1	22.5	30.1	37.9	50.8	52.3	48.5
Germany	10	14.8	25	32.4	44.6	47.3	57.1	46.8
Japan	9	8.3	14.8	17.5	24.5	32.7	36.3	38.2
UK	9.9	12.7	26.2	32.2	44.8	42.9	45.2	43.9
USA	n.d.	7.5	12.1	27	31.7	36.3	35.7	36.5

Source: Carone, Schmidt, Nicodème, 2007 (n.d. = no data)

Democratization[15] came along with an extension of social rights and thus of public spending dedicated to social protection in the broad sense. This phenomenon is valid for developed countries as a whole, including countries with a liberal Welfare State. In fact, in spite of certain particular results, sometimes contradictory[16], the major tendencies of the Wel-

15 In relation notably with the extension of the "political voice" (Lindert, 2004).

16 a) Several typologies exist (Korpi, Palme, 1998). b) The social policy led by Bismarck is a product of an authoritarian regime and not of a democratization of industrial societies. c) Comparatively, the United States seriously lags behind for social rights, explained partly by the preponderance of the "humanitarian" culture (Feldman, Steenbergen, 2001; Steensland, 2006): the liberal Welfare State state must not substitute for the responsibility of individuals, but must only help the most deprived in certain cases, and charity may also intervene. d) The power resources approach (mobilization of the working class) is not statistically verified in the case of Spain if the indicator for the working class power is only the party in power; this theory is better applied if we add the indicators of social agitation, of affiliations within the parties and of labour unions (Claramunt, Arroyo, 2000, p. 275). e) The diverse compromises around social rights invite one to disaggregate the notion of democracy by more subtle variables: type of regime, power of technocracy, coalitions in power, relations of the State with the world of business and of labour etc. f) Nevertheless, according to a study of 17 countries in Latin America between 1980 and 1992 (Brown, Hunter, 1999), the influence of the type of regime, democratic vs. authoritarian, remains a determining factor, on the condition of taking into account the "constraints": social expenditure in authoritarian regimes is more

fare State are well-known. Initially, the expenditure on social intervention was justified by the democratic criticism of the excesses of the industrial society in the 19th century. Social rights complete political rights through social citizenship (Marshall, 1950), which means a widening of democracy (Rosanvallon, 1981). The Welfare State is also linked to economic development which shifts demand towards such services such as health and education. The strength of labour movement is also put forward to explain the rapid expansion of social protection. This factor is at the core of the theory of labour class mobilization (power resources approach, Korpi and Palme, 2003) in favour of the social-democrat type of Welfare State.

Historically, three phases must be identified. The first period is the emergence of the Welfare State in industrial countries from the end of the 19th century to the Second World War. The second period is that of the golden age of the Welfare State. It corresponds to the post-war growth and to the generalization of Keynesian policies legitimizing, in addition to economic action, social action (Webber, Wildavsky, 1986, p. 562) by spending. The last period, starting from the crisis of 1970s, is the one of a certain ideological questioning of the Welfare State. Nevertheless, citizens, and we will come back to that, remain attached to the maintenance of social protection, and the amount of social spending remains high in numerous countries, particularly in Europe.

Table 5: The structure of expenditure in the United States in % of GDP

	Total Defense	Total Social	Total Other	Federal Transfers*	Federal Social	Federal Other
1952	15%	3%	6%	3%	0.8%	2%
2005	< 5%	12%	12%	9%	3.2%	3%

Source: Bayoumi, Gonçalves, 2007 (* Transfer expenditure or appropriations to member States of the Federation and to local governments)

In the United States (cf. table 5) for example, social expenditure has increased over a long period of time. The evolution of American public spending is firstly explained by the impact of the First World War. The federal income tax on natural persons created in 1913 and the corporate tax created in 1909 become the main taxes. The Second World War and the crisis of 1929 strengthen the growth of revenue and expenditure. The

sensitive to economic constraints and, in democratic regimes, to political constraints of beneficiary pressure groups. When revenue is lacking, the authoritarian regimes cut social expenditure, contrary to the democratic regimes who maintain a high level of social protection; when revenue is high, they increase social expenditure faster.

change in the conception of the role of public action, which is common to other countries, takes shape in the particular form of the "New Deal" programs. The evolution is also explained by the international role of the country, in particular with the Cold War. According to a study by Bayoumi and Gonçalves (2007), from 1927 to 1952 the size of the federal government (public spending) grows largely in connection with expenditure devoted to defense. Expenditure continues to grow until the 1980s before stabilizing in the 1990s and declining afterwards. The whole period after the Second World War is also characterized by deficits (with some rare exceptions). Total spending (all levels of administration together) increased. From the structural point of view, there is a decline in military expenditures, with the exception of the periods linked to the Vietnam War in the 1960s to the beginning of the 1970s, to Reagan's defense project in 1980s, and to the Iraq War (to be verified). As table shows, the reduction in total military expenditure was compensated by the increase in social spending (total and at every level of administration) and in transfers (appropriations to the States and local governments) which largely explains the growth of American public expenditure.

If social expenditure largely explains the growth of public expenditure in developed countries, and thus the growth of taxes, there is a more or less big impact according to the system of financing social protection which is based, depending on the country, either on public funds or on private insurance. In addition to their level, we must therefore consider the distribution of tax revenue.

2. Public Revenue and Expenditure in the OECD

Tax revenue is defined as non-voluntary payments, without direct compensation, for the benefit of public administrations. Tax revenue before 1914 remained limited. Under the combined effect of diverse factors such as the wars, the economic crisis of 1929 then the construction of the Welfare State, public expenditure increased particularly in the social field (in the broad sense). The comparative OECD data demonstrate that, over the long term, the growth of tax revenue accompanies the growth of public expenditure. The structure and functions of the system of revenue and of expenditure also undergo certain evolutions with the growing part of social action.

a. The increase of tax revenue

The financial system of every country includes specificities non reducible to other countries. Nevertheless, some general tendencies emerge, among which the increase of tax revenue in developed countries is relevant.

The rate of tax revenue provides useful informations. Sociologically, it has also become an "indicator of society" (Leroy, 2007, p. 99) used to evaluate collective well-being. However, even without talking of criticisms of the GDP as a measure[17], the gross comparison of the rate of tax revenue has considerable limits. For example the differences between the economically admissible rates of imposition depend on the degree of integration of the country in the international economy. It must especially be relativized according to the expenditure (and thus to goods and services financed from public revenue). For a big part, the differences between the countries are explained by the way of financing social security which is done either from public resources or from private insurance. Technically, a certain number of operations affect (or not) tax revenue: for instance, the salaries of French state employees, which are public expenditure, are not paid net of taxes as in other countries, a procedure which increases tax revenue. Tax expenditure diminishes public revenue, whereas they could be replaced by budgetary expenditure (subsidies, allocations).

With these limits in mind, the rate of tax revenue measured as a percentage of GDP is used, essentially for developed countries, in international comparisons. This rate reaches a high level in OECD countries even if important differences exist according to the country (cf. table). The long-term observations (source: OECD, 2008) express a continuous increase of tax revenue, with certain periods of relative stability. So, the average rate (in % of GDP) within the OECD is 25.6% in 1965, 29.4% in 1975, 32.7% in 1985, 34.8% in 1995 and 35.8% in 2005. Between 1965 and 1975, the average increase of the OECD of 3.9 points concerns all the countries except Italy which is slightly lower. Between 1975 and 1985 the average increase of 3.3 points again concerns almost all the countries, except Iceland, Turkey and (very little) the United States. Between 1985 and 1995 the average increase is 2.1 points, but this time with a lower rate in 10 countries (and a higher rate in 20). Between 1995 and 2006 the average increase of 1.2 points is lower, with again a decline in 10 countries: this situation cannot be maintained beyond the crisis context of 2008 because of the expenditures in order to support banks and of the plans to reflate the economy (hence a future increase in taxes).

Taking 2006 (cf. table 6) as the year of reference (OECD, 2008) we can distinguish (knowing that such a classification sometimes creates threshold effects):

---

17 The GDP comes from the Kuznets's work, Nobel Prize winner, on national accounting which allows one since the 1930s to measure the evolution of the wealth of a country. In 2008 France established a commission chaired by Joseph Stiglitz, Nobel Prize winner in economics, to propose other indicators than the GDP.

– Countries with a very high rate above 40%: Nordic countries (Denmark, Finland, Iceland, Norway, Sweden), Austria, Belgium, France, Italy.

– Countries with a high rate (from 35 to 40%): Germany, Spain, Hungary, Luxembourg, New Zealand, the Netherlands, Portugal, the Czech Republic, the United Kingdom.

– Countries with an intermediate rate (from 30 to 35%): Australia, Canada, Greece, Ireland, Poland.

– Countries with a low rate (less than 30%): the United States, Korea, Japan, Mexico, the Slovak Republic, Switzerland, Turkey.

Table 6: Total tax revenue as % of GDP (sample in the OECD)

	1975	1985	1995	2005	2006
Average OCDE	29.4%	32.7%	34.8%	35.8%	35.9%
Average EU	32.2%	37.6%	38.9%	38.7%	38.7%
Average difference EU and OCDE	2.8	4.9	4.1	2.9	2.8
Sweden	41.2%	47.3%	47.5%	49.5%	49.1%
Denmark	38.4%	46.1%	48.8%	50.7%	49.1%
Belgium	39.5%	44.4%	43.6%	44.8%	44.5%
France	35.4%	42.8%	42.9%	43.9%	44.2%
Norway	39.2%	42.6%	40.9%	43.5%	43.9%
United Kingdom	35.2%	37.6%	34.5%	36.3%	37.1%
Germany	34.3%	36.1%	37.2%	34.8%	35.6%
United States	25.6%	25.6%	27.9%	27.3%	28.0%
Japan	20.9%	27.4%	26.8%	27.4%	27.9%

Source: OCDE, 2008 Statistics of Public Revenue 1965-2007

The rate of tax revenue is on average higher in the European Union (EU) than in all OECD countries taken together: in 1975 the difference in ratios is about 2.8 points, but in the 1980s and 1990s the difference is above 4 points. With the expansion of Europe the difference diminishes due to the lower rates of the new member states (it is 2.8 points in 2006). So the average tax revenue of the EU at 15 is in 2006 39.8% of GDP and 38.7% for the EU at 19 (source: OECD). Since 1985 it has remained above 35%. For the EU at 27 the average is 41.1% in 2006 (source: Eurostat). It must be noted that the position can vary over time for certain countries: over 5 years, between 2001 and 2006, the level of tax revenue varies by 2.5 points at least for 8 countries out of 27.[18] For the others the level remains stable. Notwithstanding these variations and the possible threshold effects, the level of tax revenue (in % of GDP) in Europe in 2006 (source Eurostat) leads to the classification of 4 groups.

18 Between 2001 and 2006: Austria -2.7 points; Cyprus +5.4; Spain: +3.1; Ireland +3.3; Luxembourg -4.4; Malta +2.7; Portugal +2.5; Slovakia -3.9.

– Countries with a high rate, above the average (equal or above 43%): in declining order: Sweden, Denmark, France, Belgium, Austria, Finland.

– Countries close to the average (at least 38% and less than 43%): Italy, Germany, the Netherlands, Slovenia, the United Kingdom.

– Countries below the average: (at least 33% and less than 38%): Greece, Ireland, Poland, Malta, Bulgaria, the Czech Republic, Luxembourg, Cyprus, Portugal, Hungary, Spain.

– Countries with a low rate (less than 33%): Rumania, Slovakia, Lithuania, Latvia, Estonia.

The differences are mainly explained by the development of social protection since the crisis of the 1970s which created structural mass unemployment. The perimeter of public action is different in Europe with regard to countries such as the United States and Japan. In addition to the higher fiscal pressure in the EU (at 15), we note a tendency to impose labour more heavily.

It is fitting to conclude with two statements related to the impact of tax revenue. Firstly, there is no opposite relation between the level of tax revenue and economic growth: thus a good level of social protection financed by public revenue (taxes) is not contrary to economic efficiency (Headey *et al.*, 2000). The Nordic model of social protection resists well to economic globalization in spite of high rates of taxes (Steinmo, 2002). Secondly, a strong correlation is observed between the size of tax revenue and the limitation of income inequalities in developed countries, or more exactly between the rate of tax revenue and the poverty rate[19] which declines when the tax revenue rate increases.

b. The structure of tax revenue

The financial system includes a variety of resources that ensure the financing of a variety of expenditure, but also fulfill other functions. We have seen the importance of revenue drawn from the domain for the feudal regime (cf. chapter 4), then its replacement by royal taxation.[20] Revenue from war tributes, like in the Roman Empire, has always constituted a means of financing the expenditure of predatory States in order to tax their own citizens less. For certain countries, the revenue drawn from natural resources, in particular hydrocarbons, is essential. In matters of local finances, the number of taxes and duties is sometimes

[19] The poverty rate is relative because it is defined by the fact of living with less than half (50%) of the median income (which divides the population in two). The level of tax revenue is not the only factor affecting poverty.

[20] The revenue structure is at the basis of a fiscal geography and history. The part of the domain and of taxation varied and always varies from country to country.

surprising, even though local authorities are financed for the biggest part by taxation and by appropriations of the State. In most of the developed countries fiscal revenue constitutes the main source of income for public budgets (cf. table). Even if it includes a variety of revenue, the output of the financial system is based on a limited number of public takings, namely: income tax, social security contributions, consumption taxes, corporate taxes, property taxes.

Table 7: Tax structure in the OECD-area

	1965	1975	1985	1995	2006
Personal income tax	26%	30%	30%	27%	25%
Social security contributions (employers) (employees)	18% (10%) (6%)	23% (14%) (7%)	22% (13%) (7%)	25% (14%) (8%)	25% (15%) (9%)
General consumption taxes	14%	15%	16%	18%	19%
Corporate income taxes	9%	8%	8%	8%	11%
Specific consumption taxes	24%	18%	16%	13%	11%
Property taxes	8%	5.5%	5.5%	5%	6%
Other taxes	1%	0%	1%	3%	3%
Taxes/salaries and labour	1%	1%	1%	1%	1%
Total	100%	100%	100%	100%	100%

Source: OECD, 2008 (the small % are rounded off by the OECD, which makes the total vary slightly)

The modernization of tax revenue carried out in the 20th century is a real mutation: it is explained by the introduction of new synthetic taxes whose output is high (except when the basis is reduced by the fiscal advantages granted). With the exception of taxation on property which is traditional, old levies such as customs duties and specific taxes on certain categories of goods or services (specific consumption taxes in the table) were replaced by modern general public takings, or are in decline (the case of category-based taxes on specific goods and services). Here it is clear that economic development creates a variety of sources in public revenue that synthetic taxes reach better.

We must also note the traditional weight of income tax which remains the first source of revenue (on average) in the OECD area: the relation between the economic development of a country and the position of the personal income tax remains verified. Nevertheless, this source of income has been declining since the 1990s, after the peaks of the 1970s and 1980s: in 2006, income tax represents 25% of revenue. Another evolution is the increase of social security contributions which in 2006 reached the top level equal to the income tax. This fact confirms the importance of social expenditures and of the Welfare State. The social security contributions paid by employers and employees thus progressed by 50% between 1965 and 2006. The increase of the consumption indirect taxes, which must be linked notably to the generalization of VAT, is an important result. Another result emerges from this table: it is the relative stability of the corporate income taxes. The reductions of the (statutory) rates of corporate taxes (on companies) in the years 1980-1990 were partially compensated by the widening of the tax base. Finally, the relative weakness of taxes on property (and thus on patrimony) must be discuss with regard to redistribution (cf. chapter 11).

One of the essential mutations is related to the Welfare State. Social protection can be financed by public resources or by private insurance. Within the public systems of financing social protection, we distinguish the source of financing according to whether it comes from taxation or from social security contributions paid by employers and employees (on salaries, the other sources being less important). Esping-Andersen's typology constitutes a good point of departure, even though diverse reforms modified the purity of the types of Welfare State which evolved towards more mixed models.

Box 3: Esping-Andersen's typology

The sociologist Esping-Andersen (1990) distinguishes:

– Social-democrat model for the universalist Welfare State (Beveridge's model), where all the people benefit from a high level of social protection financed by taxes (Scandinavian countries), corresponds to a strong and organized labour movement.

– Conservative model for the insurance-based Welfare State (Bismarck's model), where employees benefit from social protection financed by contributions out of salaries (Germany, Belgium, Italy, Japan), is characterized by the influence of the Church and the resistance to the labour movement.

– Liberal model for the Welfare State financed by taxes, but whose interventions are targeted on the most deprived people (the American model), where the majority of people use private insurance. The balance of power is more unfavorable here to the labour movement.

Esping-Andersen's typology evolved because many systems are henceforth mixed as a result of reforms implemented by numerous countries. The burden of social security contributions on salaries (Norregaard, Khan, 2007), which enters into the cost of labour, dropped in the EU at 15 by 3 points in % of GDP between 1995 and 2005, and increased slightly in the EU at 10. In the EU at 15, social security contributions on low-level salaries decreased on average between 2000 and 2006. France, that continues to stand out because of the burden of its social security contributions on salaries, has increased the part of taxation in the financing of social security. For the OECD the average remains stable. The situations are nevertheless variable from country to country. Social contributions on low salaries grew in the United Kingdom, Japan, Mexico, Turkey.

Box 4: Classification of social security contributions 2006 In % of GDP of the EU at 27

– Countries above the average (>15.5%): 1) France (ranked 1st with 18.3%), 2) Germany, 3) Czech Republic, 4) Austria, 5) Belgium.

– Countries close to the average (< 10.5% to 15.5%): 6) Netherlands, 7) Slovenia, 8) Greece, 9) Spain, 10) Italy, 11) Sweden, 12) Hungary, 13) Portugal, 14) Finland, 15) Poland, 16) Slovakia, 17) Luxembourg.

– Countries below the average (from 5.5 to 10.5%): 18) Rumania, 19) Estonia, 20) Latvia, 21) Lithuania, 22) Bulgaria, 23) the United Kingdom, 24) Cyprus, 25) Malta, 26) Ireland.

– Countries with very low rates of social security contributions: 27) Denmark (1.9% of GDP).

Notes: *Average for the EU at 27 = 13.8%. Descending order in the classification*

Source: Eurostat.

This classification illustrates the importance of the Bismarckian model of social protection financing, based on social security contributions calculated on paid salaries. It illustrates a significant choice in particular for the 5 countries classified at the top which has the biggest amount for the social security contributions on labour. From the point of view of labour cost, these contributions are a burden on salaries (the other charges linked to taxes on salaries should also be taken into account). But we must also look on the side of taxes to see how the Welfare State is financed.

The same diversity is noticed as regards the public spending of developed countries. Next to classifications distinguishing notably operational expenditures and investment expenditures, it is useful to have a functional presentation of public spending. A distinction is made between the spending on debt costs, pensions, defense and public order, general public services, education, health, unemployment, family affairs, housing and other public actions. The functional presentation of public spending can be also used for other subsets of the financial system (national, local or social finance). It is then also helpful to refer to the scope (generosity) of the social protection. Another problem is to consider the redistributive character of the system. It is also interesting to know the implemented compromises between the nature and the evolution of the public revenue and the financing of social protection (cf. chapter 11). The structural evolution of the charges is also linked to the ageing of the population and the coverage of new risks, such as precariousness or mass unemployment which aggravate with the financial crisis of 2008.

3. The Case of Developing Countries

The evolution of the fiscal system of developed countries is not found in the case of developing countries which face difficulties in the financing of public expenditure. Historically, as we have seen, the modern State that appeared in Europe is characterized by the high level of tax revenue and by the diversification (structure) of the sources of taxation. In the 20th century the democracies of developed countries functioned, starting from 1914, on the basis of a public interventionism characterized economically by Keynesianism and socially by the Welfare State. The level of tax revenue is therefore high and remains high in spite of the neo-liberal questioning of the 1970s and the impact of globalization. As for developing countries, the financial system is not based on the historic tradition of the modern State in Europe at the origin of the liberal democracies. In addition, the differences in situations must not be minimized, as the case of countries disposing of natural resources shows. Nevertheless, in the presence of challenges common to numerous countries, the question of the political approach is put with the aim of rectifying the failures of public finance in developing economies.

a. *The weakness of tax revenue*

The institutionalization of the tax State comes up against obstacles in developing countries such as the weakness of tax revenue shows. For the period from 1975 to 1989 (Zee, 1996, p. 1660) the average level of tax revenue of developing countries (56 countries) is 16% of GDP. For developed OECD countries (24 countries) it is at least one third. For the period 1995-1997 (Tanzi, Zee, 2000, p. 8), the ratios are 18.2% and 37.9%. The level of public resources drawn from tax revenue is thus on average two times smaller in developing economies than in rich countries.

Tax structures of developing countries also represent some variations. Customs duties and diverse taxes on international exchange represent on average (Zee, 1996, p. 1661) between 26 and 30% of the total revenue for developing countries and less than 5% of total revenue for developed OECD countries over the period from 1975 to 1989 (2.2% between 1985 and 1989). Tax levies on individuals (personal income tax and social security contributions) occupy generally a small place in developing countries in comparison with rich countries. According to a study (Gambaro *et al.*, 2007) of 65 countries between 1990 and 2004, the only personal income tax reaches on average about 13% of GDP in

OECD countries, while the whole of taxes of developing countries represents on average 15.6% of GDP.

b. Difficulties of increasing taxation

It is obvious that the economic structure of developing countries imposes important limitations on the tax system. Taxation increases, according to Wagner's "law", with the level of economic advancement: as empirical studies show, "the level of fiscal pressure of a country is well explained by its GDP/inhabitants" (Moisseron, 1999, p. 104). Taxation based on property (or land) tax is better adapted in economies predominantly agricultural. The presence of an informal sector of the economy constitutes by nature a loss of tax revenue, although one must deduct revenues offered by implicit taxation (cf. below). The development of the tax system thus depends on the reduction of the informal economy, of which it is thus useful to know the size, the causes and the consequences. Concerning the size[21], it appears that it varies from country to country.

The obstacles to the tax State in developing countries are not negligible. The reduction of customs duties is part of a market conception nourished by a neo-liberal vision of economic globalization which has often been harmful for developing countries. The influence of the "Washington consensus", recommended by the IMF and the World Bank in the years 1980-1990 in order to stabilize debts, free markets and reduce public spending through privatizations in particular, was negative.[22] Market fanaticism led to the deterioration of the human capital of developing countries for the benefit of financial priorities poorly-established from an economic point of view (Stiglitz, 2002, 2006). The economic growth of China constitutes for developing countries an efficient counter-model of the democratization of the State and of the hegemony of markets.[23] Russia increasingly takes the non-democratic way of state capitalism. The banking crisis of the summer of 2008, whose "globalized" consequences make economies of the whole world

[21] Several methods, sometimes with divergent results, exist to measure the size of the informal economy: direct surveys of representative samples, the difference between national expenditure and official revenue, the difference between the official and the real amount of labour, the estimation through electricity consumption, the calculation based on the demand for currency or for cash and calculations based on several indicators.

[22] For example, according to a study of five countries in Central America from 1975 to 1995 (Jonakin, Stephen, 1999), the decline or the stagnation of spending on education is paradoxically accompanied by an increase of debt interests.

[23] The economic opening up of China has been progressive but has not generated a progression of citizen rights.

recede, risks engendering protectionist reflexes favorable to the legitimacy of customs duties.

Box 5: The size of the informal economy in developing countries

Cobham (2005) estimates the size of the informal economy in developing countries at 285 billion dollars. A study of the size of the informal sector (Vuletin, 2008) in 32 Latin American and Caribbean countries reveals big differences in the years 2000: 6 countries are not much concerned (between 15 and 25% of GDP), 6 countries are above 50% of GDP (among which Paraguay and Nicaragua reaching 70%), the others being in an intermediate position. Four causes are studied: on average for the countries retained, the fiscal pressure (tax burden: 35%), the importance of agriculture (31%), the rigidities of the labour market (26%) and inflation (8%) contribute to explain the size of the informal economy.

But the importance of every cause varies from one country to another, which has some implications for any reform aiming to reduce the size of the informal economy. For example, fiscal pressure is the main cause for 7 countries, the importance of agriculture for 4 countries and the rigidities of labour for 2 countries. Inflation remains a more marginal factor. As far as the consequences are concerned, for the three examined variables, the informal sector tends to reduce social security contributions, inscriptions in secondary education, and the rate of worker unionization.[24] Other studies confirm the revenue loss linked to the informal economy, in particular for the VAT. The size of agriculture in the economy is in inverse relation to the total amount of taxes. In a developing country, it is in fact difficult for the administration to collect taxes from the agricultural sector. On the other side, the collect of taxes in an urban environment from commercial and other enterprises is easier.

We must not forget either that the colonial fiscal system has contributed historically to delegitimize the State in a certain number of countries. The revolts and other forms of resistance to colonial taxes illustrate the historic illegitimacy of the State. Finally, State levies often appear to be not very legitimate in the presence of persisting practices of corruption. The reports of Transparency International emphasize corruption in the form of political interference of the executive power and of "bribes". For example, according to a survey conducted between July and September 2006 involving 59,661 people in 61 countries, more than 40% of people interviewed declared to have paid a bribe within the last 12 months. The most affected countries are in Africa and Latin America and the countries of the CIS (Commonwealth of Independent States). The European Union and North America are only slightly affected (less

[24] These factors are essential for the development of the democratic Welfare State.

than 5%). In Africa, the average cost of a bribe paid to the justice system is more than 70 euros (1st item of expenditure and rising); in Latin America it is about 240 euros (2nd item of expenditure).

The notion of tax revenue remains attached to religious donations or to family solidarity[25], and with much more difficulty to the State. We must finally mention the importance of funds transferred by emigrants to their countries of origin. These funds constitute flows of redistribution in the networks of parents and alliances better anchored in the socio-economic system than taxes.

c. *The rentier State*

A certain number of developing countries fall, as for their revenue, in a category of States called "rentier"[26] States. The rentier State uses two types of rents (Moore, 2004, p. 305): those drawn from natural resources, such as for example oil, and those drawn from geostrategic resources generating development aid, such as in case of France with French-speaking Africa. The relation between natural rents and received aids, on the one hand, and the type of State, on the other hand, is not easy to put into question. Economic, political and social factors are at stake. One fact is established: the rentier State disposes of resources which exempt it from asking the opinion of the majority of the citizens on taxation. The non-fiscal financial means curb the process of fiscal democratization in a "European way". Correlatively, the rentier State is linked to the outside. For a long time it has been situated at the periphery of a center dominated by developed countries that exploit raw materials for their economies. The rentier State depends on the strategies of rich countries that buy raw materials or dispense financial aid. Its sovereignty is dependent on external commitments. Even if this reality still remains true to a certain extent nowadays, the rentier State has also become an actor in the world economy. It is able to put pressure on raw material markets by regrouping producer countries and/or by modulating the quantities sold. It has become an actor in financial markets by accumulating monetary reserves. The coming into power of the left in such countries as Venezuela or Bolivia has been marked by a return of the interventionist State.[27] Petrodollar recycling illustrates this phenom-

---

25 Cf. the money paid by emigrants to their family and to the network of their "creditors" remaining in the country of origin.

26 The notion of a rentier State was mentioned in a particular sense by Schumpeter (cf. chapter 2) in the case of the crisis of fiscal State in opposition to the entrepreneur State.

27 In Venezuela and Bolivia hydrocarbon exports ensure more than 50% of tax revenue. Liberal policies have been revised and the State has controlled a good part of the petroleum industry since the renegotiation of contracts with large multinational companies. Social policies have been put into place. This policy has resulted in a certain

enon well. Capital that passes through the financial centers of the world is invested in Western economies and notably in the American economy. The impact of the rentier State on the fiscal system, in particular on the amount of receipts, is empirically investigated (cf. box). The presence of revenue drawn from hydrocarbon products reduces the revenue from taxes, while external aid has had a positive effect on the tax State since the 1990s.

Box 6: The impact of the rentier State on tax receipts

According to a study (Bornhorst *et al.*, 2008) of 30 countries disposing of hydrocarbon resources, the revenue from 1992 to 2005 increased on average, going from 49% of total public revenue (or 15% of GDP) to 60% (24% of GDP). The study proves statistically that the amount of the revenue from taxes is inversely correlated to the amount of revenue drawn from hydrocarbon exploitation. For example, an increase of 1% in hydrocarbon revenue reduces the other receipts by an equivalent of 0.19% of GDP. The rent-based State is indeed an obstacle to the tax State.

The international policy of development aid is the subject of a debate on its utilization. The empirical question is to know whether or not the aid substitutes for the revenue from the national taxation of the beneficiary countries. The empirical studies are not numerous on the subject.[28]

A study by Gupta *et al.* (2003) on 107 developing countries for the period from 1970 to 2000 concludes that external aid, defined as the sum of subsidies granted and of loans, entails a diminution of the revenue from taxes. Loans lead to an improvement of the revenue from taxes, while subsidies have a negative effect. For the recent period, these statistical results are not verified any more.

A change in the fiscal system occurred in the 1990s, probably in relation with the programs of improvement in the quality of institutions. Actually, another study (Gambaro *et al.*, 2007) on 65 countries gives new light on the impact of development aid on the fiscal system for the recent period (1990 to 2004). For the countries retained, the revenue from taxes represents on average 15.6% of GDP, 4.43% of GDP for the personal, corporate and capital taxes, 7% for the consumption taxes and 3.36% for the taxes on international exchange. A positive but weak[29] correlation is found between

decline of foreign investments, but the constitution of a network of friendly countries (China, Russia, Iran etc.) causes the situation to evolve.

28 Specialized literature is more interested in spending than revenue: investments, services (education, health etc.) to the poorest, tax relief for enterprises, productive or non-productive spending etc.

29 The effect is weak because an increase in aid equivalent to 1 point of GDP (in the form of subsidies and not of loans) is correlated with an increase of only 0.077% in revenue from taxes.

external aid (subsidies and not loans[30]) and the total amount of revenue from taxes. The effect does not have the same meaning according to the different types of taxes. For personal, corporate and capital taxes the correlation is negative: an effect of substitution arises in this category of direct taxes which is fortunately small (on average < 5% of GDP). But external aid has a positive (statistical) effect on the most important receipts (in % of GDP), namely indirect (consumption) taxes and taxes on international exchange. Corruption is an essential explanatory factor. In fact, tax revenue (output) is correlated with the quality of institutions or with what is called, according to the term in vogue, good "governance".

It thus seems that the attention given since the 1990s by international organizations and governments of developing countries to the quality of institutions is justified in order to thwart the eviction effects of external aid on the fiscal system.

d. *Which political solution?*

The development of the modern economy has created new possibilities for taxation, but also operates a complex system of management in public finance. Following the example of Western capitalism, the passage from the agricultural economy to the industrial economy offers an opportunity to improve the tax system revenue by the possibility to create taxes on the new economic activities and the new social modes that are implied: corporate taxes on the enterprises in the market sector, personal income tax settled in areas of urbanization, VAT-type general indirect taxes on consumption, social security contributions of employers and employees on salaries.

Certain recent evolutions seem to confirm this point of view. For example, the burden of indirect consumption taxes has become more important in developing countries, while for OECD countries as well as for the EU on its own a slight increase is noted. Between 1990 and 2002 (Norregaard, Khan, 2007), they went from 4.6% to 5.4% of GDP on average for African countries and those of the Asia-Pacific area and from 4.1% to 8.8% of GDP for Latin American and Caribbean countries. This phenomenon is largely explained by the reduction of customs duties and of taxes on international exchange. The VAT has been adopted by numerous countries, namely: 48 countries in 1989 and 143 in 2007, in spite of the fact that its functioning meets some difficulties (fraud), especially when the informal sector is important.

Moreover, one must remember that tax revenue designates taxes and (public) social security payments retraced by the national accounting. Now in developing countries a certain part of tax revenue is in form of

30 For external aid attributed in the form of loans, the results are less evident.

an implicit taxation. This revenue, not taken into account officially, arises in particular from regulations on unofficial foreign exchange markets and from inflation. Sometimes it represents a non negligible amount of revenue for the State.

Above all, the situation is not the same from one country to another. The economy of emerging countries in Asia is not that of Africa or of America and every country has its own particular features. A process of reinforcing the tax State is at work in numerous developing countries, at least in those that do not have natural rents such as oil. Even though current transformations are not completely attained, several countries have reduced their customs duties, especially within the framework of the agreements of the World Trade Organization (WTO). The project of the Union for the Mediterranean, initiated by France in February 2007[31], also implies the reduction of customs barriers. In order to compensate for the diminution of revenue drawn from external exchange, these countries have reformed their fiscal systems by instituting the VAT and/or by trying to improve the personal and corporate taxation.

In the 1960s, Kaldor (1963) maintained that the problem of developing countries is to learn how to tax correctly. The creation of a real tax State is a crucial financial issue in order to finance public services, which are indispensable for poverty reduction and economic development. As Bodin showed (cf. chapter 4), taxation is also a part of State sovereignty, it constitutes a way to free developing countries from external supervision. It is finally a valuable means for the democratization of the political regimes in developing countries, in particular with the establishment of a efficient personal income tax. The history of the modern tax State in Europe shows that the establishment of a permanent tax requires the consent of citizens. An improvement, urgent in a certain number of developing countries, of educational services, social security and health can thus be hoped for by a tax democratization. Indeed, in accordance with the democratic theory of political choices, the control over public spending by those who bear the cost of it implies the presence of a tax State. It is nevertheless the case that a specific (sociological/anthropological) approach must be invented in view of the mechanisms of social solidarity at work (informal economy, religious gifts, solidarity of widened families, links with emigrants etc.).

---

31 The Union for the Mediterranean aims to relaunch the policy of good neighborliness between Europe and the Mediterranean Sea countries and to get out of the failure of the Barcelona process of 1995.

Conclusion

For developing countries the political problem is to construct a legitimate tax State, economically stable and socially adapted to their particularisms. As for developed countries, the dispersal of the financial system reinforces the complexity of its interventions (Leroy, 2007), even if the national scale or the State keeps its pertinence. Taxation is linked to the spending system through the financial function of taxes. This function is also negatively presented by the multiplication of tax expenditures consisting in giving up revenue from a part of taxes in order to grant social or economic advantages. In addition to its relation to taxation, the financial system is divided into State finances, social finances, local finances and supranational finances (such as the European Union). Local finances experienced a particular development in numerous countries following the decentralization movement of the last few decades. On the other hand, the European Union finances remain little developed and national budgetary policies remain modestly coordinated at the European level.[32]

In this way the financial system is not limited any more to the finance of the State such as in the classic era of economic and political liberalism in force in the developed countries of the 19th century. However, the public finance system is still largely focused on the tax system of the State, which remains impossible to neglect in the sense of the interventionist public action associating other actors. The contemporary financial system is also characterized by the financial complexity of interventionist public action. This is well demonstrated by the variety of classifications of tax revenue and the diversity of public services that are financed. The complexity of tax law, accentuated by the policy of fiscal particularisms (derogatory taxation), accentuates this phenomenon even more as we shall see in the next chapter. This complexity is explained by the economic and social interventionism of the contemporary developed State that uses taxes and public spending simultaneously as instruments of public action.

32 The European Union budget represents approximately 1% of the total GDP of the member countries. The main part of the budget goes to the financing of the common agricultural policy and the regional policy but this system struggles to find its legitimacy (Leroy, 2004) in the absence of a coherent political project and due to budgetary limits. The refusal to establish a European tax is combined with the limitation of payments consented by the member states. The Europe of public finance also becomes apparent through the budgetary discipline aimed at by the criteria put into place by the treaty of Maastricht and prolonged by the treaty of Amsterdam. In the case of an economic crisis, that is when the GDP drops more than 0.75%, the texts admit the exceeding of the limit of 3% of GDP for the public deficit, the authorization of the European Commission being necessary if the drop is between 0.75 and 2% of GDP.

Interventionism through taxes and public spending leads to a categorization of society notably based on the social action of the Welfare State, notably in Europe. In fact, the social financial system has shaped post-war industrial societies. Its resilience to economic globalization and the current crisis is a crucial factor for social cohesion and political democracy. Despite the complexity of its interventions, the financial system is concentrated on a few large general taxes, created in the 20th century, with a big output. In the same way, social spending on health and education makes up the main items of public budgets.

Other factors could be mentioned[33], notably privatizations and the complex practices of co-financing. Privatizations (2459 operations realized between 1977 and 1999 in 121 countries) and the outsourcing of tasks have modified the financial system.[34] Privatization policies correspond to an advanced stage of economic development, that of financial capitalism with strong liquid assets. Since the crisis of the summer of 2008, an opposite movement has occurred and several countries have proceeded with the nationalization (sometimes partial) of banks threatened with bankruptcy. The traditional conception of the financial system limited to the revenue and expenditure of an autonomous legal entity is also upset by the logic of co-financing. The use of contracts ("contractualization") in the public sector, without being new, has been developed in industrial countries entailing the rise of financial partnerships. The mechanism of public-private partnership (PPP) spread, especially in Europe (Parker, Hartley, 2003, p. 98).[35] As for developing countries, the World Bank counted 2500 projects from 1990 to 2001 mobilizing 750 billion dollars in 132 countries, with a concentration in Southeast Asia and South America.

Finally, the mechanism of comparison (comparativism) has become one of the essential keys of the evolution of the financial system. Imitation as a process of change is not a new fact as such. As a tool of knowledge, the comparative method is considered by Auguste Comte and Emile Durkheim, two founders of sociology, as the best substitute to

---

33 The development of local public enterprises in Europe, real satellites of local authorities (in general the capital is held by them) also illustrates these transformations: in 2004 in the 25 member states of the European Union (source: www.dexia.org) we counted 16,350 of them with a turnover of 138 billion euros and 1,125,000 employees in a variety of activities.

34 Outsourcing does not mean selling State assets (privatization) but entrusting public tasks to the private sector. Although France has been using the mechanisms of concession and delegation of public services for a long time, the movement of outsourcing has become more pronounced with the subcontracting of activities such as military equipment.

35 The United Kingdom provides an example with 665 contracts signed between 1987 and 2005.

the experimental method in hard sciences. The sociologist Gabriel Tarde (1895) even thought that the laws of imitation were at the foundation of societies. In this way, institutional mimetism and the fascination for foreign "models" can sometimes facilitate useful reforms. Nevertheless, in the case of tax revenue, the limits of the comparison are forgotten for the benefit of an ideological presentation, drawn of the quantitative indicators, which distorts the political meaning: this general level of systemic trends has to be completed by the study of the social changes came from fiscal policy.

CHAPTER 6

The Elemental Factors of Fiscal Policy

Even though certain institutional movements such as decentralization and federalism moderate the analysis, the sovereign power of the tax State remains a reality. Since its regalian origins (cf. chapter 4), the tax State, having become interventionist, remains at the centre of choices, in spite of the fragmentation of the financial system (chapter 5). As is illustrated by the rule of the member countries' unanimity regarding the tax decisions of the European Union, its legal competence in this domain leads to keep the term of public policy. The legitimate authority is in many cases the State. Ideas, groups and partisan preference which characterize society influence tax policy through an intermediate variable: the conception of public policy. This societal dimension completes the institutional shaping of the interventionist public action which, without being centered on the State, admits a real autonomy of the State.

Specialists generally favour one or two particular factors. For example, Wildavsky (1985) develops a theory of budgetary cultures which are connected with the explanations from the role of ideas. Institutions and ideas are considered by Steinmo (2003), while Eisenstein (1961) privileges the combination of interest groups (or classes) with ideologies. Campbell (1993), considering crises as a cause for change, also emphasizes interest groups that determine the real content of tax policy. Neo-Marxists (O' Connor, 1973) analyze the crisis of the tax State within the framework of social classes. Korpi and Palme (2003) associate classes and the partisan variable etc. Sometimes a particular variable, such as the type of ballot or the nature of the coalition, is questioned: it depends however on one of general factors retained, namely the institutions in the quoted example.

Fiscal public action considered here is situated at a level of elemental analysis constituted by ideas, institutions, socio-economic groups, and the left-right division.[1] The macro-analysis of democratic and capitalist

[1] Our subject is in line with the methodological idea of Durkheim, 2001 (1912) expressed in *The Elementary Forms of Religious Life*: "therefore every time we intend to explain something human (...) it is necessary to begin by going back to its most primitive and simplest form". Nevertheless, it is not a question of going back to primitive forms, but of starting from the elemental level of the "causes" of tax policy in order to distinguish and decompose (cf. chapter 7) the complex form that public

frameworks is questioned in the chapter 7: we will see that context is the principal transition variable between the elemental and global levels of public action. Here, in the chapter 6, institutions are supposed to put into concrete form the democratic choices of a society through two causal factors, namely: the groups or classes that proceed from social stratification, and the ideas which are inspired by societal cultures. In the same way, the capitalist framework is not endogenous to the model; it can be found, in a simplified manner, in groups (the business community) and ideas (the neo-liberal ideology for example).

1. The Influence of Ideas

The noblesse of studying ideas has been existing for a long time with the well-known works of Max Weber on the cultural approach to capitalism, on religious sociology and on axiological rationality. We also saw that for Pareto modern democracies tend to govern by ruse: they justify tax despoliation for the benefit of the ruling elite by ideological reasons ("derivations"). Despite these illustrious precedents, Campbell (2002) reveals that until the 1990s scholars did not investigate very much the influence of ideas on public policies. Ideas are conceived as an alternative to the dominant paradigm of self-interest supported by rational choice theory. They brought together cultures, theories, values, beliefs, ideologies, visions of the world and ways of thinking. Ideas stemming from cultures belonging to a society, to classes or to social groups are distinguished from ideas belonging to the political field. In the case of societal cultures the influence is more indirect, more diffuse (cf. figure 2) than in the case of conceptions directly linked to the actors of fiscal decision-making. The process is therefore long and uncertain before a culture, shared by a majority of persons or by certain groups, is transformed into budgetary ideas. It also has to appear on the public agenda as the conception of a public program. This way of influencing is a process of public action which includes the societal dimension; it becomes by its effectiveness a causal factor of public policy.

a. The ideas stemming from society

A few founding principles guide the financial system in general and tax policy in particular. We have seen in chapter 4 that the formula "the king has to live from his own", namely from his domain, constituted the guiding principle of the financial system in the feudal period. In economics, Brennan and Buchanan (1977) adopt a contractual point of view

action has. The particular case of redistribution is studied in chapter 11. We do not come back to systemic changes notably due to the general increase of social expenditure in developed countries (cf. chapter 5).

in the wake of Rawls: they propose a fiscal constitution based on economic ideas in order to limit the Leviathan State which tends to maximize its revenues.

Some historic examples illustrate the influence of ideas on tax policies. For example the idea of the permanence of a progressive income tax, on the model of the English income tax created in the middle of the 19th century, became a reality in most of the industrialized countries at the beginning of the 20th century. The conception of equality through taxation, consisting in taxing the rich more strongly than the poor, enters into competition with the principle of equality before taxes. Equality before taxes implies only treating in the same way individuals placed in the same situation. The tax system was based on customs duties, taxes on consumption and on property, notably with the idea that the poor could refrain from consumption in order to avoid taxes. The creation of the income tax was the cause of an ideological battle. In the United States (Eisenstein, 1961, p. 18), the progressivity of this tax was thus denounced as a weapon of the communists, a blow on civilization, an offense against the American Constitution (according to the Supreme Court in the *Pollock Case* of 1895). In France (Leroy, 1996), the criticism against the creation of the income tax was also virulent. The well-known economist Leroy-Beaulieu (1906, p. 178-186) vilified for example the reform with ideological arguments legitimized by his "scientific" authority:

> "The progressive tax system is a simple sentimental theory (…). Proportionally it costs less to the State to protect and guarantee a big property than to (…) a small one (…). Does the elegant and light car of the rich man damage the roads infinitely more than the heavy and awkward vehicle of a lower middle-class man or than the light cart of a farmer? (…). If we consider the debt of France, for example, it results almost entirely from two series of events: the French Revolution and the First Empire which came from it; the Revolution of 1848 and the Second Empire which was a product of it. Now can we maintain that it was the upper classes that caused these events? (…). Thus, the theory of the progressive tax is not rational (…). This theory is moreover dangerous, because, starting from the principle of the equality of sacrifice, it has a tendency wanting to correct social inequalities; there is here a consequence which is fatal."

In France, we can also mention the arguments against the abolition of the "octroi", the old indirect tax (from 1795 to 1941) on certain goods entering into the towns. In 1870, the municipal council of the town of Sedan justified this tax as follows (Leroy, Tisserand, 2003): the octroi is painless, "at the same time as every citizen pays his daily expense, he pays his part of municipal expenditure". The octroi is fair because he who "consumes the most (…) is he who pays the biggest part of the tax, (…) he who is stopped by poverty, is exempt from a part of municipal expenditure, in proportion to his abstention. The truth is therefore that the divided indirect tax, paid imperceptibly, is fairer, lighter, and more agreeable for the poor man". The tariff of the octroi is moderate, and the ultimate argument is that it has good budgetary yield: "before abolishing a tax, we must know by what we shall replace it". In addition to these historic examples, we should also mention the cultural theory of the American sociologist Wildavsky that emphasizes the interdependence between the financial system and the dominant values of the society (cf. box).

Box 7: The influence of budgetary cultures

A. Wildavsky proposes a sociological theory of public expenditure founded on political cultures (Wildavsky, 1985; Webber, Wildavsky, 1986, p. 560-615). He distinguishes four types of culture capable to influence the budgetary regime. Culture points out to shared values legitimizing social practices; it is an axiological rationality that considers intentions in terms of values, and not necessarily their realization. In modern societies, no culture completely dominates the others, as it has been empirically established by studying the values of social groups. Thus, the size of the State today is a function of the political culture of yesterday, keeping in mind that the development of the equalitarian culture explains the increase of public expenditure. The social ideal of the Market Culture is auto-regulation that reduces the need for authority, while accepting at the same time social competition stemming from the division of labour: this culture limits revenue and expenditure; it refuses the equalization of differences by budgetary redistribution. The Culture of Institutionalized Hierarchy legitimizes a non-egalitarian collective order in a society of differentiated statuses: it encourages revenue and expenditure, with a weak redistribution towards the poorest, and a weak deficit. The Egalitarian Culture ("sectarians" according to Wildavsky) conceives life as a voluntary association; it works to reduce inequalities (race, parents/children, teachers/students, authorities/citizens, men/women etc.): it recommends revenue transfers from the rich to the poor, encourages social programs; but it curbs tax collection due to distrust in the authority, and thus it creates a tendency for deficits. Wildavsky adds a fourth budgetary regime, the Fatalist Regime: there is no budgetary strategy, notably because of the effect of very strong constraints. When things go wrong, the Market supporters blame the unproductiveness of individuals or government hindrances to business, the Egalitarians blame the system (the authority responsible for inequalities), and the adherents of Hierarchy blame deviants.

b. The conceptions of public finance

The ideas[2], which entered the political agenda, were realized by the construction of a budgetary law whose stages are historically linked with the rapid growth of the parliamentary regime. In order to control the government better, the parliament relied on budgetary principles[3] that are still in force in numerous democracies. The general decline, even though variable from country to country, of parliamentary power was expressed by the diminishing significance of its principles. The evolution of global budgetary conceptions is characterized firstly by transition from the classic or liberal conception of the 19th century to the generalization of Keynesian policies after the Second World War. These conceptions form a coherent set of budgetary values. In the 19th century, the liberal conception restricts State intervention by public finance characterized by the following features: neutrality of public finance, balancing the budget, limitation of expenditure and revenue, and proscription of loans. This conception prevails until the First World War. As Mann observed (1943: cf. chapter 2), a major change takes place starting from 1914: in the context of expenditure necessitated by the two World Wars and the crisis of 1929 and under the influence of the economic ideas of Keynesianism, the interventionist conception of public finance becomes prevailing. Economic action through public expenditure is encouraged. The deficit becomes legitimate in certain cases. All the developed countries will apply Keynesian policies after the Second World War. The development of the Welfare State also justifies the growth of social expenditure.

Since the 1970s, Keynesian ideas have been called into question[4]: the neo-liberal market conception extends its influence over public policies. Ideologically this conception uses globalization to impose deregulation and privatization. It recommends the control of expenditure, of debt and of public deficit, the decrease of tax revenue, and the dismantling of the Welfare State etc. The neo-liberal ideas give however rise to considerable social and political resistance. It constitutes an influential ideology rather than a consensual conception of tax policies. This ideology

---

2 On the influence of ideas on social expenditure, cf. Jacobs, 2009; on the Third Way in Germany and in the United Kingdom, cf. Hudson *et al.*, 2008; on English governance, cf. Bevir, Rhodes, 2003, 2004.

3 Annual voting and execution of the budget, unity of the budget which must be regrouped in a unique document submitted to the deliberative assembly, specialization of expenditure, presentation according to the rule of gross revenue (universality) prohibiting the compensation or the appropriation of a particular revenue to a particular expenditure.

4 Cf. the policies of the Thatcher and Reagan governments, and in France the turning point of "rigor" of 1983.

justified the supply-side economic policies of the Reagan and Thatcher governments. A new justification of this ideology was found in the intensification of economic globalization starting from 1990s by referring to the theory of "market efficiency" in order to promote the reduction of social expenditure and of taxation on capital. On the other hand, the theory of "the resilience of the Welfare State" insists on the maintenance of social expenditure as a means of compensating for the effects of globalization, notably on the most deprived. In reality, the neo-liberal ideology was realized on the international level by the "Washington Consensus" shared by the IMF and the World Bank in 1980-1990: in order to liberalize the market, these institutions recommended the reduction of public debt and expenditure, privatization, and the deregulation of the labour market etc.

Empirical findings (cf. chapter 7) do not confirm the universal retrenchment of the State as a result of economic globalization. We have also seen (chapter 5) that the level of tax revenue and of public expenditure remains high in many countries and that the European Welfare State resists to globalization. With regard to the taxation of enterprises, we note a decrease of the statutory rates for corporate tax in all countries since the 1990s. For OECD countries, the average tax rate dropped from 38% in 1995 to 28% in 2005 (Norregaard, Khan, 2007). This general decline is not the same in the different countries. The tax rate remains high in the rich countries of the G7 (decreasing from about 45% in 1995 to 35% in 2005) which remain at the top of the classification. On the opposite side, the new member states of the EU have the lowest rate: it decreased from 30% in 1995 to 20% in 2005. The rate in the EU at 15 members went from 38% in 1995 to 30% in 2005. The tax rates in Latin American countries dropped a little from 30% to 28%. In OECD countries, however, this decrease in official rates was compensated in general by a widening of the tax base[5], so that the amount of revenue drawn from the taxation of enterprises (measured as a percentage of the GDP) increased over the same period. On the other hand, in developing countries and in countries in transition towards market economies, a certain stagnation and sometimes an erosion of tax bases are noted: this observation is explained by the generalization of derogatory taxation or of flat tax mechanisms in order to attract companies. Neo-liberal ideas therefore use the pretext of economic globalization to promote a conception favourable to capital.

As for the taxation of natural persons, we observe a general decrease of the marginal rates of income tax since 1990s. On average, in OECD countries, the marginal rate went from 49% to 43% between 1995 and 2004 (Norregaard, Khan, 2007). For G7 countries, the drop is 8 points.

5 Cf. Devereux, 2006.

For the EU, the decrease is also observed, but we must note the difference between the marginal rate of the EU 15 and of the EU 10 (in 2004: 15 points lower). This time the decline in rates was accompanied by a slight erosion of tax bases in OECD countries (including European countries) but not in developing countries.

The success of the neo-liberal conception of reforms is not complete because of the provoked resistance and the other functions that taxation has to ensure. Ideas thus modify on the whole the sense of the compromises realized (cf. chapter 11), sometimes in a radical way, but not the existence of the compromises, for instance between the working classes which support the Welfare State and the capitalist classes which are pushing towards the de-taxation of big (multinational) enterprises. The increase of inequalities in the world shows nevertheless that the tax burden of the rich was reduced.

At the end of the 1990s, a new conception came to complete the neo-liberal conception, in the form of the performance of public management. Encouraged by the OECD, this management conception asserted itself in many countries, including in less developed countries, in the form of budgeting by objectives or results. It consists in measuring by indicators the results obtained with regard to the objectives pursued by the financing of public programs. The intellectual framework is that of the new public management. In France, the adoption of the idea of public performance was put into concrete form in the organic law relative to budget laws (LOLF) of 1st August, 2001. Now the government carries out general repertoire of public policies (French RGPP) in order to measure their efficiency. All around the world, the tendency is to try and justify the limitation of public services by the efficiency of management. The democratic argument of the transparency of public accounts is also used.

As a political regulation of society through its public programs, the conception of performance presents an original characteristic with regard to the budgetary conceptions of the past. Of course, it still aims to diffuse a set of values. But, contrary to classic liberal and Keynesian references, it is not analyzed any more as the financial consequences of political and economic values that are socially defended. It tends to put forward budgetary performance as a primary value of politics. By pushing this reasoning, the paradox is the following: the regulation, serving as a reference, of public policies becomes itself financial in order to construct political projects that are bargained over financially. It is disturbing to put the management reference system of financial performance forward as the main determinant of public action. In fact, this tendency takes place to the detriment of political choices (projects) based on a social theory of the regulation of the economy. In democracy, the political legitimacy of public programs must be based on the citizens. It is also important to know how this new management conception of budgets is articulated with regard to every particular public policy (the expenditures). An evolution towards a certain standardization of the indicators of performance[6] and, in some cases, towards a democratic use of this information is not to be excluded. Nevertheless, the risk of a dilution, or even a disappearance, of political systems of reference is real. In this case the management conception of public action will be reduced to a supplementary ideological weapon against public action.

c. *The reception of ideas*

The theory of relative frustration of Tocqueville (chapter 1) shows how tax inequalities had become unbearable for the French people on the eve of the Revolution, while the overall situation had improved. In this context the reception of revolutionary ideas and of the philosophy of the Enlightenment was facilitated. Nowadays, the impact of the expertise of the high-level administration (technocratisation) and of soft law is important. The media also play a role in reception of the discourses. But it is above all the nature of the argumentation that explains the diffusion of ideologies, as is shown by the case of the reception of the neo-liberal anti-tax discourse.

The technocratisation of tax policies and of public expenditure plays an important role, even if it takes up different institutional forms in different countries. In Sweden, in the years 1950-1960 (Steinmo, 1993, p. 122), the debate shifts towards the depoliticized discussion of tax techniques by the government and the representatives of business and labour unions. The expertise is more or less shared. In France, the technocratisation is seized by the government (the Ministry of Finance services) that benefits from the participation of a number of high-ranking officials called "*énarques*".[7] In the United States, it is associated with the Congress (cf. below). Technocratisation intervenes more by argumentation than by the institutional power of high-ranking officials. The mechanisms of soft power are thus to be seeked in the ability to convince more by arguments (generally, economic) than by a kind of constraint. The arguments depend on the ideological influence, in the sense specified below, and not on the power to constrain. Thus, these informal norms become one of the legal sources unforeseen in tax policies, so-called soft law.

---

6 For example, for the relation between indicators of action and of results, the general and target indicators, the indicators politically attributable or not, the place of the function of management support (purchases) etc.

7 Graduates of the French National School of Administration (École nationale d'administration – ENA).

For a long time soft law has been fed by tax administration practices. The administration produces instructions (doctrine) to interpret the law. It more and more tends to say what the law is instead of the legislator or the judge. Administrative texts very often substitute for the rules of law. As a consequence, several countries have established mechanisms for the protection of taxpayers against the changes of administrative doctrine. Globalization has an impact because it increased the complexity of tax schemes from enterprises. In response, tax administrations have strengthened their control mechanisms: following the example of the American administration (Joyce, 2008), they publish the list of the tax schemes (once again soft law) that they consider as fraudulent.

The domain of soft law has been particularly developed in international matters. The IMF in particular publishes Working Papers which, without involving it formally, are followed by specialists. The OECD, through its fiscal affairs committee, identifies the good practices of the member states. It publishes comparative statistics, reports, recommendations which are generally followed, in particular by the European Union. Tax incidence is analyzed within the framework of economic conceptions that are not politically neutral (Mahon and McBride, 2009), as those already discussed of competitiveness, governance, performance. Private organizations, such as foundations, think-tanks (Leroy, 2010) also participate in this movement of power through ideas. These organizations rely on their power of expertise to direct tax policies by denying the possibility of a political choice[8] facing economic constraints. They therefore exercise an informal influence (soft power) through the rationality of their arguments.

The forums of lobbying through expertise have an antidemocratic character given their functioning in closed networks. The phenomenon is not new in itself. Campbell (2002) quotes studies on the emergence of the social policy of the English Liberal Party showing that decision-makers frequented the same clubs as the intellectuals supporting the reforms. But the international dimension of these networks is nourished by the impact of comparativism, whose impact on the financial system was pointed out in chapter 5. Another example is given by the adoption of new international accounting standards for enterprises. A study of Capron and Chiapello (in Capron, 2005) shows how the ideas of a private board of international audit[9] were imposed upon the European Union. Financed by private capital, this professional organization, where Americans are overrepresented, exploited the inability of the EU to

[8] Cf. the adjustment policies of the years 1970-1980 for the countries in difficulty, then the "Washington Consensus" of the years 1980-1990, then the plea for economic and financial neo-liberal globalization which led to the sub-prime crisis.

[9] International Accounting Standard Board.

adapt its accounting standards (by directives) to globalization. The standards called IFRS (International Financial Reporting Standards) officially applicable to European countries thus valorize the Anglo-Saxon conception of financial capitalism: for example, the market value is retained to value the assets of an enterprise, instead of the calculation traditionally used in several States of the patrimonial value (the acquisition price). A private organization thus substituted for the sovereignty of European States.

The media also participate, according to their own vision, in the public diffusion of information on public finance. This information is more intense during the ideological periods of tax policy. During the ordinary periods, it is rather depoliticized. It follows the budgetary and fiscal agenda of public authorities drawing from official data. Nevertheless, it sometimes also uses financial expertise to catch the reader on the deficiencies of universities, hospitals etc. The risk of deviation is a lesser evil in a democracy which respects the free information of citizens. Media pluralism is a crucial challenge. In practice, the processing of financial information by the press remains to be more or less improved depending on the countries and the subjects. The presentation of arguments influences public opinion as for the situation of public finance (Jerit, Barabas, 2006).

The reception of the anti-tax discourse (Leroy, 2009) is explained by the presence (or not) of a scientific argumentation which facilitates its diffusion among decision-makers and the public. The anti-tax discourse[10] then becomes an ideology in Raymond Boudon's[11] sense. We must add that economics has become the discipline of reference for the government of post-war modern societies. The impact of the anti-tax discourse is facilitated. It is based on an inaccurate systematization of scientific knowledge joined together around the economic analysis of the Keynesian Welfare State, then the globalization of exchange. In this context, the anti-tax ideology will be received all the better for being based on economic knowledge. The ideological discourse, in case of success, tends to impose itself as truth and creates commonplaces, social clichés, generally admitted without critical examination.

---

10 There are numerous books written for wide public that convey the anti-tax discourse which is also taken over by certain associations of taxpayers. I am interested here in the ideological use of economic theories because the impact of these ideas on tax policies and on public opinion is important.

11 This ideology is a "doctrine based on a scientific argumentation and endowed with an excessive or unfounded credibility" (Boudon, 1986). This definition is important because, along with modernity, the beliefs concerning social and political matters give the authority of science as a reference.

Several social factors explain the influence of the economic ideology on our societies. The criticism is however not new; Friedrich Hayek published his well-known book *The road to serfdom* in 1944. But the context, until the crisis of summer 2008, was favorable for the reception of the neo-liberal criticism. The economic crisis of the 1970s and the difficulties of the Welfare State questioned Keynesian and social policies applied by developed countries after the end of War.[12] Since the 1990s, the phenomenon of economic globalization has strengthened this effect even more. The new[13] internationalization serves as an economic argument for supporters of Market efficiency in favour of State retrenchment.

The social reception of the anti-tax ideology is also explained by the status gained by economics in our societies.[14] The end of the hegemony of the big systems of explanation (Marxism, structuralism, functionalism, systematism) has accentuated the specialization of disciplines. Priority is given (at best) to medium-range theories (Merton) in order to verify empirically testable hypotheses (Popper), which are thus often narrow, and in order to control variables. Globalization does not signify the end of ideologies, because it also provokes a reflection against the single way of thinking (*pensée unique*). It accentuates however the decline of disciplines concerning the society and politics which constituted the hard core of social sciences, to the benefit of economic and management disciplines.

As we have seen, the conception of public finance policies has also evolved towards a neo-liberal ideology of the market and of management performance. While politics has still weighed up against economics on the ideological scale, economics, strengthened by the development of its mathematical knowledge (econometrics), has become the reference. It justifies public choices. The hegemony of economics and the influence of the neo-liberal ideology which refers to it are thus well-established. The same evolution is observed in the scientific approach to public finance. The great theories of financial science elaborated with the appearance of the interventionist State have left in place the specialization between tax and budget experts, the division between jurists and economists, the orientation towards practical kinds of knowledge, the expertise of consultants. Economists appropriated the monopoly to rule on tax policies within the framework of a utilitarian paradigm, simplistic in its hypotheses but complex in its mathematical presentation. Too many jurists bury themselves in the (remunerative) arcane aspects of the

12 It is noteworthy that Hayek and Friedman became Nobel Prize winners in Economics in 1974 and in 1976 respectively.

13 Cf. chapter 12 and Leroy, 2006.

14 For a philosophic reflection: Tucci, 2007.

positive law and of recent jurisprudence, abandoning doctrine as theorization. The complexity of public budgets discourages global approaches, while at the same time leaving the field clear to the devastating commonplaces of the neo-liberal economic ideology (cf. box 8).

Box 8: The anti-tax commonplaces of the neo-liberal ideology

P1: Taxpayer has an aversion for taxes because he has from an economic point of view no interest in paying taxes (argument of Downs, theory of risk, theory of crime, theory of collective goods).

P2: Tax revenue is too high, damages economic growth and encourages evasion (theory of the growth of the State, Laffer curve).

P3: Taxpayer is unrealistic by claiming for lower taxes and higher spending (for him), or by underestimating the weight of his tax with regard to the real cost of public services and of redistribution (theory of tax illusion).

P4: Globalization forces to reduce taxes and cut expenditure, notably social expenditure (theory of market efficiency or State retrenchment).

The circumstances have facilitated the diffusion of the neo-liberal doctrine inspired by representatives of the prestigious economic discipline.[15] In the fiscal field, it is especially the school of public choice, with the emblematic figure of James Buchanan, the 1986 Nobel Prize winner in economics, which has served as a source of the neo-liberal ideological reading from the 1970s until now.

The phenomena of technocratisation, of soft law, and the cognitive theory of the reception of ideology put forward the mechanisms of influence of ideas on public action. The level of analysis is not that of power relations stemming from the classic approaches to public decision-making. The theories of elite and oligarchy are certainly validated by the influence of high-ranked administrative officers. The theories of corporatism, Marxism or pluralism are not invalidated; but the emphasis is on the technical quality of arguments, next to more traditional variables such as power relations, interest groups and institutions.

2. The Institutional Shaping

Even though institutions do not explain everything as certain theories tend to claim, they are important. One must again refer to Tocqueville who, in order to explain the French Revolution, analyzed the centralization of decision-making by the royal power and the destruction of

15 For example, the ideas of Hayek served as reference for the programs of R. Reagan and M. Thatcher, who came to power in 1979, and these ideas found a world audience.

political freedom: tax incentives ensuring the preponderance of Paris as capital, interventionist expenditure of the State, and breaches in the fiscal competencies of intermediate institutions. The functioning of the administrative organization is studied in chapter 8. In a classic sense, the study of institutions is that (preferred by jurists) of power and formal procedures. In a broader sense, the neo-institutionalists also study the practices that structure relations between the actors of political decision-making. Institutions are thus defined as rules (in fact or in law) that shape the choices of actors: formal procedures, but also other variables (electoral system, veto points, the processes of public decision-making). The two case studies of local taxation reform in France and of fiscal federalism complete this analysis.

a. The legal power of institutions

Institutions shape the content of tax policies. Without going back to the impact of budgetary and tax law on tax revenue (cf. chapter 5), we must emphasize that the type of constitutional regime has an influence on budgetary and tax policies. In a classic sense, it is thus a question of assessing the respective powers of government and parliament: distribution of competencies, budgetary and tax procedures... Public finance is at the origin of parliamentarism as is shown by the cases of Great Britain or France.[16] Parliament thus appears as a legitimate actor of the classic financial system. Nowadays the legal analysis of budgetary power generally indicates a decline of parliamentary power. The situation is nevertheless different from country to country as is shown by the cases retained below. In this regard, the OECD notes that in 2002 41% of the countries had an effective form of amendment law, according to diverse terms and conditions.

Under the Fifth Republic in France, constitutional rationalization ended up entrusting from 1958 to 2001 the greater part of financial power to the government. The organic law of 2nd January, 1959 legally establishes the preponderance of the government over the parliament. This real decline of the legislative power leaves even so an influence of the national elected representatives over certain decisions, notably in matters of local finance (cf. below), for fiscal niches[17], or through information and evaluation reports. The organic law related to finance

---

16 Cf. chapter 4. In France, it was with the Restoration (started in 1815) that the parliamentary power finds its effectiveness in the consecration of the great rules of budgetary law, after the Revolution had introduced the principles of parliamentary consent to taxation.

17 For example, the setting of a ceiling for tax niches, foreseen in the finance bill for 2009 of the government, was largely watered-down by the parliament in order to satisfy certain lobbyists.

laws (LOLF: Leroy, 2007) reinforces the powers of the parliament. It provides the parliament with new legal means to position itself as a decisive actor in public finance. The effectiveness of parliamentary control is a key factor of the reform because it constitutes the counter-balance to the freedom granted to the managers (executive and administration). The legal means exist for a parliamentary evaluation of public action, even so they have to be used. Actually, until now, the fact for the executive to have at its disposal a obedient majority represents a considerable obstacle to execution of parliamentary power. One must really emphasize that article 48 of the LOLF which establishes the budgetary orientation debate before the parliament does not foresee the approbation of the government report. Above all, the current tendency of the regime to become more presidential, which accentuates the old phenomenon of the importance of the executive in the Fifth Republic, does not lead to optimism. The government has also set up a procedure for the general revision of public policies (RGPP) which competes, under its authority, with the LOLF. The problem is therefore to elaborate a real democratic theory of political choices in order to get away from the ideology of budgetary determinisms of public action.

Box 9: The reinforcement of the legal means of the parliament in France

Only the main provisions are quoted. Article 57 provides that the finance commissions "follow and control the execution of the finance laws and initiate the evaluation of any question related to public finance". This text foresees the investigation of documents, the investigation on the spot, the right of hearing which has a compulsory character without that the secret could be opposed[18], the communication of administrative and financial information.[19] Article 59 establishes a possibility of a "référé" (summary proceeding) to the benefit of the presidents of finance commissions in the case of hindrance to the communication of documents within "a reasonable delay". In a certain number of cases related to execution of finance laws[20] the information of the finance commissions is obligatory. We must also note the provisions of article 60 which constrain the government to respond within a delay of 2 months to the observations notified by the parliament following a

[18] With the exception of the secrets of defense, security, health and judicial enquiry.

[19] Including the reports (often well informed) of the control of the administration, except for the cases listed in the previous note.

[20] According to Article 12 of the LOLF, the payments and transfers of credits can only be made following information from finance commissions. Article 13 provides that decrees (*décrets*) on advance payments can be made following advice by finance commissions (the advice has to be formulated within a delay of seven days). Article 14 also provides for information by the finance commissions on the cancellations of credits (whose application has given rise to abuse).

control or an evaluation. The law of settlement, which allows the control of the execution of the budget, is the subject of several provisions that improve its legal scope. Article 37 specifies its content by requiring in particular the establishment of a balance sheet and an income statement subject to parliamentary approval. The delay for the presentation of the bill of settlement by the government is regulated (article 46) in order to allow a rapid parliamentary examination of the text.[21] Article 58 confirms, by strengthening it, the role of the Court of Auditors[22] with regard to the assistance of the parliament. Finally, article 54 gives a list of documents and information that must be added to the bill of settlement with notably the annual performance reports (RAP). The RAPs allow the parliament to control the execution of programmes by a comparison with the information that appears in the annual performance projects (PAP) presented in the appendix to the initial finance law. They indicate the objectives, the results obtained with regard to those that were expected, the expenditure and the credit flows by title, the costs of the programmes and the distribution of employment and staff. Article 41 seals in a certain sense the procedure by specifying that the new finance law cannot be put up for discussion before the law of settlement is voted.

In the United States, the Congress has at its disposal by its fiscal legitimacy a considerable budgetary power (Zoller, 2004). Outwardly, the emphasis put on the budget performance estimates seems to limit the budgetary power of the Congress: except creating a political crisis, the Congress seems obliged to pass the resolution (law of 12 July 1994) approving the big aggregates and the limits of the credits for the missions decided by the President. The presidential budget estimates is based on assessments made by the Office of Management and Budget (linked to the executive). The reality of power remains however in the hands of the Congressional subcommittees for the credit attributions. These committees can work on the parliamentary propositions, elaborated with assistance of an independent entity, the Congressional Budget Office (CBO) created in 1974. The law of 3 August 1993 on government performance imposes an evaluation of the execution of programmes. Not being considered as a law, the budgetary resolution is not subject to the right of veto of the president: it does not stand in the way of sector-based decisions of the subcommittees to fix the detail of expenditure by programmes and to modify expenditure; The executive's

21 The bill of settlement has to be presented by the government before the 1st of June which follows the execution. In the past it has been noted that the parliament took no further interest in the laws of settlement that were presented late.

22 Article 58 foresees the drafting by the Court of Auditors, besides the already mentioned certification of the regularity, sincerity and faithfulness of the accounts, of a preliminary report on the execution (at the time when the government drafts its report on budgetary orientation), of a report on the execution accompanying the bill of settlement, and of a report on the decrees on advance payments subject to ratification.

tax reformes are often changed, even in the case of a strong electoral victory. Changes are often inspired by political considerations.

In Great Britain, the power of parliament includes significant limits. There are two distinct procedures for expenditure and for revenue. Expenditure is examined within the framework of two-period procedure. Firstly, the vote of the "estimations" represents the opportunity for the parliament, at the initiative of the opposition, to debate pursued policies. This debate is more political in nature than financial (Baranger, 2004), but the expenditure foreseen for the current year is always voted. After that the law "of appropriation", without debate, formalizes the budgetary authorization to spend. Revenue is the subject of another procedure resulting in the voting of the finance law which thus concerns only tax revenue and rules. In this way, paradoxically for the cradle of parliamentarism, this institutional functioning shows the decline of the parliament. The executive, and in its midst the Treasury branch, dominates decision-making.

The power of the parliament is more or less important according to the constitutional institutions of the country. If the power of the government varies in the opposite direction, it is nowhere negligible. An exhaustive study of 98 democratic countries made by Cheibub (2006) from 1970 to 2002 shows that the budget deficit is better controlled (statistical correlation) in a presidential type of regime than in parliamentary regimes: the effect on the (improved) budgetary balance is on average 1% of GDP. The reason is that in presidential systems, the political accountability in the management of public finance is considered by voters as part of the responsibility of the executive; in parliamentary regimes, the electoral responsibility of the executive is on average less strong. Finally, we have to note that the respective powers of the executive and of the deliberative assembly have an impact on local budgets. Other institutional factors must be pointed out according to a less formal approach.

b. *Other institutional variables*

The neo-institutionalist approaches take into account other variables.[23] Steinmo (1993), for example, compares the history of the fiscal policies of the United Kingdom, Sweden and the USA. He recognizes that historic institutionalism does not explain the choices put into place, but certain specificities of the policies. For example, in the United Kingdom, the government has at its disposition centralized institutions with very few institutions of countering power. It has the opportunity of

[23] Concerning the neo-institutionalist approaches: cf. March, Olsen, 1984, 1989; Hall, Taylor, 1996.

conducting an autonomous tax policy, by separating itself from its election promises (a common practice), or by deciding on a reform unilaterally[24], or by radically applying a program.[25] In Sweden, the corporatist compromises between labour unions, employers and the government are structured by the relations between capital and labour. In this regard, the reform of 1938 stemming from the Saltsjöbaden conference puts into place a negotiated compromise. Taxes on income, fortune and heritage, and then indirect taxes, which affect all taxpayers, including ordinary workers, are increased in exchange for economic prosperity. Large enterprises (capitalism) are favored by tax deductions to the detriment of small enterprises. In the United States, the powerful Congressional committees (cf. above) and the vitality of a federalism aiming at, as Tocqueville said it, avoiding the tyranny of the majority, modify the tax reforms of the executive even in the case of a strong electoral victory.

The electoral system affects public expenditure.[26] This result is confirmed by the study of Thames and Edwards (2006) on the data of 17 countries from 1990 to 2000: the majority ballot is correlated with a lower level of expenditure (about 3% of GDP) than the proportional ballot. Moreover, social expenditure is lower in the case of a majority ballot. The proposed explanation is as follows: in the majority system, public spending is aimed to satisfy certain demands strengthening the majority; in proportional representation, public spending is more massively used to consolidate government coalitions. The scale of the difference between the two systems depends on number of seats held by a party: in a majority electoral system, the larger the party majority, the lower is spending; in a proportional representation system, the weight of the seats of every party is susceptible to challenge government. More generally, as numerous countries have adopted mixed electoral systems, i.e. combining in variable quantities a majority ballot with a proportional representation, the exact effect on public finance will depend on the particular rules of every country. In any case, the impact of this institutional factor is pointed out. In the case of systems including a level of proportional representation, it appears as a source of "veto point".

The impact of veto points on budgetary and fiscal decisions has been the subject of interesting empirical studies. According to the theory of veto points (Tsebelis, 1995, 1999), the higher the number of institutional

24 It is the case of the reform called *War Budget on Poverty* (1909) in order to finance a social insurance by taxing the rich; this reform was decided by Lloyd without concerted action.

25 It is the case of the Thatcher's tax reform during the period 1979-1988.

26 The parti system institutionalization (Robbins, 2010) or the party strength (Primo, Snyder, 2010) also influence government spending.

points of resistance, the more difficult is change. Veto points are constituted, as the case may be, by the system of parties, bicameralism especially when the two parliamentary assemblies are not elected in the same way or have different political tendencies, by the electoral system facilitating stable majorities or requiring coalitions (the cited case of proportional representation), or by the impact of lobbying etc. Here, budgetary policy is studied as a problem of collective action, where the government is more or less driven to negotiate, particularly according to the composition of its majority. The study of Crepaz and Moser (2004) gives precise details that are useful, based on data of 15 OECD countries from 1960 to 1996. It distinguishes[27] collective and competitive veto points. In the first case, the large "collective" diffusion of institutional power pushes public spending growth, because the government coalition sees to the respect of promises (spending). In case of competitive veto points, the tendency is to maintain the status quo because of the reciprocal blocking between institutions, and thus to maintain the stability of spending, sometimes to reduce it.

The veto points theory allows a fertile dialogue with the classic institutional approach. It introduces factors of the social and political diffusion of power. For its part, the legal analysis of institutions has admitted for a long time that the constitutional fact (the practice of the institutions) has its place. For example, in France the "majority fact" makes the parliament docile with regard to the government, even though its budgetary power was reinforced by the LOLF. New sources of rather competitive veto points have been created as a result of the broad movement of decentralization (and federalism) in the world during the last few decades.

c. *The institutional blockage of the reform of local taxes in France*

In spite of numerous criticisms, the radical reform of French local taxes seems impossible to realize (Leroy, 2004). In essence, the criticism of local taxation currently concerns the residence tax, the business tax, and two types of property tax (on builded and not builded property) which ensure a good return to local budgets.[28] The diagnosis converge in

---

[27] The indicators of *collective veto points* are: a proportional electoral system (inciting the multiplication of parties, candidates, and the coalitions); a high number of parliamentary groups; a "corporatist" influence favouring certain social groups and not pluralist (balance of requests). The indicators of *competitive veto points* are: effectiveness of federalism; and bicameralism.

[28] They represent globally 34% of the operating funds of local authorities in 2006, and, with regard to tax revenue only, 71.7% of taxes levied by communes, 55.5% of taxes of departments, and 52.3% in the case of regions.

order to denounce these taxes as archaic, inegalitarian[29], ineffective, complex, and not very transparent. The cadastral rental value, i.e. the theoretical rent of a property on the market, is used as a basis for their tax base. These taxes of a real nature are thus not created to take into account the income and personal situation of the taxpayer. Regardless of the personalization carried out for the residence tax (half of the households are partially or completely granted a tax relief), the index-based character of these taxes imperfectly apprehend the taxpayer's wealth. Above all, the rental value fixed in the 1970s has not been revised: it is thus disconnected from the reality of the real estate market, regardless of the adjustments carried out. It creates distortions, for example between new and old housing. Criticism concentrates on the local business tax: before the belated and partial reforms of 1999 and 2009, wages and investments were imposed. The inequality of tax rates between local communities was added onto these deficiencies of the tax bases. Even though this inequality is also the expression of local autonomy put into concrete form by the freedom (cf. box on France) of the vote on the tax rate, it is in particular present at the level of communes[30], because of their big number (more than 36,500).

Facing this criticism, the reform of local taxation follows the way of progressive adjustments thus emphasizing its complexity and its lack of transparency. In the context of French decentralization, the change of local taxes is blocked not because of the taxpayer-citizen, who is absent from the debate, but because of the functioning of the local political system. An institutional factor is in question, that of the cumulation of public mandates that allows elected representatives to press politically on the configuration of the problem for the local fiscal reform in direction of gradualism. The problem has moved from the conception of decentralization to the question of the financial means that the State must grant. Local elected representatives, taking advantage of their national mandates and of their influence on the Senate, refuse the "big bang" which seems electorally risky to them, as is shown by numerous examples of unsuccessful reforms.

The decentralization of 1982 thus does not take into consideration tax reform. It simply lays down the principle of the financial compensation for the transfer of competences: this principle will not always be effective in practice facing the cost of certain responsibilities transferred by the State. In 2004, the new momentum given to decentralization by

---

29 The impact of appropriations paid by the State does not adequately correct inequalities between local authorities: in the communes (where inequalities are the biggest) this impact passed from -13.2 in 2000 to -15.8 in 2006 (Source: *Centre d'analyse stratégique*, January, 2009).

30 The commune is the lowest level of administrative division in France.

the law of 13 August, 2004 (called act II of decentralization) was intended[31] to be a "real society project" based on "the democracy of proximity" through administrative modernization within the framework of a "real territorial Republic". Very quickly this reference on decentralization takes the most agreed upon form of local autonomy whose content is reduced to the debate on the financial means of this local autonomy. Article 72 of the French constitution was thus modified in 2003 by the addition of a provision guaranteeing local financial autonomy. The configuration of the problem is restricted within the framework of the local politico-administrative system: it leads to a debate on the financing of new transfers of competence while excluding the reflection on local tax reform. The logic of the adjustment has the effect of placing the State in the position of the first "local taxpayer" as a result of the compensations paid as exemptions that it grants with regard to local taxation (in 2006: a quarter of the four local direct taxes).

Box 10: The adjustments of French local taxation

The structural immobility of French local taxation is historically proven. The principle of the fixity of the cadastral value (rendered intangible), which serves as a tax base, prevailed in the 19th century. The special surtax (centimes additionnels) for local authorities, calculated on the basis of State taxes, remains in force for almost two centuries (from 1791 to 1973). After the abolition of the State taxes on which they were calculated, they were established on "fictitious principles". The octroi, an important indirect tax (for towns) levied on merchandise, restored by the Directory at the end of the 18th century remained in force until 1941 even though it was not adapted to the modern market economy any more. The local tax created in 1941, a local indirect tax of a cumulative nature (not neutral), appears incompatible with the introduction of the VAT. It is replaced by the tax on wages whose importance diminishes as the VAT is generalized (incompatibility of the two taxes). This new opportunity for radical reform is not used. The adjustment consisted in establishing a representative payment of the tax on wages, then in replacing this payment by an appropriation from the State (global operating appropriation).

The recent period is still marked by the logic of gradual adjustment. The decree (ordonnance) of 7 January 1959 abolishes the four old direct contributions which bear the label of taxes and generalizes the use of the cadastral rental value. The law of 10 January 1980 establishes the direct voting of tax rates by local authorities in order to give a sense of responsibility to elected representatives in a logic, according to the Voisin report that had preceded this reform, of the adjustment of local taxation. The other recent modifications concern the movement of the personalization of the residence tax and

[31] According to the president of the Senate in *Revue française de finances publiques*, No. 81, March, 2003.

exemptions which lead to the reduction of the tax revenue portion in local budgets. Half of the households are henceforth completely or partially exempt from the residence tax because of their income level. The vehicle tax license for private persons (in 2001), the part of the transfer duties (1998) and of the residence tax (in 2000) destined for regions were abolished, which still constitutes some adjustments. The laws of 6 February 1992 and of 12 July 1999 create a certain specialization of the local taxes, because in 2008, 1224 inter-communal structures, bringing together 16336 communes, profit from the single business tax which is not attributed to commune-members any more. The local business tax was the subject of multiple punctual adaptations (for example, setting an upper limit based on the value added of the enterprise). The budget law for 1999 put into place the abolition over 5 years of the wage portion entering into the base of the business tax. The budget law for 2010 abolished local business tax, which is replaced with the territorial economic tax (*contribution économique territoriale*). This new tax includes a taxation on the property (land, industrial buildings like in the old local business tax) and a taxation on the value-added. Despite this last reform, which rather radically changes the local taxation on enterprises, local tax system is once again not globally reformed.

d. *Fiscal federalism*

Fiscal federalism is often treated from the economic or legal point of view. It also involves a political dimension to understand the financial relations of negotiation, legitimacy and power between several authorities. Our intention here is only to show that the institution of fiscal federalism directs public action. Fiscal federalism (or decentralization) theoretically presents classic advantages justifying this choice. From an economic point of view, the goods and services financed by taxation appear to be better adapted to the preferences of citizens; they are also better controlled at the sub-national than at the central level; the competition between the sub-national entities (competitive federalism) concerning the mobile factors is considered as positive: it limits public budgets, stimulates innovation and favours economic growth.[32] In spite

[32] Economic analysis refers to two classic theories of fiscal federalism: the functional theory (Musgrave, 1959; Oates, 1972) of the benevolent government, and the theory (Brennan and Buchanan, 1980) of the leviathan that maximizes its revenue. The first theory maintains that fiscal federalism allows citizens to better express their preferences (that can diverge from one region to another) and seek to determine the optimal level of attribution of 3 economic functions: the functions of economic stabilization and of income redistribution must rather depend on the upper level, and the function of allocation of goods and services on the lower level. The second theory insists on the encouragement of fiscal competition based on the mobility of factors between the sub-national entities (cf. also: Buchanan, 1950) which limits the maximization of revenue by taxation. The Tiebout's theory (1956) concerning notably the vote with the feet of enterprises also serves as a reference.

of the contribution made by the economic approach (Ahmad, Brosio, 2006), it is still the normative dimension of federalism that is favoured to the detriment of institutional choices really carried out. In order to test the economic hypotheses of fiscal federalism, the study of concrete experience remains to be developed following the case of Belgian federalism (cf. box 11). Consequently, even though certain hypotheses are confirmed, it appears for example that the presence of numerous tax expenditures (exemptions etc.) and the differences in the adopted rate policies do not correspond to the reality of a leviathan federalism.

The legal approach to federalism analyzes the constitutional distribution of competencies between the federation and the federated States. It contributes to the questioning of the financial autonomy of the sub-federal entities. The allocation of taxes, the competencies over the tax basis, the rates, the fiscal incentives etc., form the legal framework of the tax power. The legal regime of appropriations also matters: allocation rules, global or targeted character etc. The legal regime of expenditure structures the power of every level of public authority. The rules controlling borrowing and cash reserves complete the legal analysis of financial autonomy. Before 1914, (dual) federalism was based on a clear separation of the financial powers of the center and of the member States within a minimalist budgetary logic. Modern federalism is interventionist. It represents a reinforcement, according to variable combinations, of the competencies of the federation to the detriment of the federated authorities. Contrary to the economic vision of competitive federalism, "cooperative federalism", whose archetype is given by the German example, leads, in addition to the field of their own exclusive competencies, to an important division of competencies between the Federation and the States on the one side, and the States and the local authorities on the other side. In Germany (Preisser, in Leroy, 2005), the sharing of the principal taxes is constitutionally guaranteed; it ensures a financial equalization between the *Länder*. The model of cooperative federalism was the subject of debates because of the difficulties to finance the new *Länder* lagging behind structurally. The reunification did not however prevent Germany from being classified among the leading economies of the world.

Box 11: Federalism in Belgium

According to the study of Belgian federalism by Cantillon *et al.* (2006), the distribution of competencies leads to a fragmentation of several social policies between the different levels of administration; but it maintains at the federal level the social security system, the progressive income tax and the definition of a certain number of criteria (for example, the minimum income level). The exclusive competence for the function of redistribution is thus given to the highest level. In conformity with the classical (functional) economic theory, this choice allows for a real redistribution of income from the Flemish (rich) region to the poorer region of Wallonia[33]: the inequalities between the two regions are thus reduced (1997) by 75%. The study also simulates the effects of a transfer of the redistributive competence to the sub-federal entities (which is the subject of a debate in Belgium): such reform would aggravate the inequalities (increase of the available income for the inhabitants of Flanders by 7%, decrease of the income of the Walloons by 4%, increase of the poverty rate by 5 points in Wallonia). Moreover, the theory of fiscal competition between sub-federal entities comes up here against the weakness of the mobility of enterprises and people (in particular owing to the fact of the difference of languages). Finally, the hypotheses of the regional differentiation of preferences and of the regional innovations find a certain empirical echo.[34]

A study of Rodden (2002) tests the impact of the appropriations (grants) from the State (federal or unitary) and of the legal regime of borrowing in 43 countries from 1986 to 1996. The results do not show any relation between the size of the appropriations and the financial imbalances of sub-national entities. On the one hand, the restrictions on loans limit the possibilities of deficits. On the other hand, the combination of a regime of freedom of borrowing and of an important system of appropriations (thus less own exclusive taxation) increases the risk of deficits. This way, followed by a large number of countries, notably developing countries, is thus dangerous in the long term. Another study (Khemani, 2007) relative to Indian federalism also brings some light on the role of law. In India, the States ensure at least half of public spending, but only about 30% of total fiscal receipts are their own resources. The other resources mainly come from federal appropriations and from loans (for a big part given by the federal government). Two agencies, the one constitutionally independent (the "Finance Commission"), the other attached to the federal government (the "Planning Commission"), ensure the distribution of appropriations between the States. The study shows that the action of the independent agency, whose status is guaranteed by the Indian constitution of 1950, has the effect of limiting the

33 The effect of tax progressiveness is stronger for the inhabitants of Flanders (who have higher incomes), and the beneficiaries of social transfers are mainly the inhabitants of Wallonia. The reduction of the inequalities after payment of taxes and social security contributions and after reception of social transfers, is diminished (Gini coefficient) in the two regions (in 1997, disposable revenue measured by the Gini coefficient is 0.225 for Flanders and 0.236 for Wallonia), and the reduction of the inequalities between the two regions is 75%.

34 Master's degrees are earned in two years in Wallonia contrary to one year in Flanders: Flanders thus participates in the extra cost decided by Wallonia, through the federal device of the financing of higher education. Regional innovations were carried out as regards the social integration of under-qualified young people.

impact of the partisan attribution of appropriations by the governmental commission[35] (namely the fact of belonging to the majority, the division between left and right etc.).

From a political point of view, the democracy of proximity is supported by the budgetary autonomy achieved. It can satisfy local preferences, regionalist demands, and ease ethnic tensions in certain countries. The large political movement of decentralization, going up to federalism, of these last few decades has become a reality: it accompanies the democratic transitions in Latin America, Asia, Africa, and in the former Soviet-bloc countries; it also concerns the old democracies of Europe. Henceforth the diversity of the experimented institutional arrangements leads to the questioning of the traditional theories of fiscal federalism, inspired by the particular case of the United States.[36] As we have seen, the legal analysis of competencies finds its place because it structures the power play between the different decision-making levels. For example (Leroy, 2005), in Russia the decision to appoint the governors of the Regions by the central authority (2004) puts into question the effectiveness of its federalism. A centralization of resources to the advantage of the federal budget has been implemented since 1990. In Italy, the constitutional reform of 2001 introduces a major institutional change: it reinforces the power of regions which henceforth have large institutional powers and a strong financial autonomy at their disposal. In this way, regionalism approaches a form of federalism. We must also emphasize the particular electoral context of this change: the regions held by the Northern League refuse to finance the poor Southern regions through the national budget. We should now turn to the study of interest groups.

3. Socio-economic Groups

In addition to the possibility of mobilizing themselves against the government (social conflicts), the ordinary power of socio-economic groups (Campbell, 1993) is materialized in their access to institutions: they then constitute pressure groups. An example is provided by the study of Jacobs (1987) using American data of 1960 which shows the influence of enterprises on fiscal policy: the size of the enterprises is

35 The independent Finance Commission allocates more appropriations to the disadvantaged States on account of the partisan reasons of the governmental commission. Actually, these States are more often eligible for the objective criteria of the appropriation distribution that is decided every 5 years and concerns appropriations representing about 24% of State revenue. The governmental Planning Commission allocates appropriations representing about 6% of revenue, but is also competent to grant loans (in practice aiming at 50% of State loans).

36 For example (as we have seen) with the liberal Welfare State which conveys a certain conception of public action.

correlated with the reduction of taxes that are levied on them. Another American study (Richter *et al.*, 2010) from 1998 to 2004 shows that firms lobbying in a given year pay lower effective tax rates in the next year. But the groups also intervene through the influence of their ideas and their values. They defend their interests in numerous cases, but their collective action can take the form of a wider social movement in order to challenge the dominant values of a society or of a period. In this case these opposition groups militate in favour of a contra-culture. Within the framework of the elemental analysis of this chapter, we must point out that the influence of a socio-economic group depends on the approach to public decisions. Within the Marxist conception or within the elitist conception, a dominant group sees its interests overrepresented. Within the pluralist conception (Dahl, 1961), pressure groups balance each other on the political market. Within the neo-corporatist theory (Schmitter, 1974), the State favours the relations with certain groups (trade unions). According to the Public Choice School, pressure groups try to get the financing, by all the unorganized taxpayers/voters, of the services which are to the advantage of these groups.

The influence of pressure groups depends on their access, variable according to the countries, the time periods, and the sectors, to the decision-making institutions (cf. box 12 for the size). Postwar French corporatism, rather sector-based, witnessed the influence of a modernizing ruling elite composed of high-ranking officials. In the United States, (lobbying) interest groups are officially recognized according to an "iron triangle" associating an administrative department, an interest group, and the competent Congressional committee. In the Scandinavian States or in the German State, labour unions are influential at central level of the State, especially when the left is strong. Nevertheless, in most cases, the mass of taxpayers is not organized as a pressure group. The institutional arrangement, particular to each country, is relevant, even though the places of expression of interests are varied in contemporary society. An illustration is given by a Japanese study of the revolt against the property tax of the 1990s (Jinno, Dewitt, 1998): the group mobilization of the speculators owes its success to the institutional rivalry between the ministry of Economics and the ministry of Finance.

Box 12: The influence of the groups' size

Olson (1966) maintains that the number of participants hinders group efficiency: small groups easily take action to receive public expenditure in their favour; in big groups everybody benefits from the results of an action, including those (the "free riders") who are not mobilized. Olson's analysis especially raises the problem of incentives of collective action (by coercion, reserved advantages). We must therefore distinguish the conditions of the mobilization, difficult for the latent interest groups, and the success factors, among which the number of participants can be important. Empirically, another study provides a statistical verification of the influence of the number of parents on spending on education (in 1960, 1970, 1980, 1990) in 48 American States: the higher the number of parents in the electorate, the higher the *per capita* spending of the State in this domain (Miller, 1996, p. 179); the same study (p. 181) confirms this result in the case of spending on education (in 1970, 1980) studied in 253 counties of Texas.

Pampel (1994) studies, in 18 developed countries from 1959 to 1986, spending in favour of elderly people. He emphasizes the influence of the socio-political context. In the United States, this spending is higher than for young people, which is explained by the pluralistic context (competition of groups, weakness of left-wing parties) which allows numerous groups (here, groups of elderly) to influence spending; for Scandinavian countries, which are corporatist (support of parties in the government, weight of labour unions at the central level, strength of the working class), the size of the elderly group does not intervene: the Welfare State is as generous to the young as to the elderly, if the left is in power and if the ideology is universalist. For the other countries of Europe where corporatism is weaker, the demographic variable (measured by the size of the elderly group) influences spending positively, including when the left is in power.

Lowry and Potosky (2004) study the discretionary subsidies of the American federal government to the States (from 1991 to 1998). They measure the influence of organized interest groups[37], with regard to the political supply[38], and with regard to the latent demand.[39] The effects of the organized groups are verified and they constitute the first factor of statistical explanation of subsidies, except for agriculture. The latent demand has a significant influence, but not as big as the effect of the organized groups (except for agriculture). The political supply has a very small impact, except for subsidies for the environment.

So, if the power of pressure groups is not to be neglected in order to understand tax policy, one should not overestimate this factor. In fact, a good part of the empirical studies concern American data which are particular in an institutional context traditionally more open to interest groups. Even if the pluralistic approach of public decision-making competes with other schools, it is in fact admitted that interests groups in the United States have a significant weight. If the situation varies according to the history of every country, the autonomy (more or less

---

37 Namely: private, non-profit organizations, municipal and district governments.

38 Namely: % of representatives in the Congress, % in the legislative committees, weight in the federal majority.

39 Namely: weight of the urban population, level and stability of revenue, employment rate.

substantial) of the State, or more broadly of public institutions, by nature implies a certain independence with regard to pressure groups.

It is also important to know the values, the cultures of the groups. For example, in Sweden the institutional compromises on tax policy are facilitated by the fact that the trade unions and the social-democrat parties accept the compromise with capitalism. Consequently, the recent Swedish pension reform was elaborated starting from the agreement of a committee composed of five of the seven parties represented in the Swedish parliament (or 85% of the members of parliament). This large coalition was able to establish a new mechanism for the financing of pensions[40] by relying on the idea that the reform had to ensure the equilibrium of the system over the long term. Inversely, the ideologies of certain parties or trade unions of breaking off from capitalism do not facilitate compromises.

Finally, the impact of pressure groups is for a large part explained by the influence of their argumentation on the conception of public issues (cf. Figure 2). The ideological lobbying then consists in justifying the interests of a group by using reasons of public interest. On tax matters, Eisenstein (1961) for instance considers that taxation reflects the ideologies of interest groups. He distinguishes three basic ideologies: the ideology of ability has led to the promotion of progressiveness; inversely, the ideology of barriers and deterrents insists on the disincentives to invest and on the risks for the economic growth (notably the progressiveness); the ideology of equity pushes towards the equality of treatment of individuals in the same situation. One must also consider the case of partisan ideologies.

4. The Left-Right Division

The left-right division sometimes proves to be an explanatory variable of the policies followed in the field of taxation and/or public expenditure. The left has often defended in its electoral programs a redistributive system through taxes and/or social expenditure in order to reduce inequalities. But the partisan factor actually has a relative impact, except for certain "ideological" periods and in the case of public expenditure where its impact is more distinct. Political programs, even those marked by a strong ideology, are rarely applied with all their radicality.

---

40 Source: *Conseil d'Orientation des Retraites*, Letter No. 2, February, 2009. The new system (which is gradually introduced according to the generations) replaces the regime based only on distribution by a regime based at the same time on distribution and capitalization.

a. Ideological (partisan) periods

Some periods appear more "ideological" than others. For example in the American case, a statistical analysis (of data for 1994) concludes that the left-right division, the degree of competition between the parties, and political alternation influence taxation in the direction of a more or less large progressiveness of taxes (Martinez, 1997). In England, Steinmo (1993) confirms the existence of ideological periods for the tax policy between 1946 and 1975.[41] As a study of 792 budgets of English municipalities from 1974 to 1988 shows (Page *et al.*, 1990), the confrontation between the leftist radicalism and the Thatcherian liberalism had a significant impact on local tax policies.

It is interesting to look more closely at public spending because it mobilizes tax policy in its function of financing. The partisan division is more often confirmed empirically, in particular in the field of social welfare expenditure.[42] For Esping-Andersen, the Welfare State of the universalist kind has a social-democrat character: it is "leftist" by allowing workers not to be subject to the constraint to sell their labour on the market at no matter what condition. We must also recall that a redistributive system through taxes and/or social expenditure leads to the reduction of inequalities.

Korpi and Palm (2003) defend the "power resources approach" in order to understand the Welfare State. In the 18 countries studied for the period from 1975 to 1995, economic logic plays a less important role than political factors linked to the power stemming from class conflicts on the labour market. The degree of retrenchment or resilience of the Welfare State depends little on globalization, but much more on the partisan variable which curbs social cuts more or less (according to the context): the left increases social expenditures significantly in case of worsening unemployment (theory of compensation), even if it tends to diminish them when the situation of public finance is bad. A recent study (Castles, 2009) concerning all OECD countries in 2003 confirms the impact of the partisan variable on the global social expenditure.

As it has been mentioned with regard to taxation, in the United Kingdom, the period of 1970-1990 is characterized by the left-right division in a context characterized by the ideology of the limitation of spending of the Thatcher government. Empirically the impact of the left-

41 "Each time the Labour party entered office it raised income taxes for this group, thus decreasing PDI (Personal Disposable Income). But Labour's actions were largely counteracted by Tory tax policies that reduced income taxes" (Steinmo, 1993, p. 47).

42 These studies are in general on OECD countries. We can mention for Latin America, the study of 18 countries from 1970 to 1980 by Huber *et al.* (2008) that shows that the partisan variable does not play a role in social expenditure.

right division is pointed out by several studies (Lewis (1982, p. 166); Edgell, Duke, 1982; Lewis, Jackson, 1985; Page *et al.*, 1990; Ibrahim, 1994). In the United States, an opinion survey conducted during the presidential elections of 1992 (Jacoby, 2000, p. 762) shows that, contrary to the Republicans, the Democrats and the Liberals are rather favorable to public spending. Another study on the voting of American members of parliament (Gill, Thurber, 1999) shows that the partisan variable played an important role during the struggle of the Republican Congress (1995-1996) with the Democratic President Clinton. In South America from 1990 to 2006, Hart (2010) finds that partisanship is a reliable indicator of tax revenue.

b. A rather weak impact on tax policy and more relevant in spending

It is thus not fair to say that tax policy or public spending programs are determined (in the exact meaning of the word) by the political color of the government, even if this variable can play a role. In his article, presented as a synthesis, Campbell (1993, p. 170) thinks that the left-right division has relatively little effect on taxation policy in the United States. According to the Cusack's study (1999), covering 14 OECD countries from 1961 to 1991, the effect of partisan division sometimes intervenes in an unexpected way: the left, which is nonetheless more sensitive to unemployment, conducts more rigorous budgetary policies (control of deficits) than the right, which is preoccupied by tax cuts, but is less efficient to reduce public spending. We also know that, during the 20th century, American federal governments (Republican or Democrat) always taxed enterprises rather heavily, at least until the 1970s (Morgan, Prasad, 2009). In Sweden, the introduction of the progressive income tax in 1902 is for a big part explained (Steinmo, 1993, p. 64) by the financial needs of the State and a little by pressure from the left. The tax policy of the United States, Great Britain and Sweden is characterized by social compromises. Between 1920 and 1945, high marginal rates (striking the rich) are applied to income tax and the tax on the profit of enterprises becomes more important; in return, the generalization of income tax amongst all classes of society and the growth of indirect taxes on consumption are recorded. After the Second World War, the right wing in power in the United States, in England and in Sweden does not directly call into question again the progressiveness of income tax rate.

In the case of the Indian federalism, according to Khemani (2007, p. 481) the governmental allocation commission favours the federal States that are favorable to it with regard to the allocation of certain appropriations. But this partisan division is counterbalanced (cf. the studies on federalism) by the existence of an independent commission which grants subsidies based on objective criteria. Nevertheless, another study (Nichoson-Crotty *et al.*, 2006) dealing with the spending choices in 50 American states between 1971 and 1996 concludes that the left-wing States are more favourable to social expenditure (in the wide meaning of the term). But the Mitbo's study (1999) over 100 years concerning six Scandinavian and Anglo-Saxon countries shows that public sector growth is not much explained (statistically) by this political factor. The analysis of tax policy in France does not confirm either the general impact of the left/right division.

c. *The case of tax policy in France*

It is indeed so that the creation of the income tax by Caillaux (laws of 1914 and 1917) opposed the reformist trend of the left-wing to the right-wing parties. Nevertheless, certain industrialists supported the reform by referring to the English model of taxation on income in return for a reduction in customs duties. In the same way, some conservatives thought that an income tax was a useful concession in order to avoid more radical questioning of social inequalities or economic structures. Under the Fifth Republic, the French left, when it was in power, adopted taxation advantageous for income coming from the stock-exchange which favours the rich. In addition, the tax policy debate, for a long time crystallized between fiscal redistribution recommended by the left and tax reduction wanted by the right, was put to an end during the presidential elections of 2002. A consensus between the left and the right was reached to reduce income tax. The left indeed created the tax on big fortunes, which became the solidarity tax on wealth, but its weight in the total tax revenue is not much.

Moreover, the reduction of the tax rate striking the highest income bracket is not a taboo for the French left anymore; some of its leaders defend this idea. The French fiscal doctrines of the left and of the right came closer together[43], in conformity with the convergence of policies conducted under the Fifth Republic (Leroy, 1996). For the last few years the discourse of the left has changed on some points. But the preparation for the presidential elections of 2007 also showed the divisions. Nevertheless, so big can the gap between discourse and practice be that it is difficult to foresee what would be the effective decisions if the left returns to power. In any case, in spite of certain social measures such as

---

43 On social matters, when the socialists came back to power, they did not reconsider the right-wing reform of the Balladur government of 1993 which hardened the conditions for obtaining pension. In the same way, Ségolène Royal, candidate of the Socialist Party for the presidential elections of 2007, did not include in her program the abolition of the law of 2003 voted by the right on the extension of the duration of contributions in order to benefit from a pension.

the announcement of the income of active solidarity (RSA), the program of Mr. Sarkozy, the current president, favours especially the richest people. The reduction of the wealth tax by the right-wing government, the reduction of the income tax, the tax presents to the richest people are all objects of criticism.

Under the name of "tax packet", the law in favour of work, employment and purchasing power of 21 August 2007 was voted just after the presidential and legislative elections of spring 2007. It includes a series of measures, estimated at about 14 billion euros per year. The reduction of the solidarity tax on wealth[44] constitutes a tax gift to the privileged estimated at 1.1 billion euros in 2008. The reduction of the inheritance tax[45] and the exemption of donations made by parents during their lifetime to their children, at the rate of 150,000 euros per child (possible every 6 years), also benefit the richest people. From now on, 95% of the successions are tax-exempt, instead of about 60% before the reform. Together with the exemption of donations, these measures represent a tax gift estimated at 2.2 billion per year. The reinforcement of the "tax shield", which puts the upper limit at 50% the maximum tax to be paid on annual income[46], benefits essentially the richest for a budgetary cost estimated at 800 million euros per year. This measure has the effect to limit the impact of the solidarity tax on fortune (ISF). The creation of an income of active solidarity (RSA) is destined to compensate for the possible loss of income due to the resumption of employment by the beneficiaries of certain social security payments.[47] This income creation is part of the struggle against the employment trap (costing 25 million), but also leads to a redistribution in favour of the poor. The detaxation of overtime hours, which is exempt from national insurance contributions and from taxes (including the general social contribution, so-called CSG, and the contribution for the repayment of the social debt, so-called CRDS), is estimated at 6 billion euros per year, but the current crisis should reduce this projection. The President's slogan "work more in

---

44 This is made up of a reduction of 75% of the payments made for investment in SME capital or in foundations, up to 50,000 euros a year, and of an increase of the allowance for the value of the main residence from 20 to 30%.

45 The tax on inheritance between spouses is abolished; the allowance per child increases from 50,000 euros to 150,000.

46 The tax shield has been applied since 2006. It limits the amount of taxes paid by the richest people by establishing a payment ceiling. At that time, it was applied the total tax constituted by the income tax, the solidarity tax on wealth and local taxes. Since the reform of 21 August 2007 it has included the general social contribution and the contribution for the repayment of the social debt, which are direct taxes on income destined for Social Security. The reduction went from 60% to 50%.

47 The RSA is generalized by the law of 30/12/2008. It concerns the beneficiaries of the minimum income of "insertion" (RMI) or of the single-parent allowance (API).

order to earn more" benefits especially senior executives and discourages the hiring of unemployed persons to the benefit of overtime hours. A tax exemption is also foreseen for salaried students within the limit of 3 months of the minimum wage (SMIC), for a cost estimated at 40 million. Finally, the establishment of the deduction of interest on loans for the purchase of the principal residence will cost about 3.7 billion per year.

Conclusion

The public action of the interventionist State is based on elemental factors of tax policy (cf. Figure 2). Conception and institutions occupy a central place in relation to ideas; socio-economic groups and the left-right division intervene to a more variable extent. It should be noted that the groups argue ideologically in order to influence the general societal ideas and the particular conception of the tax system. They also act, with more or less success, as pressure groups in order to lead institutions to take into account their ideas and their interests. The conception of public policy take up ideas coming from cultures, values, ideologies etc. which circulate in society. It also relies on expertise proposed or imposed by the high-level administration or certain networks of development of informal norms (soft law). The weight of groups and of the left-right division has a variable intensity according to the countries and the time periods, while conceptions, ideas and expertise play a sustainable role. Tax policy schematized in Figure 2 links up general factors, even if its functional concretization has been specified in this chapter. By being placed in the wider context of interventionist democracy and globalized capitalism, certain structural tendencies can be specified as is shown in the next chapter.

Figure 2: The elemental factors of tax policy

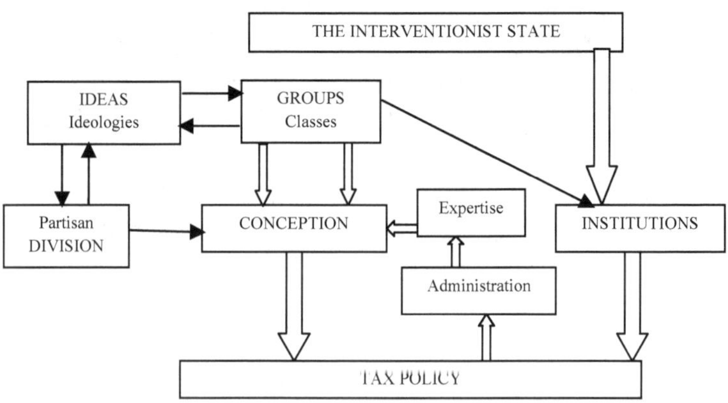

CHAPTER 7

Obstacles to Fiscal Democracy

The role of context is important, even though, as we have seen in the previous chapter, we can put this variable aside in order to target the elemental factors of tax policies. It is obvious that the general situation of capitalism and of democracy, or more commonly, the periods of elections, of ideological debates, of crisis etc. influence the configuration of public problems to be resolved by taxes and/or public spending. All the same, the use of contexts, which opens up opportunities for reflection, changes and choice, is noted by decision-makers in an ideology of deterministic constraint. If the phenomenon is not new, as the case of war financing by the tax State illustrates, it experienced a decisive turnabout with the global diffusion of the neo-liberal concept of the market. Periods of "crises" (oil crises, financial bubbles, raw materials, social welfare etc.) are reinforced here by the intensification and "financiarisation" of global capitalism, and are used to mask the real decisions of the interventionist State. Democratic consultation on possible choices is thus limited, in particular by the lack of clarity in the relation between tax revenue (loans, taxes) and public policies (expenditure).

It is not easy to include financial action in the classic typologies of public policies: indeed taxation is used as an instrument in a complex way within fragmented issues which are related to practically all the aspects of life in society and of the economy. By its function of financing expenditure, but also by applied incentives and disincentives, it participates in a primary or complementary way in all public policies. The social stratification of wealth is modified (fiscal redistribution, financing of social benefits) and a social categorization is created by the distinction between sources of income (storekeepers, employees, owners, company leaders, professions, farmers etc.). Taxes encourage the creation of enterprises, investments in certain sectors, innovation and research; they classify and organize territories into a hierarchy (tax exemption zones, ecological conservation etc.) etc. They indeed constitute the hardcore of interventionist public action in rich societies. Consequently, the ideological staging of the determinisms of the constraint of the globalized market crises leads to a biased "configuration" (scheme) of public action which weakens democracy.

1. Against the Determinism of Contextual Factors

Certain exceptional circumstances, such as wars or socio-economic difficulties, are treated as crisis constraints, while they also offer opportunities for change. The same determinism characterizes the exaggerated interpretation of the incremental importance of the past. In reality, the contexts have a variable character (crises, ideological periods, new elected officials, electoral cycle etc.) and leave a margin of manoeuvre to public action, as the cases of the economic globalization and of the European Union norms in public finance show.

a. The cognitive approach to the changes of crises

As we have seen in chapter 4, crises are often considered as a key factor of the change of tax policy. The tax crisis is that of a fundamental (structural) dysfunctioning of the financial system as a socio-economic framework in the process of transformation. As for Schumpeter, the crisis of tax State is not very likely, even in the context of a war economy. However, in the context of the late Middle Ages, the economy of a domain did not anymore correspond to the appearance of a distinction between the private sphere (encouraged by the repurchase of the military obligation by the noblemen) and the public sphere. Historians confirm the financial crisis of the domain where the king cannot anymore "live by his own domain" and needs revenue drawn from taxes (Chaunu, 1977, p. 147; Favier, 1978, p. 170; Genet, 1990, p. 266). Even if Campbell (1993, p. 167) refers to it, the thesis of the crisis of the tax State was especially supported by neo-Marxists with the earlier quoted symbolic essays of Goldscheid (1917, 1967) and of O' Connor (1973).

In the context of the developed countries, the thesis of the tax crisis is doubtful. Without taking up again the criticism formulated in chapter 4, we must remember that the increase of tax revenue, linked to a large extent to the explosion of welfare expenditure, has up to now not resulted in the bankruptcy of the big States. New sources of income exist, for example with the suppression of tax exemptions (niches), or as in France with the creation of taxes (CSG, CRDS) in order to finance the social security (Leroy, 1996). The future of the Welfare State is above all a socio-political problem. But one should also emphasize the relevance of cognitive factors. The context of a crisis serves as an argument to convince people of the necessity to increasing the weight of taxation on the biggest number of people; it facilitates the reception of the reform justified by constraint, even when the reform goes against the interests (in the sense of the utilitarian rationality of economists) and/or the values of citizen-taxpayers. It is thus indeed through cognitive rationality that the legitimacy of reforms in time of crisis is explained.

The other crises, namely of an economic or social nature or related to war (Peacock, Wiseman, 1967) constitute other contexts whose direct impact is systemic (cf. chapter 5). As Pareto pointed out, a context of economic growth creates supplementary revenue which open up choices. Inversely a recession restricts tax collection while at the same time pushing for the increase of welfare expenditure (scissors effect). As figure 3 shows, the budgets of the interventionist State are sensitive to environment but are not determined by economic constraints. In a context of an economic crisis, the real choice, whether it is efficient or not, of a reflation through public spending or inversely through rigor (cuts) is political. The social crisis can proceed from the poor economic situation which is represented by a deterioration of employment (unemployment). It can also have other sources, as in the case of the French Revolution where, as Tocqueville shown it, a number of factors accumulated to change the political regime and its unfair tax system. Tax revolts (cf. chapter 9) are symptomatic of a social crisis: collective action denies the political legitimacy of taxes and sometimes succeeds in having public policy modified (except where the way of repression is chosen). War leads to particular financial choices. For example, the English income tax was established in 1798 to finance the war against France; abolished afterwards, it was restored in order to face up to a recession that affected ordinary workers particularly (Ardant, 1972, p. 382). This change, valid for the first country to have established the income tax in a lasting way, also exists in the United States: the origin of the first federal income tax is linked to the financial needs created by the American Civil War (Leroy, 1996).

Here again the true causal variable is of cognitive nature. The context allows for the modification of the way of reasoning. A crisis, together with other variables, acts on the general aspects of the problem and leads actors to modify the tax policy. One must cite again the case of the "Washington Consensus" which served as the ideology for the intervention of the IMF and the World Bank in the years 1980-1990. The argument was that in order to take countries out of the economic crisis, it was necessary to diminish debt and reduce public spending, free the markets, and privatize. This choice presented as an absolute economic necessity turned out to be disastrous in most cases. For example, a study (Jonakin, Stephen, 1999) of 5 countries of Central America from 1975 to 1999 shows that spending on education (human capital) declined or at best stagnated. The analysis of Stiglitz (2002, 2006), a Nobel Prize winner in economics, has also insisted on this criticism of the deterioration of human capital to the benefit of financial priorities economically badly founded. The economic argumentation of experts of the Washington Consensus corresponded in fact to a neo-liberal conception which once again used the constraints of the context (a crisis). The reception of this program was facilitated ("cognitively") by its economic core.

War can be financed by other means than taxation, namely by borrowing, the sale of assets, and the reduction of certain expenditure. It does not always imply financial needs, as it can also constitute a source of revenue (cf. the Roman tribute mentioned in chapter 4). For example, under the reign of Louis XII (1498-1515), war outside the borders produced a decline in taxation in France. We also saw that war in Latin America did not entail the extension of the tax State (Centeno, 1997, p. 1598). Taxes can weigh on poor or rich, on households or enterprises through the modification of the bases and/or rates and through exemptions granted. It is thus indeed a question of legitimacy (that depends on an approach based on cognitive rationality) which is at stake. Moreover the alternation of periods of crisis and of slowdown is not new.

Hence, the determinism of the socio-economic contexts of crises appears doubtful when facing available choices. The crisis of the summer of 2008 has thus brought forward again the question of the financial bankruptcy of the State. The systemic globalization of the economy explains that the subprime crisis of the American property market propagated from banks to stock exchanges, then from stock exchanges to economic activities, and that it provokes a social crisis in several countries. We saw in the previous chapter that States intervened through public finance first to support banks then to reflate the economy. Debt is thus going to increase for many countries to a great extent. It is however unlikely that the public finance of the big States will collapse.[1] The context leaves political choices open, even for the countries with the most difficulties.[2] It offers an opportunity to follow the precepts of Goldscheid by nationalizing of the banks, instead of merely granting loans: in this case, the State will be able to recover a part of its spending (through the profits of the nationalized enterprises) once economic growth is back. Likewise, the stimulation by consumption or by investments can be privileged. In the absence of serious regulation, the failure of financial capitalism is more severe, especially if the international monetary, stock-exchange and banking order is not reformed and if the social crisis of employment is not addressed: indeed, the big sum of

1 In a study of 44 countries (1790-2009), Reinhart and Rogoff (2010, p. 7) find that "it is evident that there is no obvious link between debt and growth until public debt reaches a thresholf of 90 percent" of GDP. Thus Public debt, even if it is an important challenge, is not a constraint (determinism) for political choices.

2 For the countries who appeal for IMF loans, the imposed constraints, such as to reduce public spending in order to keep in check the deficit, are justified by diverse arguments which recall the ideology of the "Washington Consensus" of the 1980s. In reality it is a question of privileging lenders to the detriment of political choices to be made in order to ensure the economic future of countries democratically.

public money engaged in saving the caste of the privileged creates a situation that reminds one of the context of the French Revolution studied by Tocqueville. But the contexts of crises do not always lead to radical disruptions; they are often related to quiet times of public policies.

b. The false evidence of incrementalism

The theory of incrementalism (Lindblom, 1959) indicates that changes are carried out with small-scale adjustments. The sociologist Wildavsky (1964), already quoted for his cultural theory (chapter 6), is the authority referred to in the case of budgetary incrementalism. Analyzing the decisions by the Congressional committees on the distribution (appropriations) of credits of the American federal budget within the administrations from 1946 to 1963, he maintains that the budget is renewed on the basis of the previous year with few modifications (less than 10%). In a comparative study (Wildavsky, 1975), this sociologist considers that incrementalism is applicable to all public budgets, which is also maintained by other researchers for the United States (Fenno, 1973), Norway (Cowart *et al.*, 1975), England (Rose, Davies, 1994), and France (Siné, 2003).

Incrementalism relates at the same time to the inertness of decision-making and of results with regard to the previous year, something which should be appraised critically. The size of the programs of stimulation by public expenditure, which follows the crisis of 2008, shows the limits of the incremental theory. Of course, it is obvious that in some particular contexts, budgets do not vary much from one year to another. In the same way, nobody contests that changes are sometimes (but not always) slow. The problem is that the incremental theory does not limit itself to these banalities, which is often however common practice of all scientific knowledge; it lays claim to the generality of this constraint of the past and does not hesitate to reify a form of determinism by describing why public policy cannot change. According to a study based on systematic comparisons of 9 governmental units (Jones *et al.*, 2009), if budgets are often incremental, large changes are found. The theory of incrementalism, similarly to related theories of past constraints or of budget inertness, denies in this way the possibility of a radical reform, of a "big-bang" of public policies. Nevertheless, the impact of the crisis of 2008 (public plans to reflate the economy) show that limits of incrementalism to predict large changes in the volume of public budgets (debt, expenditure and, later, taxation). Incrementalism was moreover tested empirically especially for expenditures, and less for revenues.

In tax matters, next to small-scale changes by adjustments, which are preferred by certain governments or in certain periods, there exist radical reforms with important effects. We saw that crises often serve as a pretext for creating new tax revenues and/or accentuating fiscal burden. History testifies to tax changes brought about. For example, in Great Britain, the taxation of British experienced 38 important changes between 1945 and 1972 (Steinmo, 1993, p. 46). Radical reforms of the Thatcher government led to important modifications of tax system, with notably the reduction of the marginal rate of income tax and the cuts in (social) public spending: between 1979 and 1988 the effect of the reform was to increase from 32% to 40% the burden (net of social-security benefits) of the most deprived quintile, while the ratios declined from 37% to 35% for the richest quintile (Steinmo, 1993, p. 173). Poll tax reform was also a radical reform which moreover provoked a revolt. In the United States, the reforms of Reagan in 1981 and 1986, which were also inspired by supply-side economics, had no incremental character, even though their real effects were much more limited.[3] In France, during the last twenty years of the 20th century, several new (or rediscovered) taxes were implemented: wealth tax, proportional income tax (CSG) in order to finance social security.

Sometimes changes are slower to observe than the simple comparison with the previous year. The continuous rise of tax revenue since 1914 (cf. chapter 5), and the appearance of general synthetic taxes illustrate this fact. It is also necessary to mention the increasing importance of derogations which constitute "tax expenditures" for economic and social purposes. Incrementalism in decision-making that supposes proceeding by gradual adjustments often has important medium- or long-term effects, as the case of the reduction of income tax rates demonstrates: between 1995 and 2004, it is important to remember, the marginal tax rate was reduced from 49% to 43% in the OECD countries. The relative stability of the tax revenue structure, which contains the same group of taxes classified in a similar way over long periods of time, must not either hide the reality of the changes brought about in the tax base or tax rates: the distribution of the tax burden between citizens is affected, as is attested by the increase of inequalities, which the tax redistribution does not succeed in containing anymore (chapters 11 and 12).

As for public expenditure, reservations must also be raised (Leroy, 2007, p. 41), even if it is not a question of denying that expenditure of high inertness exists (debt, remunerations, social action). According to the incrementalism of decision-making, negotiation automatically renews the budget of the previous year. But in the case of the American federal budget, the administrations ask for big increases in credits (LeLoup, 1978, p. 495) which are not reflected in the President's document (used for incremental studies). A budget can be incremental at

[3] The reduction of marginal rates and the suppression of certain tax niches were mitigated by the tax rebates and exemptions created by Congress.

some point, but not afterwards. A study by Ryu *et al.* (2007) for example points out that in 1998 the requests of 1,175 administrations in the 50 American states were divided as follows: 5% decreasing, 21% identical, and 74% increasing, even though only 14% asked for a sharp increase (more than 10%). These numbers correspond to certain degree of incrementalism over the year considered, but the facts can change very quickly, as the scale of 2009 American program of stimulation by public spending illustrates. The generalization of such results leads to a determinism of the renewal of budgets. Propositions for expenditure are part of a dynamic budgetary process which implies distinguishing between preparation, vote, implementation, and control. For example, the study (Potoski, Talbert, 2000) of 3,000 decisions of the Congress from 1994 to 1996 on redistribution policies shows that, during the preparation, bills are multidimensional, in order to obtain wide political support. At the voting stage, they are reduced to a determining dimension for the ballot. During the implementation we find a variety of dimensions of preparation (texts are not applied literally).

In France, under the regime of the organic law of 2 January 1959, the procedure legally gave an importance to the credits to pursue the execution of public services ("voted services" of article 33): this budget of financial means constrained especially the Parliament, and less the ministries, by establishing a global single vote for the voted services of the general budget (Leroy, 2007). As for the preparation, the renewal is not identical to the previous year. Moreover, the framing letters of the Prime Minister always insist on the curbing of expenditure, and the negotiation is based on this renewal and on the new procedures requested by ministries. With the organic law (LOLF) of 1 August 2001 the notion of voted services does not exist anymore (except in the absence of a vote on the budget act). The adoption of this reform shows that radical change is possible. The gap (Lambert, Migaud, 2005, p. 13) between ministerial requests and governmental framing (16 milliard on average before the reform) became more pronounced (23 milliard in 2006). In terms of local finance, a study of the Rhône-Alpes region in France (Leroy, 2001) shows that, despite a big financial margin of manœuvre, political choices of stability are carried out by the regional executive: refusal of the increase in local tax rates, limitation of the debt with repayment increasing by 269% in 1997 with regard to 1996. Considering the number of amendments tabled by elected representatives, we also notice that the contest of the regional budget is sometimes important. As for French departments, which are in fact in charge of heavy social action expenditure, Maurel's (2006) study shows that their margin of manœuvre in 2006 remains strong for 1/3 of the departments. Finally, as a study of 234 cities in France (Le Duff, Orange, 1997) shows, the margin of manœuvre depends on the political choice (strategy) of the decision-maker (mayor) with regard to financial risk (loan, taxation and spending). It is also necessary to note that in many countries, following the requirements of the European Union on deficit limitation in member states, budgetary choices are multi-annual. These results contradict to the incremental inertness of decision-making by a more refined conception of budgetary change.

Result incrementalism makes the most of the weakness of annual variations in the volume of public budgets, but retains a too high level of aggregation of spending. For example, Anglo-Saxon studies focus on the level of agencies (ministries or big administrations), and the French study of Siné (2003) concerns 7 aggregated categories of spending. Sometimes, only the global volume of the budget is measured. In general, at this level of aggregation, the annual modifications are actually weak with regard to the total amount of credits in question. But modifications exist at the non-aggregated level of data. At a finer level of the French budget (Siné, 2003, p. 187), 7 out of 28 budgets vary significantly, a fact which weakens result incrementalism; likewise, if the annual variations in actual spending are weak, the variations in the initial credits of finance acts are important: there is a place for the political game of the actors. French incrementalism is also a product of parliamentary weakness; following the LOLF of 2001, the State budget becomes a budget of objectives and not anymore a budget of means renewed annually. Another methodological problem results from the fact that considerable changes may occur within a stable budgetary volume. According to several American studies (Kanter, 1972; Natchez, Bupp, 1973; Moreland, 1975), the reallocation of credits modifies the structure of spending. LeLoup (1978) even talks about the myth of incrementalism. It is also necessary to take into account the modifications of the perimeter of the budget (privatization, decentralization etc.) and the rhythm of changes. Sometimes a decision has weak budgetary consequences for the following year, but significant consequences afterwards. In empirical studies the dependent variable is the volume of the budget of the previous year, a fact which smooths, and sometimes occults, multi-annual changes: stating that there is not much variation in the global mass of the budget becomes a truism which does not prejudge the margin of political manœuvre over several years. It is evident that the modifications of the working time or of the period of contributions for pensions, the sector-based or global stimulation plans etc. have real budgetary consequences. One should therefore restore the diversity of the effects and of the open choices created by the economic and political situation.

c. *The varied impact of economic and political contexts*

Public finance is sometimes used in the context of political instability resulting from conflicts in society. Relying on a global index of the ethno-linguistic and religious fragmentation, Annett (2001) for example emphasizes that public spending is used to ensure political stability. This empirical result validates the economic theory of social fragmentation which predicts a spiral of growth of spending: the fragmentation of society creates a political instability that public spending combats by trying to calm ethnic and religious conflicts.

The theory of the varieties of capitalism insists on the complementarity of the forms of social welfare and the types of economy within the framework of the same socio-economic system. In this vein Hall and Soskice (2001) distinguish capitalist economies with coordinated or non-coordinated (liberal) markets. Sometimes this theory appears as a criticism of the typology of the Welfare State founded on the strength of the labour movement, typology such as it was notably established by Esping-Andersen (1990). Indeed, the analysis of the Welfare State is blamed for not taking into account differences in economic contexts. The theory of the varieties of capitalism is itself put into question when it uses a rigid conception of the (closed) system, whose internal logic poorly explains the diversity of the processes of social change (except for change by incrementalism). The systemic reading of the interdependence of the economy and the social sector implies accepting the opening of the system to a plurality of factors (Becker, 2007). It is also important to emphasize that the sub-system of social welfare does not always have functions for the sub-system of economic production, since it responds to other kinds of dynamics such as that of the extension of social democracy (cf. chapter 5). The conception of economic (market) and social (welfare) relations structures the agreements that the actors try to make prevail, based on compromises that are actually variable (cf. chapter 11): the functional reading of the Welfare State has to start with the tax State which is constituted by its own political definition in Western democracies, and not by the competitiveness of the economy. It should also be noted (Schröder, 2009) that the theory of the varieties of capitalism can be combined with the typologies of the Welfare State.[4] In fact, all these approaches acknowledge a liberal model, but distinguish themselves within the number of models that coexist with it.[5]

---

4 The connection of the theory of the varieties of capitalism and of the Welfare State was also tested (Iversen, Stephen, 2008) in the field of human capital (skills for the economy, and public action in the field of education).

5 From the perspective of the French school of regulation (Boyer, 2004), four forms of capitalism are distinguished: the (liberal) market model (Australia, Canada, the United States, New Zealand, the United Kingdom etc.) becoming financial in the 1990s;

The response to the political or economic context may vary as the case of the New York budgetary policy illustrates. In this field Kantor and David (1983) propose a typology of budgetary decision-making by having 2 variables that intersect: the local economic situation and the political support to the municipality (cf. table 8). "Incrementalism" (of decision-making and of results), sometimes considered as a key variable of budgetary decision-making, appears as a particular case where political support is stable within a favourable economic context: it is then possible to satisfy the groups of support to the municipality without too many budgetary modifications. Empirically, incrementalism is verified for New York from 1945 to 1962. If the political support of the team in power declines and if the economic situation is favorable (which generates revenue), the budgetary policy becomes "pluralistic", in the sense that it uses, by bargaining with social groups, (increasing) spending in order to gain new support. That was the case for New York from 1962 to 1975.

Table 8: Budgetary practices according to the local context

Local political support Local economy	Stable	Unstable
Growing	Budgetary incrementalism (New York 1945-1962)	Budgetary pluralism (New York 1962-1975)
Declining	Budgetary elitism (New York 1975-1980)	Budgetary control

Source: according to Kantor, David, 1983

If the economic situation is deteriorating, which reduces the margin for manœuvre, and if political support remains stable, budgetary policy becomes "elitist": it is influenced by economic leaders, in order to avoid the relocation of enterprises notably, to the detriment of the bargaining with the other social groups whose demands are neutralized by certain stratagems (a targeted and temporary increase in certain items of spending). In 1975 the financial crisis of New York City is precipitated by the conjugation of a deteriorated economic situation and of a distributive budget, which results in the intervention of the State and of the federal State who put into place new supervising institutions dominated by businessmen. This period of elitist budgets, which is also marked by cuts in spending, ends in 1980. The fourth type of budgetary policy is

State capitalism (Germany, Belgium, Spain, France etc.); the particular (meso-corporatist) model of Japan (and of Korea); social-democratic capitalism (Sweden, Finland, Denmark, Norway). From a strictly empirical perspective, Amable (2003) proposes 5 types of capitalism: liberal, continental, Mediterranean, Asian and social-democratic. Cf. also the essay of Albert (1991) distinguishing the Alpine-Rhenish capitalism from the neo-American model.

that of public finance "control" (curbing) within the context of decline of the economic situation and of political support: spending is focused on the revitalization of the local economy, but without being under the influence of the local economic elite who is contested. This situation appeared in New York, notably with the dissatisfaction of municipal employees and of certain groups of beneficiaries of social security, but an economic upturn has cut short this budgetary phase.

According to the theory of political cycles, the budget follows a cyclical rate in order to satisfy voters, an idea which is supported notably by the school of public choice. The idea of an electoral cycle thus implies the autonomy of elected officials in the use of tax revenue and spending. It marks the dependence of the budget on electoral dates. For the team in power, the "opportunist cycle" consists in diminishing taxes and increasing expenditure on the eve of elections. The "partisan cycle" corresponds to the budgetary implementation of the political program in the year following the election of the team in power. This theory is attractive, but is only very partially confirmed, as table 9 shows.

Table 9: The influence of the electoral cycle on the budget

Sample	Period	Results	Authors
Denmark, Finland, France, Italy, Norway, Sweden	1978-1986	Yes for expenditure increase No for revenue	Mouritzen, 1989
92 American cities > 100,000 inhabitants	1978-1985	Yes: especially increase in revenue and increase in expenditure.	Strate, Wolman, Melchior, 1993
20 American cities		Yes: revenue and expenditure increase No: weight of past decisions	Bhattacharyya Wassmer, 1995
10 Canadian provinces	1951-1984	Yes (but weak) for social and infrastructure expenditure	Blais, Nadeau, 1992
105 cities > 50,000 inhabitants	1988	No, expenditure depends on fiscal policy	Bosch, Suarez-Pandiello, 1995
10 Israeli cities	1964-1982	No, candidates who do not run for election increase expenditure more than the others	Rosenberg, 1992
883 French cities > 10,000 inhabitants	1988-1999	Yes for capital expenditure and for debt	Binet, Pentecote, 2004
Local public admini-strations (France)	1965-2000	Yes for expenditure on investment	Besson, 2002
91 French cities > 50,000 inhabitants	1977-2001	Yes for public expenditure, especially investment	Foucault, François, 2005

Source: According to Foucault, François, 2005, completed by Leroy, 2007

These debates on the forms of public decision-making, without being negligible, have become less visible as a result of the ideological diffusion of the constraint imposed by economic globalization.

d. The economic ideology of globalization

According to the theory of market efficiency (Tanzi, 1995), economic globalization obliges political decision-makers to remain competitive for investment by reducing taxes: the Welfare State is undermined by globalization because of the flight of capital, fiscal dumping, fiscal competition (relocation of enterprises) and the diminution of the power of parties and trade unions. On the contrary, the theory of compensation (Pierson, 1994; Garret, 1998; Scharpf, 2000) maintains that the tax State fights against the negative effects of globalization (insecurities, inequalities) in order to satisfy the work force, vested interests, the veto of established powers, or the dependence on regulations and institutional agreements of the past. Despite certain methodological difficulties linked to the indicators used, empirical studies prove that economic globalization does not necessarily destroy the Welfare State because it often resists. The determinism of the globalized market is invalidated.

Empirically, the effects of globalization depend on indicators of reference that are used. The study by Garret and Mitchell (2001) of 18 OECD countries (1961-1993) gives the following results. Firstly, measured with regard to the volume of exchange or to the openness of financial markets, economic globalization does not reduce the taxation of capital, a fact which invalidates the determinist theory of market efficiency. As for public expenditure, even if globalization slowly reduces its total, this result is not pronounced enough to support the thesis of State retrenchment (market efficiency). Secondly, when the indicator of dependence towards countries with low salaries is retained, public expenditure grows, which confirms the theory of compensation by resistance of the State. Thirdly, measured by the indicator of foreign investment, globalization has no effect on welfare expenditure progressing proportionally with unemployment, which also corresponds to the theory of resilience of the Welfare State.

The data of Crepaz and Moser (2004) on 15 countries from 1960 to 1996 show that globalization, measured by trade and capital deregulation, is positively correlated with amount of spending on social transfers, which is within the framework of the theory of compensation; but this effect is sometimes blocked by current institutional arrangements, the competition of different established powers leading to a tendency to a status quo. The study by Ha (2008) of 18 developed countries from 1960 to 2000 confirms this result: globalization, measured by the volume of imports/exports and the mobility of capital, increases welfare expenditure even if, this time, the number of "veto players" (institutional blocking points) tends to moderate the effect in the opposite sense.

Korpi and Palm (2003) discuss the use of the weight of social expenditure in the GDP as an indicator of the Welfare State. They defend this approach by "the resources of the power (in place)" to explain the withdrawal (retrenchment) of the Welfare State in 18 countries for the period from 1975 to 1995. Economic logic plays a less important role than political factors linked to the power coming from the class conflicts on the labour market. The extent of the withdrawal of social action depends a little on economic globalization, but much more on the partisan variable (cf. chapter 6). The theory of compensation is also verified by the study of Castles (2009) on the social expenditure of all the OECD countries in 2003: by taking into consideration the disintegrated level of social expenditure, it indicates the inverse correlation between globalization, measured by size of imports/exports, and social expenditure in favour of the working-age population (unemployment, handicapped, family etc.). On the other hand, no correlation is found with the other categories of social expenditure (health, elderly people etc.).

Dreher (2006) confirms the importance of both globalization and social and political integration. Rudra (2002) points to the strong decline of the Welfare State in the least developed countries, whose extent of withdrawal depends on "the resources of the power (in place)" in the sense given above; but in another study (Rudra, 2007, p. 32) he emphasizes that the least developed countries always have diversified social protection systems, a situation which demonstrates a capacity to formulate autonomous social policies.

A study by Kite (2002) of 14 countries from 1973 to 1999 uses the indicator of international economic openness and does not find any clear relation between economic openness and the level of social protection (measured by spending on social transfers and social public services). Very open rich countries with a generous Welfare State do exist. Consequently, the determinism of the theory of market efficiency is invalidated: the idea that the minimal Welfare State associated with a weak power of the (unorganized) labour milieu is an advantage in a global economy is not verified, except for the United States, but still only in the 1990s.

Swank and Steinmo (2002, p. 643) emphasize that, in advanced democracies, the official tax rate for commercial companies (namely, the tax rate foreseen by the tax legislation) went down between 1981 and 1995, going on average from 45 to 35%. But the effective rate of capital taxation (which takes into account diverse tax rebates and reductions) went from 38% to 36%. Likewise, the effective rate relative to the taxation of companies and of financial activities went from 26% to 24%.

One must also note that the distribution of the tax burden between capital, labour and consumption (the structure of the tax revenue as a percentage of GDP) remained stable. Many countries compensated for the reductions in the tax rates by a widening of the taxable basis (basis of taxation): for example, the tax credit given for investment was eliminated in all countries in 1992 (Swank, 2006, p. 848).

The study by Mahler and Jesuit (2006, p. 500) confirms the resilience of the *Welfare State*: while the inequality of income before taxation and social transfers worsened in the private sector from 1980 to 2000[6], fiscal redistribution (by taxation) and social redistribution (by transfers) also increased the disposable revenue during this period. The study by Vis (2007) of 16 capitalist democracies from 1985 to 2002, which takes into account both quantitative changes (amounts of spending) and qualitative changes (social legislation), also confirms the thesis of the resilience of the Welfare State.

Hence, the over-generalization of the theory of market efficiency leads to a determinist ideology of the constraint of globalization. This ideology, developed since the 1990s, came to reinforce (cf. chapter 6) the neo-liberal conception of public finance. In the eyes of public decision-makers it legitimized the rapid growth of a financial capitalism without rules whose excesses led to the global crisis of the summer of 2008. Playing on the (false) logic of the necessities of the world market (cognitive rationality) for the economy and thus for employment, the ideology of globalization allowed one to restrain public opinions. In Europe, it coexisted with the instauration of legal constraints on public budgets.

e. The political character of the constraints of the European Union

We have already mentioned the rules laid down by the Treaties of Maastricht and Amsterdam for the member states of the European Union (EU). Public debt must be contained within the limit of 60% of the GDP and public deficit within the limit of 3% of the GDP. Here as well the determinist vision of the impact of European constraints is false. The statistical study by Hansson (2008, p. 1022) from 1970 to 2002 finds no impact of these constraints on the structure of spending of the studied countries. Moreover, we know that France and Germany had deficits in 2003 and 2004 superior to the authorized limit. Yet, in spite of the decision of the Court of Justice of the European Communities (CJEC), these countries were not sanctioned. The Treaty of Amsterdam, which eased the initial rules of the Treaty of Maastricht, clearly shows

---

6 The average Gini index increased from 0.404 in 1980 to 0.441 in 2000.

the political character of community constraints. In the case of economic recession, exceeding the limit for the deficit is authorized. Thus in March 2009 the European Commission gave big time limits to the countries threatened by a procedure for excessive deficit. We can even predict that European constraints will again be lightened if they become too constraining for the countries. The process of decision-making of the EU is essentially political contrary to the narrow vision of Community law.

In fiscal matters the rule of unanimity is required with the result that every member state has at their disposal a veto power with regard to any decision. The model is one of political bargaining. An example is provided by the context of the current crisis which also served as a pretext for "clientelist" measures with regard to the VAT on restaurant services. The demand comes from French restaurant owners who insisted on a VAT reduction in order to be able to hire more staff with the savings made.[7] It received the support of the French government, but nevertheless came up against the refusal of Europe who was competent in matters of VAT. In the context of the willingness to assist the economic stimulus policy, following 7 years of blocking, the 27 member states of the European Union accepted on the 10th of March, 2009 the reduction of VAT on restaurant services. Incidentally, according to the European model of regulation by bargaining (Leroy, 2004), several other activities were targeted at the same time: services to persons, construction, morocco-leather goods, hairdressing, bicycle repairs, toll bridges in Lisbon, gas cylinders in Cyprus, food in Malta. Hence, the determinist use of the ideology of constraints is at the root of a model of complex public action where the configuration of the problem of fiscal intervention is distorted.

2. The Distorted Configuration of Fiscal Public Action

Taxation has a special nature: it is an object in itself of public policy (tax policy) and an instrument of other public policies. Taxation is rarely considered as a global social problem turning on the democratic intervention of the State. In the ideological context of market constraints, causal biases weaken the popular consent to socio-economic instrumentation by taxation. The complexity of public action, which already proceeds from the systemic characteristics of the financial system, is aggravated to the detriment of the democratic transparency of the choices made by the decision-makers in power.

7 We should incidentally note that the stock of collective action here is that of argumentation (ideas) and not conflict (pressure).

a. The weakening of democracy by causal biases

Public action is the object of causal biases that depend on three levels of analysis whose interdependence is schematized by the figure below. Firstly, the market, institutional blockings (veto points, incrementalism etc.), crises, and economic globalization are (wrongly) presented as the over-determinants of tax policy (wide arrows on the Figure 3). These factors are strategically used by decision-makers to legitimize in the eyes of citizens a conception of determinist constraint. While providing some room for institutional limits imposed by incrementalism, veto points, Europe (for the countries concerned) etc., constraints are largely put forward at the general economic level as a necessity of the globalized market and of the crises that result from them.[8] In reality, this ideology, i.e. this exaggeration of causal determinisms (biases), conceals a certain number of real relations.

Secondly, the choices made by decision-makers (narrow arrows on Figure 3) are not presented, except in the form of answers to the constraint of public action. The important power of decision-makers, which is distributed in a different way (with certain tendencies) between institutional bodies, is not emphasized.[9] Taxation policy, which results from this biased configuration of public action, becomes a simple technical and administrative problem of adaptation to economic market constraints. The action of the interventionist State, by the redistribution of income and the categorization of society, is denied. The advantages granted to certain social groups, because of the choices of tax categorization of decision-makers, are just as much concealed, or justified by the particular economic constraints of the market: creation of enterprises, support to small enterprises, fight against relocations etc. After all, it is indeed the reality of the autonomy of the power of decision-makers and of the political choices of the interventionist State for the society that is dissimulated by this administrative configuration of public policy.

Thirdly, the biased fiscal public action weakens the classic mechanisms of democracy (arrows in dotted lines on the figure 3) by concealing the choices made and the power exercised. The variety of contexts is restricted to the two situations of constraint, namely crises and the globalization. But crises, like economic globalization, also open up the

---

8 Crises involving oil (example: the 1970s), raw materials, stock exchanges, real estate markets; crisis of a specific sector etc.

9 The power is the real power which includes but goes beyond the (formal) legal power of decision-making of the government, the parliament, administrations and tax judges. Within every institutional body, one must look at the real actors of fiscal decision-making: for example, the parliamentary commissions in the United States, the head of the executive power and the minister of finance in many countries, the central tax administration.

opportunity for citizen debates and for societary choices leading to tax interventionism (and spending). The pluralism of conceivable changes is thus crushed by the monolithic dramatization of the solutions provided by decision-makers who use the pretext of the market to escape from the control by citizens. The power of the people over institutions and the political legitimacy of the conceptions of public action, on which democracy is founded, are distorted by the causal biases of public action. The configuration of the taxation problem is reduced to the ideology of constraints which excludes the democratic field of possibilities: the political choices of the ruling elite are concealed (cf. above) by the technocratic presentation of the economically "necessary" decisions.

Figure 3: The causal biases of fiscal public action

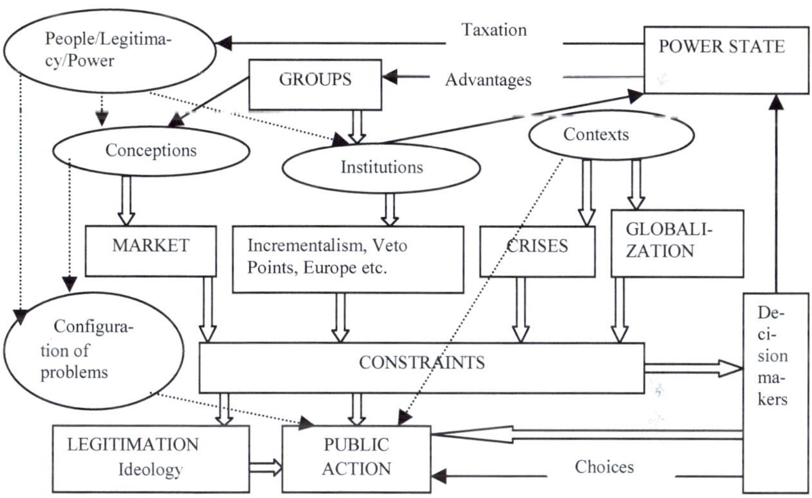

Legend: thick arrows indicate causal biases, thin arrows indicate concealed real relations, and dotted lines represent weakened relations (3 levels of analysis)

Thus the great functions of taxation for the financing of public services, the economy, the reduction of inequalities (redistribution), and the sustainable development of territories tend to leave the field of democracy. The political function of taxation stemming from the historic evolution of the tax State is flouted: formally, the consent of people to pay taxes is validated by the electoral mandate granted to institutions. But, at heart, this mandate is blank, and the citizen debate is more and more avoided within the rhetoric of constraints. The relation between taxation and spending is forgotten or perverted: political compromises made between revenue and expenditure, the taxation of capital and income, social expenditure and economic expenditure, socio-economic groups that are encouraged and subjugated etc., tend to be placed out of the reach of citizens.

Here one should insist on the (more or less strong) autonomy of decision-makers with regard to socio-economic groups. If access to institutions plays a role, as we have seen with the basic model of fiscal policy (chapter 6), the categorization of society by particular advantages constitutes an attribute of State power exercised by the elite in power. This power of derogation which delegitimizes the tax State as the general authority of taxation is the basic mechanism of political support, and not of democracy.[10] The question of the "pluralist" openness depends on the number of groups that accede to institutions: the answer is variable according to countries, periods etc. in brief, according to contexts. The paradox of the interventionist State of the rich democracies of the global market becomes clearly visible: the ideology of economic constraints leaves to decision-makers a power of appreciation of the categorial solutions to be provided. Within this configuration, we understand that the efficiency of a group largely depends upon the quality of its argumentative lobbying, which, in the current context of ideologized constraints, must be economic in order to attain a higher efficiency.

With regard to the citizens as a whole (people in Figure 3), taxation is difficult to decode because of the categorization carried out notably in favour of groups. We also understand that, without validating the determinism of incrementalism, decision-makers often give their preference to adjustments (important in its consequences at the end) to the detriment of radical reforms. Likewise, the increase in the importance of indirect taxation, whose general archetype is the VAT, goes in the direction of the decline of democracy. Similar to the labyrinth of tax derogations, this process of taxation has the advantage of being discreet (painless according to economic wording); it is associated with a consumer price and not with social issues, which are however essential because of their effect on income redistribution. For that reason, it is very difficult for an individual to calculate the real tax burden which weighs on him. We finally understand the attention given to financial relations between the central (or federal) State and local authorities (and the States of a federation): the institutional debate on financial means phagocytes the democracy of proximity.[11] It is thus the financial social

[10] This analysis allows one to specify, by providing a few distinctions, one of the ideas of financial sociology of Pareto: in democracies, the government resorts by ruse to the ideology ("derivations") of market constraints and of risks for crises, but that does not consist in satisfying the elite in power according to economic possibilities. The autonomy of the interventionist power of decision-makers is preserved, including, to a large extent, in the derogations (favours) granted.

[11] Preference supported by the specialized literature which has often defended financial decentralization.

contract (cf. chapter 11) which is amended, modified and finally forgotten by biased public action that leads to a complex instrumentalisation of taxation.

b. The use of taxation as an instrument

Taxation is more and more used as an instrument to deal with economic, social, cultural, and territorial particularisms. The global appreciation of the coherence and justice of the tax system has become difficult. The tax law of the interventionist State foresees numerous specific mechanisms whose presentation would require a whole book. As illustration we can take the favourable fiscal measures destined for the small business sector which is seen as propitious to the creation of employment and to innovation. But other mechanisms aim at other enterprises, like the investment in certain sectors or the development of certain activities (research for instance). A tax incentive for job creation is for example a widespread social tool of the fight against unemployment (Faulk, 2002). In the social domain, philanthropy, donations to charities, to associations or to foundations are encouraged; but the use of tobacco and alcohol is discouraged by an elevated specific taxation. The idea of a social control by taxation put forward by Mann is widely attested. In cultural matters, tax incentives exist in favour of patrimony (Leroy, 1997). Taxation is (timidly) becoming an issue of ecological policy. It foresees advantages for the actions of environmental protection (energy saving, nonpolluting fuels etc.). Territorial attractiveness appeals to fiscal competition between States or between sub-national territories. The French policy of regional planning also grants tax advantages in favour of rural zones loosing activities and of deprived urban neighbourhoods. Following the crisis of 2008, tax havens have thus become the object of renewed attention of governments seeking to limit tax fraud. The current period is characterized by the dispersal of the great functions of taxation.

The tax policy also accompanies other policies, in a major way or not, in order to create systemic effects with other tax revenues, such as social security contributions, or with expenditure, or loans (cf. chapter 5). We can quote here an American study of 1988-2001 (Reed, 2006) which indicates that new tax legislation counts for about half of the weight of tax payments on the income of individuals, the rest resulting from other factors. It is especially with social expenditure that taxation plays a role as a joint instrument. Hence, the reduction of income inequalities appeals both to the redistribution by progressive taxation (which hits more strongly the rich) and to the redistribution by social transfers paid to the poorest. Likewise, the policy of "Workfare" recommended in the 1990s by the OECD, then by the European Commission, leads several countries to exempt low-salary individuals from social security contributions and to re-emphasize the return to work by social incentives (increased minimum wages) and fiscal incentives (negative taxes).

Despite the methodological difficulties of measurement[12] (Burnam, 2003; Burnam *et al.*, 2008), numerous countries use tax expenditure for social purposes and for economic purposes (cf. chapter 10). A legal framework for supervising these mechanisms exists however. As for the member states of the European Union, they are subject to the Community law applicable to State aids.[13] The European Commission sees to it that fiscal aids do not distort competition, and the case-law of the CJEC supervises the regime. At the world level, the WTO can also be led to control tax advantages granted by a country to enterprises in international trade.[14] In practice, this framework, justified by the good functioning of markets, remains insufficient (it is not its purpose) to check the interventionism of States.

These particularisms accentuate the causal biases of public action by the dilution of the great socio-political functions of the role of taxation. We have to remember that the scale of fiscal spending by definition reduces tax revenue. This configuration of the problem is all the more dramatic because the financing of social expenditure appears as one of the achievements of the evolution of the democratic Welfare State. Fiscal sectorialisation is also carried out to the detriment of the function of economic macro-regulation. Finally, the redistribution function has some difficulties to be accepted on the agendas of public authorities since too many fiscal niches facilitate the avoidance of tax contributions by citizens, notably (we shall come back to this), for the most privileged. The fragmentation of issues thus feeds the complexity.

c. *The complexity of fiscal public action*

The complexity of public action is already of a systemic nature because of the relations of interdependence of the system of tax revenues (cf. chapter 5). An indicator is given by manuals and by the divisions of the administration which distinguish specific rules of taxation for indi-

12 More particularly, we cannot calculate the total of tax expenditure because, for example, their abolition would entail a return of exempted taxpayers in the ordinary categories of taxation which often benefit from a standard tax relief. Moreover, differences in definition complicate comparisons. In France, the *Conseil des impôts* tax council (2003, p. 56) considers that 75% of tax expenditure are not correctly estimated.

13 Articles 87 to 89 of the EC Treaty. On the legal regime of fiscal aids, cf. Lambert, 2005.

14 Cf. for example, the *Foreign Sales Corporation* (FSC) decision of 7th May, 2003 of the Dispute Settlement Body (DSB) of the WTO which considered that the tax exemption granted to American FSCs in the field of exports was irregular.

viduals, for real estate, for small and big enterprises etc. The complexity is then aggravated by the diversification of the instrumental use of taxation by the interventionist State. The sophistication of tax expenditure (Orsoni, in Leroy, 2005) technicizes tax law even more (tax exemptions, tax rebates, cuts in tax rates, tax allowances or tax credits).

In spite of the wise recommendations given by Adam Smith in the 18th century, tax law is therefore less and less clear, as is attested by the number of texts that are implemented every year. Legal security is threatened and fiscal citizenship is thwarted. Specialists often point to the complexity of the American tax code (Tillinghast, 2003, p. 62). It affects the poorest in particular who accumulate several problems (Holtblatt, McCubbin, 2003): a lower level of education, more difficult family lives that appeal more to social transfers (taxable or not). The big number of errors in tax returns thus becomes evident. In France, between 2004 and 2007, the annual average number of laws with tax provisions comes to 17 (Sénat, 2008). The number of articles of laws having fiscal features was 230 per year over the same period of time. Tax law is more and more technical (Lopez, in Leroy, 2008) and very often, as in the case of Sweden (Brokelind, in Leroy, 2008), imprecise. Derogatory taxation emphasizes this complexity in many countries. The application of legal norms is thus difficult, especially since law and the facts are poorly distinguished in this domain. This complexity facilitates schemes, tax avoidance, and tax fraud (evasion) by the most skilful social categories which are economically privileged in general. A transversal study (Richardson, 2006) using data from 54 countries thus shows that the complexity of the tax system is the principal statistical determinant of tax evasion. For the categories that do not want to (or cannot) commit an offence (fraud), the complexity is a source of error and leads to blur the legibility of the system.

Public action conducted by fiscal policy leads to a contradiction which consists of making law more complex by wanting to direct behaviour. The solution to this perverse configuration is in general looked for in the simplification of formalities, the intensification of administrative assistance, and in e-administration (Sacchetto, in Leroy, 2008). These answers will nevertheless remain insufficient without calling into question the fragmentation of fiscal intervention. The elimination of particularistic tax expenditure to the benefit of classic budgetary subsidies appears to be more efficient from this point of view. Furthermore, this solution would bring along a non-negligible extension of the tax base. In the meantime, the absence of legibility of the legal setting is a supplementary obstacle to democracy.

Conclusion

In the tradition of Max Weber's ideal-type, one of the central tasks of the scientific process consists in elaborating models. Through the selection of pertinent factors, variables and indicators, it is a question of obtaining sufficient precision in order to conform to the Popperian requirement of the empirical falsification of theories. Methodological exclusions, by means of data selection and simplification, are thus necessary for verification. Consequently, one level of analysis is often privileged to the detriment of others. The specialization of sciences, which followed the rejection of the great self-sufficient systems of explanation, emphasizes this phenomenon. A process of over-generalization of empirical results which justify economic theories is at work. The reception of the anti-fiscal discourse or of the ideology of constraints illustrates this process. The determinism of the economic constraints of markets, crises or globalization conceals political decisions and other possible choices. It is also true for diverse theories of institutional determinism which deny the reality of changes brought about, notably in the compromises between revenue and expenditure. The analysis of the system of tax revenue and of public expenditure already attests however the reality of the mutations of the financial State. The facts and arguments presented above complete the invalidation of the intellectual posture of the impossibility of democratic choices.

The articulation of different levels of analysis, beyond its interdisciplinary requirement (cf. chapter 3), asks for careful thinking in order to generalize, without exaggeration, about particular empirical results. It is also a question of searching for variables of transition (at the intermediate level) between levels (micro and macro but also theoretical and empirical) in order to give some place to qualitative factors next to statistical correlations etc. In the case of fiscal public action, the epistemological positioning of the context serves as a variable of transition between the level of basic factors and the other levels addressed in this chapter. Socio-economic groups form an important variable, not so much of the power of society or the economy, as of the State power of decision-makers. They are also there in a position of a variable of transition (intermediate) between taxation and the people. The degree of access to institutions by the groups[15] is here only one of the aspects of the process of taxation which expresses the State power[16] as the occultation of democracy in the ideology of constraints. The elitism of choices is justified (and concealed) by the arguments of a technocracy nourished by economic studies of the market. As functional complement this

15 Which differentiates pluralistic, neo-corporatist, Marxist, elitist theories etc.

16 Beyond formal election of rulers and power of coercion attached to public institution.

technocracy uses an arbitrary instrumentation of the power of derogation. The biased model of the public action of the interventionist State does not leave the people without voice nor without arms, but it impoverishes, and often denies, the functioning of democracy. Bureaucracy then finds itself in a difficult position of regulating the implementation of laws without a real social compass.

CHAPTER 8

Bureaucratic Regulation

Bureaucracy is a difficult concept to define as it mobilizes different approaches. To begin with, the scientific vision of the administration by economists, sociologists, historians, business managers, lawyers etc. depends on what disciplinary and methodological glasses they wear. Next, bureaucracy is analyzed from three points of view, namely as a formal structure of interconnected services with official missions defined in an organization chart, as a process of organization making a group of people function, and as a set of outputs to be evaluated. Certain theories combine the three dimensions. This is the case of Max Weber's famous model containing structural features, functional features related to the Western history of rationalization (of a "legal-rational" type), and an efficiency requirement. This is also the case of the French-style model of bureaucracy proposed by Michel Crozier, to which our analysis of fiscal organization represents a critical counterpoint. Another way consists in using the approach of public policies to define the particular role of the administration in the formulation (the objectives) of public actions and in the implementation of solutions.[1] This general approach emphasizes the importance of the administrative implementation phase of the public action.

We will put aside vague or reductionist theories conveyed notably, in opposite traditions, by certain Marxists or by the school of public choice.[2] In fact, the "critical" conception of bureaucracy, presented as a general mechanism of oppression in service of the bourgeoisie or capital, wrongly denies (cf. previous chapters) any autonomy of the State apparatus and decision-makers. In a similarly simplistic way, the "utilitarian" conception put forward by Public Choice (Buchanan, Tullock, 1962; Downs, 1957) sees the administration as a unique agent whose rationality consists in maximizing its human, material and budgetary means. A bureaucrat tends to maximize his budget (revenue-maximizer) according to a model of the Leviathan tax State (Brennan, Buchanan, 1977, p. 273; 1980), which leads to a bureaucratic deviance (Niskanen,

1 According to the analytical model of Jones (1970), a public policy includes the problem identification, the formulation of solutions, the decision, the implementation, the evaluation and the termination of the action.

2 In its extreme version which nourishes widely represented scientific orthodoxy.

1971) since economic performance is neither encouraged nor sanctioned.

Bureaucracy is considered here as a set of processes which allow one to render the "real" decision consistent with organizational choices, i.e. with the official objectives of the management of the organization.[3] In the same organization (enterprise, association or public administration) certain decision-making processes may be bureaucratic and others may not. This definition allows one to problematize change by confronting the impact of official reforms with the concrete functioning of the decision. As a bureaucratic process, management performance is studied through its means to be consistent to the action of the members of the organization. As a process of modernization, the public management of taxes is viewed in the light of bureaucratic regulation with reference to the general interest which legitimizes public action. The two retained fields are constituted by the history of the modernization of the French tax administration and by the organization of tax control in the context of economic globalization.

1. Fiscal Bureaucracy in France

Until the creation of the *Direction Générale des Impôts* (Directorate General of Taxes noted DGI: the French tax administration) in 1948, the public management of taxation was shared between three administrations with different kinds of logic. The unification of the structures and organization of the new hierarchical line took twenty years. This first reform participates in the post-war policy of modernization of the country. It aims to adapt the administrative structures to the evolution of the tax system from then on composed of synthetic taxes of a higher (potential) return and of an interventionist character. The second important modernization intervenes in 1990s. It takes into account the new phase of the European construction of a single market which abolishes borders and leads to the creation of the intra-community VAT. By privileging the amelioration of material resources and careers, it also responds to demands of tax agents and to the government policy of public service revitalization. Another reform intervenes following the adoption of the organic law on the Budget Acts of 2001 (LOLF). This reform does not directly concern the structure or revalorization of resources but aims to measure public performance in a context of delegitimization of public spending.

3 This definition is close to that of Merton (1965, p. 196) when he underlines that "in a true bureaucracy, we are in the presence of a big regularity of behavior and of a high degree of conformity to the prescribed types of action."

a. The affirmation of a modern tax administration

The creation of the DGI on April 16, 1948 aims to merge three administrations – administrations of direct and indirect tax revenue, and of registration. Merging external services was not simple as it continued for a little longer than twenty years, from 1948 to 1970. The essential lesson of this reform lies within the framework of much wider reference which is that of the modernization of French society after World War II. In fact, while the tax State becomes interventionist in all countries, in connection with the development of Keynesianism and social welfare, the issue of French post-war modernization entails some specificities. The new norms of the French system of public action are supported by the administration and elite of the country: this new conception draws on the tools of French-style planning and advocates State interventionism as a value to the detriment of the market norm. That is the time of the policy of great industrial projects of France led by the grand corps of the State; it is also the era of the "*énarques*", of technocracy. The State and high-ranking administration are thus at the heart of this process that characterized, according to some political analysts, the French model of public policy which entered into a crisis following the twofold evolution of decentralization and European construction.

As for tax policy, the motivation to improve tax revenues in order to balance post-war budgets again comes, according to the general model of modernization, from a group of finance inspectors who are high-ranking civil servants that graduated from the prestigious national school of administration (ENA). The progressive reform of structures is carried through, but the radical change of the tax system is refused, notwithstanding strong propositions from the CGT (a French trade union). The tax administration slowly comes round to the idea of an economic use of taxes. Tax revenues are also improved by the creation of VAT, in 1954, by Maurice Lauré, based on the principle of neutrality towards enterprises.

The tax revolt, led by Poujade in 1953, marks a pause in reforms however, and in particular in the policy of tax control. The genesis of many-sided control, which replaces the (not very effective) control by type of tax carried out by the three administrations, is characterized by the following controversy: the sociological compromise between productivity and negotiation (cf. later) and the equilibrium of procedure between taxpayers and tax inspectors are not disconnected from the fear for anti-tax movements of the past.

The modernization movement starts up again within the framework of a new policy aiming at creating a mass tax system (with a liability of a large number of people): the generalization of income and corporate taxes, and of VAT in 1968, the modification of taxation techniques with the development of the tax return system and of accounting requirements and the rapid expansion of fiscal interventionism profoundly modify the tax system. The modernizing reference system inspires the attempts of change in the tax administration related to the procedure of rationalization of budgetary choices (RCB) inspired by the American PPBS. It was a matter of applying modern management principles[4] that would not be denied today. This management principle is one of the constants of organization; it is represented by the control of results a posteriori of tax control in the form of productivity cards.

In 1970, the merger of the services finally succeeded by the transformation of the external tax services: all echelons of command are unified: 107 services of the tax administration take the place of 247 specialized departmental services; 152 offices of tax base assessment and control, covering a quarter of the country, are combined in a functional unit the old services of the three administrations, which are now merged. From the point of view of the structure of the tax administration, Fayol's model (1962, p. 19-47) of the administrative function[5] is applied (Leroy, 1994, p. 822), notably through the establishment of a unity of command ("an agent receives orders only from one single head") and of a "unity of management" ("one single head and one single programme for all the operations pursuing the same goal"). This period gives birth to the vision of a centralized, rigid and formal tax bureaucracy that multiplies regulations. In reality, if this model indeed constitutes one of the historical strata of the administration, it is necessary to point out that other important features modify the statement.

The "modernizing" genesis of the French administration is thus characterized by its capacity to manage the tax system for the masses in the process of being constructed: the logic of change is focused on the relation between the modification of the bureaucratic structures and the new tax policies put into place, starting from the creation of synthetic taxes. This model lasted until the transformations of the 1990s.

---

4 "The Mission was largely inspired by what is appropriate to call the modern principles of change (...), a doctrine that goes little by little beyond the ambit of the private enterprise (...). Concerning public administrations in particular, simple common sense shows all the interest there would be to: define objectives clearly; facilitate the delegation of responsibility; verify the validity of the action thus delegated by a posteriori control" (source: Mission RCB, "Inquiry into the Central Administration of the Ministry of Finance," Paris, Ministerial Archives, 1969-1971).

5 As in the OST (scientific organization of work) of F.W. Taylor (1990), the organization is conceived as a social body that has to perform certain essential functions in order to survive. According to Fayol, the administrative function includes the tasks of prudence, organization, command, coordination and control. The general principles of administration of this mining engineer valorize the superiority of the unity of command, which corresponds to the structure intended at that time for the tax administration.

b. The management change of the 1990s

The intention to adapt the organization of the tax administration is in keeping with the context of the appearance of three concomitant challenges:

– the new European order, following the creation of a new regime of intra-community VAT applicable on January 1, 1993 resulting from the directive 91/680/EEC transposed into French law by the law of July 17, 1992;

– the unrest of administration agents expressed during a large-scale strike action in 1989;

– the improvement of services rendered to users that must be related to the general process of "revitalization of public services" introduced by the written directive of Prime Minister Michel Rocard dated February 23, 1989.

It is difficult to reconcile these challenges. At that time the DGI (Directorate General for Taxation) defined four principles of action: "give responsibilities to all levels, provide teams with the support they need, hold a better dialogue between us, manage the human resources better".[6] If this general formulation is not very contestable in itself, it does not prejudge a change in logic. Through the material means put into place, this modernization is especially interpreted as an improvement of the managing capacity of the administration accompanied by a new wave of computerization of services (including micro-computers for agents) and the intensification of training. As in the case of the reforms of 1948-1970, bonuses were established in order to facilitate the acceptance of change and respond to social demands directly.

This modernization also depends on an enterprise of communication – that certain consider as ideological – to soothe the unrest that followed upon the social conflict of 1989. From the point of view of decision-making, a certain deconcentration of credits and decisions is also tried, but it is especially the creation of a rank of divisionary inspector in 1995 that modifies the hierarchical order: from that time onwards the person in charge of the tax bureau is the real head of the local services. In 2001 a new organizational change occurs as a result of the adoption in parliament of an organic law which was voted by the right and the left.

c. The administrative performance in the framework of LOLF

The organic law on the Finance Laws (LOLF) of August 1, 2001 introduces a big reform of the State management. As a complement to the

6 Source: Direction générale des impôts, *Nos principes d'action*, Imprimerie Nationale, Paris, 1990.

reinforcement of financial transparency and the role of parliament, the new logic puts forward the responsibility of public program managers who must account for costs, objectives and results. The modernization of public management has the ambition to allow France to join the league of countries that practice the culture of performance (OECD, 2007), with more or less success (Schick, 2008): the budget of means for services and the control of conformity are substituted by a logic of objectives and of evaluation of the performance of public programs. Thus the French post-war modernizing concept, that had integrated the European frame of reference and had been completed by the market concept coming from the 1970s[7], is from now on completed by the implementation of a budgetary management by results. This new concept challenges the classic legal concept of administrative action by placing the management and evaluation of human and financial resources at the center of public action.

Table 10: Architecture of the French tax administration

Mission	Program	Objective	Number indicators
Management and control of public finance	– fiscal and financial management of the State and of the local public sector: PR 156	– fiscal civism – tax facilitation – fight against evasion – revenue and expenditure management – services to agents	3 3 3 3 3
	– guidance of economic, financial and industrial policies: PR 218	– services to agents – human ressources – support function	1 2 3
Tax Refunds and tax relief	– of State taxes: PR 200	– rapidity	2
	– of local taxes: PR 201	– rapidity	1

Source: Budget Law 2006

The new budgetary architecture establishes a balance between the freedom of a manager, who has at his disposal a global budget (fungibility) for the programs under his responsibility, and the control/evaluation

7 In 1968 customs duties are abolished in Europe. In 1986 the Single European Act foresees the four freedoms of circulation – for goods, services, capital and people – by the end of 1992. Customs formalities are abandoned and the intra-community VAT is applied from 1993.

of his results with regard to the objectives defined in his annual performance project (PAP). The missions of the State (about 30) work towards public policies and comprise about 130 programs. There are about 8 inter-ministerial missions.[8] The objectives are evaluated according to 3 large categories of indicators: socio-economic indicators of efficacy or of general interest which concern citizens, indicators of efficiency which concern taxpayers, indicators of the quality of public services for users. We can also identify the indicators of action (of means) and the indicators of results.

From now on the action of the Ministry of the Economy and Finance is represented by 9 missions, 3 of which are inter-ministerial, with 21 programs. For the initial finance law 2006 (taken into account here because it is the year of the implementation of the reform), DGI, the French tax administration, is implied in 2 ministerial missions consisting of 4 programs (PR) for 23 objectives (cf. tables 10 and 11). The indicators of performance have the merit of trying to render operational the approach of transparency wanted by LOLF, even if they remain perfectible in order to allow for a genuine evaluation of tax policies.

The indicators of the "tax civism" objective are still to be improved. The first indicator measures compliance with legal deadlines for payment by enterprises, which refers for them to a basic element of any fiscal strategy in order to avoid penalties. The second indicator is related to respecting income tax obligations. Here again it is especially a question of a bureaucratic measure that ignores the basic control of the content of tax returns. In the absence of an indicator of the sincerity of tax returns, intentional fraud, which is certainly difficult to measure, is not directly taken into account. The third indicator, the rate of collecting taxes on the list (roll), is important but does not represent a real change. We know that 90 to 95% of taxes (income and corporate taxes) are collected during the first year, and the percentage is 97-98% at the end of 3 years. Here it would be interesting to measure, and thus explain, the regional differences that persist in order to establish a geography of tax evasion (fraud) and to test the impact of economic variables (unemployment for example) and of social, religious and other variables.

The objective of "fighting serious fraud" is important in order to justify the efficiency of tax control, the credibility of the tax return regime, the equality in front of taxation, and the legitimacy of tax State. The indicators of the rate of tax returns are pertinent here and will perhaps help to question the particular logic of statistical output described further on. It would be interesting to establish indicators on litigation: taxpayers concerned, types of fraud (for example, points of law and of

8 Such as the policy of territories, the pension schemes, research and higher education.

fact), results etc. The percentage of controls repressing the most serious frauds is an indicator that would also show a progress in principle. This indicator would become clearer by the diffusion of explicit criteria of fraud seriousness in order to avoid the bureaucratic construction of a statistical amalgam.[9] Finally, the best would be to propose a full analysis of the results of tax control.

The objective of "facilitating taxes", which formalizes a government decision of June 2003, contains nine commitments especially related to delays in response, reception, information, user committees, the automatic payment of taxes, the establishment of a tax mediator, and the sending of pre-filled income tax returns. A good part of these measures (responding to demands, giving printed forms, identifying oneself etc.) fortunately corresponds to former practices of a normal public service: they do not upset the administrative organization. The performance thus reaches excellence without effort since the initial indicators are already above 95%. Tax reconciliation, even though the function is entrusted to a member of the administration, constitutes a new level of dialogue. The establishment of a pre-filled income tax return shows a real progress. We must again remember that France is one of the rare modern countries not to use withholding at the source (pay as you earn) when taxing salary-earners, which would be an even simpler solution for users.

Two provisions part of the "facilitating taxes" objective are positive from the point of view of tax sociology. They concern the improvement of administrative language, for example (for the tax adjustment) by speaking of propositions of tax "rectification" instead of tax "correction", and of the "amicable reminder" procedure, in place of the notification of tax corrections, in case of discordance between the income tax return and cross-checking coming from third parties (employers, banks, pension funds). By taking up these formulations, the administration avoids stigmatizing taxpayers' errors as "fraud", and thus delegitimizing taxes. The analysis of the typology and of the concrete factors of tax minimization (Leroy, 2003 and chapter 9) shows that, even when the stakes are small[10], the administrative style of error rectification matters as much as the legal nature and the amount of money in question.

---

9 Amongst these criteria, apart from the amounts involved in and the nature of fraud methods as well as the qualification of sanctions, it would be advisable to retain: the rate of criminal prosecutions (initiated and effective) and the nature of the convictions, the percentage of international fraud, of different kinds of traffic (money laundering, terrorism etc.), the accepted and contested tax adjustments etc. It is also advisable to estimate that which we do not find by relying on the results of tax control when measuring (certainly difficult) the black economy.

10 A deduction for insulation work not corresponding to the norms, a revenue complement in the case of an undeclared illness, an error of filling in the wrong box on the tax return form etc.

The objective of "managing revenue and expenditure" aims to measure the management costs of the administration by a synthetic indicator. To be optimal, this information must be compared to the situation of the other countries. Here the French administration remains rather poorly placed: its intervention rate[11], measured by the relation between the net cost of management of tax missions and the net collected tax revenue, is 1.6% in 1997.[12]

Table 11: The performance of the French tax administration

Objective	Nature of the indicator
Tax civism (PR 156)	– % enterprises paying within the legal deadlines – % conforming to income tax obligations – rate of collecting taxes on the list
Facilitating taxes (PR 156)	– rate of program advance – rate of dematerialization of procedures
Fighting fraud (PR 156)	– % of controls repressing serious fraud – rate of collection by tax control – rate of collection of fines
Management of revenue and expenditure (PR 156)	– rate of intervention in revenues (cost) – rate of intervention in expenditures (cost) – synthetic index of productivity
Services to agents (PR 156)	– % of urgent retirement files treated within 15 days – % of reversion pension files treated within a week – % of letters treated within 3 weeks (48 hrs for electronic mail)
Services to agents (PR 218)	– % of agents having access to a collective restaurant
Human resources (PR 218)	– % of interviews of evaluation and notation conducted during 1st semester – % of C agents who had training within the year
Support function (PR 218)	– gain from purchases – operating expenditure for technical equipment per agent – number of servants for human resources and logistics
Rapidity (PR 200)	– rate of VAT reimbursements paid before 30 days – rate of IR claims treated within a one-month delay
Rapidity (PR 201)	– rate of TH claims treated within a one-month delay

Source: Finance Law 2006

The objective of "services to agents" is found in two programs and includes social indicators of delays in the treatment of retirement demands, mail, and indicators related to the number of agents having

11 Source: Inspection générale des finances, "Mission d'analyse comparative des administrations fiscales", No. 98, March 1999, p. 11.

12 The United States are at the top of the list (0.49%); then we find Sweden (0.52%), Ireland (0.83%), Spain (0.89%), Canada (1.05%), the United Kingdom (1.12%), Netherlands (1.23%), Italy (1.52%), France (1.60%), and Germany (1.71%).

access to a collective restaurant. These indirect indicators are not really part of the major objectives of performance measurement, but they possibly contribute to the satisfaction of the agents encountering problems. The "human resources" objective, with the number of interviews in the first half of a year and the number of non-top civil servants (C agents) undergoing training, also seems to be somewhat different from what one could expect. The objective of the "support function" proposes three indicators – globalization of purchases, cost of an agent's equipment, and the size of the staff in the human resources function. The first indicator is standard in management; the two others are rather indicators of the importance of the means and not of efficacy and efficiency. Finally, the objective of "rapidity" is defined in two programs by using indicators of delays.

This brief analysis of indicators is enough to show the accent put on the formal capacity of the management of the administration. The reform is therefore not negligible from this point of view, even though it does not yet allow us to have a global vision of public policy implemented administratively. The choice of making programs coincide with traditional ministerial structures deserves to be reconsidered within an improved logic of budgeting by objectives. Tax policy functions (cf. chapter 11) are not evaluated, for example by indicators measuring the impact of fiscal spending for the economy, territories, redistribution, social categories etc. Knowing the taxpayer's rationality in the presence of taxes is not questioned (cf. chapter 9), for example by an analysis of the content of tax litigation. The exploration of the complex phenomenon of fraud is rightfully based on the indicator of the struggle against serious fraud. This indicator could be refined by putting it in perspective with the degree of complexity of tax law and with the impact of tax procedure.

The French administration has shown its historic capacity for management for a long time: management of the tax return system, introduction of new taxes, computerization of services etc. It would be appropriate to continue measuring this dimension with precision as it is important. The logic of the elaboration of LOLF is however especially to know its impact on tax policies. But up to now the evolution of the tax administration is especially seen as a sequence of three modernizations, each one in a different context but who all present a certain continuity in the evaluation of management through means. The post-war modernizing frame of reference led to the adaption of administrative structures to the interventionist role of taxes, in particular for economic growth. The resistance to change (we saw that the merger of services took about twenty years) was overcome by granting advantages to the personnel. In the 1990s, the impact of the European construction, the issues of public service reform and of social struggle allowed the administration to strengthen the material means of management.[13] The recent introduction of performance indicators of bureaucratic modernization tends to replace the elaboration of a political conception of public programs by insisting on management performance (cf. chapter 6). But the administration still evolves. A reform of its administrative structures is thus in the process of being carried out with the merger of the DGI and the Directorate for Public Accounts, which results from the government decision of October 2007. The establishment of a new Directorate General of Public Finance (DGFP) will allow for the creation of a unique interlocutor for all taxpayers.[14]

More than a real evaluation of public policies, the tendency, well-aligned with the functioning of taxation organization, is to generalize management control. More than a culture of results of tax policies and of a struggle against tax deviances, it is primarily a culture of means that is still valorized for the moment. It is true that budget transparency wanted by LOLF implies the quantitative measurement (through indicators) of the means implemented by administrative action to reach objectives. But this transparency also requires the analysis of the logic of bureaucratic functioning with regard to a critical definition of administrative objectives. A big part of the problem comes from the weak coherence of tax policies (cf. chapter 11) which complicates the performance of control as a pillar of the credibility of the tax return regime at the heart of the democratic tax system.

2. The Organization of Tax Control

The study of tax control is essential both for understanding the functioning of the administration and for the effectiveness of tax policy. Dated April 2, 2009, the decision of the G20 (the 20 leading economies of the world) to fight against international fraud in tax havens shows the importance of this issue. In France, the emergence of a new taxation, particularly of the income tax (the Caillaux laws of 1914 and 1917) is accompanied by the progressive implementation of tax controls. But the period that goes from the 1920s until the end of the Second World War remains characterized by the ineffectiveness of the fight against the resistance to taxes (including fraud). It is only after the creation of the DGI in 1948 that tax controls are equipped in a serious way with organi-

---

13 Whereas the market reference, which undermines the legitimacy of taxes, justified changes in legislation (corporate and capital taxation) subject to control by the administration (cf. chapter 10).

14 In 2003, a first attempt to merge these administrations faced opposition from local elected politicians and from personnel who wanted to preserve rural services. The current reform maintains rural treasuries by attributing partial tax missions to them. The unique interlocutor already existed for enterprises.

zational resources (the creation of "multi-purpose" agents) and legal resources. The powers of getting information and of controlling of the administration provide it with important privileges that in 1986 gave rise to the reinforcement of the rights and guarantees of the verified taxpayers. From then onwards the dialectical issue consists of making the point of equilibrium between these two forces evolve. The sociological analysis of the administrative decision-making brings to the fore the originality of the bureaucratic organization with regard to classic models. The central role of controllers (audit inspectors), who do not belong to the hierarchal echelons, is analyzed as a decision-making compromise between the output, standardized by the statistics, and more or less formal negotiation. This bureaucratic model is replaced within the comparative perspective of the administrative regulation of enterprises implied in economic globalization.

a. The dialectic of the tax procedure

Following the propositions of the Aicardi parliamentary commission, appointed by the right-wing government in 1986 to improve relations between the tax and customs administration and citizens, a change is brought about in favour of verified taxpayers. Without going into the detail of the legal measures of the law of July 8, 1987, it should be noted that this reform was made possible by a reinforcement of the control of the hierarchy and by actions of raising awareness and of training. A consequence of this reform is the appearance of a sort of organizational norm, of a social representation proper to the administrative corps, which is expressed in the form of an exaggerated attention given to procedural errors. Nevertheless, the formalism of protection, which concerns the rights and guarantees of taxpayers, has relative scope.[15] On the contrary, the formalism of constraint, linked to tax return obligations and to the necessity of responding to demands by the administration, seems to be rigorously sanctioned both by texts and judges. Sociologically, this fear for errors of form, exploited by some advocates, specialists of errors of procedure, encourages the administration to negotiate.

More generally (Leroy, 2008), a dialectic on procedure is at work. It opposes, on the one side, the demand of the administration to increase its powers of getting information, of investigation and of control, without giving rise to reactions susceptible of diminishing its prerogatives, and, on the other side, the movement of improving the guarantees of taxpayers. This second movement is often legally and politically justified as general principles (theoretically). It is a matter of guaranteeing

[15] It is enough to see the variable, and sometimes very restricted, character of sanctions pronounced by judges against the administration in cases of errors of form or procedure.

the rights of taxpayers as a particular case of the defence of the rights of citizens. But one must also look from a sociological point of view at which social groups are the best protected or the best positioned to use the rights and guarantees of taxpayers. Here one must state that the protection benefits especially enterprises and the richest classes. The guarantees especially concern verification of accounting (enterprises) and verification of physical individuals (the contradictory procedure, i.e.: after due hearing of the parties, for the examination of the personal tax situation), which normally target big revenues.[16] Ordinary taxpayers are subject to a control of documents (only based on the tax return file of taxpayers), with smaller legal guarantees. In reality, this control sometimes tends to establish a kind of high-handed action by the administration that is not much disputed, also because of the economic cost of resorting to the services of a tax lawyer.

Sometimes the administration, in its doctrine and its practice, adopts certain measures in order to facilitate dialogue or establish guarantees beyond the law. For example, for local taxes, a kind of procedure with cross-examination is applied while no text foresees it. During procedures of arbitrary taxation, the arguments of taxpayers are in some cases taken into account. More recently, a tax mediator was installed at the initiative of the administration for matters of controlling documents. But these practices do not allow one to conclude on a general attitude of administrative benevolence when considering the persistence of counter-examples. As for the control of documents, the administration does not indicate the financial consequences of tax adjustments; sometimes it uses in a immoderate way the procedure of asking for information (form 754), which is not much controlled as regards guarantees for taxpayers.[17] From this point of view, one must acknowledge in its principle the establishment of a departmental mediator in order to re-equilibrate relations with taxpayers who are objects of a control of documents. His official mission is to improve relations between the administration and taxpayers and to observe the compliance with the quality of services. The culture of reconciliation for ordinary taxpayers thus constitutes a progress. Nevertheless, uncertainties remain because the tax mediator belongs to the administration and he sometimes cumulates his functions with that of a director of tax controls and/or of litigation.

---

16 The organization notably splits up different kinds of taxation: that of enterprises, and handling services separately in the case of big enterprises, that of the professions, and that of employees; the negotiation is facilitated for enterprises and the most privileged people.

17 It thus avoids the more difficult procedure of the request for justifications which is subject to a strict regulation based on articles L16 and L65 of the Book of Fiscal Procedures and through the control of the judge.

Another example concerns the duty of loyalty, a kind of code of conduct which the administration should respect when carrying out its investigations and fix tax corrections. In 1996 the *Cour de cassation* (the highest court of the French system) recalls the importance of this principle[18] present in the taxpayer's charter since 2005 (p. 25); but the systematic practice of substituting legal bases in front of the judge, or of changing the motives, in actual fact contradicts this principle. It is the position of the *Cour de cassation*[19] that must be generalized, and not that of the *Conseil d'État* (State Council and highest administrative court) that validates this practice not much conforming to the principle of the contradictory procedure (i.e.: after due hearing of the parties): the sending of a new notification of tax corrections, which authorizes taxpayers to present their observations, should be generalized.

The role of the judge is essential in order to balance administrative action: thus the visit and seizure procedures are subject to strict legal norms that limits the risks of arbitrary intrusion into private life at the time of searching. But even if a case is rarely submitted to a court, as in the case of controls based on documents of ordinary taxpayers, the risk of an imbalance is more probable especially since the legal framework (requests for information) is not binding. An error of appreciation by the administration is possible if the organizational logic is that of the productivity of controls (cf. below). In this kind of situation, discretionary power does not face sufficient limitations anymore. Finally, the administration sees to it that points, lost before the judge, are regained by getting the law to be modified. For example, with regard to the verification of physical individuals, the *Conseil d'État* considered that non-residents must not be verified[20] but the supplementary budget law of 1996 rejected this position. The legislative validation of positions of the administration is current practice.

This analysis should not make us forget that the dialectic of power of tax procedure is opposed to the strategies of the administration towards diverse groups of society, among which some, as we have already pointed out, are endowed with important economic and social advantages. Economic globalization has accentuated the de-functionalization of the tax State to the benefit of the privileged groups (cf. chapter 11). The struggle thus turns to the logic of bureaucratic decision-making.

---

18 *Cassation, Ch. Com.*, June 18, 1996, No. 1166, *Revue de Jurisprudence Fiscale*, November 1996, No. 1363.

19 *Cassation, Ch. Com.*, January 8, 1991, No. 88P, *Revue de Jurisprudence Fiscale*, March 1991, No. 377.

20 *Conseil d'État* (State Council), July 20, 1996, No. 127982, *Droit fiscal*, 1996, 43, 1310.

b. The originality of the French model of tax control

The elaboration of this model results from research work inspired both by the sociology of organizations and by cognitive sociology (Leroy, 1993, 2002, p. 38-42). The functioning of tax controls in France contains features that are "original" for a public bureaucracy. This conclusion is notably based on the following major fact: placed at the center of organizational logic, the tax controller (audit inspector) establishes a compromise between the logic of statistical output and negotiation.

The dynamics of "statistical output"[21] implies that the tax inspector has to render to his hierarchy a precise number of cases (12 annual controls) with a significant average amount of tax corrections. This "law" of output appears to be more important than the other issues such as the quality of the control, the number of cases of litigation, the penal repression of fraud, and the frequency of rendered cases. The logic of statistics logic constitutes an organizational deformation of the objective logic of the policy of tax control which supposes two principles: from the legal point of view, it is a matter of the strict application of tax law rules without trying to produce, first and foremost, tax corrections for the sake of statistics; from the managerial point of view, it is a matter of targeting administrative action on the fight against serious fraud. These two aspects are also related to the equality in front of taxation, which is a political principle, legally recognized, whose sociological basis constitutes the legitimacy of tax levies.

The measurement of the action of bureaucracy by statistics puts very different situations in the same basket: error, intentional violation of the law, abuse in the use of law, non-respect of conditions of procedure and substance, transfer of profits etc. It adds up important and/or serious fraud and breaches of little consequence; it is little concerned with the real collection of rectified taxes and the tax reliefs pronounced after litigation. The typology of tax minimization (cf. chapter 10) shows that the risk of administrative error is structurally (organizationally) encouraged by this logic of output that leads to even formal tax correction. By these statistics, apparently satisfactory, the administration justifies its fight-against-fraud action in the eyes of the public opinion and the authorities. By demonstrating that it represses fraud, it also preserves its autonomy that the government, certain members of parliament or certain social categories could call into question. It must nevertheless refrain from the opposite excess by avoiding the abuse of its powers of control. The retained solution consists in facilitating negotiation with controlled enterprises.

21 Which summarizes the amount of tax corrections requested by the tax controller following his control.

The constraint of negotiation constitutes another element of the organizational logic of tax control. It is a matter of avoiding the multiplication of conflicts and of managing the reactions of taxpayers because the powers of the administration could be put into question. The social mobilization against taxes also includes contesting the practices of the administration, as the history of tax revolts shows (Burg, 2004). The organizational choice can be expressed as follows: a tax controller has to know how to have his tax corrections accepted and how to avoid being subject of systematic litigation (difficult to manage) in order not to raise doubt in his competence and not to waste his time. In law, negotiation is the responsibility of the hierarchy within the framework of legal remedies. In practice, the role of the tax controller is also to negotiate arrangements during a control on the spot. The tactics of negotiation are diverse; often, the controller increases his tax corrections in order to better negotiate the agreement with the controlled enterprise, by abandoning afterwards a part of the additional tax deficiencies or the penalties. It should be noted here that the sociological analysis of the constraint of the informally negotiated output completes, and even corrects, the traditional legal analysis of the formal equilibrium between the powers of the administration and the guarantees of taxpayers. The power of negotiation of social groups and the strategic capacity of the use of tax procedure are not identical for all, bearing in mind that the economic and/or cultural possibility of resorting to a tax consultant is not fairly distributed in social categories. It is also necessary to take into account the geographical distribution of services, the portfolio of dossiers and of course the selection of dossiers for tax control.

The study of work methods specifies the implementation of tax law in the field of the sociology of organization: the legal categories are interpreted within the framework of schemes of the concrete elaboration of tax corrections that structure the negotiation.

Four methods give account of the manner in which a tax inspector constructs the tax corrections which illustrate the organizational reality of fraud. The first method, which we can call mathematical, concerns fraud in revenue. It rather targets small businesses whose turnover is reconstituted by the tax controller from an analysis of the purchases that are resold and of a calculation of the realized margin. This construction is to the advantage of the tax controller because of its almost scientific character linked to the objectivity of numbers. However, the analysis of data and the quantification of certain information are difficult (for example tips and broken objects in a bar). It necessitates the use of several methods of reconstituting revenues, which is not easy. Negotiation is thus based on these issues.

The second method is directly legal in the sense that it refers, not to law in general, but to an indisputable violation of the law: the non-compliance of a formality of a time limit or of a tax return; specific exemptions of VAT deductions etc. Its frequency remains limited because of the peculiarity of the taxation that mixes up elements of law and of fact that are complex to interpret because of tax interventionism. This case incarnates the obvious mission of tax control but is sometimes debated with regard to the legitimacy of the legal provisions involved, for example for the breach of formalities.

The third working scheme is called managerial as it consists of appraising the consequences of the management of the enterprise: in law, the administration cannot interfere in the management of the enterprise who is free in its decision-making, but it can criticize the consequences of it. Here we find the cases of expenses that are not in conformity with the interests of the enterprise or abnormal acts of management. The strength of the managerial model of tax control is less obvious than the other models because it depends directly on the sphere of competence of the enterprise, and not only on the tax expertise of the controller. Its legitimacy is fragile in the context of the economic and social valorization of employment and in that of economic globalization (cf. chapter 12).

Finally, there are mixed cases that combine several registers. For example, the deduction of a provision for a doubtful customer implies that the loss is probable (the strict legal aspect) and that the diligence of the failing customer is exhausted (the managerial aspect).

The tax inspector appears to be the central actor of the organization. We can speak of a profession, in the sociological sense of the term, particularly in the presence of a control of results and not of the activity itself, of specialized jargon, of a competence of expertise, and of independence with regard to the hierarchy. Of course, the hierarchy has certain means of structuring the controller's work, namely: the existence of regulations formalized in the instructions, the possibility to personalize rewards and sanctions[22] according to results, the cultural valorization of the role of the tax controller. But the tax controller amply masters the process of tax control on the spot (he is alone in the enterprise). He finds himself in a position of sociological exchange (Homans, 1958) with the organizational hierarchy. He submits himself to the constraint of output but he sees that his expertise and the freedom to organize his work is recognized. He controls the information and the results that follow, whereas his superior privileges his role of animation over his hierar-

22 By improving the notation or evaluation, by increasing certain bonuses, but the impact on the career remains limited, with all the agents progressing (of course more or less quickly) in the echelons by seniority.

chical role, which can however manifest itself in the form of a notation and/or evaluation.

The organization of tax control thus corresponds to an original bureaucratic model in front of certain classic analyses (Leroy, 1994). This "kingly" administration does not comply with a strictly legal rationality consisting in applying mechanically tax law by using the prerogatives of public power. It points out the limitations of structural approaches. The famous characteristics of bureaucracy described by Max Weber (1971, p. 226) have a certain general pertinence[23]: the status of the public service with its rights and responsibilities (for the servants) applies, the hierarchy exists, the tax procedure is written and foreseen in a special code called the book of tax procedures, the competence of the tax controller is both technical and geographically defined. As we have seen, the administrative function of Henri Fayol also seems to characterize certain aspects of tax organization. Nevertheless, the logic of decision-making is not deduced from these structural conceptions. In case of tax control, one must look for it in the compromise between output and negotiation, which is implemented by an essential actor, the tax controller, who has a rank not very high in the official hierarchy. There is also a form of organizational rationality (that of negotiated output) which is opposed to the idea of an "organized anarchy" modeled by Cohen, March and Olsen (1972).

Likewise, the classic model of the French-type bureaucracy of Michel Crozier (1963; 1987, p. 98) is badly applied to the case of the French tax administration. The model of Crozier contains four general features applicable to any organization and to any country: the impersonality of the rules, the centralization of decision-making, the isolation of every hierarchical category and the pressure of the group on the individual, and the development of parallel relations of power. A cultural feature is particularly applied to France according to Crozier, namely the fear of face-to-face relations. In the model of the French fiscal bureaucracy, rules, then, are not applied in a general and impersonal way, but are adapted to the considered case; the decision during the tax control depends more on negotiation between the tax controller and the taxpayer than on the hierarchy: it is made during the control within the enterprise and not according to a centralized process as in Crozier's model; there is a form of evaluation by the measurement of the statisti-

[23] According to Weber, the structural characteristics are related to the historic process of rationalization (of the "rational-legal" type) of the West. This functionality of bureaucracy has relative relevance in the case of the tax administration which, as we have pointed out, lumps together in its statistics very different situations of "fraud."

cal output[24]; the tax controller operates in the enterprise facing the head of the enterprise and his council (he does not fear face-to-face relations). He is considered to be an expert, including the use of tax procedure. There exists indeed a particularism of the profession of tax controller.[25] The existence of negotiation is combined with the dimensions of output, of expertise and of cultural management.

These results must be put into perspective together with certain (potential) factors of change. As we have seen, the recent implementation of LOLF has found a concrete expression by the inscription of the objective of "the fight against serious fraud", whose real scope depends on the evolution of the decision-making logic of tax control. From this point of view, the French model must be confronted with the diffusion of an international model of administrative regulation, in favour of the big enterprises of the globalized market, which could call into question the particularities of the French model.

c. The administrative regulation and the new public management

Without proceeding with a systematic comparison[26], we shall rely on the case of the control of transfer pricing by the administration (Sakurai, 2002) which constitutes one of the most important issues in the fight against tax avoidance (and fraud) in the current context of economic globalization. This field offers an opportunity to compare national forms of administrative regulation. Regulation is questioned here in the meaning of the putting into compatibility of the issues and the priorities of the actors, and in the meaning of the derivation of the formal principles towards operating rules of public action.[27] Adaptation to globalization is used as an argument (cf. chapter 7) in order to justify the diffusion of a cooperative mode of "administrative regulation" of the control of multinational enterprises (i.e.: responsive regulation). In this perspective, the logic of tax control is supposed to adapt to market efficiency by applying in a flexible manner tax law that leads to the assessment of the profits of world groups.

---

24 Tax bureaucracy is not an organization "incapable of correcting itself according to its errors" (Crozier, 1963, p. 239) with some "dysfunctions that come from its rigidity" (p. 250). We cannot say either that tax controllers "do not succeed in imposing their ideas" (p. 254).

25 In *État modeste, État moderne*, Crozier confirms the pertinence of his model and notes: "everything that could be a counterbalance, like the particularism of the profession (...), has become weaker" (1987, p. 98).

26 Data available on this subject data are still incomplete; Sakurai's survey cited above is based on 55 interviews (managers of multinational enterprises, tax consultants, administrative authorities).

27 For a more distinct conceptualization, cf. chapter 10.

Up to now three forms of administrative regulation have put into concrete form the labelling of fraud or legality. In the United States, regulation is conflictual because the administration (*Internal Revenue Service*) tends to adopt an "aggressive" approach towards the financial schemes of multinational enterprises with regard to transfer pricing (re-invoicing between entities of the same group of companies located in different countries). American inspectors are evaluated by their hierarchy with regard to proposed tax corrections (Sakurai, 2002, p. 183), which must be compared with the French constraint of statistical output of the tax control. But, in contrast with the French case, negotiation seems to be more difficult due to a strong culture of litigation: the judge rather often finds himself in a position of arbitrating tax disputes, as the number of appeals related to the amount of transfer pricing shows.

In the United Kingdom, administrative regulation is cooperative according to a flexible approach. Informal agreements are strived for between the inspector in charge of the dossier and the enterprises, a situation which tends to bring prejudice to small enterprises which do not have sufficient capacities to negotiate with the administration. In Japan, regulation is hierarchical (Sakurai, 2002, p. 187) in conformity with the consensual culture of this country. The administration is considered to be placed in a prestigious statutory position: its social power is superior to that of taxpayers in general and of multinational enterprises using transfer pricing in particular. Negotiation with the administration, socially situated above enterprises, is customary, while referring a case to court still appears to be contrary to the values of the Japanese society who considers litigation as a sign of tax evasion or fraud. The hierarchical regulation avoids conflicts, but stands in the way of interpretative adaptations of the law by the judge. The implementation of public policy follows the ways of a complex and hierarchical administrative structure which generates delays in decision-making. The Japanese administration appears to be reluctant to change, interprets restrictively the possibilities opened by tax law, and is thus rather unfavourable to multinational enterprises which appear to be submissive to its position.

The Australian way of regulation, called "responsive regulation" (Braithwaite, 2007), is cited as the best synthesis of international practices, bearing in mind that economic globalization undermines differences between national styles of administrative regulation. It appears as an ideal to reach for the new public management. In Australia, a reform in 1997 encouraged the cooperation with taxpayers and thus the abandonment by the administration of "aggressive" management practices. Two stages are distinguished: that of information, dialogue, persuasion, and of auto-regulation for taxpayers who want to cooperate (Braithwaite, 2003, p. 4); and that of punitive strategy based on a growing scale of penalties when the cooperative way fails. Responsive regulation abandons repressive management by "stick" based on threat and legal coercion, since this style of regulation is considered to be ineffective, especially facing complex fraud. In this sense, Murphy (2004, p. 203) shows, based on a study of 2292 Australians accused of tax evasion, that the fact to be mistreated by administration reinforces the willingness to fraud in relation with the decline of trust in the administration.

The idea which underlies the valorization of cooperative regulation is that big enterprises require a specific way of management. It thus appears that several administrations reform their management in order to adopt this new form of regulation of the business world (Job *et al.*, 2007) which favours that what the Marxists would call the big capital. Likewise, the adoption of specific organizational structures, following the example of the direction of big enterprises put into place in several countries, participates in the same movement. Certainly, the reasons for this reorganization are serious, whether we refer to the complexity of tax problems raised by multinational groups, to the centralization of their tax management (parent company and subsidiaries) in the country of the parent company, to the specificity of some of their legal regimes (like profit consolidation), or finally to their importance for tax receipts in the context of public finance deficit. One must mention here the resort to the model of agency (different from the administration) to ensure a certain volume of tax revenues, while at the same time subcontracting the problems of management and of tax control. As the case of Italy shows (Adda, in Leroy, 2008), these management, which establish a link between the remuneration of the agency and the level of tax collection, encourage cooperative regulation with big enterprises. In fact, the generalized quest for an agreement with taxpayers puts the social categories the best equipped to negotiate their taxes (such as multinational enterprises) in a strong position, even if this logic preserves the financial interests of the State.[28]

Nevertheless, responsive regulation raises the question of the ethical relation to be established between the State and the market in the field of taxation. Here, even though it is for the administration a question of better controlling the strategies of tax optimization of multinational groups through this new organization, the solution tends to legitimize the right to a privileged treatment in favour of the economic actors of globalized capitalism.[29] In the context of economic globalization, the

[28] Tax revenue collection improved in Italy following the implementation of this new organization in 2001.

[29] In a study of Swiss cantons with a strong direct democracy, Feld and Frey (2002) find that the taxpayer is better treated by the administration: he is not systematically suspected of defrauding in case of an error and is less severely punished in case of a

cooperative regulation of the big multinational enterprises expresses the submission, not to the norms of tax law, but to the ideological percepts of the new public management which affirms the superiority of the market.[30] A parallel can be established with the new international accounting norms (IFRS) that favour financial capitalism. We can also cite the case of the reforms of the relations between the administration and taxpayers. In several countries, voices are raised (rightly so) to improve the rights of tax citizens facing the administration. These demands draw on the movement of public performance measurement which pushes people to call on administrations to account for their management.

We therefore cannot but state that in the case of tax control, this type of reforms of tax procedure benefits big enterprises especially which have better advisers. The link with the reforms of the 1980s is clear: following the transition from the political sphere to the administration (reduced by privatizations), it is today a matter of reforming bureaucracies by establishing performance management (Leroy, 2007). This managerial illusion is well illustrated by the valorization of tax planning which ensues from it: under the pretext of legal security encouraging cooperative agreements between big enterprises and the administration, tax avoidance is justified as a strategic element of business performance conceived in fact, not within an economic logic, but as a frenetic race of improving of the financial gains of the actors of capitalism. We understand that the labelling of the financial schemes of taxpayers by the administration is fundamental for tax deviance (cf. chapter 10).

Conclusion

The "modernization" of the tax administration refers to a process of polymorphic bureaucratic change by the variability of the contexts and by the plurality of the explanatory levels. In case of France, the merger of diverse pre-existing structures was coupled with a transformation in order to adapt to a tax system that has become interventionist and is from now on based on declarative general ("synthetic") taxes. This change is part of the global modernizing reference system of the postwar period. The second transformation realized in the 1990s also aims at bureaucratic modernization in order to address European, social and public service issues. The recent third stage introduces the logic of performance, established by the LOLF of 2001, into the organizational objectives. The indicators of performance represent a certain progress but need to be improved in order to attain a real evaluation of tax policy.

---

minor violation of the tax code. In this case, related to the level of democracy, cooperative regulation is not reserved for the business world.

30 With reference to the theory of market efficiency: cf. chapter 7.

The study of these decisive reforms is completed by the study of cases relative to tax control, essential for the credibility of the tax return system of democracies. Tax procedure is the subject of a dialectic of power where the prerogatives of the administration come up against the movement of improving the rights of controlled citizens. The particularities of this bureaucratic model with regard to classic analyses are explained by the polymorphism of the organization of the work of control. The statistical measurement of output recalls the logic of a private enterprise, but it does not entirely comply with the legal rationality of the fight against (serious) fraud. The negotiation depends on an actor whose power is linked to expertise and the mastery of the information. His role is valorized even though he is not positioned in the superior echelons of the hierarchy.

The analysis of bureaucratic modernization supposes the combination of different levels of analysis in order to arrive at an evaluation. Without neglecting the structural reforms, it is advisable to focus on the mechanisms of the organizational functioning. In this sense the new indicators of performance, such as the traditional statistics of the number of managed tax returns, the output of the control etc., tend to neglect the decision-making processes too much. Contrary to the administrator, the researcher has to construct this critical distance from the object by opening up certain "black boxes". This work is difficult when the question and the results are complex and when some changes are recent as it is the case here. The interpretation of perspectives includes some limitations. The tendencies brought up to date by means of the international context of administrative regulation can change, and even inverse themselves because of the opposition forces that they provoke.

Therefore, even though it is still premature to judge it, we can ask ourselves if the world crisis that erupted in the summer of 2008 is going to change the organization of international tax control. The publication of the list of tax havens by the G20 meeting in London on April 2, 2009 could, if followed by an implementation, reinforce the fight against international fraud: the conventions of administrative assistance between countries, that currently come up against the existence of offshore zones, of bank secrecy, and of the refusal of some states to pass on information, could find a new momentum. For the time being, the "black" list established by the OECD contains only 4 countries[31], and we have to be

[31] Costa Rica, Malaysia, the Philippines and Uruguay, but the Channel Islands (Jersey etc.), Macao, Hong Kong (dependent on China), the American states of Delaware, Wyoming and Nevada, the (American) Virgin Islands, known for constituting territories with privileged tax systems, do not appear on the list. The "grey" list of the OECD contains 38 countries, who committed themselves, some of them recently, (Switzerland, Luxembourg Liechtenstein, Austria, Belgium etc.) to cooperate. We

prudent about the long-term effectiveness of the political dynamics set in motion in order to regulate fiscally the financial flows.

With this reservation in mind, it seems important for us to emphasize the risks of the diffusion of the liberal precepts of the new public management applied to tax management. The incoherencies and the contradictions of tax policies that undermine the exercise of (full) democracy are coupled here with the reduction of the tax obligation for capital. The cooperative regulation of the control of big enterprises creates an inequality incompatible with the political and social principle of a "contribution-tax" helping public policies. The demand for a privileged treatment of enterprises involved in globalization delegitimizes the redistributive taxation of the richest. It neglects the problem of the coherence of tax policies at the level of a country, Europe, and (even if it seems to be in the distant future) the world. It ignores the question of the amelioration of the social justice of the tax system. In the line of the neo-liberal ideology, management by administrative performance could serve as a pretext for new tax privileges. We have known however since the time of Tocqueville that "tax inequality is the most pernicious and most appropriate to add isolation to inequality."

---

must wait to see the contents of the (bilateral) conventions that will be signed, or amended in the sense of a real cooperation.

CHAPTER 9

The Individual's Logic in the Face of Taxes

Although taxation is an old topic of reflection, we find few operational details concerning the taxpayer in classical texts (cf. chapter 4). As we have seen in chapter 2, the founders of fiscal sociology were more interested in the tax State, even though Goldscheid (1967, p. 202) proposes to distinguish fiscally between working classes and capital classes. The analysis of tax policy (chapter 6) treats mainly pressure groups. In an approach extended to other disciplines, it is therefore necessary to use the works of history, economics, social psychology and economic psychology to obtain a body of empirical data concerning the logic of the individual in the presence of taxes. As the title of this chapter shows, our questioning is part of the methodological individualism, but it is not exclusively based on rational choice theory (restricted to the logic of self-interest). Moreover, it takes into account the collective action of individuals, who through their socio-economic position can form a group or a class, in view of certain factors of the tax revolt. But the characterization of tax deviance as a socio-economic macro-phenomenon including fraud is discussed in the next chapter.

So the history of tax revolts has its place here because it sheds light on the diversity and complexity of the factors that the sociology of the individual tax decision must integrate. Beyond their economic, social, cultural and cognitive dimensions, the rebellions against taxes are political in nature. In fact, even though the economic and social frameworks shape collective action, and though there are various pretexts for protest, tax revolts ultimately constitute a political refusal of the institutional authority. Secondly, the empirical studies on the individual minimization of taxes are taken into consideration in order to elaborate a theory of the practical rationality of taxpayers. Contrary to a widespread opinion, the individual does not systematically abhor his tax obligations. Even if the individual benefit drawn from tax evasion seems immediate from an economic point of view, the possibility of an altruistic taxpayer, convinced of the importance of citizens for financing public policies, does exist. Economic interest (self-interest), in the sense of an optimal calculation based on the objective factors in decisions, does not (always) determine the actor whose rationality is certainly limited, but logical with regard to his values, and especially to his reasoning (cognitive rationality). The inadequacy of the approach through the utilitarian economic rationality used by the (narrow) rational choice theory (RCT) leads to the valorization of the citizen's contribution-tax.

1. The Factors Involved in Tax Revolts

Historically[1], tax revolts have often accompanied revolutions, as Tocqueville and Mann (1947) pointed out. In fact, with taxation being constitutive of the State, protest against them is at the heart of numerous political movements (Ardant, 1971, p. 400, Tilly, 1986, p. 121, Bercé, 1991, p. 23-35, Campbell, 1993, p. 175). This section aims to present, by means of a few illustrations, the principal factors involved in the history of tax rebellions: beyond the complexity of the possible causes, such as the class struggle, the legitimacy of the State and the socio-economic transformations, the collective rejection of taxation is interpreted as a political act.

a. The class struggle

Tax revolts can be considered in terms of social groups and classes involved. The Marxist schema, illustrated by Porshnev's study (cf. box 13), sees in taxes a class struggle, much like the Goldscheid's conception, one of the founders of fiscal sociology. For Porshnev, in the 17th century French taxation oppresses the peasants and the urban plebs who rise up, in particular against the salt-tax collectors ("*gabeleurs*").

Box 13: A Marxist interpretation of tax revolts

The Russian historian Boris Porshnev (1963) adopts a Marxist[2] approach to explain the popular uprisings in France from 1623 until 1648 with the class struggle. Peasants and the urban plebs cooperated in the tax revolt in order to struggle against the feudal and absolutist regime. Being the true pre-proletariat (without property and working physically for a wage) of the feudal society undergoing transformation, the urban plebs was composed of artisans, small merchants, declassed peasants and a lumpenproletariat. The uprisings were no longer movements of artisanal corporations as in the past,

[1] Cf. the English Revolution of 1648, Portugal's independence (from Spain) in 1668, the American Revolution of 1783, the French Revolution of 1789 etc.

[2] Controversy opposed Porchnev to Roland Mousnier over the interpretation of the 17th century revolts, with the French historian refusing to consider them as the expression of a class struggle. Mousnier in fact thinks that the society of that period is hierarchical: it is based on relationships of social status, with honour and prestige being more important than wealth; the classes are pertinent only with the intensification of the market economy (from the 18th century onwards).

but aimed at the social order defended by the nobility, the clergy and, despite a certain ambiguity, by the bourgeoisie.[3] Two real forces opposed one another, that of the people who resisted being exploited by taxes, defined as a centralized feudal annuity ("rent"), and the "class front" who supported "the tax system (...) of the State" (p. 292). The other factors (opposition of parliaments, religious issues, struggle of the nobility against the monarchy, corporations etc.) did not have real importance. The State was in the hands of the ruling economic class[4] and through the tax yoke ensured three functions: it maintained oppression (the judiciary and law enforcement system); it associated a part of the bourgeoisie with the State (offices) in order to avoid an alliance with the popular classes; it ensured a centralized (tax) annuity (rent) for the nobility by means of the various benefits (pensions). These "tasks were more or less secrets of the nobiliary monarchy (...) Disclosing them would stir up a class struggle in the country. It was thus necessary to persuade public opinion, by justifying this tax yoke exclusively by referring to military needs" (p. 458). The deeply-rooted causes of the revolts were economic, with the situation of people's poverty making the tax yoke unbearable.[5]

The Thirty Years War, which monopolized the armed forces, and the power of the popular movements stood in the way of the complete repression by the royal power which was led to compromise, while at the same time strengthening the fiscal pressure. But people had lost confidence in the institutions, which would become the background of the Fronde after 1648: "all plebeian movements that had taken place in France for 25 years were reflected in the political crisis of the Fronde" (p. 277). Here the bourgeoisie (and the parliaments), then the nobility alternatively tried and used popular discontent against the tax yoke: they manipulated (and betrayed) the people.

This analysis is not that of the political logic of the construction of the tax State studied in chapter 4. It increases the influence of the economic determinants, wrongly reduces the State to a simple instrument of the dominant classes and neglects the real importance of the nobility and

---

3 The bourgeoisie participated or sometimes showed sympathizing neutrality, but later often contributed to the repression. Similarly, some members of the lower clergy sometimes participated in the revolts.

4 "The State is above all the instrument of the ruling economic class to keep in check the exploited classes. It was the power of the State which accomplished the functions of exploiter, collecting a centralized feudal annuity ('rent') for the Court service. Thus the absolutist monarchy was precisely the system which held in check the exploited majority (...) Two powerful forces opposed each other: the resistance to exploitation of the popular masses of several million people and the force that repressed this resistance" (p. 293-294).

5 "In rural areas, taxes only completed the ruinous situation of peasants already exploited by feudal lords; in towns, poor classes were deprived as a result of a capitalist exploitation which progressed little by little. The tax yoke (...) brought the poor to a state of pauperism" (p. 269).

the bourgeoisie. It has however the great merit to show that the institutionalization of the tax State, at that time in France, not only largely excluded the people, but also exploited them, on the pretext of the needs of the war. Once the conditions and the specific pretext for mobilization are reunited, revolt is the logical response to the absence of consent to taxes by the majority (the popular classes). When the levy destined for the authority becomes an economic tribute and when the political way of reform is impracticable, revolution is not far away.

Caron (2002, p. 300) concludes his study of the tax revolts of 1841 by interpreting them as a claim for political citizenship in the context of a regime where the right to vote was reserved to the rich paying a certain amount of tax (cense-based regime): "In the case of the riots of 1841, the use of violence can also be interpreted as one of the forms of the demand for access to citizenship, itself reflecting a long process of politicization of the popular, urban and rural classes, at least since the French Revolution."

b. The political legitimacy of the tax State

The history of tax protests provides indispensable lessons. The legitimacy of the tax State was built up slowly from the transformation of the feudal system. Thus the decisive action of Philippe le Bel to establish a permanent taxation gave rise to resistance: the establishment of a permanent tax on the sale of goods (a general tax payable by the buyer and the seller called *maltôte*) was abandoned in 1295 in favour of the return to feudal aid (Vuitry, 1883, p. 147). Concerning the tax revolt of 1548 in the Charente and Bordeaux regions in France, Bercé (1991) points out that this peasant movement starts from a reaction to the extension of the regime of the salt taxes, so-called *gabelles*; it forms part of a context where taxes are (still) considered by the doctrine and the common opinion as exceptional, with the monarch supposedly living on (cf. chapter 4) the proceeds of his domain. This reasoning is completed by the idea that the obligation to pay for an abundant produce in these regions near salt-marshes was not fair. A decisive motive for the tax resentment is also found in the scandalous enrichment of the agents collecting the gabelle. The willingness of the royal authority to detach the tax State under construction from the old social formations of feudality therefore constitutes a historical context for the anti-authority activity. But in this context some permanent factors are stimulated, namely the (fair) concrete relation with tax management and with the nature of the taxed commodity.

The political dimension of tax revolts is important. The lack of legitimacy of taxes nourishes tax revolts. In England, the rebellions are not directed at the principle of royal taxation, especially when war justifies the needs; in rural areas they concern the exactions and the collectors' corruption or else are targeted at the levy and the attributions of the lord, for example for legal expenses (Hilton, in CNRS, 1987, p. 171). Analyzing the French mobilization in 1841 against the reform of the "tax on doors and windows" launched by the (liberal conservative) minister of finance, Caron (2002, p. 124) notes that the tax revolt in Toulouse has a political character: it mobilizes "the people, the workers or the populace, the rabble whose social and political motivation is repressed, denied, and therefore invisible in these dominant discourses". Certain processes of taxation foster the injustice and therefore the illegitimacy of taxes. We can mention here the solidarity between all the inhabitants of a parish established under the Old Regime in France for the payment of the taille (a direct land tax levied on the peasantry and non-nobles). Certain people's failure to pay was thus attributed to taxpayers who had already paid their share. It was only in 1775 that Turgot, who had grasped the iniquity of such a mechanism, abolished this measure.

c. *The economic and social factors*

The role of the economic determinants of tax revolts is favoured by Ardant who defines tax as a liberal technique of the exchange economy. The author considers taxation to be an "awakener of revolts" (Ardant, 1971, p. 408) for two reasons: first because of its novelty, and then with regard to the conflict between the monarchy, oriented towards the monetary economy, and feudalism which persists in the closed economy. If the exchange economy, notably trade, is insufficiently developed, taxes, payable in money, become more difficult to raise. That then requires "evaluation methods at the same time uncertain and irritating" (p. 409). For example, the slowing down of exchanges in the Europe of the 17th century, which is caused by the gradual drying up of the imports of precious metals, explains many tax revolts of this period. This structural thesis of economic exchange seems fundamental. It sheds light on a variety of tax phenomena, but constitutes a doubtful model[6] as for its deterministic basis.

Thus, as we have seen in the first chapter, Tocqueville proposes another interpretation of the factors for the collective movements based on the study of the French Revolution. While Ardant once more analyzes the causes of the Revolution, especially the failure of the tax reforms (1972, p. 119), in terms of the structure of economic exchanges, Tocqueville (1986, p. 1058) shows on the contrary how economic prosperity accelerates discontent. Using a variety of cumulative factors related to the theory of relative frustration, he proposes a cognitive

[6] Even though this model is open to other factors such as the tax technique or the attitude of the privileged.

model of tax revolt[7]: as the economic situation is improving, tax inequalities are even more unbearable. Ardant's geography of tax revolts is centered on the (objective) obstacles to economic exchanges entailing irritating practices of taxation; Tocqueville's geography of revolution is that of prosperity and the improvement of tax levy[8] which stirs up the (sensed) frustration of the inhabitants of the richest regions. In these regions, the residual defects of taxes (such as the exemptions) become all the more unbearable the better the socioeconomic position of the inhabitants. If the theory of relative frustration appears more relevant than the deterministic theory of economic exchanges, it is because it illustrates a particular application of the cognitive approach (cf. below) to the relation between the concrete context and the feeling of fiscal injustice.

Taxation may give rise to a movement of rebellion by affecting the central processes of the social and economic life of a society. For example in France, the revolt of 1707 against the increase of stamp duties is explained by its consequences on the cost of jurisdictional proceedings which occupy a privileged place in the society of that period. Another example is given by a study of the tax revolt of the Swazis (Southern Africa) against the British colonial State[9] (Crush, 1985). The contradiction between coercion and legitimization is highlighted here. The main objectives of the taxes established in 1903 on this African people are to complement the public revenue of the colonial government and to create an incentive for work (in order to pay tax with the wages received from the masters). But the new taxation causes complete disorganization of the traditional social order: the peasants are obliged to sell part of the harvest reserved for their own consumption; the families arrange marriages, not any more as a strategy of enlarged kinship, but to obtain money; children are sold or obliged to keep the income of their work in order to pay their own taxes. In view of these changes imposed by the level of taxation, tax evasion becomes widespread. The response of the colonial power is first to intensify the controls and the sanctions, but the yield does not improve, all the more because inventive practices of tax

7 "It is primarily in the collection of all the taxes where the change which took place among those who govern can be seen the best. The legislation is still as unequal, as arbitrary and as harsh as in the past, but all its defects become more moderate during the enforcement (…). It is not always going from bad to worse that on falls into a revolution (…). The evil has become less, it is true, but the sensitivity is more intense."

8 As in the administrative district (so-called *généralité*) of Île-de-France: "the parts of France which had to be the principal hotbed of this revolution are precisely those where progress is most visible" (Tocqueville, 1998).

9 The history of colonial taxation remains to be revisited from the perspective of revolts.

minimization are put into place (false certificates of payment, absence during inspections etc.). Finally, as coercion not being sufficient, concessions claimed by the Swazi chiefs are granted: they lead to a reduction of the level of taxation. This example shows that the needs of capitalism (accumulation through the work of wage earners) and coercion do not suffice to account for the individual's relation to tax. The (relative) restoration of the legitimate social order is a complementary dimension.

d. The complexity of the political mobilization against taxation

Many factors intervene in the explanation of tax revolts. A good case study is given by the adoption of Proposition 13 in California in 1978 and the establishment of various upper limits on taxes in other States (Cox, Lowery, 1990). These measures are the results of a protest in the public opinion against the level of taxation. To explain the success of this reform, Buchanan (1979) uses the theory of the "free rider": the presentation of the reform, approved by referendum, targets exactly the real limitation of taxes (the amount, the type of tax), but it does not specify the expenses that will be cut out, which leaves the possibility for the taxpayers who benefit from the tax reduction to hope for an avoidance of reductions in public services (expenses) which they are interested in. It must be noted that for the future winner of the Nobel Prize in economics this situation is an exception because, according to the public choice school (Buchanan, Tullock, 1962), in democracies the way is generally in favour of expenses whose beneficiaries are fixed while taxes are generalized. Musgrave (1979) puts forward another argument by referring to the increase of taxes in relation to inflation: the burden of property and income taxes is aggravated even though real income does not progress. He also mentions the discontent towards the public services and the government.

These explanations postulate a direct relationship between the taxpayers' self-interest and the mobilization against taxes. As we have seen however, the factors of tax revolts are more complex than these too simplistic economic theories on the self-interest rationality. Lowery and Sigelmann (1981) show that the abundant literature on the American revolt (in the line of the Proposition 13 in California in 1978) retains eight little tested variables: self-interest; the elevated global level of tax pressure; the inefficiency of taxes in relation to the services provided (public waste); the inequity of the distribution of the tax burden; anxiety with regard to the personal impact of the general economic situation; partisan ideology; distrust towards the government; the lack of information. Statistical analysis reveals a certain correlation between the tax revolt and the disillusion (distrust) with regard to public authorities, which confirms the involvement of the legitimacy of the institutions as a political factor of fiscal civism. No explanation however, considered separately or in combination with others, is validated rigorously (at a significant level): the reason must be sought, according to the authors, in the fragility of the hypothesis common to these explanations, namely that the revolt is a function of the socioeconomic position of individuals. It should rather be seen as a social movement of political expression of a dissatisfaction, which finds conditions for mobilization deemed favourable by the individual in the concrete context. It must also be noted (Cox, Lowery, 1990) that the impact of this tax revolt upon the growth of the public budgets of this period was very limited.

The analysis thus emphasizes the complexity of the causes of the taxpayers' decisions, the political character (in the last instance) of tax revolts and the (relative) autonomy of the choices made by the public decision-makers. The sociology of tax revolts must also investigate the conditions of mobilization, and notably the "repertoires" of collective action (Tilly, 1986, p. 16) which may vary historically. Today the debate interested in the impact of the new social movements, as is shown in the case of the revolt against the poll-tax (cf. box).

Box 14: The collective action against the poll-tax

The poll tax is a local capitation tax which asks the same amount from all the taxpayers without taking into account their income. It was introduced by the Thatcher government in 1988 as a leading measure of its neo-liberal programme to limit local public expenditure. It resulted in an important movement of tax revolt in Great Britain. A study (Bagguley, 1995) shows that the opposition between the old and the new social movements is not necessarily pertinent. The factors at stake are economic (which is classic) but also moral (injustice which favours the rich and hits the poor). The organization of the revolt relies on an informal network of protests, but also involves Labour Party activists and trade unions (at the local level) who disposes of a variable influence. The majority of the active members in the revolt are people who have never been involved in previous social movements. The social groups involved combine at the same time the middle class of the public sector and the (traditional) class of the low-income workers. Women are particularly mobilized, especially mothers at home who find themselves for the first time confronted with a personal tax in the case of the poll tax. There are diverse forms of action (meetings, letters etc.) but they are especially expressed by the non-payment of this tax. So it appears that this tax revolt combines the old and the new traits of social movements.

Finally the socio-historical context must be considered in order to understand tax revolts. If the cost of a collective strategy seems too heavy, the individual may turn to other forms of tax minimization (evasion/fraud, avoidance, lobbying for exemptions) in relation to the policies of the interventionist tax State.

2. The Concrete Rationality of Taxpayers

Starting from the "broad" approach to rationality from R. Boudon (1989, 2003), the analysis of the taxpayer's decisions marks the limits of the standard utilitarian approach used in the literature of economics: self-interest, in the sense of an optimal calculation based on objective factors, does not (always) determine the decisions of actors whose logic depends on their values and on cognitive rationality that expresses the concrete link to taxes.

a. The limits of the approach of "utilitarian" rationality

The utilitarian interest to minimize taxes is not the only point at stake. This is important[10] because the interventionist tax system cannot survive if tax incivism is the only behavior. For the approach by utilitarian rationality, paying taxes is not linked to a general social contract concerning the provision of public services, but is seen as a form of exchange-tax, i.e. as the price paid by a taxpayer in exchange for services that he receives. The main economic models of fraud[11] use the Expected Utility Theory (Allingham, Sandmo, 1972; Yitzhki, 1974; Cowell, 1985), a research framework based on utilitarian rationality in the sense of the rational choice theory (especially with the analysis of costs and benefits): the minimization of taxes is seen in turn as taking a risk linked to the methods of taxation and of control, as a criminal category, and as a refusal to finance public goods.

For the theory of risk, tax minimization (evasion and avoidance) is a function of the expected objective gain which is calculated in relation to the tax rate, to the probability of being controlled and to that of being detected, and to the amount of the penalties legally applicable. It is often maintained that high tax rates encourage evasion, and therefore that official growth is undervalued. This approach leads to the "deterrence theory", by recommending strong repression with frequent inspections and high penalties, which appears difficult to achieve in developed democratic States where the moral condemnation of fraud is weak (cf. below). The second approach uses the economics of crime (Becker,

---

[10] This section and the following contain parts of my article "The concrete rationality of taxpayers", *Sociologia del diritto*, March 2011. We have also seen that citizens are in favour of the social spending of the interventionist State for reasons unrelated to the selfish egoism of the social groups benefiting from them (cf. chapter 4).

[11] Economists do not always distinguish tax fraud (evasion), which is legally defined as a violation of the law, from the general behavior of minimizing taxes notably by a clever use of the legal ways (rules) to pay less tax (avoidance).

1968) which measures the expected utility of fraud (tax evasion) compared to that of other activities and also recommends deterrence. The third approach is based on Olson's paradox (1966) whereby free riders, members of the latent group of taxpayers, do not have any interest in financing collective goods from which they will benefit anyway.

These theories, which conclude that taxpayers have objectively a tendency to minimize their taxes, in a legal way or not (except if sanctions are severe), come up against several objections. The relationship between the objective factors of risk and the actual behaviour of taxpayers is not mechanical.[12] Economists ignore in general the variables constituted by the attitudes that intervene between the economic stimulus and the response (Lewis, 1982). They overestimate the impact of self-interest. Concerning the effects of the level of public takings, and contrary to the idea, already put forward by Schumpeter, of a limit to fiscal capacity, the results remain uncertain. At the macro-economic level, there does not exist an empirically verified relationship between a high global level of takings (taxes and social security contributions) and a low rate of economic growth (linked to tax evasion). For example, despite very high marginal tax rates, the United States experienced a strong post-war growth. At a micro-social level, it is not empirically demonstrated that the tax civism of the richest people is weaker than that of other people. Some find a correlation between income and tax evasion, others dispute this result.[13] From the socio-political point of view, one should therefore take into account the rate of taxation socially tolerable. In his study of the Swedish social-democratic system of the 1970s, Vogel (1974, p. 501) shows[14] that 53.5% of the people assess as reasonable the amount of taxes that they pay, despite a particularly high rate of taxation. In Germany, Schmölders (1970) concludes that the opposition to taxes is not a direct function of the importance of the

12 For example, Lewis (1979, p. 253) concludes from his surveys that the exchange model does not explain all the data. Similarly, Beck *et al.* (1990, p. 88) note that to understand the tax preferences of citizens economic and socio-political explanations of behavior must be used.

13 The correlation between the amount of income and tax evasion is defended by: Dornstein, 1976; Clotfelter, 1983; Pommerehne, Weck-Hannemann, 1996; Hanousek, Palda, 2003; but it is not found by: Mueller, 1963; Spicer, Lundstedt, 1976; Citrin, 1979; Grasmick, Scott, 1982; Wärneryd, Walerud 1982; Beedle, Tayor-Gooby, 1983; Furnham, 1984, Richardson, 2006, Gërxhani, 2007.

14 In a pioneering survey in Sweden, Vogel considers as explanatory factors: the risk to be caught out, the norms of the reference group and the individual's own values. This typology is incomplete because it leaves aside (cf. table on tax deviance in chapter 10) errors (non-voluntary behavior labeled as deviant by the authority). It has the merit of showing that tax compliance takes several forms and that the classical theory of reference groups, appreciated here in terms of tax evaders personally known by taxpayers, has an impact.

objective burden. In England, Lewis (1979, p. 255) confirms this thesis. For the United States, Etzioni (1986, p. 183) indicates that tax fraud (evasion) is linked to the sense of injustice of the tax system in the public opinion (for the years 1960-1980) even though the rate of taxation remained stable. According to the survey by Dubergé (1990) in France, 60% of the people take into consideration the "psychological costs" of taxes (for example, the complexity of the tax return), and not the amount that they must pay. Torgler and Schneider (2007) do not find a statistical correlation between tax rates and tax morality (known from surveys on values) in Belgium, Spain and Switzerland. Thus the idea taken from Laffer's studies that "too much tax kills tax" is not verified.

Concerning the risk of a tax inspection, an important fact is that the average frequency of tax audits is generally low, and thus that the respect for tax return obligations should be less than it is in reality: this observation contradicts the approach by the maximization of utility. Experiments and surveys[15] show that the percentage of tax evasion is not linked to the objective probability of a tax inspection, except when the information given to the person on tax inspection is precise (Spicer, Thomas, 1982). The heuristic logic of fiscal duty distorts the representation of his personal interest by the taxpayer, including the one who is well informed. The probability for a tax audit is estimated subjectively by those taxpayers who have already undergone an audit of their tax returns[16] (Spicer, Hero, 1985; Maciejvosky *et al.*, 2006; Mittone, 2006, p. 823). Empirically, it is also put forward that the propensity to evade depends on the number of tax evaders personally known by taxpayers (Vogel, 1974, p. 505; Spicer and Lundstedt, 1976, p. 300; Dubergé, 1990, p. 230). Within the framework of their reference group, the estimation of the number of persons engaged in a process of tax evasion is linked to the estimation of the risk of sanctioning (Welch *et al.*, 2005, p. 24). Tax morality is correlated with the perceived probability (and not objective) by the individual for the risk to be caught out (Verboon, van Dijke, 2007, p. 720). According to the prospect theory (Kahneman, Tversky, 1972, 1973), the objective factors of being caught out in case

15 Spicer and Lundstedt, 1976, p. 300; Spicer, Hero, 1985; Vogel, 1974, p. 505; Dubergé, 1990, p. 230; Webley *et al.*, 1991, p. 84; Reckers *et al.*, 1994, p. 832; Scholz, Pinney, 1995, p. 497.

16 Experiments lead to contrasting results on the exact effect of subjective probabilities by the taxpayers who have already been audited: Spicer and Hero (1985) put forward an over-estimation of the probability of inspection (and thus an improvement of fiscal civism), but Maciejvosky *et al.* (2006) as well as Mittone (2006, p. 823) insist on the opposite result, at least in the period immediately following the inspection ("the bomb crater effect": the idea that the inspection in the image of a bomb cannot come twice in a row on the same place in the same period). Notwithstanding these clarifications, it appears that the probability for inspection is not estimated objectively.

of tax evasion[17] have a weak influence on "the subjective probability" calculated by the taxpayer in his decision to evade: the superiority of the prospect theory over the expected utility theory is demonstrated notably by Dhalmi and Al-Nowaihi (2007). For example, many people estimate that the probability to be caught out by the tax authorities is greater when the amount of tax evasion is high. People are more tempted by tax evasion in a situation when they have to pay a tax (perceived as a loss) than in a situation of a tax credit which is felt as a gain (on this "bias": Kirchler, 2007, p. 133-142).

There is thus no direct relationship between the objective calculation of the risk linked to tax evasion and the actual behaviour of the person. The economic approach does not take into account the subjective rationality of the taxpayer, in particular concerning the issue of the legitimacy of taxes.

b. The Axiological rationality and the political legitimacy of taxation

Taxpayer does not react solely in a utilitarian way (based on interest), but appreciate taxes also regarding moral attitudes, their axiological rationality in the sense of Weber. At their origin, even though there is still little information on this aspect, the establishment of taxes seems to be related to the transformation of a religious payment to God into a payment to the State. We know today that, in the presence of the tax State, social norms do matter (Keenan, Dean, 1980; Reckers *et al.*, 1994; Torgler, 2004; Wenzel, 2004; Alm, Torgler, 2006), especially when the taxpayer identifies with the group that bears his norms (Vogel, 1974; Wenzel, 2004). The data of World Values Surveys just as laboratory experiments of social sciences show that, even if moral attitudes vary from one country to another, they have an influence on the civism of taxpayers. For example, Richardson (2006), in his cross-sectional study using data from 45 countries, confirms the influence of "tax morality", such as it is assessed in world surveys on values. Among these values, the impact of religious convictions constitutes an empirical question difficult to solve (cf. box 15).

17 Frequency of inspections, difficulties to audit certain incomes, possibilities for fraud or tax evasion etc.

Box 15: Religion and taxpayers

Studies on the attitude of taxpayers belonging to a religion still remain scarce.[18] While Furnham (1983) shows in a British survey that people who adopt the Protestant work ethic are rather opposed to taxation, Grasmick *et al.* (1991), in an American survey including Protestants, point out that religious conviction, measured by the frequency of religious practice and by identity, reduces the tendency to cheat with taxes. According to a Dutch survey by Verboon and Van Dijke (2007), Protestants has more fiscal civism than Catholics and people without religion (the latter being the last in the ranking). Torgler (2003, p. 297), with data of the World Values Surveys focused on Canada, concludes that religiosity is correlated with tax morality, but in a way that is variable according to the religion (Catholic, Protestant, others). Still using the World Values Surveys, he confirms (Torgler, 2006) this result in a study of 32 countries from 1995 to 1997. For Spain, by retaining as an indicator the fact of attending a religious service, Alm and Gomer (2008, p. 84) find no correlation. Torgler and Schneider (2007, p. 466) confirm the absence of correlation between religiosity and tax morality for Spain, while it has a significant impact in Belgium and Switzerland. Finally, Welch *et al.* (2005), in a study of American Catholic parishes, show that personal religious conviction has little impact on tax evasion when most people think that there is a low level of tax compliance in their religious community.

Nevertheless, if moral values sometimes intervene, the moral condemnation of tax evasion (cf. box 16) is rather weak (Leroy, 2003, p. 232). Tax seems fairly little perceived by the individual as a moral or social obligation.

Box 16: The weak moral condemnation of tax evasion

According to world and European surveys on values[19] between 1981 and 2004, "cheating with tax" is seen as "never justifiable" by only 53% of respondents (average rate for all countries). These results are confirmed by the available empirical research. For the Germany of the 1970s (Schmölders, 1973, p. 106 and 137), 4% of respondents compare the tax evader to a thief, while 43% consider him "a cunning businessman". For Sweden, Vogel's survey (1974, p. 506) confirms the tendency of indulgence towards tax avoidance, the loopholes of the tax system being considered as an excuse. For the United Kingdom, Lewis (1979, p. 249) mentions a certain tolerance of the surveys for small tax omissions, and concludes that these attitudes

[18] There are a few studies on the relation between religion and the tax system.

[19] A scale of 1 to 10 is provided, where 1 comprises the mention "never justifiable" and 10 "always justifiable", in order to answer the question "cheating with taxes if you have the opportunity is etc."

depend more on the amount of the sums involved than on moral values concerning tax evasion. A survey of Keenan and Dean (1980) covering 424 persons indicates that the moral condemnation of tax evasion is little expressed compared to other forms of deviance, including other financial deviances. For France, according to the surveys of Dubergé (1990, p. 225), 12% in 1958 and 30% in 1986 condemn tax evasion, knowing that polls confirm these results. For Australia, according to data of 1998, Evans and Kelley (2002, p. 253-254) point out that tax cheating is considered very serious by 32% of the people, a result much lower than for social (welfare) security fraud where the ratio is 59%. For the United States, Grasmisk and Scott (1982, p. 227), who test the impact of the deterrence theory, conclude (p. 227) that there is little sense of guilt with respect to tax evasion. Another American survey by questionnaires on 205 persons (Burton *et al.* 2005) confirms these results: tax evasion is not considered as a serious problem (occupying the fourth position among five in the descending scale of gravity); it is seen as less serious than other business crimes.

Other values, as for example, respect for obligations in general, adhesion to the attitudes of the group to which one belongs or refers (on the role of occupational cultures: Ashby *and al.*, 2009), can intervene. The individual may also condemn tax evasion for good non-moral reasons, for example if he himself cannot evade, or because tax evasion transfers the tax burden onto the non-tax-evaders. Tax compliance, so difficult to probe in its foundation, expresses very little moral duty, in the sense of an interiorization of the rule; moreover, an individual may judge tax evasion as reprehensible and practice it all the same (Vogel, 1974, p. 511; Dubergé, 1961, p. 102 and 1990, p. 226).

More than the moral values, it is the political legitimacy of taxation which is essential: the feeling that the tax system is unfair favours tax evasion (Etzioni, 1986; Richardson, 2006, Torgler *et al.*, 2008, p. 329). The political dimension of taxation is historically well established in relation with the birth of State (chapter 4). Taxes contributed to draw the figure of the modern State in Europe, often in the sense of a centralization of power (Tocqueville, cf. chapter 1). The political legitimacy of taxation is therefore central in order to understand the axiological rationality of taxpayers. In this sense, tax compliance (here fiscal civism) constitutes a form of support for the party in power and, in certain historical circumstances[20], it expresses a commitment to a political regime. Empirically, it is demonstrated that pride with regard to one's

20 For example, George Sand calls for the support of the Republic of 1848 by paying taxes (in an anonymous brochure: "Words from Blaise Bonnin to the good citizens"). A survey conducted in Israel (Dornstein, 1976) shows that the tax compliance of recent immigrants, notably those coming from underdeveloped countries where the use of taxes is contestable, appears weaker than that of former immigrants convinced of the legitimacy of contributing to the financing of a modern Jewish State.

country (Torgler, 2003, p. 295; Torgler, Schneider, 2007), trust in the government and public institutions[21] (Slemrod, 2001, p. 20; Bergmann, 2002; Torgler, 2003; Alm *et al.*, 2005; Torgler, Schneider, 2007; Torgler *et al.*, 2008, p. 332 and p. 334; Rudolf, 2009; Torgler, Schneider; 2010) and the use of public money[22] are correlated with tax compliance. Vice versa, in the absence of these criteria of political legitimacy, the disillusionment with regard to the authorities has a negative impact on tax compliance (Lowery, Sigelmann, 1981; Beck *et al.* 1990, p. 86, Alm *et al.*, 2005). We have also seen that tax revolts often express an opposition to the legitimacy of taxation, which is felt as arbitrary, a feeling which is not mechanically connected with the socio-economic status of individuals. In the last instance, the cognitive rationality of the actor (Leroy, 2003) must be considered in order to reconstitute his real reasoning.

c. The Cognitive rationality

The cases retained here shows that the decision of the taxpayer is not solely based on his objective interest (self-interest) or his values, but that it expresses a cognitive theory of the taxpayer which considers the way in which he treats information.

The cognitive rationality of the taxpayer explains the estimation of the risk of a tax audit. In general, the taxpayer does not know the objective factors for being caught out in case of fraud or tax evasion, factors which are retained by utilitarian economists. He reasons according to the concrete information available to him (number of known tax evaders, lessons from previous inspections etc.); he proceeds to calculations and bets called "subjective biases" in the psychological literature, but which are in reality logical with regard to the situation. It is thus rational (from a cognitive point of view) to think that the bigger the tax evasion, the more risky it is, even if this does not correspond to the standard calculation of probabilities. Besides, we have seen that tax administrations often target "big" tax evasions. In the same way, taxpayers who have already been audited logically fear a new inspection, even if the mathematical probability has not changed. In fact, they estimate, often quite rightly moreover, that henceforward their dossier is more administratively watched. Finally, to take up again another one of the examples given before, it is rational when one prefers to limit an amount to be

---

21 For example, Torgler and Schneider (2007) find a statistical correlation between tax morality (measured according to European and world values surveys) and trust in the government, the parliament, the legal system.

22 Examples: the satisfaction with public services (Bergmann, 2002), the feeling resulting from the benefits received by society through the financing of public goods and services (Alm et Gomez, 2008, p. 84).

paid, which weighs down on one's cash flow, than to take a risk on a tax credit that relieves it. Nevertheless, the risk and thus the gain are "objectively" the same in the two cases.

Tocqueville's theory of relative frustration, set out in the first chapter and used in explaining the French Revolution and tax revolts, also forms part of this model for the cognitive rationality of the taxpayer. In the context of improvement, it is logic to be even more frustrated by persisting fiscal injustice. Sociologically, taxation (like satisfaction, happiness etc.) cannot be studied only from the point of view of the "objective" burden represented by public takings (tax revenue). It must also be viewed with regard to its felt burden, as well as in its concrete relation to public services (expenses).

Cognitive rationality also provides a solution to the paradox of the relation between taxes and public spending. The theory of fiscal illusion, presented by Puviani (cf. chapter 2) and taken up notably by the school of public choice (Buchannan, Tullock, 1962), wrongly insist on the unrealism and the taxpayer's irrationality, because he demands lower taxes and the maintenance or the creation of public services (and thus expenses) at the same time. This theory may avail itself of certain surveys (Lewis, 1982, p. 49; Winter, Mouritzen, 2001, p. 120), or of the argument of Downs (1960) which wants that taxes are the object of aversion in democracy because one sees the money going out of one's pocket, while public services received are less visible. Other surveys refute this theory however.

We must first point out that this paradox is not systematic. According to the Welch's survey (1985, p. 314), the "unrealists", who want less taxes and more expenses, are not in the majority: the majority of people declare themselves in favour of either an increase in taxes in order to finance the wanted services, or a reallocation of expenses, or a reduction of public wastefulness. Courant *et al.* (1980, p. 3), on the basis of 2001 responses to a questionnaire (State of Michigan), had already put forward that the unrealists were not many and that most people are prepared to pay for the financing of the additional services they desire. Another survey (Hadenius, 1985) also shows that discontent decreases when the link between taxes and expenditure is indicated to the people. Sometimes political campaigns or the media make citizens aware of the relation between the taxes and the services provided, as in the case (Citrin, 1979, p. 114) of the debates around Proposition 13 in California. If, in the surveys, the support for the Welfare State is weaker when people are being asked how much they are prepared to pay (taxes), that does not necessarily express a general rejection, but rather a question of priorities (Beedle, Taylor-Gooby, 1983, p. 18). The demand for a reduction of taxes and an increase of expenditure is not necessarily irrational, as confirmed by the Australian survey of Blount (2000, p. 287). an aversion for taxes may express the conviction that the State can (and must) finance the desired expenses in another way.[23] Schmölders (1973, p. 40) had already pointed this out for the Germany of the 1970s where four out of five persons think that in the case of a budget deficit, the State must reduce its expenditure, with 15% being in favour of an increase in taxes. Kemp (2002, p. 146) also underlines the same phenomenon.[24] A Belgian survey (Schokkaert, 1987) on 1824 people covering real projects of expenditure shows, with respect to the size of the public sector, that the majority prefers the status quo for the overall expenditure, which invalidates the theory of fiscal illusion (which implies a growth of public expenditure by the underestimation of taxes).

In this way the theory of cognitive rationality integrates this data well by explaining that the citizen considers that his demand for public services can be financed by various means: by taxes certainly, but also by loans, the reduction of waste, the reallocation of appropriations, subsidies from other authorities, the pricing of services etc. Therefore, asking for more public services and less taxes is neither unrealistic, nor irrational, when the citizen proposes other resources (Leroy, 2007, p. 92), even if he is mistaken in the exact estimation of the cost of public choices. Finally, the political function of "contribution-tax", which implies the possibility of an "altruistic" citizen, contradicts the economic theory of fiscal illusion.

The framing of the problem is also important for determining the attitudes to public finance. A study of the 1992 presidential campaign in the United States shows that citizens are more favourable to the increase of public expenditure in the case of a specific presentation of the sectors concerned (63%) than in the case of a general presentation (37%) (Jacoby, 2000, p. 757): in the first case, the effect of the variables measuring the attitude towards the groups benefiting from the expense is stronger; in the second case, the scheme of the motivated thought concerns the government itself, notably in accordance with the general economic situation. The partisan variable tends to play a role in the two cases. Income is an important factor for global expenses, but not for specific expenses, which is in line with our cognitive theory. In the case of a global expense, the schema of reasoning is financial (how to finance

23 The State, even in a context of crisis, is capable of providing diverse responses and therefore of innovating in financial matters (Gold, 1995).

24 "Responses tended to suggest that the government should spend more (…) while at the same time holding taxation stable or reducing it. However, analysis (…) revealed that this was not necessarily a case of fiscal ignorance since often the respondents wanted to reduce spending on some areas in order to increase it in others" (Kemp, 2002, p. 146).

the demand for public expenses) with the result that income influences the response; in the case of a specific expense, the schema turns on the preference relative to the project, and not on the level of public spending. An American survey (Hansen, 1998, p. 519) also indicates that individual choices lead all the more to coherent collective preferences since the questions asked are realistic and since they include alternative propositions: contrary to the Condorcet-Arrow paradox, the majority of preferences here are transitive (and therefore logical).

In the same vein, we can explain by cognitive sociology the presence of a "bias" pointed out by the literature on the frames on framing. This bias is the following: the support for the redistribution of incomes through a progressive tax schedule seems to be experimentally more important (McCaffery, Baron, 2004, p. 698) when the choice concerns the rates rather than the amounts of the taxes. The explanation is simple: in the same way that nobody buys his bread with rates, the amount of the tax, compared to its concrete situation, is more typical than the choice of an abstract percentage of taxation. The concrete idea of justice is indeed that the rich must pay (reasonably) more tax than the poor: the differences of incomes must remain justified, which is not the case in the context of the neo-liberal globalization that has led to the crisis of 2008 (cf. the excessive remuneration of the managers of the banks who have suffered losses). Another example is given by a study on the evaluation of a fiscal bonus. With reference to the prospect theory, the results show that the framing effects are relevant (Lozza *et al.*, 2010): if the fiscal bonus is described as a tax rebate (a loss reduction), the respondents attach a higher importance to the fiscal bonus and are keener to save it when it is described as a tax rebate (a loss reduction) than when it is presented as an income increase (a gain). I interpret this result as following. In line of the cognitive rationality, the respondents consider that the loss of money in the case of a tax rebate is lesser, but it is a loss: thus, they prefer to save the bonus (perhaps in order to pay the next taxes). And vice versa, they use the bonus for everyday purchases (they do not save it) when it is viewed as an additional income.

The painless character of indirect taxes on consumption also raises an enigma that the cognitive approach allows one to solve. It is notably a question of explaining why persons with modest incomes declare themselves in certain surveys (Dubergé, 1961, p. 140 and 1990, p. 280; Schmölders, 1973, p. 79) in favour of indirect taxes, even though these taxes penalize them.[25] The answer is clear: unless there is precise concrete information, indirect taxes are not perceived as a burden because they are associated with consumption costs by the taxpayers who are

25 They consume all of their income and therefore the tax is levied on its totality, while the richest people can make savings.

badly informed about the nature of the taxes. Consumer expenses are considered by individuals as total amounts, without distinction between the purchase price exclusive of tax and the amount of VAT. The individual therefore has a concrete knowledge (or ignorance) of the tax, logical but false. Besides, cognitive rationality explains that the painless character of indirect taxes is relative. For example, in France, taxpayers have claimed (opinion polls) a reduction of (indirect) taxes on gasoline, in relation with the media coverage of the conflict of the truck drivers in road transport of September 2000, which insisted on the importance of these taxes. Similarly, the debate on the reduction of taxes, which has agitated several European countries, provides information for the citizen-taxpayer. Concerning the VAT, the painless character of this indirect tax is thus less and less verified as a result of the successful media coverage of the debates and of the criticism coming from certain opinion leaders.

The case of ideologies, attribution errors and myths point out to a variety of situations where citizens implicate taxes, even though the taxes are objectively not responsible.[26] In chapter 6 we saw that cognitive theory explains spreading of the anti-tax discourse which underlies the neo-liberal ideology: within a context of the "crisis" of social protection which the argumentation of economic globalization reinforces, it is logical for the individual to believe in the necessity for the retrenchment of the tax State which is defended by reputed economists. The causal attribution error also explains that the individual rebels against taxes, even when he is not involved, because he maintains the following reasoning (cognitive rationality): the State is responsible for my economic situation, but taxes are used to finance the State; therefore I do not have to pay taxes if my personal situation is precarious. This syllogism, inexact in its involving of the State, logically explains the error made by the taxpayer regarding the cause of his situation[27], especially since even the most liberal conception recognizes a role for the State in the economy. For example, the Poujadism of the 1950s is explained economically by the poverty of small traders and craftsmen, while taxes and the tax administration were violently attacked. We can finally mention certain myths of the Old Regime such as the tax on life (Bercé, 1980), supposed to tax the birth, marriage and death: an illiterate society that observes that taxes are imposed on administrative obligations

[26] Ardant had already pointed out this "transfer phenomenon" or "imputation error" (1972, p. 654)

[27] The causal attribution error has been well described by social psychology (Heider, 1944; Jones and Davies, 1965; Kelley, 1967; Weiner, 1979). This theory has been applied to the attitude of the taxpayer by Kaplan, Reckers, Reynolds, 1986 and Hite, 1987.

(notary deeds, stamped paper) has good reason, in the sense of R. Boudon, to believe in the taxation of life. The same cognitive rationality is found in the myth of the end of taxes, which is historically recurrent especially during a military victory of the monarch. Since permanent taxes were fairly recent in nature, and since they were outside the logic of the feudal system, it is reasonable to think that they have a temporary character only like in the past. Taxpayer's rationality, which is often "limited" in the Simon's sense (1982), is thus explained by the logic in the concrete reasoning of the taxpayer in his real-life situation.

d. Taxation as a concrete relation

A principle of concrete expression (Leroy, 1992) structures the taxpayer's decision: the individual reasons according to his concrete situation, to his subjective knowledge of taxes, on looking at the sources of information which seem typical and accessible to him. This idea of the fiscal sociology is corroborated empirically.[28] The low level of citizens' information and the complexity of tax law impoverish the cognitive rationality of the individual who forges his opinion from his circle of acquaintances, the media, experts who advise him, his vision of public services, of the role of the State[29] and of his contacts with the tax authorities etc. Thus the relationship, "experienced" by the individual, with the tax authorities (Leroy, 2002; Kirchler *et al.*, 2006; Alm *et al.*, 2010)

---

28 For example, Schmölders (1973, p. 74) in his surveys on Germany underlines: "the word tax give rise more to an association with something experienced than to the idea of the State." Dubergé (1961, p. 57) shows that elderly taxpayers have a more accurate assessment of tax inspection based on lifestyle because of their experience with previous controversies concerning the income tax. We have also seen that the contacts with tax evaders guide the taxpayer in his decision whether to comply or not with his tax duties. Citrin (1979, p. 118) maintains that concrete programmes are more easily controversial than abstract goals. Roberts *et al.* (1994) show that the preference of individuals in favour of a progressive tax scale (which hit the richest harder) diminishes when one passes from abstract questions to concrete questions. Scholz, Pinney, (1995, p. 508) point out that the subjective estimate of the risk of tax inspection depends on the concrete nature of this risk. Blount (2000, p. 287) indicates that when one gives a detailed breakdown of the targeted spending, only a minority of people are in favour of a reduction of taxes and spending. Kirchler (2007, p. 65) confirms that the attitude towards tax evasion depends on the individual's reference group, which is also in line with our principle of concrete expression. We should finally note that this principle had already been brought up by Durkheim (1984) in *On the division of social work*: it is very difficult for the government to act in favour of common solidarity if the concrete (pathological) specialization of tasks moves the individual away from this feeling: he "cannot do anything against the vivid, concrete impressions that his professional activity arouses at every moment in everyone of us."

29 The classical results of the theory of reference groups apply here (Leroy, 2002, p. 68-69).

influences the tax compliance.[30] Torgler *et al.* (2008) also show that tax morality is correlated with the feeling that the tax administration is honest, and that it works accurately when helping taxpayers. Alm *et al.* (2010) show (laboratory experiments) that the assistance information from the tax administration has a significant impact on the compliance of the taxpayer.

The taxpayer thus commits representation and decision errors. He badly estimates the taxes that hit him[31], sometimes fails to recognize the link between taxes and spending on public services and often strays into technical details.[32] For example, in France, opinion polls show that many people consider that local taxes are intended only for the municipality (while it is mot the case). We have also seen that taxpayers declare themselves in favour of the reduction of taxes while at the same time claiming the extension of public services because they think that other means of financing are available. Certain high income households are sometimes favourable to taxes in order to reassure institutions[33] and avoid deficits (Mueller, 1963, p. 232).

As the study of the concrete relationships to taxes, fiscal sociology provides an original field to discuss the standard economic approach based on the individual utilitarian rationality. In fact his decision does not only depend on interest, but also proceeds from (political) values and the concrete knowledge of the social phenomenon of taxes; the utilitarian model of "exchange-tax" has a limited pertinence, since the social phenomena of taxation also bring into play other sociological configurations. Fiscal sociology thus crosschecks the advances of rational sociology and economic sociology. By endorsing the deontological figure of "contribution-tax", citizen does not seek his own interest and does not optimize a utility function. As I have shown, since my first studies on fiscal sociology (Leroy, 1992), five figures representative of taxes exist in a concrete way, among which the citizen's contribution-tax must be encouraged.

---

30 Torgler *et al.* (2008) also show that tax compliance is correlated with the feeling that the tax administration is honest, and that it works accurately when helping taxpayers.

31 According to the survey of Schmölders (1973, p. 80), only a third of the people estimate their tax burden correctly. For Spain, Martin, Lopez, Lobo (2000, p. 145-149), who study the subjective tax pressure, indicate that 56% of the people (in 1999) find that they pay a lot of tax, even though the rate of tax revenue is 39%, which is relatively low compared to other European countries.

32 Dubergé (1961, p. 53) shows that it is especially the tax technique which presents problems to non-specialists: for example, 75% of the people know the principle, but not with the schedule, of the taxation of income based on lifestyle.

33 This is the basic argument of Montesquieu that taxes are levies on property for the State, which ensures the safety and the use of private goods: cf. chapter 4.

3. The Citizen's Contribution-Tax

Fiscal sociology demonstrates that the citizen is favourable to the financing of legitimate public action by taxes. He is capable of altruism, which is denied by the clichés of the neo-liberal ideology that has been raging since the 1970s. The cultural or universal tax aversion, the limitation of tax revenue due to the efficiency of the market and economic globalization, the irrationality of irresponsible taxpayers in their demands for public services, are not inevitabilities. Even if there are several representations of the role of taxes in society, the figure of the citizen's "contribution-tax" is a reality whose extent depends on the characteristics of the financial public action.

a. The sociological representations of taxes

Except in those cases where the tax is painless (invisible), for example with certain indirect taxes on consumption where the taxpayer does not represent for himself the taxation included in the prices, five representations of taxes must be retained (cf. table 12).

Table 12: Representations of tax in the society

Invisible-Tax	It is not a social representation (for example, but not always, indirect taxes: VAT)
Tribute-Tax	The felt tax burden is intolerable
Constraint-Tax	The felt tax burden is too heavy
Obligation-Tax	Tax paid to public authorities (one of the two bases of the formation of the tax State in Europe): legal concept
Exchange-Tax	Price paid by the taxpayer for the benefit (services) which he receives from society: economic concept
Contribution-Tax	Taxpayer judges it legitimate to finance public institutions or policies: political form of tax consent

The "exchange-tax", used by the followers of the school of public choice, takes up one of the economic conceptions of taxes considered as the price to be paid by the individual for the benefits[34] that he receives from the State (or from another public authority). This tax dominates when the tax system does not justify its interventions by the contribution to the authority. Olson's paradox, according to which the individual has no interest to personally finance collective goods since he can benefit from them without paying tax, is based on this approach. The historic example of cense suffrage, where the payment of tax determines the granting of citizenship, also illustrates the sociological pertinence of

[34] This figure of tax could be also called: benefit-tax, expense-tax, price-tax.

utilitarianism. Today the dues paid for the use of certain services illustrate sociologically the idea of the interest-based consent to taxes. The conception of exchange-tax is finally congruent with the theory of pressure groups claiming tax benefits. Theories based on self-interest do not suffice however, as we have seen, to explain the taxpayer's decision.

The "obligation-tax" is inspired by the legal definition of a tax: it is a unilateral act of a sovereignty-based nature involving a financial levy of the public authority, without consideration (compensation). The individual has the feeling, more or less explicitly, that it is not possible to avoid paying the tax. The reasons for this feeling of tax obligation are nonetheless various. The resigned taxpayer considers that the individual strategies (fraud) or the collective strategies (revolt) of avoiding tax, as too risky, although legitimate. The indifferent taxpayer does not ask himself questions on tax change, for example due to lack of information, of opportunities for tax minimization, or of financial needs. The ethical taxpayer deems it normal to comply with his obligation, without prejudging the use of the tax etc. The obligation tax, like the following figures, thus concerns the person liable to tax more than the person paying tax. It does not suffice to legitimize the tax duty.

The "constraint-tax" and the "tribute-tax" refer to cases where the tax burden is considered heavy to bear. These figures are not radically distinguishable from the obligation-tax, but are situated on a continuum: if the perceived constraint is weak, the tax constitutes an obligation; if it is felt as very strong, the tax is seen as an arbitrary "tribute". Between these two situations one finds the constraint-tax. The tribute-tax finds its origin in Roman history.[35] It may lead to anti-tax reactions, in varying forms ranging from tax avoidance to tax revolt, because of its objective financial weight, but also if it is experienced as unjust. In fact, contrary to the utilitarian vulgate, taxation is not felt solely as a constraint for objective financial reasons (cf. before).

The "contribution-tax" refers to the political form of consent to tax in the sense where the taxpayer considers it legitimate to finance institutions or public policies. This figure of political legitimacy includes a formal aspect of procedural democracy: from this point of view recent studies show that democracy improves fiscal civism (cf. box). In addition to the already mentioned examples of adherence to political regimes, various cases justify this figure of legitimate tax. In France in towns benefiting from a charter, the practice of approving the budget accounts (that are written) by local taxpayers spreads from the 13th century. From the four "old" revolutionary contributions up to

---

35 In the beginning, the tribute was due by Roman citizens to pay the costs of war, but subsequently this charge was transferred onto conquered countries because of the reticence of Roman citizens.

today, the governments have moreover attempted to promote the social representation of the fair contribution-tax.[36] The troubled history of consent to the tax State (cf. chapter 4) by assemblies representing tax-payers also illustrates the validity of this sociological figure. In its struggle against England, the American Revolution puts forward the principle of consent ("no taxation without representation"). Periods of socio-economic crises and wars often justify the acceptance of the increase in tax pressure[37] (cf. chapter 7). The history of democratic parliamentarism, according to the English model, relies on the power to consent to and control public expenditure financing. The experiences of direct local democracy, with participatory budgets, also valorize this conception

Box 17: Participation in choices (democracy) improves compliance

Financial democracy, defined as the participation of people in the choices of public finance, has positive effects on fiscal compliance. Torgler (2004, p. 34) shows experimentally that the fact of being able to choose the level of deterrence (number of inspections and level of penalties) improves the respect for tax obligations (compliance). This study is confirmed by other experiments (Alm, McClelland, Schulze, 1999; Feld, Tyran, 2002) on the relationship between the power to decide democratically and tax compliance (tax citizenship). Direct (real) democracy is more positive for tax compliance, as is shown by Pommerehne and Weck-Hannemann (1996). This result is confirmed by Torgler and Schneider (2007) in the case of Switzerland where the cantons that grant more rights of participation are correlated with stronger tax ethics. Financial transparency is also correlated with the diminution of the impact of electoral cycles on the balance of public budgets (Alt, Dreher Lassen, 2006). Tax involves the legitimacy of public action (Leroy, 2002); the relation to institutions explains, according to the experiments carried out on the basis of the global surveys on people's values, the differences in tax compliance (Cummings *et al.*, 2004).

Empirically, it has been proved that a significant part of the people are ready to pay additional taxes for programmes that seem important to them (Mueller, 1963, p. 224, Beedle, Taylor-Gooby, 1983, p. 29, Welch, 1985, p. 316, Taylor-Gooby *et al.*, 1999, p. 192). Contrary to the theory of the public choice school, it appears that certain people are in favour of a tax on gasoline for ethical reasons[38] (Brodsky, Thompson, 1993),

36 Cf. the examples of the "*vignette*" (a vehicle tax license) for elderly people, the drought tax of 1976 for farmers, the solidarity tax on wealth etc.

37 The condition is to present the possible political choices without using deterministic ideological biases.

38 They thus adopt a conception of public interest that does not correspond to the utilitarian theory of values.

even though they often use their vehicles. Slemrod (2001, p. 13) points out that in the United States a certain number of citizens voluntarily pay sums of money (in addition to their tax due) to the treasury to reduce the public deficit. Moreover, taxpayers appear more favourable to taxation when they can establish a concrete link with the expenses for public services (Hadenius, 1985, p. 351). These established facts lead one to reject the idea of an insurmountable aversion to taxation.

b. *Against the cliché of the cultural aversion to tax*

Concerning the commonplace of the general aversion to taxation, we must first put aside the theories, more or less sophisticated, referring to an allergy of a cultural nature.[39] The explanation by means of cultural determinism remains engaging, notably with the vicissitudes of the dubious notion of the "tax mentality of peoples", extolled by Schmölders (1970) in order to interpret his surveys (in other respects pioneer). For example, according to this idea, Latin countries would be distinguishable by their propensity to tax evasion because of their mentality.

To discredit the cultural theory of tax aversion, we can go back to the results of the European and world surveys on values. Let us first recall that tax evasion in general meets little moral condemnation, which seems to uphold the theory of a general tax aversion. It is however also noted that tax evasion is sometimes condemned more strongly, which invalidates the thesis of a general tax aversion[40]: 67.6% in Denmark in 1981, 63.9% in Hungary in 1999, 80.5% in Japan in 2000, 67.7% in 1995 in Spain, 69% in 1982 in Sweden, 73% in 1995 in the United States[41]. This first analysis seems then to support the idea of a variable tax mentality depending on the country (proper to each nation), but in reality this is not the case.

According to the data available over a long period, only Japan and the United States maintain high figures of reprobation of tax evasion, thus seeming to illustrate a culturally virtuous tax mentality. Yet, even

39 With the progress of social sciences, the explanation by means of the nature of man, inclined to evil, is rarely invoked.

40 Similarly, if tax evasion is encountered in all countries, we know (despite the difficulty of its measurement) that it reaches variable levels according to the country.

41 On the basis of the data of the International Social Survey Programme's Religion, Evans and Kelley (2002, p. 255) confirm this observation. They point out that cheating in matters of income tax varies from one country to another. In 1998, the order of classification, that starts from countries which express the least disapproval of tax evasion, is the following: Russia, Austria, West Germany, Latvia, Ireland, France, East Germany, Cyprus, Switzerland, the Netherlands, Northern Ireland and Great Britain (at the same level), the Philippines, Hungary, Italy, Chile, Slovakia, Norway, the Czech Republic and New Zealand and Portugal (same ratio for the 3), Australia and the USA and Slovenia (same ratio for the 3), Sweden, Bulgaria, Spain, Japan.

for these two countries, the figures vary, going for example from 73% to 62% in the USA between 1995 and 1999 and from 74.2% to 80.5% in Japan from 1981 to 2000. Above all, for the other countries, the results invalidate even more clearly the theory of the mentality of peoples. Sweden, often quoted as a model, reports a rate of 48.9% in 1996 and 50.4% in 1999. Spain, a Latin, Catholic and supposedly more complacent country, has a rate of 67.7% in 1995, a rate of 59.7% in 2000, and a rate of 65.7% in 2006.[42] The ratio of West Germany is 29.5% in 1990 and 39.6% in 1997. France condemns tax evasion rather little (47.8% in 1981, 45.9% in 1990, 47.2% in 1999), but Germany is even less severe (1990: 39.5%; 1997: 39.6%). The figures thus confirm that the rates of response vary according to the years, as these examples further illustrate: the Czech Republic has a rate of 39.6% in 1998 and then 58.3% in 1999; Hungary 58.3% in 1998 and 63.9% in 1999; Germany 39.5% in 1990 and 56.4% in 1999.

These results raise the question of the role of moral values but do not justify an (ideological) explanation based on the general aversion more or less strong according to the peoples' mentalities or based on a kind of determinism of the national culture.[43] The differences between the countries are therefore a result of a set of variables that influence citizens in a more or less durable context. Currently, as we have seen in chapter 6, the economic theory of aversion has a much larger credit.

c. *Altruism against the commonplace of the universal aversion to tax*

The economic theory of aversion is based on the idea that the individual has no interest objectively to pay taxes, all the more so as the objective risk of being caught out and of being sanctioned is generally low. Now taxpayer is not always motivated by his self-interest in the sense of the utilitarian rationality; he is capable of altruism if the tax State is legitimate. Therefore aversion to taxation is not general. When it does exist, it often expresses the conviction that the State can and must finance the desired expenses by other means; it depends on the political justification of the functions of taxation in relation to expenditure; it diminishes when the concrete link between taxes and expenditure is evident. One must also remember that taxpayers, in their majority, fulfill their tax obligations in the developed democracies.

---

42 For 2006, source: Alarcon Garcia *et al.*, 2007, p. 500.

43 It goes without saying that cultural variables must not be excluded, but the question is indeed to explain these "cultural" values according to the rationality of the actors in a precise socio-historical context.

The utilitarian idea, which says that the interest in minimizing taxes is all the bigger the higher the taxpayer's income, is not statistically attested by all of the empirical studies. The estimation of the risk of a tax inspection does not depend on a simple utilitarian equation, but prolongs rather the "bounded rationality" (Simon, 1982). Concrete factors, such as experience of inspections and of tax evasion, nourish the taxpayer's cognitive rationality. There is therefore no direct relation between the objective (utilitarian) calculation of the interest in evading (the risk, the comparative opportunity) and the actual behaviour. The utilitarian model (RCT) thus explains badly the real estimation of the risk of a tax inspection (audit), certain errors of causal attribution (tax revolts) where tax is not involved, the belief in the myths and ideologies of taxes, the preference of a part of the deprived people for indirect taxes.

The economic approach to evasion neglects the importance of the political legitimacy inherited from the historical tradition of the European tax State. We have also noted the political character of tax revolts. Nowadays the complexity and the instrumentalization of the tax system blur the choices on the functions of the interventionist State, which renders the contribution-tax less visible. This figure is also less spread out in the countries where the State interventions are not legitimate for the citizens: the extreme example is given by the corrupted States, knowing that the wasteful State also meets difficulties to legitimize tax.

Citizens are capable of altruism, contrary to the utilitarian conception of values popularized by the theory of tax aversion. Though the causes of altruism are still debated, the reality of the phenomenon is undeniable. Since *L'essai sur le don* by Marcel Mauss, we know that "potlatch" does not refer to a purely utilitarian logic of self-interest, even if the discussion remains open as to the exact part of disinterestedness. Recent studies propose to explain human altruism in relation to evolution that has fostered cooperation between people (Bowles, 2006). Natural selection pushes people to cooperate, so that the individual knows how to evaluate that which is merited (justice) through social norms. Certain authors also invoke (Heinrich *et al.*, 2006, p. 1770) the presence of sanctioning mechanisms that punish non-cooperation and the violation of the norms of one's social group (cultural group selection), which would also result from the evolution of mankind. Other specialists (André, 2008) refer to reputation that everyone wants to preserve, in order to account for altruism.

In the economic field the ultimatum game consists in asking one person to share a sum of money with another person that the latter can accept or refuse. If the person accepts, each retains his share; if he refuses, the money is lost. The interest, in the utilitarian sense, wants that the proposed sum be minimal and that it be accepted (better having a small gain than nothing at all). Nevertheless, the results differ from the forecasts: the proposed sums are sometimes significantly higher than the (narrow) rational requirement, which validates altruism. On the side of the recipients of the proposals, refusals appear either for too small amounts or for too big amounts, contrary to the economic self-interest. These experiments, however, concerned especially students from developed countries, which introduce the possibility of a bias (ethnocentrism) as to their validity. To remedy this problem, Heinrich *et al.* (2001; 2006) conducted experiments[44] in 15 non-industrial societies, diversified by their characteristics. They confirm that the canonical model of self-interest does not explain the results in any of the societies studied (Heinrich *et al.*, 2006, p. 1767). Economic altruism is therefore present[45] on a broad scale, even if it varies from one society to another. As pointed out by this study, economic choices are not explained by the exogenous variable of objective interest, but by the social and economic interactions of everyday life (Heinrich *et al.*, 2001, p. 77). In other words, the concrete context influences behaviour.

In the field of taxes, we can take the simple example, suggested by Gershon (2004, p. 206), of gifts to charities that correspond to a widespread practice: and yet, a person does not have an interest economically to hand over (pay) money, even if a generous tax reduction is granted, since the net cost of the operation still shows a loss. Experiments conducted by Ackert *et al.* (2007) with 110 participants lead to less clear results, but confirm the reality of altruism: out of 110 persons having to decide (1,430 "votes") on the amount of income before and after tax within a group, 20% reduce (altruism) their own gains for the benefit of the group. We must point out moreover that this type of experience leaves aside the link with public spending and with politics, which tends to diminish, as we have shown, the intensity of altruism.

The sociological figure of the contribution-tax (Leroy, 1992), which is analyzed as a payment consented to general public policies, confirms the possibility of altruism by the taxpayer. We have seen that citizens are prepared to pay for legitimate public programmes, even if they do not benefit from them and even if ethical reasons can justify the taxation. There is a consensus to admit the need for the financing by taxes of

44 Namely: the ultimatum game already described; the dictator game which introduces a variant to the ultimatum game by not giving the second player the possibility to refuse the sum proposed by the first player (the latter does not propose a zero sum by following his pure interest); the game of punishment by a third party which introduces a mechanism of sanctioning by a third player in the ultimatum game.

45 Even if we must remain prudent regarding the manner of generalizing laboratory experiments towards real choices concerning the financing of public goods: cf. Laury, Taylor, 2008.

basic services for underprivileged groups, notably as regards the spending for social protection which are widely acclaimed (cf. box). The legitimate State is therefore resolutely interventionist because citizens are in general claimants for public services, notably in the field of healthcare and of education. The amount of income of a person seems to produce only a limited effect on the demand for expenditure (Schokkaert, 1987, p. 179), and has no relevance at all in the case of specific spending with well-targeted beneficiaries (Schokkaert, 1987, p. 179; Jacoby, 2000, p. 761).

Box 18: The attachment of citizens to social protection

Surveys show that public opinion assigns significant value to social services, even if there are differences from one country to the next, from one period to the other, or from one policy to another. The surveys on the European values confirm, despite national differences, the attachment of citizens to the Welfare State. In the case of England, a study (based on 800 interviews) indicates that, while at the same time wishing to render individuals much more responsible in the presence of risk, people are in favour of the intervention of the State for the most deprived and are prepared to pay higher taxes to finance these spending (Taylor-Gooby *et al.*, 1999, p. 192). In the case of France, the favourable opinion towards social security conveys existential concerns as well as the attachment to the fate of the most deprived. In the case of Sweden, a study of opinion polls from 1981 to 1992 (Svallfors, 1995) shows that the support for the universal and generous social model financed by taxes remains stable (from 66 to 75% according to the types of policy), even if criticism of bureaucracy and individual abuses appear. Another study (Steinmo, 2002, p. 853) reveals that only a minority of Swedes is in favour of tax reduction if this must result in a reduction of public expenditure. According to a survey in Norway (Bay, Pedersen, 2006, p. 425), the possibility of introducing a basic income for everyone is approved by two thirds of the respondents. For Chile (Bergmann, 2002, p. 296), a study by questionnaires yields the following results: 76% of people (N = 1160) (rather) agree to pay more taxes for the benefit of the poor and 88% think that the intervention of the State for the elimination of poverty is "indispensable." Finally, we know that public spending in the social sphere (education, healthcare etc.) is in general widely acclaimed (Lewis and Jackson, 1985; Bergmann, 2002, p. 297; Kemp, 2002, p. 100).

d. Against the economic commonplace of the limitation of levies

Here the point is to remember that tax revenue is not contrary to economic growth and does not necessarily encourage tax evasion (cf. 3-a). Regarding the effects of the level of tax revenue, the results remain uncertain, contrary to Laffer's curve: there is no reliable empirical correlation between the global level of tax revenue and the rate of growth. At the micro-social level, the surveys show that we must take into account the tax burden that is socially bearable, in other words such as it is felt. The link with the objective weight of tax revenue is not direct. We must also take account of the use of tax in its cognitive relationship to public spending.

e. Against the commonplace of the unrealistic (irrational) taxpayer

We have seen that (3-c) the taxpayer is not unrealistic, even when he demands less tax and more expenses (public services). The political function of the contribution-tax contradicts the economic theory of tax illusion, which says that the irrational individual claim more expenses and less taxes. Empirically, despite a few confirmations, tests refute this theory. The approach through cognitive rationality explains that the citizen considers that his demand for public services may be financed by various means: taxes, but also loans, the reduction of wastefulness etc. Therefore, asking for more public services and less tax is neither unrealistic, nor irrational (in the broad sense), when the citizen proposes other resources.

Conclusion

Up against the commonplaces of the neo-liberal anti-tax ideology (cf. chapter 6), the scientific answers of tax sociology correspond to reality (cf. box 19).

Box 19: Against the anti-tax neo-liberal ideology

R1 (versus P1 studied in chapter 6): General aversion to taxes does not exist: the taxpayer does not reason (only) by self-interest but (also) in accordance with his political values and his information experienced; he is capable of altruism.

R2 (vs. P2): Tax revenue is not contrary to economic growth and does not necessarily encourage tax evasion.

R3 (vs. P3): The taxpayer is not unrealistic, even when he asks for less taxes and more expenditure (public services).

R4 (vs. P4): Reminder[46]: Globalization does not oblige a retrenchment of the State in order to satisfy the diktat of the market.

---

46 This proposition was demonstrated in chapter 7: the resistance of the Welfare State to compensate for the effects of economic globalization does exist and is possible, contrary to the theory of market efficiency, which maintains that globalization undermines social spending. We find rich countries largely open to globalization with a generous Welfare State (example of the Nordic countries). Globalization does there-

The concrete relation of the individual to taxation marks the social dimension of the taxpayer's decision. The social phenomenon of taxation is not reduced to a calculation of self-interest according to the price for the services received, but refers to a cognitive representation of the just levy in a given socio-historical context. The functions of tax in the society are essentially political, even if the citizen's cognitive relation to tax State combines this socio-political issue of legitimacy with the economic dimension of trade. The renewed rational theory of the actor can in this way reconcile the normative aspect with the empirical because the citizen's conception of the contribution-tax is validated as real or realizable. But the complexity of taxation and its increasing use as a policy instrument conceal the stakes of public action. The stereotype of the taxpayer recalcitrant to all taxation serves as an alibi for the exclusion of the citizen from the evaluation of the equity in tax policies (Leroy, 2002, p. 110). Rather than betting on voters to be satisfied, on pressure groups to be treated with consideration, on public opinion to be flattered and on the privileged to be preserved, the government must offer political choices to the citizens: the link between tax and expenditure, the direction of social justice through tax, the strategy of economic intervention must notably be approved democratically. Otherwise individual or collective reactions through tax avoidance will spread out. Here the justified success of the methodology of cognitive rationality must not exempt one from a theorization of the general logic, from an empirically-founded "ethical" point of view. In fact, in the context of the modern finances of the State, the legal form of parliamentary consent to taxation does no longer suffice to forge the political principles of a democracy. The concrete figure of the citizen tax within the framework of a social contract establishing the contours of the interventionist State must be valorized.

---

fore not lead to a systematic reduction of taxes, especially on capital, and reinforces even, in certain cases, social spending.

CHAPTER 10

Fiscal Deviance Becoming Commonplace

Regardless of whether it adopts a legal form or not, be it individual or collective, fiscal deviance is a phenomenon bringing politics into play, on the collective level of society. It constitutes the reverse side of taxes, seen as a contribution to public policies, resulting from the historical creation of the State. The delicate equilibrium between the juridical and political principle of "obligation-tax" and the procedure of parliamentary consent witnesses a decline in its democratic significance owing to the debilitation of the main functions of the interventionist fiscal system. The classification of the behaviour of taxpayers by the authority into "legal" or "illegal" categories coincides less and less with the socio-political acceptance or refusal to participate in the common good. In order to escape from taxation, the economy uses the unofficial sector, tax havens and generalizes the tax optimization (planning) by means of schemes cleverly placed with regard to the law. Capitalism is deviant because of its rejection of the "contribution-tax" to public action, but, and this is the "ruse"[1], it pretends to remain inside the legality of the formal obligation to the State. Symmetrically, public action acknowledges the value of the market in an ideological way: it encourages legal tax avoidance through its incentive policy which puts States in positions of competition in the context[2] of economic and financial globalization. Another process of defunctionalization of policy takes place through the fragmentation of the fiscal "categorization" of society into dispersed stakes. The proliferation of detailed rules disorganizes fiscal normativity. The global compromises of fiscal policy are thwarted by the multiplication of economic indulgences granted by the State. Taxation based on derogations tends to be developed as a norm of public action, thus making the very concept of economic deviance void of any meaning. After exploring the information concerning fiscal deviance, the focus shifts to the evolution of regulation by the State in

1 As opposed to Pareto's vision, ruse is attributed not only to the ruling elite, but is found in the symmetrical relation between capitalism which has accentuated its tax avoidance and evasion strategy (optimization) and the public action of States who have granted special national and international exemptions (offshore places).

2 In certain aspects the process resembles Durkheim's economic anomie: cf. chapter 12.

order to demonstrate how the societal normativity of the functioning of the economy has been questioned.

1. The Phenomenon of Fiscal Deviance

Despite methodological difficulties, the measurement of fiscal deviance shows the magnitude of the phenomenon which could be viewed as a part of the underground economy or as the tax evasion alone (fraud to taxes and social contributions). Beyond the problems of measurement, one should point out the process of the authorities (mostly administrative) of classifying the ways to escape from taxes into legal or illegal categories, and then try to classify the forms of deviance according to the categories of taxpayers.

a. The measurement of the unofficial economy and of tax evasion

The measurement of fraud is uncertain because of its concealed nature. The principal methods used give different results and put methodological questions. Certain (indirect) methods measure fraud (tax and Social Security evasion) using the unofficial economy as a basis, i.e. all the income which is not taken into account in national accounting. Several approaches are used in order to measure the underground economy, in particular those based on: the volume of monetary transactions; the (abnormal) demand of cash money which serves the underground market; (abnormal) electricity consumption; conspicuous errors in national accounting (for example, between revenues and expenses). Certain calculations are based on a combination of factors in accordance with a multi-varied approach. These calculations provide an estimation of the hidden economy which is a wider concept than tax evasion because it includes undeclared work, smuggling etc. Other (direct) methods use statistical data of tax and social adjustments, or surveys aimed at tax evasion or social fraud. But this second technique comes up to the difficulty of obtaining trustworthy responses.

According to Kirchler's synthesis[3] (2007, p. 16-19), in the year 2000 the underground economy represented: 41% of GDP in Africa and South America, 38% in ex-communist European countries, 26% in Asia, 17% in OECD countries. The countries with the lowest percentages are: Switzerland, the United States, Austria (< 10%). For the OECD countries, the classification is as follows: USA (8.7), Switzerland (8.6), Austria (9.8), Japan (11.2), United Kingdom (12.7), Netherlands (13.1), New Zealand (12.8), Ireland (15.9), France (15.2), Canada and Germany

[3] Cf. also Braithwaite, Schneider, Reinhart, Murphy, in Braithwaite, 2005, p. 95; Bajad, Schneider, 2005.

(16), Denmark (18), Finland (18), Norway (19.1), Sweden (19.2), Belgium (22.2), Portugal and Spain (22.7), Italy (27.1), Greece (28.7).

For 21 OECD countries, according to Schneider's calculations (2008, p. 106), the GDP ratio for 2007 in % is: USA (7.2), Switzerland (8.2), Japan (9), Austria (9.4), New Zealand (9.8), Netherlands (10.1), Great Britain (10.6), Australia (10.7), France (11.8), Canada (12.6), Ireland (12.7), Finland (14.5), Germany (14.6), Denmark (14.8), Norway (15.4), Sweden (15.6), Belgium (18.3), Spain (19.3), Portugal (19.2), Italy (22.3), Greece (25.1).

Cobham (2005) estimates that in developing countries the informal economy is equivalent to a loss of 285.8 billion dollars of public revenue.

The evaluation of the unofficial economy thus leads to important differences, but marks the magnitude of the phenomenon:

– If we take the (very incomplete) ranking of the United Nations[4] drawn up with the results of a survey, we find that in 2000 Belgium had a ratio of 4% of the GDP instead of the 22% in the previous survey, Canada had 3% instead of 16%, Italy 15% instead of 27%, the United States 1.2% instead of 8.7% etc.

– If we look at studies of the informal sector, the estimations vary as well (cf. chapter 5). According to Vuletin's study (2008, p. 25), for Brazil, for example, we find that it represented around 29% of GDP in 2000 instead of 39.8% in Kirchler's study, for Chile it is 33% instead of 20%, for Uruguay 37% instead of 51%, for Venezuela 42% instead of 34% etc.

– According to the research of Schneider and Enste (2000), the variations vary over the period 1986-1990 depending on the methods used: for Canada from 1.4% to 21.2%, for Germany from 14.5% up to 31.4%, for Great Britain from 9.7% to 13.2%, for Italy from 9.3% to 21.3%, for the United States from 6.2% up to 10.2%.

– For Germany Schneider (2008, p. 102) finds a difference of about 12% in 2005, going from 3.1% (direct method by surveys) up to 15.4%.

In the more limited field of tax evasion, the problems of measurement are a delicate issue as well. For the United States, in 2001 the IRS (Internal Revenue Service) estimates the tax gap, the loss of public revenue resulting from eluded taxes at 345 billion dollars (Shropshire, 2009). For France, in 2007 the *Conseil des prélèvements obligatoires* (the Council for taxes and social contributions) estimates the amount of evaded taxes and social contributions to be between 29 and 40 billion euros, or 1.7% to 2.3% of GDP. For Sweden, social fraud and tax eva-

4 Source: United Nations, *Non-Observed Economy in Nations Accounts*, Geneva, 2003.

sion are evaluated to be 5% of GDP in 2000 (McManus, Warren, 2006, p. 62). These figures must however be used with caution: it is not easy to determine the distinction between error, avoidance and evasion. The results depend on the policy of selecting the files to be studied, and sometimes take into account only the notified tax readjustments (tax corrections: cf. chapter 8) and not the actual adjustments (after litigation). There is a big variation between the studies, sometimes representing a difference of 4% of GDP. An original result is presented by Watrin and Ullmann (2008) showing (in an experiment) that consumption tax (a type of VAT) causes more fraud than income tax. This pioneer survey widened the debate between the defenders of the economic efficiency of indirect consumption tax and the defenders of income redistribution. Indeed, in addition to its political legitimization in defence of social justice, progressive income tax (if this result is confirmed) would tend to avoid the economic damages of fraud.

Fiscal law has an impact: for example, granting a tax allowance for expenses related to accommodation (which supposes the presentation of bills) will entail a drop in black-market work. It also affects the definition of fraud directly. Defining fraud is not that simple, despite the apparent clarity of distinctions. If we follow the legal criterion for the violation of fiscal law, we must exclude tax avoidance which constitutes a skillful use of the law; if we take overall minimization of taxes, we include tax evasion; finally, errors are just an involuntary way of eluding taxes. Fraud (evasion) is situated on a continuum constituted by various forms of eluding taxes. Fraud figures also cover very different situations of eluding taxes: fraudulent maneuvers, fictitious financial schemes, misuse of law, concealment, omissions, different types of errors etc.

b. "Labelling" fiscal deviance

The elaboration of a general typology of fiscal deviance (cf. table 13) is freely inspired by Becker's sociological theory of labelling[5] (1963). It allows one to initiate a dialogue with the legal and economic approach starting from these two questions: on the side of taxpayers, does a scheme exist in order to minimize taxes? On the side of the competent authorities, is this act being qualified as legal or illegal by the public administration?[6] Introducing the notion of tax scheme defines a dynamic conception of fiscal deviance seen as the encounter between the legal administrative qualification of the act and the logic of the taxpayer. A

---

5 The sociologist Becker defines deviance using as basis the idea of reciprocal independence of action and reaction.

6 In fiscal matters, the administration "expresses" the concrete law, under the control of judges.

premeditated scheme for eluding tax, qualified as legal, constitutes *tax avoidance*, In other words the skillfulness to use the possibilities or the loopholes of the law in order to reduce the sum that has to be paid. A premeditated scheme defined by the authorities as illegal constitutes *tax evasion*, comprising a variety of more or less sophisticated procedures. The absence of a premeditated scheme associated with the respect of legal obligations constitutes *tax compliance*. The absence of a premeditated scheme leading to the violation of tax law constitutes an *error*.

Firstly, we have to note that the taxpayer sometimes adopts a passive position towards taxes (Caroll, 1987; Webley *et al.*, 1991, p. 80). The visibility of tax problems implies specific events such as the period of income tax returns, or the media coverage of reforms or of social protests. The essential point is that the opportunity to minimize taxes plays an important role (Vogel, 1974, p. 507; Lewis, 1982, p. 158; Wärneryd, Walerud, 1982, p. 205; Webley *et al.*, 1991, p. 102), which depends on the legal methods of taxation and on the economic conditions of the activities of taxpayers (cf. below). It is very difficult for a salaried employee, whose income is declared by his employer, to reduce his tax. For a multinational enterprise there are a large number of methods for reducing its tax burden etc.

Table 13: Typology of tax decision

Taxpayer Decision	Authority Decision →	Legal	Illegal
Scheme to minimize taxes		AVOIDANCE	EVASION
No tax scheme		COMPLIANCE	ERROR

The more complex[7] the law is, the more possibilities it leaves to the actors of fiscal deviance for interactive games: favoured (almost fortunate) taxpayers create schemes which they defend as legal tax avoidance categories while the administration tends to want to label tax decisions in the category of evasion (fraud). The socio-political game consists in getting the boundaries to shift between what is legal and what is illegal on the level of tax law elaboration as well as on the level of tax examinations (audit). The way of presenting the scheme, in particular through vocabulary (McBarnet, 1991, p. 341), is chosen by the taxpayer, or his adviser, in order to fall in the legal category of avoidance. New legal forms of tax avoidance are invented, while tax advantages are claimed by socio-economic groups (cf. chapter 5) At another level, these results

[7] In fiscal law, the crossing of boundaries has been established according to the categories of evasion, avoidance and abuse in the use of law (Leroy, 2008).

call into question the influence of "privileged" taxpayers, especially of business circles (Jacobs, 1987), on taxation.

As regards to authorities, by giving a central position to the criterion of legality, this approach is part of legal sociology. It determines the effective possibilities of action which the law and the judge leave to the administration. It is a question of understanding how the authorities in a concrete way makes the decision of "labelling" deviance, how administrative regulation is implemented[8] (cf. chapter 5). The politicization of tax control sometimes leads to deviations (Leroy, 2007, p. 39): public action is thus phagocytosed by the political power.[9] In other cases, the politicization of tax control takes on the more discreet form of political intervention in favour of friends of those in power in order to prevent the examination or reduce its scope. But the politicization of tax control should also be questioned in its relation to the legitimacy of the State, to the justice of the tax system and to the substance of policy translated into law. What is the point of the duty of paying taxes in a corrupt State which labels evasion (fraud) in an arbitrary manner? What is the point of the fiscal examination of ordinary citizens if the policy grants unjustified tax privileges to the richest?

The complexity of tax law refers to the instrumentalization of taxes by the interventionist State and to the difficulty of separating law from fact. It provides opportunities to avoid taxes while at the same time blurring boundaries between avoidance and evasion. This distinctive characteristic complicates the evaluation of the gravity of the deviance with respect to the law, as well as with respect to society: the State offers legal forms of tax avoidance (tax allowances, tax exemptions etc.) and then confers to the administration the control of the regularity of the taxpayer's tax return. In the absence of a coherence of public action, tax control accentuates the organizational game of the labelling of deviance as an obligation defined by the bureaucratic interpretation of the law.

The criterion of legality has diverse effects depending on the level of analysis under consideration. For the system of tax revenue, legal decisions (tax avoidance, relocation) and illegal decisions (tax evasion breaching the law) have the same negative impact by reducing public

8 From an ethical-normative point of view, the administration must avoid arbitrary decisions by verifying objectively whether acts of taxpayers are legal or not, while at the same time guaranteeing their rights. From an analytical point of view, the implementation of tax policy by the administration, the organizational interpretation of tax law, the logic and work methods of the actors in this field determine the decision of administrative labelling.

9 Russia gives the typical example with the tax control of the petroleum groups Yukos and TNK-BP, and of the troublesome NGOs (for the NGOs, within the framework of a law promulgated in 2006). It is not about supporting the embezzlement of certain oligarchs, but emphasizing the need to respect the rights of taxpayers.

budget receipts. As social representations, an empirical study concludes that tax evasion is considered in a rather negative way, relocation for tax reasons in a neutral way and tax avoidance in a positive way (Kirchler *et al.*, 2003). These positions correspond to the nature of "tax-obligation" promoted by authorities on a legal basis in order to distinguish between what is permitted and what is not. We should however also consider the methods of economic deviance.

c. *Forms of tax deviance according to socio-economic categories*

Fiscal deviance is a universal social phenomenon but it does not concern all "classes" in the same way, since the opportunity and the methods to avoid taxes are not identical from one socio-economic category to another. The categorial definition of tax evaders using the classical socio-demographic variables is not very pertinent: empirical studies do not show consistent regularities (cf. box 20).

Box 20: The uncertain impact of socio-demographic variables

With regard to *age*, certain authors affirm that young people are more indulgent towards tax evasion (Keenan, Dean, 1980, p. 214, Wärneryd, Walerud, 1982, p. 200; Spicer, Lundstedt, 1976, p. 300; Torgler, Schneider, 2007; Alm, Gomez, 2008, p. 85). Others, however, do not validate the influence of age (Mueller, 1963, p. 233; Beedle, Taylor-Gooby, 1983, p. 27, Torgler *et al.* 2008, p. 336). Richardson (2006, p. 160), in particular, in his transversal study conducted in 45 countries does not find any correlation (multivariate analysis). In the case of local referendums (in Florida) a generational division has been observed concerning school financing, with old people showing disagreement with tax increase (Button, 1992, p. 793), but this division has not been found in other areas.

With regard to the *educational level*, the results are equally contradicting: certain authors think that the most educated people use tax evasion more than others (Wärneryd, Walerud, 1982, p. 200; Richardson, 2006, p. 164), while other studies maintain the opposite (Wallsschutzky, 1984). Torgler *et al.* also find a correlation between education and tax morality. The level of education does not seem to matter much for the expectations concerning public expenditure (Courant, 1980, p. 9), but it encourages the tendency to adopt an ethical representation of general interest in local referendums (in the USA) (Brodsky, Thompson, 1993, p. 293).

With regard to *gender*, the results are identical. Certain studies find that women are more favourable to the financing of public expenses than men, in particular concerning schools (Courant *et al.* 1980, p. 9, Button, 1992, p. 793). According to the survey of Hasseldine and Hite using questionnaires (2003, p. 526), men appear to be more tolerant of tax evasion than women (the survey includes 430 subjects), which confirms Vogel's results (1974,

p. 507). The influence of gender is also revealed in the experiments conducted by Cullis *et al.* (2006), men being more sensitive to "framing" which leads them to decrease the importance of taxes when they are in the form of a sum to be paid (as opposed to a tax credit). For Turkey (survey), Torgler *et al.* (2008, p. 336) highlight that women's attitudes (tax morality) towards tax evasion are more negative than men's. According to Torgler and Schneider (2007), in Switzerland, Belgium and Spain women's tax morality is also stronger. The experiments used by Kastlunger *et al.* (2010) confirm this result. But for Furnham (1984, p. 544) and Alm and Gomez (2008, p. 85) there is no correlation between gender and tax morality. Richardson's (2006) international study, conducted between 2002 and 2004 in 45 countries, does not confirm either the influence of gender on tax evasion. Likewise, some studies show (Courant *et al.*, 1980, p. 9) that the people who live with their family are more in favour of public expenditure, but in this case the problem also consists in linking taxes to expenditure.

With regard to *partisan preference* (identification with a political party) seems to have no impact: Lewis (1982, p. 87), Mueller (1963, p. 233), Alm, Gomez (2008, p. 85) do not validate this factor.

With regard to *revenue*, the empirical studies are again contradictory, negating the general impact of this variable (cf. below).

With regard to *social class*, while Keenan, Dean (1980, p. 214) note that the social class has an effect on the opinion expressed with regard to tax evasion, Vogel (1974, p. 507) indicates that blue-collar workers show a favourable tendency towards tax evasion (attitude) but do not practice it very much.

It is therefore appropriate to distinguish the socio-economic categories of taxpayers concerning tax evasion and avoidance. We can retain Merton's (1949) idea to question the link between social structure, anomie and deviance[10], set out in chapter 5 of *Éléments de théorie et de méthode sociologique.* Merton builds up his reflection with respect to the acceptance of the goals proposes by society, for example to earn a lot of money, and of the means to achieve them. Starting from this double question, he distinguishes on an individual level five types of adaptation depending on whether the response is positive or not with respect to goals and means.[11]

10 Merton explains on the subject of deviance with regard to means (potentially illegal innovation) that white-collar criminality is tolerated because of the valorization of financial success in our civilization, while ordinary criminality is more the case of the poorest layers of society.

11 Acceptance of goals, acceptance of means: yes, yes (conformism); yes, no (potentially illegal innovation); no, yes (ritualism); no, no (avoidance: the fringe elements of society). To these four cases Merton adds rebellion which aims at changing society's goals.

The variable “revenue” cannot directly be retained insofar as empirical studies do not prove a systematic correlation between income and tax evasion (cf. chapter 9). But it is clear that the very rich, who are notably at the head of big enterprises or banks, have the means to avoid taxes by using the flaws of the tax system. Here we have to insist on an essential factor of tax minimization (legal or not), namely the opportunity for evasion. This factor has to be related to the possibilities given by the complex instrumentalization of tax policy[12] (chapter 7; Richardson, 2006).

Several “classes” of taxpayers must be distinguished:

– *Big enterprises (notably the multinationals) and the richest.*

Taking into account the presence of institutions of internal audit and the number of salaried employees, it is difficult for big enterprises[13] to cover up income, to illegally employ salaried persons, to carry out cash transactions etc. On the other hand, they use tax optimization strategies (planning), by trying to exploit (and to get around) national legal rules through complex schemes. They may also choose to relocate their establishments and create subsidiaries for tax reasons. The existence of territories with privileged taxation (cf. tax havens) encourages the flight of capital and the minimization of taxes. The economic crisis in the summer of 2008 highlighted the detrimental role of the deregulation of the financial economy and of tax competition. We have to remind ourselves here that 50 to 60% of global transactions are carried out within multinational companies. One of the techniques consists in manipulating transfer prices (cf. chapter 8), in other words altering the price of the transactions between the parent company and the subsidiaries within the same group in order to reduce taxes to be paid.[14] We have also seen that big enterprises try to influence tax policy by lobbying institutions (or Think Tanks). Tax optimization also concerns the richest people, who are often owners and/or leaders of enterprises, certain members of the professions, salaried employees etc. With regard to Merton’s typology, we find ourselves in the case of a deviance with regard to the purposes of the tax which is seen as an obstacle for the enterprise that it manages by using legal means (or by trying to make as we have already seen the boundaries of legality shift in its favour).

---

12 Torgler *et al.* (2008, p. 330) confirms for the United States that complexity reduces tax morality, but the correlation is not statistically significant. Nevertheless, this result does not invalidate the idea that complexity encourages (legal) tax avoidance by the most skilful or the best advised.

13 A big enterprise is an enterprise which has a big turnover (of more than 150 million euros exclusive of taxes in the case of sales or 76 million in the case of services and/or employing more than 200 salaried workers).

14 Purchases, financial costs, costs of studies etc.

– *Small- and medium-sized enterprises and independent professions.*

Tax evasion is often simple: concealment of revenues (sales without invoices), undeclared work, reimbursement of unjustified expenses, cheating[15] with cash or goods etc. The study of Ahmed and Braithwaite (2005) based on a questionnaire (2,040 people answered) representative of the Australian population confirms the analysis: this category of taxpayers (small business taxpayers) engages in tax evasion more often than others (private or public salaried employees) and is less in favour of the use of taxes for social action (but more in favour of its use for the police and the defence force). This class of deviants refuses both the goals and the means of taxes, but does not correspond to the idea of fringe elements of society.

– *Salaried employees (except for managers).*

Their possibilities for tax evasion are restricted insofar as their salaries are declared (or confirmed) by the enterprise or the public administration employing them. It is difficult to do undeclared work, especially if they are employed full-time. These salaried employees sometimes benefit from the niches offered by fiscal policy. Due to conviction and/or lack of opportunity, fiscal deviance in this category is more rare.

– *Labour market outcasts.*

Undeclared work is possible but implies a socio-economic network in order to attain an economically viable scale. In the absence of taxable income, they are not much concerned by the issue of fiscal deviance. On the other hand, they are subjected to VAT on their consumption, and as a consequence their contribution (taking into account the importance of this indirect tax) to the fiscal State is significant. Sometimes they enjoy social security benefits when such rights are foreseen by legislation (another possible deviance).

– *The economy of crime.*

It constitutes a particular sector (drugs, blackmail, forged documents, different illegal traffics etc.). It has to be said that this category sometimes uses the same channels as the international finance of large capitalist enterprises. To put it simply, the term “laundering” refers to illegal traffic activities, because of violence and/or direct trespass to persons or goods, while the sanitized notion of tax optimization (or planning) is preferred in the case of international finance. They fall under the category of tax delinquency and are closer to the idea of fringe elements of society used by Merton.

---

15 Certain types of tax evasion are easier in certain sectors. For example, undeclared work is facilitated in the hotel and restaurant business, construction, the custom clothing industry. On the opposite side, doctors whose income is known by the social security (reimbursement of medical acts) cannot cheat on their earnings etc.

Box 21: Tax havens

It is difficult to know the exact sum of amounts passing through tax havens. According to the Tax Justice Network, in 2005 the income of physical (rich) persons placed in tax havens was estimated to be 860 billion dollars, or a loss of tax revenue of 225 billion. The flight of capital is especially serious for developing countries. It contributes to impeding the creation of a true fiscal State, able to provide democratically chosen public services. According to an econometrical analysis by Ndiumana and Boyce (2008) in 40 African countries, the (legal or illegal) capital flight between 1970 and 2006 was estimated at 420 billion dollars, while the external debt of these countries amounted to 227 billion. Of course, not all capital movements are illegal, but their transition through tax havens leads to tax minimization entailing the loss of public revenue.

For the United Kingdom, Richard Murphy (2009) estimates that the loss of tax revenue linked to tax havens amounts to 18.5 billion pounds per year, broken down into 8.5 billion for (very rich) individuals, 3 billion for enterprises and 7 billion for (illegal) tax evasion. In Canada, according to the study of Lauzon and Hasbani (2008), tax avoidance used by the five biggest banks through their 89 subsidiaries, owned in tax havens, represents from 1993 to 2007 16 billion (Canadian) dollars, or 30% on average over 15 years of the sum of their income tax to be paid. In the case of the United States, the estimates of the IRS (which nevertheless does not dispose of direct statistics on international tax avoidance) for 2001 are from 40 to 70 billion dollars for tax avoidance that went to off-shore zones, and from 2.8 to 53 billion for tax avoidance linked to transfer prices between multinationals (Shropshire, 2009).

The problem (cf. chapter 11) is to reflect on the relations between the different categories, which may involve conflict, compromise or exploitation. We link up with the general issue of the existence and the nature of socio-political compromises. In particular, the challenges concern the integration of the middle class, subjected to considerable taxation, although they also benefit from certain tax advantages, as well as income redistribution to the poorest classes. Here it has to be especially pointed out that in Merton's analysis the absence of a critical reflection on goals, which are reified as an obvious fact, limits the reflection on anomie.[16] We might be surprised that the functional method, so appreciated by our author, has been ignored when gauging the coherence and the legitimacy of the norms and objectives which public action proposes for society. On a collective level, we should look into the disruptions of

16 Even though Merton rapidly evokes the functions of the myths which justify or reject institutions.

the prescribed models of conduct and thus try to understand the normative meaning of public action.

2. The Deviation of Fiscal State Regulation

The regulation is conceptualized on the basis of three characteristics of public action: harmonizing stakes and priorities of actors whose logic diverges; transforming coherent formal principles into operating rules; exact positioning on the power and political legitimacy scale, intermediary between the government as unique authority imposing public rules and governance marked by the retreat of the State in favour of the private sector.[17] It must be specified that the regulation may be controlled by a single political centre which manages to orientate widely (and not to determine) the actions of the others: this is the case, the figure, of the regulatory State.[18] The regulation in a strict sense aims at the case where the stakes and priorities of several public authorities, the national State, Europe, and local governments for example, are taken into account in a negotiated compromise. This analytical approach allows one to emphasize the transformation of the normativity that accompanies the evolution of the regulatory power exercised by public action on market. The ideological context of economic globalization has highlighted the deviances of normative power which tends to lose its reference to the major functions (for society) of tax policy. This gives rise to the phenomenon of tax minimization becoming commonplace.

a. The deterioration in fiscal normativity

In the first place, it has to be remembered that in most countries the State is not the only political actor anymore or the only legal authority. In the tax matter, the State sees its sovereignty confronted by various powers: the Community law for the EU member States, the fiscal power of the federal States in countries with a federal structure, and more and more the power of local governments. Nevertheless, it generally retains important powers.

Regulation that harmonizes stakes and challenges has henceforth changed in scale and nature. It is less and less brought into effect by means of global political arbitrations between the main functions of the

17 When the authority is totally devoid of legitimacy and has absolute power, it transforms itself into a tyrant. At the bottom of the scale, the case of the complete absence of rules refers to the notion of anarchy. This theoretical framework has been applied to the study of conventional public action based on my work on the planning contract (Leroy, 1999) and to the European Union (Leroy, 2004, 2009).

18 The case of regulatory authorities is a false problem because their independence is founded on a text which politically corresponds to the renunciation of the State to directly regulate a domain (but this is a reversible process).

tax system, like in the case of the compromise on the Keynesian Welfare State (cf. chapter 11). It does not take into account the democratic dimension of taxation whose main choices are more and more separated from the people, in breach of the genesis of consent to the contribution-tax of the tax State in Europe. These functions are certainly still present, especially in rich countries, according to variable compromises around the financing of economic and social expenses. We can also note that fiscal policy maintains coherent blocks more or less extended according to countries and circumstances. But the regulatory function of the interventionist State is becoming more and more fragmented. The financial function has been rivaled and questioned by the massive use of loans. In countries where fiscal expenses are used to the detriment of the widening of the taxable base (like in France), this function is degrading. The macro-regulation of economic trends by taxation has been downgraded to the benefit of dispersed economic micro-interventions. By borrowing the neo-liberal method to cut the rates of certain taxes, the financial function has delegitimized the role of taxes, moreover without always leading to a real reduction of taxes because of the increase of indirect taxes. Tax redistribution is less efficient in the struggle against inequalities which have soared together with neo-liberal globalization. The territoriality of taxes, which formally refers to State sovereignty, does not succeed in finding coherence in the presence of the globalization of fraud and of the failures of supra-national tax harmonization.

Since national and international harmonization of stakes is brought into effect in more restricted formulations of public action, the global logic of the regulation is diluted in the socio-economic particularisms. The choice and organization of tax functions have lost their general normative scope. The degradation of normativity, which piles up specialized and sectorally applied tax systems, undermines the "contribution-tax" to public action for society. It confers an important position to the market norm. But here as well concrete measures in favour of enterprises are often detailed in complex rules devaluating the tax norm as an expression of general legal principles. We observe an asymmetrical relationship between the evolution of the normative concept of public expenditure and the weakness of novations in tax policy principles.

Concerning budgetary matters, as we have seen, many countries have since the 1990s adopted budgeting systems of targets and results, focused on the performance of public management (chapter 6). This management frame, encouraged by the OECD, prolongs the neo-liberal questioning of the Keynesian state, initiated in the 1970s. The nature of the financial "constitution"[19] thus proposed has its coherence, even though it raises doubts regarding its socio-political objective and its self-referenced positioning. The main idea is to watch over the efficiency of the use of public means.[20] The relationship with market ideology is found in the use of performance as a norm of limiting public services. Eliminating the expenses which do not correspond to the indicators of performance is a possible way for State retrenchment in accordance with the ideology of market efficiency. In spite of this connection, the norm of budgetary performance refuses any reference to external political and/or social values. Its normativity is internal and totally instrumental: the means become the values of politics, with public management substituting public action (of the general interest). Methods designed for enterprises[21] are applied, opening the door to a radical neo-liberal use. This budgetary regulation also generates other possibilities by the establishment (or reassertion), at the highest level of the legal hierarchy, of a general norm of transparency of public accounts and by the methods of control and evaluation given to Parliament. The evaluation norm thus contains the seeds of a counter-power for the citizens, even though the institutional flaws of the functioning of representative democracy attenuate its scope to a great extent. The way of this real democracy is not easy and implies another positioning concerning socio-political objectives.

In tax matters the picture is different although the ways followed have been for a long time linked to the same (supra-normative) meta-concept. The period of liberal finances, in the meaning of the 19th century, prohibited financial interventionism because of an economic and political concept (dominant bourgeois values) of a State limited to its functions of sovereignty. According to the dominant bourgeois values of this era, the tax system, loans, taxes and public expenses should be held in check as far as their amount and functions are concerned. The big budgetary principles of unity, annualization, universality and specialization establish the peak of liberal parliamentarism. The consent of the representatives of taxpayers to taxes, whose basis is linked to the birth of the modern State, is legitimated. These principles constituted both tools of legal techniques (budgetary law), as well as political procedures. They were based on a restricted political normativity (as a dogma) and on a market anomie which were materialized in commercial

19 The financial constitution refers here to the philosophical acceptance of the founding principles of the political order, but also finds a legal meaning in the rules of constitutional value that are in force.

20 We find in an ideological form the specter of the figure of a wasteful State.

21 This movement is of course older, but the normative breach is situated in its generalization and, the most often, in its consecration in the hierarchy of legal norms.

and industrial freedom and in the absence of social democracy.[22] Nevertheless, it could also be pointed out that democratic expansion has been speeded up by the existence of this budgetary constitution.[23]

The interventionist concept of public finances emphasizes relations opposed to budget neutrality and parliamentary power. The economic role of the State (Keynesianism) when there are crises and its capacity to solve social problems (Welfare) against which classical liberalism came up are valorized. The success of the social compromises of Keynesianism confers a normative (external) coherence in economic, political and social fields at once. Budgetary principles are adjusted, more or less in accordance with each state, for example in order to facilitate public investment in equipment that requires procedures for several years. The planning of public policies is developed etc. As for the fiscal aspect, the financing function is reinforced by the creation of a system based upon major synthetic taxes of a general nature that authorize expenses (especially social expenses). The redistribution of revenues is set up. The principles of legality, of equality (through taxes) and of necessity find a renewed, but coherent meaning when there is fiscal interventionism. The decisional reinforcement of the executive, which mobilizes technocratic expertise in line with post-war socio-economic changes, marks a decrease in parliamentary power (yet varying for each country).

With the neo-liberal period (since the 1970s), the questioning of the interventionist State does not bring a real drop in public expenditure and tax revenue. Their progression is at best stabilized, or sometimes they decline slightly in isolated cases in several countries. Social security, health care expenses and labour legislation are the object of reforms that modify the types of Welfare State, without succeeding for the time being to dismantle it. On the fiscal level, we have seen that the policies of income tax reduction of the years 1970 to 1980 had a mitigated impact. Like the attempts to reform social expenses, they followed the neo-liberal conception of the market. Since the 1990s, while performance brings a renewed normative synthesis of budgetary law, tax policy is problematic. It has been characterized by an increasing competition between States and an interventionism, not harmoniously diversified in great functions anymore, but fragmented. The great tax principles[24] of the interventionist democracy get emptied out of their general

22 Marx describes the absence of real democracy as an inherent feature of capitalism, political liberty being that of affluent people, whereas Durkheim describes economic anomie firstly as a pathological effect of the division of labour, then as a chronic element of the economy (in *Le Suicide*): cf. chapter 12.

23 With the vote on the budget being an important event of parliamentary democracy which had evolved towards an expanded suffrage (women still being excluded) with the abolition of the voting system based on the poll tax.

24 Cf. the constitutional value of the principles of fiscal legality, equality and necessity.

and social content (for society). The European construction, which had succeeded in harmonizing the VAT, has broken down. The economic globalization of the 1990s still lacks a social axiological compass (chapter 12). The tolerance of tax havens, which was revealed by the media coverage of the 2008 crisis, also illustrates the degradation of the tax norm. With the globalization of tax avoidance (and evasion), which is facilited by the competition between States in order to attract enterprises, the axiological disfunctioning of public policy calls the foundations of power into question.

b. The transformation of the regulatory power

As a concept, political regulation refers to the logic of public action, in particular to the meaning of the general interest and of public services. On the contrary, governance signifies that the search for lucrative market profit predominates. It depends, as demonstrated by the recent crisis of banks and stock exchanges (2008), on the neo-liberal base of market supremacy and makes common cause with the ideology of State retrenchment and of "market efficiency." The classification of power on the political scale is therefore a question of fact, which finds one of the best responses in the area of fiscal sociology. This conceptualization thus stands apart from the use of the vocabulary of public policies for the purposes of communication, ideology, negotiation, popularization, notoriety etc., by institutions and/or personalities whose objectives are not primarily scientific. It also aims to show the abuse of references to the notion of governance and to its ideological use as a neo-liberal dogma of financial capitalism.

The power of regulation of the tax State has evolved in its capacity to produce norms respected by taxpayers at the time of the neo-liberal turning point of the 1970s and the economic globalization of the 1990s. In the first place, parliamentary consent through the principle of tax legality does not ensure on its own anymore the political pertinence of the State. The real norm of the contribution of citizens to legitimate interventionist public action is impaired by the dilution of great socio-political functions of the tax system (cf. chapter 11). The questioning of the functional contract of the social Keynesian state has broken the social foundation of the political and legal dimensions of tax normativity. The concealment of possible choices by the ideology of market constraints has vitiated interventionist democracy (cf. chapter 7). This democratic deficit, which characterizes the manipulation of the choices of society by the governing elite constitutes a form of political alienation.[25] As we have seen, biased public action tends to exclude citizens

25 Or in Pareto's terms, a new ruse in order to satisfy economic elite.

while benefiting a social categorization in terms of taxes which covers up the real meaning of political decisions. We come here to a limit of the study of the individual approach to tax minimization[26], which refers to an extremely limited problematization of deviance situations as a relation to the market and the State.

In fact, and this is the second point, by giving a very important place to the market norm, public action has made tax policy to shift towards the governance of capitalist profits. Multinational enterprises and the financial sector are advantaged to the detriment of regulation by the great socio-political functions of the tax State. This is notably the meaning of the action of the European Union (EU) or of big international organizations like the OECD who have interpreted the market norm in the sense of accepting the principle of tax competition between States.[27] The logic of fiscal dumping, illustrated notably by the reduction of corporate tax rates or, using a more aggressive method in certain countries, by mechanisms of flat taxes, is an example of tax competition. Interventionist tax law, based on the functional norms of the Keynesian Welfare State, has thus accentuated the incentive law to attract enterprises and capital. The general norm is indeed that of minimizing taxes for enterprises and the rich capable of investing in the economy.

In developed countries, however, if the market norm has become important and has taken the twisted road of competition between States as regards taxes, it leaves intact the regulatory authority of the State. The State defines the tax obligation applicable in its territory.[28] The problem is that particular norms created in this way have weakened the relation of coherence (without even speaking of subordination) with values of the society. The reference to the market and the complexification of the categories of instrumentation of the tax system for the society (taxation of families, proprietors, inheritors, wealth, salaried workers etc.) henceforth spread confusion in the tax norm in its link with the great functions of the tax system. The process of axiological de-functionalization of the tax policy has eroded the normative content of the social contract drawn up during "the glorious thirty" years. Naturally, the compromise concerning the Welfare State, which has made mass taxation possible, has so far shown quite a resistance to dismantlement, no matter how real its

26 Methodological individualism expanded to axiological and cognitive rationality remains valid for disclosing individual tendencies in the face of taxes (cf. chapter 9).

27 That one tries to limit by prohibiting harmful fiscal competition (cf. chapter 12).

28 In developing countries or in countries who recently adopted the market principle, the viability of the tax State often remains precarious, because of the influence of international financial backers (the IMF, the World Bank etc.), of the importance of foreign enterprises (cf. derogatory tax privileges concerning investments) and of the weakness of the legitimacy of the tax State.

erosion may be. But the reorientation of the regulatory normativity of the fiscal power is effective. It results from three dimensions: the democratic alienation; the market injunction; the loss of sense of societal functionality during the hyper-categorization and the legitimatization of the derogation concerning the "contribution-tax". The legitimacy of various syntheses of the period from 1945 to 1975 is put into question. The more or less well-balanced normative congruence between law, politics and social aspects, concerning in this case the financing of public services and of economic action through taxes, has been made fragile by the neo-liberal wave.

The consequences of this evolution are important. When the law is not general any more but tends to become a juxtaposition of particular cases, the political base of the norm, which is found in the society-oriented functions, dries up: the only thing remaining is the formalism of the obligation. Respect for the law is then based on submission to the authority and on the (subjective) appreciation of its methods of repression (cf. chapter 9), and less and less on the legitimacy of the tax State. In societies which mistrust the authority[29], this norm, even though it may conform to formal parliamentary approval, cannot be sufficient. Biased public action maintains and justifies taxation of the majority of citizens, and notably of the middle class, by intervening in several ways. Biased public action also justifies taxation with the ideology of globalization. It thus avoids questioning the arbitrations made in the classification of society by the economically incentive State and its class arbitrariness. For the majority of citizens, taxes continue to be accepted, at worst as an obligation which they have to be subject to. By valorizing public services related to social issues, education and health care, citizens remain imbued with the need for the socio-financial compromise of public policies, even though the system of political decision-making excludes their participation and question the fiscal contract of the State. Although they mistrust institutions and political elites, they are still convinced (at least the majority of citizens) of the usefulness of financing good-quality social services (in a broad sense).

The ideology of market constraints feeds the cognitive rationality of tax policy which misleads citizens about the possibilities for democratic choices. The use of (more of less) painless taxation practices, such as the

---

29 Here we come across Wildavsky's cultural theory of budgeting, except that "culture" is not presented as a cause, but as a participant in the political legitimacy whose influence on tax policy is distorted by the model of biased public action (cf. chapter 7). We should also point out that the degree of distrust towards the authority varies depending on the country and the period, but that the evolution of our societies sets the norm for justifying the authority which amounts to mistrusting the ruling power as an authority non-legitimated by public action. For a reflection on "policy in the age of mistrust", cf. P. Rosanvallon, 2006.

VAT included in prices or the deductions made from salaries at their origin in the form social security contributions or income taxes, reinforces the alienation of citizens. The social categorization (classification by taxation) has abandoned functional legitimacy by overvaluing the market norm as justification, while at the same time making policy more and more particular with a complex fragmentation of tax rules. These factors allow one to conceal new neo-liberal tendencies of fiscal public action. The formation of popular protest is thus held in check for the time being.[30] We now understand that this situation of (cognitively rational) alienation explains why citizens, who do not abhor the politically legitimate tax State, (in general) continue to comply with their tax return obligations, contrary to the Utilitarian model which emphasizes the interest for minimizing taxes (chapter 9).

For large enterprises and wealthy people, the shortcomings of a coherent harmonization of national tax policies and legislation facilitate the circumvention of State authority. Legislative complexity also encourages a game of power and interpretation in the relations with the administration in order to label evasion, avoidance and error. For ordinary citizens, the tax authority of the State is more difficult to circumvent. But it is especially the legitimacy of the tax State which is questioned. It is no longer recognized as being superior to the legitimacy of the market. As we have seen, large enterprises choose a strategy of tax optimization by including the management of risk, in other words by approaching the probability of an unfavourable "labelling" by the administration of the tax scheme applied by them.[31] Tax minimization is reinforced by the dissemination of the neo-liberal ideology of financial profits and by possibilities offered by economic (and financial) globalization.

c. *Tax minimization becoming commonplace*

Finally, tax policy legalizes tax minimization by using various formulas, according to the country: general reduction of statutory tax rates, tax advantages, tax relief mechanisms etc. By encouraging the political delegitimization of the social functions of taxes, market ideology has led to tax competition between States. Economic incentive law has gained autonomy within tax law at the expense of social interventionist law (for society). Laudable efforts to restrict harmful competition between States on an international level[32] are mere palliative measures in the absence of a questioning of their legitimacy in principle. Symmetrically, the legal

30 The 2008 economic crisis has changed the situation.

31 The big law firms specialized in taxes thus sell international tax schemes etc.

32 The "codes" of good conduct of the EU and the OECD.

"labelling" of tax evasion by the tax administration becomes an increasingly delicate issue insofar as tax optimization practiced by big companies is considered as normal. The legitimization of the norm of tax minimization by policy (and thus by law) and its central position in the management of enterprises distort the definition and delimitation of fiscal deviance. Deviance is not delinquency because the latter indicates a violation of the law, whereby deviance implies a deviance from the norms of society, and from the values that underlie them. However, neither of them could ignore the legitimacy of the rights and duties that they define.

Tax control was justified historically by the establishment of big synthetic taxes which made the financing of the Keynesian Welfare State possible. It took part in the credibility of the tax return regime as a technique for citizen participation in socio-political objectives defined for the society of the 20th century. Tax control proceeded logically from the system of public finances which put into concrete form the economic and social compromise aimed at by public action. Economic activity was subordinate to social (societal) objectives among which taxes and social security contributions occupied a place closely linked to social expenses (cf. chapter 5). Up to now, administrative regulation oscillated between a more or less satisfactory logic of yields and a more or less important negotiation which corresponded quite well with a period when the mobility of economic factors remained restrained. With regard to principles, interventionist law used taxes as an instrument within the framework of a legitimate general social contract, in the context of post-war economic and social modernization. The non respect of the law constituted a deviation with regard to this socio-political norm. Tax minimization can only be authorized if it strictly meets the objectives and conditions (interpreted restrictively) foreseen by interventionist law. The question was reduced to the simple problem of implementing efficient tax control in order to rectify errors and justify that the deviance was dealt by the tax office, without provoking troublesome anti-tax reactions of enterprises (systematic litigation, revolts, and especially the questioning of the tax return contract).

In this configuration of interventionist democracy, tax avoidance is not problematized as a delinquency since the business world has its place in the social contract. The small number of criminal proceedings for tax evasion, in a certain number of countries, shows this perfectly well. Despite official statements, the repression of economic fiscal crime does not constitute a priority for public policy. In such a regulatory system, criminal judges only try a few fiscal delinquency cases.

With the appearance of the axiological de-functionalization of the tax State in the 1970s and its intensification in the 1990s as a result of globalization, tax control (audit) becomes the only barrier to the denormalization of public action. We understand the intensity of the dialectic struggle related to the procedure determining the legal powers of the administration and the defense methods (rights) of taxpayers (cf. chapter 8). For enterprises and the richest people, the challenge concerns the security of tax evasion schemes, explicitly foreseen by tax policy or implicitly encouraged by its complexity. It is less and less a matter of discussing the contents of a public policy that has to a large extent acquiesced to the management norm of tax minimization.

The sociology of fiscal litigation (Leroy, 2008) shows that, for the majority of people, the administration expresses the law; it automatically repairs errors, with a minimum intervention from the judge. In the business world, we have to distinguish between big multinational enterprises and the others. As we have already said, for the others, tax evasion, when it exists, often consists in brutal procedures of tax minimization (concealment of revenue, black market purchases, unjustified expenses). In the case of big multinationals, incentive law combines with the possibility of taking advantage of international competition between States. The validation of tax minimization schemes is placed in the field of the economic management of the enterprise. From this point of view, the legal mechanisms envisaged by the law to allow the tax administration to restrain excesses in tax avoidance/evasion are indispensible; but these remedies[33] do not tackle the origin of the trouble which is situated in the deviance of normative regulation practiced by public action in (tax) policy. Even if the enterprises and their management boards sometimes complain about the restrictions associated with the possibilities promised by the tax policy, the administrative regulation cannot condemn tax planning. Instead, it may simply curb some of its abusive practices, because State encourages tax optimization.

As exposed in chapter 8, nowadays there is a movement initiated in favour of "responsive regulation", cooperating with big enterprises. Inspired by the precepts of the new public management, an argumentative pressure is exerted with the objective to reform the functioning of the tax control of the administration that, despite intervening reforms, still operate very much within the logic of a struggle against deviance with regard to the interventionist State. It is a question of putting an end to the hiatus between the management model of tax "planning" (i.e., minimization) serving as a norm for enterprises, reinforced by national incentive regulations (tax competition between States), and the very idea

[33] Abnormal acts of management, breach of law, the regime of transferring profits to territories with a privileged tax system are the main legal instruments.

of the administrative regulation of deviances.[34] In this respect, words are deceitful because this cooperative regulation, favouring big enterprises, marks an evolution in the direction of fiscal governance, in the sense defined above (the preponderance of the global market). Certain commentators thus claim that, in the case of multinationals, the negotiation of taxes (for example, of transfer prices) should become systematized and recognized in the Community law applicable to EU member states. The conclusion is clear: we must abandon the bastion, already weakened however in the context of the globalization of tax minimization, constituted by the fiscal control of the big enterprises. The argumentation of legal security of the schemes of flight from taxes serves as an pretext for the refuse of questioning the flaws of fiscal normativity, distorted by the competition between the incentives policies of States. The notion of fiscal deviance tends to lose its meaning for society.

Conclusion

The evolution towards a de-functionalization of fiscal normativity is not irreversible. The introduction of performance budgets has led certain administrations to establish as a priority the struggle against large-scale fraud. It should also be reminded that the financial function of taxes, already impaired by the incentive law of fiscal expenses and the globalization of tax optimization, implies that the participation of enterprises remains credible. The crisis of 2008 has awakened public awareness of the evils of tax havens. In this way the summit of industrialized and emerging economies (G-20) which took place in London on the 1st and 2nd of April 2009 made public a black list of tax havens established by the OECD. The deviances of the neo-liberal globalization of financial capitalism have been properly emphasized. Popular protest has until now been restrained through the mechanism of cognitive alienation of fiscal democracy, based on the neo-liberal ideology of market constraints. Nevertheless, as Tocqueville proposes it regarding the French Revolution (chapter 1), powerful ferments nourish popular discontent: the isolation of classes by tax categorization (classification), the spectacle of tax privileges reinforcing inequalities, the demystification of the market constraint (with support programs for unscrupulous financial executives), the political failure of the elite in maintaining the financial foundations of the social contract.

[34] We can understand the success of the Utilitarian rationality model applied to tax avoidance, which is in perfect congruence with this evolution towards tax avoidance becoming commonplace and sterilized under the notion of tax planning. The scientific validity of this model is not universal, but gives a good account of the evolution of the business world with regard to the socio-political de-functionalization of the regulatory power of the State.

Nonetheless, in the absence of a social movement, this change in normative logic seems uncertain: the method of patching up the system of profits (here taxes) and its inegalitarian logic is more probable, even though we may be witnessing a return of the State. The struggle against large-scale fraud can be reduced to the staging of a few illegal traffic networks and to a statistical construction leaving the problem as it is. The recourse to loans and the increase of tax burden borne by working classes and the middle class are means of finding new revenues to finance public expenses. On the organizational level, it is possible to adopt the agency model (cf. the case of Italy in chapter 8) in order to ensure a certain volume of revenue, while at the same time reducing regulation to a more or less balanced negotiation according to the categories of taxpayers. The policing of certain practices used by tax havens leaves aside the very problem of "normal" tax optimization in accordance with territorial advantages. The territories with privileged taxation are fundamental for the capitalism of multinational enterprises and financial institutions. We must underline that the interdiction of relations (possession of assets, joint ventures) with tax havens was not decided at the G-20 summit in April 2009. They were content to include only 4 counties on the OECD's black list. A better cooperation, such as the commitment of certain countries to lift the bank secrecy and the improvement of information exchange between administrations, marks a progress. But the problem is indeed that of reexamining the sociopolitical functions of tax policies within a supranational framework and of creating a socially just fiscal contract.

CHAPTER 11

The Destabilization of the Functions of the Interventionist Tax State

The genesis of the modern State is explained by the establishment of permanent taxation. The tension between the submission to the authority of the sovereign and the legitimacy of the consent by the representatives of the taxpayers characterizes, as we have seen, this evolution. The climax of liberal democracy in the 19th century is based on parliamentarism which is inspired by a limiting conception of financial political action. The liberal dogma extols the neutrality of expenditure and hence of taxes which are limited to the financing of the sovereignty competences of the State. The increase of tax revenue (taxes and social contributions) indicates a radical change of the weight of the tax State: it always represents on average for the OECD countries more than one third (cf. chapter 5). From the Second World War the financing of social protection has accentuated this tendency, while at the same time creating significant differences between countries according to the type of fiscal structure and Welfare State. The role of taxation has changed with the Keynesian and social interventionist State: taxes are not only an object of public policy but also an instrument of other public policies. In accordance with Mann's presentiment (1943), a functional approach to taxation is thus justified.

In sociology, functional analysis is classical since Emile Durkheim recommended it in *The Rules of the Sociological Method* (1982, chapter 5), on the condition of distinguishing between the cause and the function of social phenomena.[1] Without going back to the causes of tax policy (chapter 6), it is a question of the reconstruction and evaluation of the evolution of the role of taxes through its great functions for society. This reasoned usage does not suppose accepting that every institution has a social function in the vein of the hyper-functionalism of the anthropological school (Malinowski). Indeed, as Merton (1949) explains it in *Social Theory and Social Structure*, functional analysis is justified on

[1] "Thus when undertaking to explain a social phenomenon, one must search separately for the efficient cause which produces it and the function which it fulfils (...). But if one must proceed only in the second place to the determination of the function, it is necessary all the same so that the explanation of the phenomenon is complete." Cf. also the work of Parsons (1977, for example).

the condition to specify the social units to which it is applicable. This leads to the study, by following Durkheim, of "social types". In our case, a socio-political typology of the tax State is proposed in order to complete the classic economic analysis of Musgrave (1959) centered on financial functions, economic regulation and tax redistribution (Leroy, 2005, p. 78).

Table 14: Socio-political functional-tax approach

Financial function	– Revenues from taxes to finance expenditure
Economic regulation function	– Economic action by taxes: priority sectors, exports, research etc.
Social function	– Redistribution by progressive income tax towards the poorest – Tax categorization of the society: family taxation, some social groups, products, socially developed or discriminated sectors
Ecological territorial function	– Legal territory of competence in tax law – Territorial tax inequalities – Territorial development: tax exemptions of certain "weak" rural zones, urban districts, tax incentives for "competitivity" zones – Safeguarding of the environment: eco-taxes, expenditure taxes
Political function	– Citizen contribution-tax to general interest policies – Political legitimacy – Tax State compliance (civism) – Tax democracy with direct tax consent

1. The Financial Function

Historically, the tax State appeared in Europe based on the financial function, at first in relation to the financing of wars and then according to its own dynamics. It has become and remained interventionist by diversifying the tax instrument. In all developed countries, taxation constitutes the main revenue that finances the other public policies (expenditure). The growth of public expenditure in developed countries, which the literature links to industrial capitalism (Wagner) or to democracy (Tocqueville), explains the rise of tax revenue used in its financial function. More precisely (cf. chapter 5), the increase of social expenditure in OECD countries after 1945 constituted the key factor, until the neo-liberal calling into question whose effects are complex.

A recent change is related to the massive utilization of loans which competes with the financial function of taxes. Public debt has been increasing in several countries for about twenty years. It is today even higher because of the stimulation plan[2] ensuing from the crisis of the summer of 2008. Now it is indeed taxes that must finance the reimbursements of the loans, even though the real charge may vary notably with regard to inflation and with regard to the gains of the State which will be taken from investments in enterprises in the case of economic growth.

The financial function is also called into question by derogatory taxation, used in various ways in all the countries. The advantages granted in this way (tax rebates, exemptions, reductions and tax credits etc.) in view of categorial social and economic objectives form the tax "expenditure" (cf. below). Apart from the level of tax revenue, we must also look at the evolution of its structure which is based on a limited number of "taxes" (in a wide sense) and contributions among which income tax and social contributions occupy an important place. The recent evolution is marked by a tendency of an increase of the weight of taxes on consumption (mainly VAT).[3] The relation between taxes and economy is also important.

2. The Economic Function

Tax policy may target a global (cyclical) regulation of the economy or a (structural) orientation of certain sectors or agents which may or may not pass on the fiscal effect (incidence and transfer). In this second case, tax incentives are often used, even if it is also possible to use a surcharge, or to limit or prohibit the granting of certain tax advantages. The advantageous derogations for a category of taxpayers are considered as tax expenditure because they diminish budget revenues.

a. The decline of global economic regulation

The cyclical measures of combating inflation by raising tax revenue (reducing the money supply) have not been used any more since the 1980s: the monetary policy of the European Central Bank, the only competent institution for fixing the interest rate, and the introduction of the euro allowed one to bring inflation under control. Tax reduction policies (on the supply side) have on the other hand been used by left-wing as well as by right-wing governments, without always leading to a global decrease in tax revenue. In certain countries, such policies were accompanied by a widening of the tax base but this is not the case of countries that maintain numerous tax niches (loopholes) which have the effect of narrowing the base. With the decline of Keynesian economic

2 For a global comparison: Saha, von Weizsäcker, 2008; Jamet and Lirzin, 2009.

3 In France, we also note a evolution towards the financing of social protection by taxes which appeal to national taxpayers along with employees and employers.

policies (related to the social spending) and the deviances of the policies of reducing taxes[4], economic macro-regulation is not functional any more.

The economic sectorization of fiscal measures is carried out to the detriment of the function of macro-regulation of economic cycles. The mutation of the economic function of fiscal policy from a function of macro-regulation to a function of micro-sectorization is important: it participates in the defunctionalization of the role of tax which is divided in a categorization of society which aims at directing the behaviour of specific groups. The neo-liberal discrediting of the State started in the 1970s, and which will perhaps end with the crisis of 2008, has not really destroyed the tax power. By supporting the fragmentation of the tax instrument it has rather led to the questioning of the reference to general social objectives in favour of a categorization without any global coherence.

b. Tax expenditure

In spite of the methodological difficulties of definition and measurement (Burnam, 2003; Burnam *et al.*, 2008), we know that tax expenditures (tax deductions, exemptions, reductions, tax credits etc.) are used for social purposes in many OECD countries.[5] Tax incentives for the economy can be defined, in opposition to general measures such as the reduction of a tax rate, as a more favourable treatment of certain sectors or certain activities compared with the law applicable to all the enterprises. They may take various forms.[6] An incentive tax for the creation of jobs is also a widespread social tool for combating unemployment (Faulk, 2002). We may also quote tax incentives for research and development which are often used. Small and medium-sized enterprises are also the subject of favourable tax legislation in numerous countries. Tax competition between States has accentuated the recourse to tax incentives in order to attract (big) enterprises. The evaluation of

---

4 Cf. also the widespread failure of flat tax policies which concerned the income tax of natural persons but which led to increases in social contributions, weighing down on labour costs (Keen and others, 2008).

5 The decline of other economic instruments (such as monetary policy reserved for the ECB) is one of the explanatory factors. Tax expenditures moreover diminish tax revenue.

6 That is to say, principally: accelerated depreciation of invested assets, special reserves, temporary exemption from certain levies for new enterprises (tax holiday), advantages for certain zones, tax credit or deduction of a certain fraction of the base of imposition on the value of investments, (targeted) reduction of the tax rate for certain activities or certain transactions such as the injections into the capital of the enterprise.

the economic effects of tax incentives, which depend on the situations, nevertheless remains mitigated (Klemm, 2009).

However that may be, the recourse to tax incentives for economic purposes is widespread. In 2003, for Canada, France and the United States, the economic objectives represent 65% of tax expenses (income tax, corporate tax and VAT) against 35% for social purposes (Godbout, 2006, p. 252). In these three countries corporate tax is little used for social purposes (more than 93% for economic goals), but income tax is used in a varied way as a social function (Canada: 34.6%, the United States: 38.5%, France: 44.3%). The number of kinds of tax expenditure (tax deductions, exemptions, reductions, tax credits etc.) varies very much from country to country. In 2002, by harmonizing the definition of tax expenditure based on the case of France, it is thus 420 in France, 300 in Spain, 225 in Canada, 175 in Germany and 140 in the United Kingdom (*Conseil des impôts*, 2003, p. 20). On the other hand, the weight of tax expenditure, measured in % of GDP, places Canada at the top with more than 16% of GDP, followed by the United Kingdom with 15.5%, Spain with 6%, France with 4%, Germany with a little more than 2%.

In Sweden, tax expenditure of an economic nature, which is understood as a result of the compromises of social-democracy commitments, benefits the investments of big enterprises. In 2008, in France the 486 tax niches (loopholes) represent approximately 70 billion euros of revenue losses; their number went from 320 to 420 between 1981 and 2002. The amount of tax expenses for which we have an estimate represents more than 50 billion euros in 2001, that is to say more than 3% of GDP and more than 20% of the tax revenue. In the United States, tax expenditure is very detailed, benefiting enterprises or individuals sometimes nominally designated, because the interests of their constituencies are privileged by commissions of the Congress. According to the study of Burman and Toder (2008), American tax expenditure between 1980 and 2006 represents from 4.2% to 6.5% of GDP according to the years retained. In 2007, tax expenditure of a social nature in the field of income tax, taken separately, represents 750 billion dollars, that is to say more than the American defense budget. This tax expenditure increased between 1980 and 1985, then dropped following president Reagan's reforms, between 1986 and 1990, before increasing again from 1990 to 2001, then decreasing slightly between 2001 and 2006. As a whole, this period has been marked by an increase of tax expenditure of a social nature compared to those of an economic nature.

Globally it appears that this social expenditure benefits the rich more. A study of American tax expenditure between 1980 and 2006 (Burman *et al.*, 2008) shows that elimination of tax expenditure in the field of income tax would lead to a decrease of income after taxes of

6.5% for the most modest (the 20% situated in the first quintile of the distribution of incomes) and of 11.4% for the most well off (the 20% of the last quintile). Much more than that, the income after taxes of the 1% most privileged people would decrease by 13.6%. The tax receipts recuperated by the elimination of tax expenditure would be better employed by directly financing social expenditure in favour of the most deprived people, which would reduce the inequalities even more. In France several important kinds of tax expenditure benefit mostly the richest people. This is the case of the tax relief, to the amount of 50% of the sums paid, for the employment of a wage-earner at home.[7]

Since the 1990s employment policy has been using tax revenue to urge a return to employment and diminish labour costs. In this way in capitalist democracies (Vis, 2007; Dingeldey, 2007), these reforms change the direction of the traditional Welfare State in the sense of *workfare* by targeting social action against poverty on persons still working. The struggle against inactivity, supposedly self-chosen, aims at the beneficiaries of the "*minima sociaux*" (minimum guaranteed incomes), for example by reducing social contributions on little qualified employment. Tax law thus lays down numerous specific provisions in favour of enterprises (creation of employment, innovation, research, reduction of rates etc.), but also fulfils social objectives of public policy.

3. The Social Function

The social function integrates the redistribution of revenues by taxes because it modifies the social stratification. But it extends to interventions, in favour of or in opposition to social groups, predefined or not, by tax policy that tries to orientate behaviour. In spite of neo-liberal policies of the limitation of certain taxes, the social function of tax remains important; but the priority traditionally given to tax redistribution appears modified by the rise of non-progressive taxes, and sometimes even regressive ones, and by the accentuation of the social categorization of society.

a. The variable impact of redistribution

Redistribution uses either social transfers or taxation to reduce the inequalities of incomes. It leads to the narrowing of the differences between the richest and the poorest.[8] Here classes are defined by their

---

7 Notably for the following reasons: half of the households is not taxable in France (and many among them cannot finance an employment at home); the reduction cannot exceed the amount of tax paid.

8 The other inequalities (gender, health, ethnical origin, territorial origin etc.) that sometimes justify policies of action in the field of equity (measures favouring certain

incomes. In general, tax redistribution is carried out through the progressive income tax of physical persons or through the taxation of the fortune of the richest. It also depends on tax exemptions provided for by the law. Many countries have used reductions of the marginal rate of the income tax, which undermines the redistribution from the (very) rich to the (more or less) poor people. Historically, the creation of the progressive income tax in Europe has been associated with the creation of the Welfare State in order to respond to the social question of industrial capitalism (Leroy, 1996). So the purpose of the tax is to diminish the inequalities[9] of incomes and to finance the social interventions of the State.

Table 15 shows for the period 1980-2000 what the impact is of fiscal and social redistribution on inequalities for 13 OECD countries. The first column classifies the countries according to the importance of inequalities (measured by the Gini index). The second column classifies the countries in accordance with the importance of redistribution by taxes and the third column according to social redistribution (through transfers). The fourth column classifies the countries in accordance with the importance of total redistribution (fiscal and social). The fifth column classifies the countries according to inequalities (Gini index) after redistribution.

We note that inequalities before redistribution are high in the United Kingdom, France, Belgium, the Netherlands and Sweden and low in Norway, Switzerland, Canada and, to a lesser extent, Denmark and Finland. As for disposable income after redistribution, measuring real inequalities, the United States, the United Kingdom, Switzerland, Australia, Austria and, to a lesser extent, France are classified at the top of the list. The countries where inequalities are the smallest are without surprise the Nordic countries. There is also Belgium which puts into practice the biggest redistribution since it passes from the 3rd place as for the inequalities to the 10th (out of 13). Apart from Belgium which takes the first place, redistribution (the 4th column of the table) is important in Sweden, the Netherlands, Finland and France. Switzerland,

groups) are not part of our subject. Let us simply note that in general inequalities accumulate, so that the problem of inequalities in incomes remains central.

9 Many specialists see the Welfare State as the result of power relations or of class struggle, but this interpretation is only partially right because it neglects the importance of cognitive rationality: the creation of the income tax (in Europe) is a compromise between the capitalist class (Leroy, 1996), which thus avoids the (real) risk of a social revolution in the 19th century, and the working class, supported by the left-wing parties, which considers these advantages as a stage in the transformation of society. The case of the creation of the English income tax in 1842 by the Conservative Peel also shows that the Conservatives have accepted the creation of the progressive income tax in exchange for the reduction of customs duties.

the United States, Canada and Australia use redistribution less. The priority given to the type of redistribution is variable from one country to the other. France and Switzerland use tax redistribution only a little whereas other countries such as Belgium resort to it to a bigger extent.

Table 15: Redistribution in an international perspective (1980-2000)

Gross Income Inequalities	Tax Redistribution	Social Redistribution	Total Redistribution	Disposable Income Inequalities
1 UK 0.475	1 Belgium	1 Sweden	1 Belgium	1 USA 0.345
2 France 0.469	2 Australia	2 Belgium	2 Sweden	2 UK 0.323
3 Belgium 0.465	3 Finland	3 Netherlands	3 Netherlands	3 Switzerland 0.299
4 Nether lands 0.458	4 Germany	4 France	4 Finland	4 Australia 0.297
5 USA 0.447	5 USA	5 Finland	5 France	5 France 0.292
6 Sweden 0.441	6 Netherlands	6 Denmark	6 Denmark	6 Canada 0.290
7 Australia 0.423	7 Norway	7 UK	7 Germany	7 Netherland 0.257
8 Germany 0.421	8 Sweden	8 Germany	8 UK	8 Germany 0.254
9 Finland 0.417	9 Canada	9 Norway	9 Norway	9 Denmark 0.245
10 Denmark 0.412	10 Denmark	10 Switzerland	10 Australia	10 Belgium 0.242
11 Canada 0.406	11 UK	11 Canada	11 Canada	11 Norway 0.235
12 Switzer land 0.396	12 France	12 Australia	12 USA	12 Finland 0.223
13 Norway 0.379	13 Switzerland	13 USA	13 Switzerland	13 Sweden 0.223

The figures to the right of the country = ratio according to the Gini index. The figures indicate the average of the results collected in 1980, 1985, 1990, 1995 and 2000 by LIS (*Luxembourg Income Study*).

Source: Based on Mahler, Jesuit, 2006, p. 490

We must however consider the explosion of high incomes[10] in numerous countries and observe the inequalities of wealth and patrimony

[10] In France, the work of Piketty (2001), based on declared incomes, retains a hazardous estimation of fraud and thus of inequalities and of the effect of redistribution: cf. M. Leroy, *L'Année sociologique*, March 2006.

(cf. chapter 12). We should also recall that the policy of tax expenditure, which categorizes taxpayers by rather favouring the rich, has an effect on redistribution. The VAT has a distinctly anti-redistributive effect as is shown by French studies[11] (Forgeot and Starzec, 2003).

Apart from redistribution, the social function also concerns several challenges for society. In fact, numerous sectors of society are the subject of a specific treatment through the use of tax expenditure (cf. above). Income tax thus no longer has redistribution as its sole objective and has evolved towards social particularisms in order to deal with specific issues for society.

b. The other social issues

Traditionally the family is encouraged by taxes in the form of tax reductions or the application of lower tax rates, or furthermore a general tax break for married couples such as in France. Mann (1943, p. 226) noted that Nazi Germany or Fascist Italy overtaxed unmarried people. Recently, tax discrimination with regard to marriage in the United States is seen as a blow to the legal neutrality of marriage, that is to say: to the equal treatment of married couples in each State and the equality of married couples and unmarried couples (Berliant, Rothstein, 2003).

The analysis of the tax policy of the family thus constitutes an interesting case (Leroy, 2009). In the 19th century, the family remains largely ignored by public interventionism which is, on a general level, condemned by the liberal conception of public finance. In the context of the individualism of the industrial revolution, the principle is that of the neutrality of the minimum State towards the family. Much more than that, the State seeks its legitimation in the family taken as a model of government in the image of the good father, head of the family. It is preoccupied by the contribution of the family to the social order. In this sense, it simply remedies the deficiencies of the family with regard to hygiene, an idea that appeared at the end of the 18th century and then in the field of education with the development of schools.

At the end of 19th century in France, pro-birth movements militate for a family policy either for demographic reasons, or to defend the values of the family as an institution of the social order. The Caillaux laws of 1914-1917 introduce the notion of a tax household which still constitutes the unit of imposition of the family (art.6 CGI *Code Général des Impôts*). In 1945 the family quotient mechanism (tax advantage) is introduced in order to put the pro-birth policy after the war into concrete

11 VAT increases the Gini coefficient by 1.3%. The standard of living of the poorest diminishes by 22% because of VAT whereas that of the richest diminishes only by 8%. Cf. *INSEE, France Portrait social 2008*.

form. The legitimate model is that of the nuclear family. In the 1980s a bonus mechanism for the so-called family "*parts*" (when calculating tax) is put into place for the large families. Since 1986 the State has been rewarding in a certain way morally the fact of having brought up children by also granting an increase of "*parts*" to widows and widowers having brought up children.

The State has at its disposition different tools, remedies and arms, among which tax policy is not always the most important. It also intervenes to alleviate, encourage or hit by the policy of social transfers, the school and educational policy, the supply of services (crèches etc.), the security policy (police and judicial systems) etc. The context is that of the mutation of the family in relation to the development of woman labour, the increase of divorces and the recompositions of families. In view of this context, the configuration of the public response to the problem varies according to the country, in terms of the conception of the family policy which is influenced in a variable degree from one country to another by the values of society. The demographic study of the family policies of OECD countries (Thévenon, 2008) shows that there exist contrasting models of public action. Globally public spending consecrated by developed countries to families went from 1.6% to 2.4% of GDP from 1980 to 2003. The Nordic model provides an important support in the case of young children.[12] On the other hand, the amount of financial benefits granted to families is rather lower than the average and is targeted on low-income families. This model, of which Denmark is the archetype, is founded on a strong public intervention in order to allow parents and in particular women to reconcile professional life and the education of the children.[13] From a tax point of view, the counterpart is a high rate of imposition of people who enter into the labour market or take up their post again.

The second model brings together the Anglo-Saxon countries, Japan, Korea and the Southern European countries. There is less aid to the reconciliation of work and young children. The different kinds of leave of absence are shorter and poorly remunerated or not at all. The supply of child day care services is globally smaller, even though the situations are variable. The spending per child under the age of 3 is lower. In this group, we distinguish on one hand the Anglo-Saxon countries with

---

12 Generous parental leave of absence equivalent to 53 weeks of full-time work is allowed in Sweden, 47 weeks in Denmark against an average of 27 weeks for OECD countries. Children are taken care of by reception services: in Nordic countries almost 50% of children under the age of 3 are received in day care centers against 25% on average in the other countries. In Denmark this rate is 62%, in Iceland 59%.

13 Contrary to a widespread idea, it appears that the fertility rate is the highest in countries where the rate of employment of women is the highest.

Japan and Korea and on the other hand the Southern European countries. Social benefits and tax deductions are higher, representing 1.9% of GDP against 1.6% on average in OECD countries. The United States are a case apart with only 0.8%. This aid is targeted towards low-income families in accordance with the goal of fighting poverty. Day care centers for young children do exist, even though they are often private, taking care of 28% of the children. The idea is that the flexibility of the labour market must allow the necessary adjustment for the reconciliation of private life and working life. If the poverty level of families remains high, the fertility rate is high. Southern Europe is characterized by more limited benefits. The fertility rate and the employment rate of women are low. There is no real tax policy. Sometimes parental leave is long, but poorly remunerated or not at all.

Eastern European countries are in an intermediary situation. In Southern Europe it is admitted that families may take on certain costs themselves. France stands out as an exception. Spending on families amount to 3.8% of GDP after taking account of tax incentives (Thévenon, 2008), which puts France in third position among OECD countries (where the average rate is 2.4%).

The tax categorization of the family, which is separated from the social groups (cf. 2), distinguishes the relational family (the case of tax households), the economic or patrimonial family (the case of the taxation of inheritance), the professional family (the case of transmission of enterprises), the alimony family (the case of maintenance paid to children of separated couples), the demographic family (encouragement of the birth rate). It also creates the categories of the legitimate tax family (married couple), the child-centered family (example of the linking up or of the deduction of alimony and/or maintenance), the grandparents and grandchildren family (example of donations), the single-parent family, the "civil"-partnership family, the common-law family (cohabitation) etc.

There exist other examples of the categorization of society by the tax policy. The negative income tax policy (income guarantee), which participates in the workfare[14], by aiming at public action, tends to distinguish between the "good poor" which deserve public aid and those which must be urged on to work (Dean, 2007). It gives a concrete form to a compromise between the neo-liberal idea of the struggle against the employment trap, in order to remedy the economic disincentive of working for the beneficiaries of social transfers, and the social-democratic idea of redistribution towards the poorest. In this case, the

[14] This policy is initiated in the 1990s exonerating low wages from social contributions and revalorizing the return to work by social and tax incentives.

evolution of the cognitive rationality of political leaders and citizens changes, following the example of the American attempt to create a negative tax in the years 1960s-1970s (Steensland, 2006).

Many countries adopt tax measures to encourage philanthropy, even though some countries do not use tax reductions or else set limits to deductions. The social function sometimes also aims at moral dissuasion such as with the taxation of tobacco and alcohol which also fulfills a financial function by generating complementary revenue (Johnson, Meier, 1990; Paton *et al.*, 2004). In the United States, the taxation of gambling has a moral purpose, while gambling involving money are socially accepted in the United Kingdom. Another example is given by the tax rebates granted to associations to support civil society or to foundations. We can furthermore mention cultural policy which sometimes provide for tax incentives in order to protect the cultural heritage, but which taxes culture when it becomes a lucrative activity (Leroy, 1997).

The social function therefore comprises a general redistributive part, which stratifies society in terms of available income, and particular measures, which categorize it, sometimes including a territorialized aspect.

4. The Ecological Territorial Function

The first legal application of the territorial function consists in defining the sovereignty of the tax State from a geographical point of view. The second application relates to the territorial inequalities which result from taxation and constitute a territorialized social function. For example, in the case of Belgian fiscal federalism (Cantillo *et al.*, 2006, p. 1051), the systems of social security and of income tax diminish the inequality of incomes by about 75% between Flanders and the Walloon region. In France, the professional tax (before the reform of 2009/2010) paid by enterprises is the main cause of the inequalities between local authorities. The third application is determining the differences in the attractiveness of territories, in relation to the problem of the tax competition between States and other sub-national authorities. For example, globalization leads to tax avoidance by the relocation of enterprises and the flight of rich people through the intermediary of tax havens. Another case is given by territorial development policies which provide for a zoning of tax deductions (rural zones losing economic activities, deprived urban areas). These issues contribute to the splitting up of tax policy. Environmental (or ecological) taxation constitutes the fourth issue related to the territorial function of tax.

Environmental taxation aims to protect the natural resources of territories within the framework of sustainable development. Inspired by ecological demands, it is the subject of several international agreements:

the polluter pays principle is acknowledged by the OECD and the European Union (art. 174 of the Treaty). The tax is used either to penalize activities which destroy the environment (pollution), or to encourage actions which are beneficial for the environment. Certain contradictions exist: first between tax incentives in favour of the (polluting) economy and those in favour of the environment; then between the incentive and punitive conceptions of green taxation. The current crisis gives rise to reflections to implement an ecological taxation likely to favour another model of economic growth based on sustainable development.

5. The Political Function

The political function of taxation lies at the heart of the legitimacy of the tax State. As shown in chapter 4, tax is a constituent element of the birth of the Western European State following the transformation of feudalism.[15] Fiscal revolts express an opposition to the legitimacy of taxation, perceived as arbitrary (cf. chapter 10). Taxation is an essential indicator of the legitimacy of the State (Cheibub, 1998; Lieberman, 2002; Leroy, 2003; Gilley 2006). The problem is thus to encourage the emergence of the contribution-tax in order to finance public policies in a legitimate way. The non-democratic solution of the cense-based regime which reserved the right to vote to the rich taxpayers is not acceptable. The solution of the parliamentary democracy (tax voted by the Parliament) does not suffice any more (cf. chapter 7) in many countries to fulfil the political function. In fact, the complexity of taxation, the general tendency of the reinforcement of the executive power to the detriment of the legislative power and the influence of experts create obstacles to the debate on taxes by the elected assemblies. The social-fiscal compromises made during the period of "the glorious thirty" years have since then been largely put into question as far as their axiological value for society.

a. The socio-fiscal compromises of "The Glorious Thirty"

In line with Tocqueville's forecast, in the long run the democratization of industrial societies has brought an increase in public expenditure. A socio-financial democratic contract is thus initiated from the end of the 19th century based on an extension of the social public action financed by the tax State. A general link is established between mass taxation and social rights which will lead to the Welfare State. On the

[15] Cf. also Schumpeter's analysis in chapter 2. the nobility's refusal to go to war so that they could look after their fiefs (private sector) explains the recourse to an army of mercenaries that the economy of the domains (demesnes) could no longer finance. The royal taxation created within this context is one of the competences of the tax State which gains autonomy as a legitimate public sphere.

basis of the genesis of this political contract, different compromises will be put into place in order to determine the levels and types of social expenditure and taxes: it is a question of finding a political balance between the rights of the different socio-economic categories and their responsibilities (contribution-tax) as taxpayers. Lindert (2004) has thus really shown the central role played by the political voice on the growth of social expenditure. In the same way, Aidt and Jensen (2009), on the basis of the data of 10 Western European countries over the period 1860-1938, show that the extension of suffrage is correlated with the increase in expenditure, but also in taxes: a country which adopts universal suffrage sees an increase of its total public expenditure of about 8 points of GDP and 2 points for the total sum of taxes. This political right also has an effect on the tax structure, because a correlation is also found with the progression of direct taxes. Nonetheless, this is conditioned by the possibilities of tax collection in order to allow for a system of controlled tax returns (that is to say a sufficient level of education, measured by the rate of enrolment at school between 5 and 14 years).

After the Second World War, the generalization of Keynesian policies is accompanied by the development of social public action. During "the Glorious Thirty" period which ends with the economic crisis of the 1970s, taxes, apart from their function to finance social expenditure in a wide sense, also fulfill the interventionist functions of economic macro-regulation and of income redistribution. Beyond the differences, the conflicts and the failures of this regulation, interventionist democracy finds in this period a foundation in the socio-political functions of taxes. Axiologically, this foundation consecrates the legitimacy of the regulatory power of the tax State (cf. chapter 10) as a conception of public action. In reality, of course, the compromise has taken various forms according to the countries as is illustrated by the national diversity of Welfare states and of the structures of public revenue and expenditure. It is marked by the more or less strong decline of the financial power of parliaments to the benefit of the more or less distant executive authorities listening to technocrats. But, in its essence, the increase of taxation was justified by the construction of a social protection, by spending on health and by the rapid growth of public education. The economic and social interventions maintained a global objective for society in keeping with the conception of social Keynesianism. The modernization of the tax system logically relied upon the establishment of big (synthetic) general taxes hitting all income. Mass taxation accompanies the Welfare State within a context of strong economic growth.

In this way, the categorization of society, even though it complied with other types of logic such as that of the family, ownership (vs. renting), occupation (commercial, salaried, independent, in arts and crafts), was carried out on the basis of the fundamental functions. At another level, provided that we refuse all the determinism of the systemic complementarity of the economy and of social issues (cf. chapter 7), we may interpret the literature on the diversity of capitalisms (Albert, 1991; Hall, Soskice, 2001; Amable, 2003; Boyer, 2004) from the perspective of arrangements made between the market and the economy. Schröder (2009), for example, emphasizes the statistical correlation between the degree of decommodification[16] and the coordination of the economy (Hall, Soskice, 2001). He also underlines the link between the law of employment protection, or also the level of social expenditure, and the degree of coordination of the economy. Arrangements between the type of production regime (coordinated or liberal) and the type of Welfare State are also observed in the field of education (Iversen, Stephens, 2008)

For the rich Western countries, the compromise on the post-war Welfare State consecrates a general relation between the level of social protection and the method of financing. A socio-political consensus emerges concerning the forms of the Welfare State which more or less come close to the ideal-typical classification of Esping-Andersen (1990).[17] But the compromise also involves various tax functions, which are not treated in *The Three Worlds of Welfare Capitalism*. In fact, tax policy must be considered in its interventionist functions, and not only as a passive instrument of financing social policy. So there are two important criteria for the analysis of the choices made which concerns here not the causes but the results, namely: the subject, or more precisely the perimeter, of the compromises characterizing the more or less large configuration of the problem[18]; the process of consent which allows one to clearly show the democratic nature of the arrangement. The political function finds its full consecration as a democratic contract when a global compromise is found between the main functions of the tax State and when this compromise is submitted to the consent of the people. In real history the two criteria are difficult to fulfill completely. The consensus is sometimes simply implicit or partial. But the political function must be valorized as a normative ideal of interventionist democracy (and of its limits), even if, in practice, the social-fiscal public action of developed countries has used various arrangements.

16 It is higher in the Scandinavian model of the Welfare State, according to Esping-Andersen, 1990.

17 Esping-Andersen uses the term of capitalist Welfare State because all Western countries have a level of taxation and public expenditure situated between 30% and 60% of GDP and because they spend more than half of their budget on social policy or welfare.

18 Cf. Figure 3 in chapter 7. On the epistemological and ethical level, the positioning of the configuration of the problem, which refers to the pertinence of the level of analysis, is essential (cf. chapter 3).

The socio-democratic model of a universal character, where taxes finance a high level of social protection for all, is that of Scandinavian countries. Here the compromise has indeed had a global character (1st criterion) and puts into concrete form a rather successful (social) kind of democracy (2nd criterion) by achieving an accord between trade unions (labour), the State and enterprises (capital). This social democracy leads to the generous Welfare State accepted by capital in exchange for the moderation of salaries[19], the significant taxation on the incomes of labour, and a moderation of taxes on economic and financial profits. The Scandinavian model of dual income taxation involves a low rate for the mobile factors (capital) and a high rate for the immobile factor of labour. What is less known is that it also relies on indirect taxes. The compromise between State, market and society has thus indeed a global character here. It relies on a tax system with high financial yields. With regard to the decision-making process, we saw that in Sweden the Saltsjöbaden conference of 1938 (cf. chapter 6) had established a negotiated compromise to tax in a significant way all taxpayers, including those earning modest wages, on income, wealth, inheritance and consumption (indirect tax) in exchange for economic prosperity which allowed the Welfare State. This agreement is a bigger advantage for large enterprises (tax allowances) as compared to the others, keeping in mind that, as a whole, capital is not much imposed. It relies on relations based on power, in connection with the mobilization of the working class as required by the power resources approach. It especially expresses a historical logic of socio-political argumentation on the functions of tax. The idea is that tax must serve to finance an elevated social protection while at the same time allowing enterprises to remain competitive[20] on the world market, which implies a (relatively) less important priority for tax redistribution (cf. above).

In democracies with (corporatist) social security systems, the total level of social spending remains high. But it is the social security contributions of the employers and employees that finance a social protection (originally) reserved for wage-earners. This conservative model is found in countries like Germany, Belgium, France, Italy and Japan. The achieved compromise aims for a regulation of the labour market where social rights depend on the integration of employees.[21] By focusing on

19 And for social peace.

20 Cognitive rationality, which is defined with regard to the logic of treatment of the information of the actors within context, explains the compromises better than the logic of interest (utilitarian rationality): it is often the validation of the reasoning which then explains the attachment to the values of the Welfare State (axiological rationality) which in some sort has been proven from 1945 to 1975.

21 This includes, from the point of view of social expenditure, a priority for unemployment benefits and for retirement pensions.

employees, the compromise is less global and especially concerns the function of financing social spending (in the wide sense) by social security contributions. The economic and redistributive functions of tax are not included within the perimeter of the compromise. For example, Belgium uses tax and social transfers to ensure a big redistribution of income, while France makes less use of taxation for this purpose and obtains average results in the field of social redistribution. More sectoral compromises may exist like in the case of the taxation of families in France. In general, these democracies are elitist[22] by excluding citizens or their representatives from the debate on the compromises to be made as for the major functions of the tax State. They are also corporatist when they grant tax benefits to selected groups.

Liberal democracies valorise the private financing of the insurance of social risks, with the exception of interventions for the most destitute. This market model is that of the United States which have a low fiscal pressure and relies on an individualistic ethos.[23] It leaves the place for much targeted fiscal compromises within the framework of an institutional structure relatively open to socio-economic groups. With regard to the perimeter criterion, the limitation of a high level of intervention by spending and by taxes constitutes, in a negative sense, an agreement with a wide scope. Regarding the criterion of the process of consent, the debate depends on the appreciation of the scope of the American pluralistic democracy. It appears in any case that leaders take into account public opinion, in particular in the field of tax policies (a fact which remains valid: cf. below). Until 1986, the American tax system shows high statutory income tax rates and exonerates through allowances the incomes of the poorest people. But the reality proves to be more complex because we have to take into account numerous specific tax advantages which Congress commissions grant to their voters. On the one hand, the traditional resistance of the other social groups with regard to the rich and to business circles explains why high rates of taxation have been maintained until Reagan's coming into office. On the other hand, short-term electoralism, more or less kept in balance by the pluralistic competition of socio-economic groups, leads to the multiplying of tax expenditure which modifies the effective rates of imposition.

22 In a vein in which Pareto worked, the oxymoron is necessary because numerous decisions elude the direct consent of the people or of their representatives.

23 This ethos explains the big growth of private foundations which intend substituting public action to alleviate the misery of the world, according to moral criteria whose principles and application methods are excluded from the democratic sovereignty of the people.

In the era of globalization, diverse forms of compromise continue to exist with regard to the system of relations between the State, taxes and public services, but they abandon their social direction.

b. The defunctionalization of socio-fiscal contract

The diffusion of the neo-liberal ideology of the constraints of the market having become globalized[24] has been undermining since the 1970s the axiological foundation of social contract guaranteed by the tax State. The regulation of the compromises between the market and society tends to invert the relations between politics and the economy, the latter trying to become more autonomous from the first. The coordination of the market economy by the State, according to the types studied by the theory of the varieties of capitalism (Hall, Soskice, 2001) or by the French regulation school (Boyer, 2004), is devalued in favour of the liberal model of capitalism. The general link between taxation and the Welfare State is criticized, wrongly as we have seen (chapter 7), with reference to the efficiency of the market. The resilience of Welfare States and of tax structures[25], which differ from country to country, must not lead to underestimating the tendencies of the bringing down of interventionist democracy. We have seen that taxation loses its primacy as financial function of social public action to the benefit of loans. Fiscal macro-regulation has been discredited, at least until the current economic crisis; the action on the stratification of classes through the redistribution of incomes is thrown into confusion by a categorization of society in too many particularisms. The territorial function has come under the impact of fiscal competition.

Empirically, the axiological defunctionalization in favour of the market remains within limits according to the more or less explicit arrangements of the ruling elite. We thus note a strong relationship between the source of the revenues and the nature of the "actions" (sending) of the State. According to Timmons (2005), in the OECD countries from 1975 to 1995, regressive taxes (hitting the rich less than the others) are associated with increased social spending and indicators of social development but not with the protection of property rights. Cusack and Beramendi (2006) show that the governments of the "coordinated market economies" tax labour more than capital in exchange for a generous Welfare State. But, as we have indicated, the idea of the

---

[24] And, to a lesser extent, the institutionalist avatars of other deterministic theories: cf. chapter 7.

[25] This axiological defunctionalization of interventionist democracy has not entirely produced its practical effects on public action, but it can change (in this last line: cf. Busemeyer, 2009). At the end, it tends, if it is not reversed, to subordinate politics to the economy as is argued by Marco Tucci (2007).

coordination of the capitalist economy is put into question by the ideological valorization of the neo-liberal model. According to a study of 59 surveys conducted from 1980 to 2000 in 13 developed countries (Malher, Jesuit, 2006, p. 493), a compromise is established between the importance of transfers and the focusing of social programmes for the poor; in other words: the more the social policy is focused, the less the extent of transfers is important and thus the less the poverty and inequality are reduced. In numerous countries the decrease of some taxes (for example: the income tax) are financed by the increase of taxes on consumption (or of social security contributions: Steinmo, 2003, p. 225): reinforcing the use of "painless" tax, this financial arrangement is non-democratic by nature and modifies the distribution of the tax burden to the detriment of the poorest. The approach by what is known as "flexicurity", adopted in Austria and Denmark, constitutes an evolution of the financial contract. We have also seen the progression of the neo-liberal idea of Workfare in comparison with the traditional logic of Welfare State.

Box 22: Classification of compromises according to the structure of social spending

Castles (2009) shows, by breaking down the social spending of OECD countries for 2003, that the arrangements on social spending vary nationally. For example, for spending on retirement, Italy occupies the first place (13.8% of GDP) and Iceland the last (2.4%). For spending aimed at the labour milieu (unemployment, family etc.), Denmark is at the top of the list (10.4) and Japan at the bottom (1.8). For spending on health, Germany is first (8) and Austria last (5.1). For the other types of spending (services not related to health), Sweden occupies the top position (7.4) and Italy the last (0.8). Beyond any differences, families (clusters) of nations do exist, but they do not tally exactly with the ternary typology of Esping-Andersen.

Liberal countries indeed display low levels for total social spending and for spending on pensions. But they have contrasting positions as for spending on the labour milieu (unemployment etc.) with Ireland and New Zealand situated above the OECD average and the others below. Regarding spending on health, Australia and Ireland are below average and the others above. For the other types of spending, we find a variety of measures.

Scandinavian countries have indeed a big total amount (above the OECD average) of social spending and a big amount of spending on the labour milieu (even though Finland has 7.6% compared to an OECD average of 7.9%) and an amount above average for the other types of spending. We may simply point out that spending on pensions is below the OECD average, except for Sweden which is situated a bit higher than the average.

Continental countries ("conservative"), if we exclude the Netherlands whose profile is atypical, have a high level of total spending, with high levels of spending on pensions, and spending above the OECD average for the labour milieu and for health. But the other types of spending are varied.

A group not expected in the typology of Welfare States is formed by Southern European countries (Greece, Italy, Portugal and Spain). It is characterized by a low level of spending for the labour milieu and for services (other than health). As for total spending, the group also stands out because of the contrast between Italy and Portugal which are above the average (like the conservative continental countries) and Greece and Spain which are below. Spending on health is rather contrasting.

Lastly, four countries are unclassifiable, namely Iceland, Japan, Luxembourg and Switzerland, because the structure of their social spending does not match any of the foregoing groups.

In Scandinavian democracies, the use of indirect tax intensified with the economic globalization of the 1990s, restricting tax redistribution within the limits of respecting the compromises made between labour and capital. The Nordic countries have thus, on average, a higher level of indirect tax: in 2006 (OECD, 2008), taxes on goods and services represent 16.3% of GDP in Denmark, 13.5% in Finland, 12% in Norway, 12.8% in Sweden compared to an OECD average of 11.1%. The study of Beramendi and Rueda (2007) on 16 OECD countries between 1965 and 1995 confirms the importance of indirect tax, measured by its effective rate, in the Scandinavian countries governed by left-wing parties. The method of functioning of the social contract remains in force within the context of economic globalization. For example, in Sweden the retirement reform still relied on a compromise based on the idea, accepted in 1994 by 5 of the 7 parties represented in the Swedish parliament, that the long-term equilibrium of the system of financing had to be ensured. The new system (the new social contract) introduces a component based on distribution next to the traditional mechanism of distribution.

The compromises of the model based on insurance have also evolved under the impact of mass unemployment and the phenomena of new poverty and of exclusion. An example is given by the case of France which has introduced a taxing for social security, but also a certain privatization of the coverage of risks (suppression of the reimbursement of certain medicines, franchises etc.).

Special attention should be given to the liberal model which serves as a reference for the ideology of globalization. By focusing on the American case, it appears that the ambiguous structure around the intervention of the tax State remains largely valid. For example, Steinmo (1993, p. 168) notes that the reduction of marginal income tax rates under Reagan's presidency indeed caused the elimination of tax niches, but was called into question by the creation of other derogations by the Congress and by the reinforcement of the effective taxation of enterprises. We are really here within a political logic, and not an economic one as the reform intended; but the political function of the contribution-tax, whose global level remains limited, is led astray in particular arrangements whose complexity does not seem very democratic. In the fiscal field, the economic neo-liberal model is in line with a form of interventionist State that does not correspond to the classical version of an institutional action on the environment of the market: it is indeed a question of intervening in order to protect or encourage certain economic sectors or certain enterprises. An illustration is given by Hayes (2007, p. 471) who quotes a compromise made in 1996 under the Clinton administration within the context of a control of the Congress by the Republicans and of a decline of syndical organizations: the increase of the minimum salary finds in return side the granting tax and budgetary advantages to enterprises, which amounts to transferring the cost of the reform from employers to taxpayers. We are far from the limited image of a public authority seeing to it that a fair competition between enterprises and a climate of confidence are ensured.[26]

At the electoral level, liberal democracy remains vigorous, as is illustrated by president Obama's election in 2008 which creates a political alternation. We also know that in social matters, according to a study of 14 OECD democracies over the years 1980 to 2000 (Brooks, Manza, 2006), that the preferences of the masses with respect to public politics are important for maintaining the Welfare State, very particularly within the limits of the liberal Welfare State. Now, in the American case, public opinion was until now rather favourable to targeted social programmes in close contact with humanitarian socio-political ethics (Feldman, Steenbergen, 2001). A certain consensus was thus created on social public action. On the other hand, fiscal democracy, in accordance with the model elaborated in chapter 7, is on the whole avoided in the activities of the socio-economic groups. The deficit of fiscal democracy also characterizes the liberal model, without being able to evoke a consensus on the functions of public action as we have found it comparatively in the field of social policies. With economic globalization, the neo-liberal model, which managed to compensate for the deficiencies of the Welfare State by the creation of employment, comes up against the insufficiencies of the regulation of economic profits: the crisis of 2008

26 A study of 30 countries (Riahi-Belkaoui, 2004) shows a correlation (statistically meaningful) between, on the one hand, tax compliance and, on the other hand, the fairness of competition on the market (measured by a synthetic index of 23 elements), the equity of the market (measured by the fairness of access by enterprises to the financing of their activities) and the strength of moral standards (measured by low levels of violent crimes).

marks the failure of a financial capitalism whose real motor is the increase of inequalities to the detriment of social rights (cf. chapter 12).

The transition towards the market economy of a certain number of countries that belonged to the Soviet block also constitutes a field of observation of the evolutions in progress. For example, flat tax policies have been applied within a liberal logic. In reality, a compromise has been reached as is shown by the study of Keen *et al.* (2008, p. 714): "in many of the countries that have adopted flat personal taxes on labour income, substantially more revenue is raised by social contributions". Here the compromise, which intended to push to the extreme the liberal policy of cutting taxes put into practice in the 1990s by numerous countries, follows the same schema of an undemocratic financial arrangement.

In the last place, we have to recall that the fundamental functions of tax have been undermined by two factors of fragmentation of the tax policies. Firstly, the use of the tax instrument has become too targeted to the detriment of the logic of the major functions of the interventionist State. Secondly, in relation to the first factor, the complexity of the tax system accentuates the dilution and the confusion of the tax functions by concealing the logic of the tax system as a whole. The financial function is submitted to the competition of the recourse to other budgetary resources such as loans and privatizations. The economic sectorialization of tax policies is carried out to the detriment of the function of macro-regulation. The redistribution function has difficulty in being part of the agendas of the public authorities.

Conclusion

A new fiscal democracy must therefore be imagined within the framework of a new social contract on the contribution-tax in the interventionist democracy. We must in fact recall that the "citizen-tax" is possible because self-interest (utilitarianism) does not account for the whole behaviour of the taxpayer (cf. chapter 9). Citizens are capable of altruism if the public action of the tax State is legitimate. The political function of the tax State has a central place here and is opposed to the theory of the universal aversion to tax. The contribution-tax contradicts the economic theory of fiscal illusion, according to which the irrational individual demands more spending and less tax. It is really a question of justifying democratically the fiscal public action for society in relation to expenditure in the presence of the neo-liberal crisis of the economic-financial globalization.

Chapter 12

Globalization, Europe and Taxation

The field of taxation, situated at the crossroads of the State, the economy and society, is essential in order to understand "globalization" (Leroy, 2006). The univocal conception of globalization evokes a phenomenon inexorably determined by an iron law of the capitalist economy. The complex conception, full of nuances, insists on the vagueness of its three dimensions, economic, political and cultural. On the cultural level, globalization concerns networks and technologies of information and communication[1] which favour a global culture[2]. On the economic level, globalization indicates an old process of capitalism which has accelerated for the last few decades. The Roman Empire had already experienced this type of phenomenon around the Mediterranean. The "economy-world" of Fernand Braudel (1949, 1979) also describes the areas of development of capitalism which followed one after the other from the 15th to the 18th century. From 1870 the Atlantic becomes the place of a globalization, where colonization has a role, until the national withdrawal of the First World War. The current economic globalization has its origin in the intensification of international trade and started back in 1945 with the global commerce.

Since the 1990s the emergence of a global financial sphere, where speculative capitalism swept in, has been associated with various effects: integration of markets and stock exchanges, deregulation, relocalisation, interdependence, fiscal dumping. It is interesting here to ask oneself whether this process corresponds to the economic anomie described by Durkheim. On the financial level, it should be noted that the movements of capital, which have increased, are composed both of private capital (invested notably in emerging markets like China) and institutional investments (pension funds, insurance etc.). We must also recall the importance of transactions internal to multinationals (about half of global trade), involving members of the same group, and fiscally materialized by the technique of transfer prices. The world scale is not

1 There is also the economic aspect of the technologies of information and communication.

2 This is the "global village" formula elaborated in 1962 by the Canadian M. McLuhan in his book *The Gutenberg Galaxy*, which at that time targeted radio and TV for having an isolation effect on groups subjected to the messages of the global mass media.

always pertinent. We should rather reason in terms of large geopolitical regions when considering the articulation of local territories with the world economy. The involvement of certain countries at the periphery of the process is not easy: this is the case of Africa, Central America and even countries of the old Soviet bloc.

On the political level, globalization presents the question of the role of the State, whose capacity of action or operating margin would be increasingly reduced: the interests of multinational enterprises and of international finance would be privileged compared to the traditional categories and social classes and compared to national enterprises. In fact, the States, far from being outside the process, are actors of the globalization and remain strongly involved in the negotiation of international agreements. The resistance of the nation-state shows that the concept of sovereignty remains effective, even if the role of the other transnational actors (OECD, World Bank, IMF, WTO, EU etc.) is from now on difficult to avoid. Europe's capacity to impose itself as a leading actor of globalization must also be questioned through the construction of EU tax law.

1. Durkheim's Model of Economic Anomie

It is interesting to use as a starting point the discussion of economic anomie introduced by Durkheim in *The Division of Labour in Society* (*DLS*) and restructured in *Suicide.*[3]

a. Anomie as an economic pathology

In the *DLS*, anomie is presented as an abnormal (pathological) form of the division of labour which does not produce functional (organic) solidarity between individuals any more. Three cases are retained: the economic crises (the example of bankrupts), the antagonism between capital and labour, and the disorganization of science which does not directly concern our topic. Normally, the division of labour which characterizes industrialized society leads to an organic solidarity[4] by the repetition of certain ways of acting which correspond to functions that are specialized but linked between them (mutual dependence): the repetition of exchanges consolidates the spontaneously created rules and, from the moral point of view, makes the worker understand that he

---

3 We will not be dwelling on the excesses of biologism (organicism) and of moral conservatism which weaken the scientific value of the theory, notably on the moral value of poverty, religion, the legal interdiction of divorce.

4 "If the division of labour does not produce solidarity it is because the relationships between the organs are not regulated" (p. 304), which means that they are in a state of "anomie."

"is of some use (...) that his actions have a goal beyond themselves" (Durkheim, 1984, p. 308).

Exceptionally, however, the rules are not made or else are unfair. In the first case which is of concern to us, the economic anomie is pathological (noted A1 in box 23). It comes from disorganization caused by the economic and social effects of the extension of markets (this cause is noted C1).[5] In fact, the extension of markets leads to a misappreciation of demand (an effect noted E1) because producers are not in direct contact with consumers any more, a situation which results in economic crises (E11). The market extension (C1) also leads to big industries (E2), characterised by mechanization and manufacture, which rapidly upset old labour relations (E21), without a new organization of (socio-economic) labour relations being effective: the market extension is followed by a loss of references of the individual (E211) who sees himself reduced "to the role of a machine (...) a lifeless cog" (1984, p. 306). The solution (noted S) supposes a certain time of adjustment (S1) so that the natural benefits of the division of labour (cf. above) stabilize the new rules (S11).

The second case of pathological economic anomie (A1) concerns the unfairness of the socio-professional stratification, at the basis of the distribution of tasks and of the professional position, when it does not follow the logic of capacities (C2). It leads to the division of labour as a constraint[6] (E3) which is based only on force. The remedy is to ensure what we could call by anticipation of *Suicide*, the justice of access to the functions of society (S2) or in the terms of the *DLS*, "equality in the external conditions of the struggle" (p. 313). It concerns a complex notion, not because of the concrete examples given, but because of the link with the discussion of contractual exchange and of freedom. The solutions given as examples are constituted by the assistance to the poorest (S21) and the opening up of careers (S22), particularly for public employment, which aims at, using current terminology, the equality of chances.[7] The contractual solution (S23) is more problemat-

5 "As the organised type of society develops, the fusion of the various segments entails the fusion of the markets into one single market, which (...) tends to become universal (...) The result is that each industry produces for consumers who are dispersed over the lenght and breadth of the country, or even the whole world (...) The producer can no longer keep the whole market within his purview (...) Production lacks any check or regulation (...) Hence the crises that periodically disturb economic functions" (p. 305).

6 "Constraint begins only when regulation, no longer corresponding to the true state of affairs and consequently without any moral foundation, is only maintened by force" (p. 312).

7 The limit of the reasoning resides in Durkheim's position which defends the normal order of the division of labour (organic solidarity) which ensures the social rules of

ic: it implies at least that the contracts be guaranteed by social legislation (S231). It requires a real consent, and not constraint[8], which refers to the equity of the social value of exchange (S232): "the contract is not fully agreed to unless the services exchanged are equivalent in social value" (p. 317).[9] Inequalities of merit which justify inequalities of social position must not be distorted by other causes, like the inheritance of wealth (S24) (or social status). Finally, it must be pointed out that Durkheim evokes the need for the "the regulatory action" (p. 297) of the State, based on Comte, and in another paragraph makes a brief reference to the necessity of social legislation. He privileges, however, the beneficial role of the functional division of labour.

b. Chronic economic anomie

Chapter 5 of *Suicide*, which is about anomie, starts off by putting forward the importance of the power and regulatory action of society on individuals. Apart from the case of the institution of divorce, not included here, two situations are envisaged. The first one constitutes an intermittent economic anomie (A2)[10] that aims at sudden economic disruptions (C3) relating to, like in the *DLS*, economic disasters (C31), but also including periods of big prosperity (C32). The effect is similar[11]: the classification of social positions (socio-professional stratification) is disturbed (E4): "the limits are unknown between the possible and the

---

liberty reduced to the display of "those forces that are socially useful" (p. 321). The conflicts relative to social stratification are dissolved in the natural order of the inequalities of competences (which are at the base of merits) such as intelligence, taste etc.

8 "If one class in society is obliged, in order to live, to secure the acceptance by others of its services, whilst another class can do without them, because of the resources already at its disposal, resources that, however, are not necessarily the result of some social superiority, the latter group can lord it over the former" (p. 319).

9 That is "the amount of useful work (…) not the total labour that it may have cost, but the part of that effort capable of producing socially useful effects (…) that correspond to normal needs" (p. 317).

10 This anomie comes close to pathological anomie by its irregular nature, but is different from it, although Durkheim does not expands on this problem, by what is currently known as the cyclic nature of economic growth. The opposition between intermittent and chronic described in *Suicide* does not exactly correspond to the distinction, cherished by Durkheim, between "pathological" and "normal". Durkheim moreover writes: "in normal conditions the collective order is regarded as just by the great majority of persons" (Durkheim, 2006, p. 212). Chronic anomie indeed seems to be as pathological as the regular malfunctioning of the market economy. In the *DLS* Durkheim also writes, concerning cooperative law: "we might ask wether it could not be ascribed to temporary causes that perhaps were even pathological" (Durkheim, 1984, p. 102).

11 "It is the same if the source of the crisis is an abrupt growth of power and wealth" (*Suicide*, 2006, p. 213).

impossible, what is just and what is unjust" (Durkheim, 2002, p. 213). In the case of disasters, a declassification is produced for the individuals affected by the crisis; in the case of an economic boom, which favours certain classes, "overweening ambition always exceeds the results obtained (…) The struggle grows more violent and painful, both from being less controlled and because competition is greater" (p. 214).[12] We note that Durkheim recovers here a cognitive factor at the basis of Tocqueville's theory of relative frustration, which he summarizes in this way: "the less limited one feels, the more intolerable all limitations appears" (p. 214). Economic disruptions thus generate personal disruptions (E41). The solution is (like in the *DLS*) to wait for adjustment through time (S1) so that a new classification of the social value of positions be established by society's moral consciousness[13] (S12).

But *Suicide* breaks here with the isomorphism of the moral economy which in the *DLS* assimilated the specialization of economic functions with the justice of social norms.[14] The accent is put on the sentiment of justice in society, and not any more on the natural beneficial effects of economic specialization whose moral value is to show that everyone is useful for society (organic solidarity). "At every moment of history there is a dim perception, in the moral consciousness of societies, of the respective value of different services, the relative reward due to each (…) The different functions are graded in public opinion" (*Suicide*, 2006, p. 210). This break, which has already allowed a broadening of the notion of economic crisis to all rapid changes, also opens up the possibility of reflecting on the effects of economic progress. A complementary solution, already discussed in the *DLS*, is to ensure a just access to the functions of society[15] (S2), which is what the given example of the abolition of heritage[16] aims at, even though the heredity of natural talents will remain.

The second situation of economic anomie is "chronic" (A3), in other words, it has a regular character in industrial society.[17] It is caused by the functioning of the world of commerce and industry (C4), whose first

---

12 Suicides thus increase during these periods, keeping in mind that poor countries are less affected by suicide.

13 "Time is required for the public conscience to reclassify men and things" (p. 213).

14 Even though in the *DLS* certain structural phenomena such as the expansion of the markets were taken into account.

15 "But it would be of little use for everyone to recognize the justice of the hierarchy of functions established by public opinion, if he did not also consider the distribution of these functions just" (p. 211).

16 So that "everyone began life with equal resources (…) on a basis of perfect equality" (p. 212).

17 "For a whole century, economic progress has mainly consisted in freeing industrial relations from all regulation" (p. 215).

factor is the deregulation of industrial relations linked to economic progress (C41), and second factor (present in the *DLS*) is globalizing market expansion (C1).[18] The second cause is particularly interesting because it criticizes the absence of the regulatory power of the State (C5): "government, instead of regulating economic life, has become its tool and servant" (p. 216). Economic anomie which rages at the collective level brings about an absence of the limitation of passions at the individual level[19] (E5). It spreads out in all sectors of society which "is accustomed to think them normal" (p. 217). An analysis of the classes is then proposed next (in relation to the number of suicides) in order to distinguish the professions according to the degree of affectation "by the state of anomy" (p. 219). The solution includes a regulatory power of the State over the economy[20] (S3).

In his analysis, Durkheim does not put violence at the centre of the definition of power, even though he does not exclude it. The power of the State must be respected, by associating domination and legitimacy (S31).[21] Here, Durkheim refuses to give advantage either to liberal conceptions (orthodox economists) or to marxists (socialists) who share "the dogma of economic materialism" (p. 216) aiming at growth (industrial prosperity). Hence the State is neither "the guardian of individual contracts" (p. 216), nor the body in charge of the organization and the distribution of the income of production. It must "subordinate other social organs to itself and to make them converge toward one dominant aim" (p. 216) in order to bring economic anomie to an end where industry, "instead of being still regarded as a means to an end transcending itself, has become the supreme end of individuals and societies alike" (p. 216).

---

18 Like in the *DLS*, Durkheim evokes in *Suicide* the globalization of markets which "may assume to have almost the entire world as his customer" (p. 216).

19 "The appetites thus excited have become freed of any limiting authority. By sanctifying them, so to speak, this apotheosis of well-being has placed them above all human law. Their restraint seems like a sort of sacrilege" (*Suicide*, p. 216). But "unlimited desires are insatiable by definition" (p. 208), and "the passions first must be limited" (p. 209).

20 Since religion and/or ancient professional crafts no longer play this role in industrial society.

21 "In normal conditions the collective order is regarded as just by the great majority of persons. Therefore, when we say that an authority is necessary to impose this order on individuals, we certainly do not mean that violence is the only means of establishing it. Since this regulation is meant to restrain individual passions, it must come from a power which dominates individuals; but this power must also be obeyed through respect, not fear" (p. 212).

c. Summary: Durkheim's model

The anomie theory presented in the *DLS* is recomposed in *Suicide*: certain variables such as crises change their status from cause to effect; others appear such as periods of high prosperity etc. (cf. box 23). The model proposes several interesting ideas, also justifying the functional approach to social facts. The distinction and the articulation between the individual level and the social level are essential, even though Durkheim's holism is here an obstacle to a detailed analysis of the rationalities of individuals, except through the category of axiological references coming from society.

At the collective level, it is fair to consider the double question of the regulatory State and the logic of the market economy. The role given to the State is based on a theory of power, morally respected by individuals, which has to determine and impose the goals that the economy must pursue. The question of the State as regulator of the economy is thus linked to the reflection on social justice. On the other hand, Durkheim does not come so far as to think about conflict (fundamental for society) and considers, in the *DLS*, the antagonism of classes as an abnormal form. The social functions of conflict are neglected and power-based relations are denied by the theory of accepted constraint. Finally, Durkheim's theory of social justice, which refers to the social value of the services rendered by the individual (the example of work) coming from the normal functioning of the economy (*DLS*) or from the social conscience (public opinion), discards by definition the possibility for "alienation" and ideological manipulation of classification criteria.

Box 23: The Processes of economic anomie according to Durkheim

A1: Pathological economic anomie (in DLS)

– Causes (C): Market extension C1 and unfair socio-professional stratification C2

– 3 Processes: C1 E1 E11; C1 E2 E21 E211; C2 E3, namely:

* Market extension C1 → Misreading of demand (Effect noted E) E1 → Economic crises E11

* Market extension C1 → Big industries E2 → Upheaval of labour relations E21 → Loss of references for individuals E211

* Unfair socio-professional stratification C2 → Constraints for individuals E3

A2: Intermittent economic anomie (in Suicide)

– Causes: Economic disruption C3, namely Disaster C31 and Boom C32

– 1 Processes: C3 E4 E41, namely:

* Economic disruption C3 (disaster C31, Boom C32) → Deregulation of socio-professional stratification E4 → Disruption of individuals and classes E41

A3: Chronic economic anomie (in Suicide)

– Causes: Functioning of the economy C4, namely Deregulation C41 and Market extension C1 and Absence of regulatory power of the State over the economy C5

– 2 Processes C4 E5, C5 E5 namely:

* Functioning of the economy C4 (Deregulation C41, Market extension C42) → Absence of limitation of individual desires and passions E5

* Absence of regulatory power of the State C5 → Absence of limitation of individual desires and passions E5

The solutions to economic anomie

S1: Temporary adjustment (solution noted S) given in DLS and *Suicide*, namely:

S11: Stabilization of rules by the natural action of the division of labour (in DLS)

S12: Stabilization of rules by society's moral conscience (in *Suicide*)

S2: Fair access to functions (in DLS and *Suicide*), namely:

S21: Assistance to the poorest (DLS)

S22: Openness of professional careers (example of equality of access to public employment) (DLS)

S23: Fair contract, namely: S231: Legal guarantee of execution (DLS)

and: S232: Social value of socio-professional stratification (DLS)

S24: Abolition of wealth inheritance (DLS, *Suicide*)

S3: Regulatory power of the State (*Suicide*), namely:

S31: Legitimacy (respected and unfeared power) (*Suicide*)

2. Neo-Liberal Globalization of the Economy

Some of the processes described by Durkheim that we have modeled above apply to economic globalization, even though the role of the State is more complex to analyze. The diffusion of the neo-liberal ideology tends to destroy all social foundations of the economic values and the legal principles of the international public order which remains to be constructed. The legitimation of tax competition limited the possibilities for public regulation to the advantage of an international informal law (*soft law*) incapable of coping with the deviations of financial capitalism. The archetypal example of the OECD illustrates the weakness of the results obtained when facing tax havens which participate in the growth of inequalities in the world. Here, contrary to the "new" theory of the growth of public spending, the reduction of inequalities will not be brought about in a natural way by a mechanic demand for redistribution in situations of severe inequalities. In fact, this theory omits an essential variable, which is that of the force of democracy. The reduction of inequalities is explained by the democratic theory of political choices[22], and not by a sort of law of the demand for redistribution that would compensate in a natural way for the effects of economic globalization.

a. The social devalorization of the global economy

On the economic level, even though the phenomenon is not new, current globalization has its origin in the intensification of international exchanges, starting in 1945 with world trade. This process corresponds to the extension of the world market discussed by Durkheim. Since the 1990s, a global financial sphere (financialization of the economy), where speculative capitalism swept in, has been developed. The diffusion of the American real estate crisis of 2008 to the banking sector and then to stock exchanges and economic markets is a good illustration of the integration and interdependence of markets and stock exchanges as a result of economic globalization. Certain tendencies of this process are quite anomic in the sense of Durkheim.

The financialization of the economy thus leads to the preference for short-term financial return in view of the remuneration of shareholders and leading managers: it disorganizes economic production, for example by valorizing the stock market value of assets to the detriment of long-term productive investment; a disruption of labour relations is produced, as is illustrated, at the bottom of the socio-professional stratification, by the increase of precariousness and at the top of the scale, by the over-remuneration of leading managers. The aggravation of the inequalities of revenues expresses at the collective level this loss of references for individuals. This process indeed corresponds to the type C1 E2 E21 E211, even though its "pathological" nature is refused by the defenders of the iron law of globalization. The excessive place given to "capital" (which have become speculative), in the triple sense of their volume, their (stock market) value and their socio-economic hegemony, characterizes the economic disorganization. The "bubble" had to burst because it was more and more cut off from the real economy.

If the current crisis has been triggered off by the malfunction of the American real estate market, in reality, this particular event has activat-

[22] Including the revelation of the perversion of the theory's choices by the ideology of market constraints and of the influence of other variables (institutions, partisan division etc.) studied in chapters 6 and 7.

ed a general process, of the C1 E1 E11 type in the Durkheimian model: the misreading of the risks (the example of the subprimes, of the "toxic" securities) on interdependent markets at a global level explains the propagation of a national sectoral problem to all banks, stock markets and economies. One can of course also focus on the process of the increase of inequalities which has accompanied economic globalization in order to emphasize a (shorter) process of the C2 E3 type which arises from the injustice of socio-economic stratification.

One can also consider that the economic anomie of globalization is chronic in the sense that it refers to the functioning of the neo-liberal economy. A certain number of elements go in this direction, namely the extension of markets in the sense indicated above, the deregulation notably indicated by the agreements of free competition in trade matters (GATT, then WTO), the end of the stability (linked to gold) of the parity of exchanges between currencies (1971), the liberation of capital flows. One should also mention the technological progress which has facilitated the financial globalization (instant interconnection of stock markets). These same elements allow one to discard the process of intermittent anomie which does not correspond to this chronology. In this way the economic, monetary and financial deregulation has taken away the limits of individual passions for easy money (speculation, stock-options, golden handshakes) by following a process of the C4 E5 type.

But the question is really to know whether this type of anomie was produced in tax matters and hence whether the State has abandoned its regulatory power exercised through taxes as it has deregulated the markets. In other words, to follow our codification of the anomie theory in *Suicide*, is a process of the C5 E5 type under way? The answer is more complex. On the one hand, it is true that economic globalization has facilitated tax minimization for big multinational enterprises and has encouraged tax competition between States. The logic followed is that of tax optimization which consists in managing economic exchanges so as to pay the least possible tax. It is not a matter of an iron law of globalization, but of a tendency which has been encouraged by the (partial) tax impact of economic (and especially financial) deregulation. On the other hand, the interventionist tax State remains a reality in the era of globalization, which invalidates the idea of the absence of regulatory power intrinsic to this process. Other factors relative to the tax obligation complete Durkheim's theory of anomie by considering the meaning of public regulation and not simply its presence (or its absence).

As is shown by the proliferation of detailed tax rules, or, on another level, by the tax competition between States, it is not the lack of institutional regulation, but the disorganization of tax normativity which matters (chapter 10). It is of course indeed a matter, for the part linked to the impact of the neo-liberal regression, of a denaturation regarding the goals of society which is congruent with Durkheimian theory; but the analysis of the regulation by the tax State is more complex than a simple economic anomie due to a lack of social goals in the absence of public rules.

At the level of ideas, the ideology of the constraints of globalization (cf. chapter 7) has valorised the limitation of the social tax State which justifies optimization as a norm of economic competitivity. It has come to reinforce the reference to markets as a general norm (and not confined to the business sphere) that the neo-liberal wave had initiated since the 1970s against the compromise carried out by the Keynesian Welfare State. As we have seen, the diffusion of this anti-tax discourse has sparked off resistances and has not always resulted in the retrenchment of the State. But the resilience of social public action, more or less strong according to the cases, has not managed to impede the modification of normative reference points, of that what Durkheim called the "social value" of economic activities. De-taxation (tax optimization) has become the rule for the business world which can use the threat of the relocation of activities, of dismissal and of the closure of enterprises. The existence (real or imaginary) of market sanctions transform the value of profit intrinsic to the economic sector into a superior general norm. When the goal is to minimize taxes, the question of economic deviance then becomes, in order to decide whether or not there is fraud (evasion) according to the (tax) law, that of the labelling by the authorities of the means used by the business circles (cf. chapter 10). We have also seen that the "big capital", to employ a Marxist expression quite appropriate here to the financialization of the economy, prefers to use the (numerous) possibilities of the texts, while SMEs drift with greater ease into direct violation of the law. In fact, the sophisticated rules of the fictitious profit transfer schemes used by multinationals are not accessible to the second economic class.

The market standard, which for the economic actors of globalization reduces more and more to short-term profits, aspires to universality. This ideology, by putting itself forward as an objective, thus intends to subordinate State action to the normativity of the freedom of markets. This freedom is at the same time instituted as a constraint in order to sever the social roots of the democratic public action and modify the legal norms that arise from it.

This process has not ended and combines with other factors which have their own dynamics. In order to measure the advancement of this process, one must analyze the evolution of the functions fulfilled by the tax policy (cf. chapter 11) by following the resilience of the compromises in tax revenue, while at the same time taking into account the evolution of the Welfare State. The importance of tax expenditures of an economic nature in comparison with programmes having social objectives illustrate the progress of tax deviance becoming more commonplace (cf. chapter 10). Likewise, the market standard is at the origin of policies of the reduction of taxes on enterprises, like in the emblematic case of the reduction of the company tax rate. Nonetheless, we must remain prudent because the effective company tax rate does not always reflect the decrease observed in all the countries with official (statutory) rates because of the widening of the taxable base (elimination of tax exemptions, tax allowances etc.). We have also seen that tax policy does not result from a univocal and complete application of the economic market standard. It also expresses a process of categorization of the society which continues to rely on compromises between the respective taxation of capital and of labour, between social spending and taxes weighing on the households of wage-earners etc. The social tax State is still present.[23] although its global defunctionalization is under way in the double process of the particularization of problems and the reference to neo-liberal capitalism.

Finally, what Durkheim did not want to conceive in his functional conception of the division of labour[24] is that the law he calls restitutive could reinforce economic anomie by means of a cooperative regulation with capitalism. Thus the law that crystallizes tax policy in the age of globalization becomes more sensitive to market constraints. This upsets the social contract of interventionist democracy. The tax administration is thus entrusted with the difficult task of moderating the abuses of tax deviance, while the incentive law of States emphasizes the international transfers of profits. This administration tries to reinforce its procedural

23 From this point of view, the post-modern analyses of Giddens (1990, 1991), or of Beck of the individualization of society, the reflexivity of social trajectories and the perspective of cosmopolitism (Beck, 2002, 2006), or that, more critical, of Bauman (2000) of the liquid modernity that reunites neo-liberalism and consumerist individualism, do not take into account the resilience (solidity) of the social tax State: the tax public action continues, even if this is not the sole nor even the principal objective, to redistribute revenues among the classes; it shapes social categories, more and more particularistic, but without achieving an individualization; it accedes to certain social groups by stabilizing their status, even though their hierarchization is not always pertinent and/or just. There are indeed challenges of public action that question the general interest (the functions for society in our case).

24 One must remember that in the *DSL* law is retained as a field of proof characterizing the appearance of the organic society. According to Durkheim (1984) restitutive law expresses the cooperation of modern societies, in other words in societies based on organic solidarity (differentiation of individuals in complementary social roles resulting from the division of labour): "a fairly well-defined system comprising family law, contractual law, commercial law, procedural law, administrative law and constitutional law. The relations regulated with it (…) express a positive competition, a cooperation derived essentially from the division of labour."

means in order to control the tax optimization of the multinationals which on their part claim new rights for verified taxpayers (Leroy, 2008). This dialectic struggle over the law of procedures is also an ideological struggle. Next to the traditional association of the rights to tax defense with the rights of citizens, it calls up "new management" precepts in order to generalize the administrative implementation of a cooperative regulation (so called "responsive regulation") favourable to big enterprises (cf. chapter 8). But as is shown by the case of tax competition, in the absence of a regulation by the public action of the national policies, the legal normativity loses its relation with society to the advantage of a perverse market ideology.

b. Tax competition

Tax competition between States or sub-state authorities, which refers to the dilution of the territorial function, participates as we have seen in the disorganization of tax normativity. We can here again follow Durkheim by maintaining that the norms enacted by the State tend to dry up the source of their legitimacy, namely the respect for their "social value", by referring more and more to economic profit and less and less to society. From this point of view, the economic argumentation in favour of the beneficial effects of tax competition does not resist to this analysis. It is not economic globalization that determines the tax competition policy of States, but, as is shown in chapter 7, the neo-liberal market ideology. The unbridled context of economic globalization then authorizes multinational enterprises to take advantage from the transfer of profits towards territories with privileged taxation (tax havens), from the mobility of their own capital or from the possibility of relocation. Tax competition between States has lead to the reduction of company tax rates in all countries and to the adoption of some of the mechanisms of the "flat tax" with the aim of attracting or maintaining enterprises within national boundaries.

Relocation is not a new phenomenon, because for example, in France of the *Ancien Régime*, certain proprietors left the countryside for the towns where the imposition was generally less. Today, the burden of taxation is a factor often invoked as encouraging the departure of the richest taxpayers or of enterprises. The reality is not so clear-cut. The location of an enterprise depends on several factors related to the quality of the environment (infrastructures, quality of the workforce, size of the market, industrial base etc.) among which taxation is not the most important. It should therefore reason with regard to the global economic attractiveness of a territory (national, regional, urban etc.). Often it is not the tax borne in reality which is compared by enterprises, but the official (statutory) rates which are quite different. A "signal effect" of tax pressure does exist, which motivates the declaration of not too high tax rates, but with a large tax base in order to maintain financial return (public takings) indispensable for the functioning of the State. For each type of tax incentive one must therefore take into account several elements relative to the size of the country, the type of its economy, the mobility of capital etc. A country that has a guaranteed income from natural "rents" (like petroleum, for example) disposes of a resource that the mobility of multinationals cannot circumvent.

Econometric literature thus maintains that small countries have no interest in imposing taxes on capital, whereas in big countries capital taxation is compensated (at least up to a certain level) by other competitive advantages of the environment. Among the big countries, the case of France is emblematic (Leroy 2006). In fact its level of tax revenue is high in comparison to the average of the OECD (6th place) or, which is more pertinent, of the EU at 15 members (difference of 4 to 5 points); but its advantages[25] authorize a 6-point difference in matters regarding company tax, income tax and savings tax (CAE, 2005, p. 80). We must not forget either that this difference permits the financing of a high level of social protection. Moreover, if we look at the experience of Eastern European countries (cf. box 25), we note that flat tax policies have not met the anticipated success.

Box 24: The incidence of the flat tax

This policy consists in providing for a single low tax rate on the income of physical persons (instead of a progressive scale increasing with income), knowing that this principle is also applied in several countries to the taxation of the profits of enterprises. The effects of the flat tax are not obvious, all the more so as the mechanisms vary from one country to the other. Nevertheless, as is shown by a study of 8 countries (Keen, Kim, Varsano, 2008), this reform has especially constituted a useful political signal in the economies in transition towards the market (Eastern European countries). It has in general not resulted in an improvement of the output of tax revenue (no Laffer effect). It has been accompanied by a variety of tax compromises which sometimes have led to a widening of the tax base due to the reduction of exceptions, sometimes to an increase of social contributions out of salaries, or to that of indirect taxes. It has not diminished the complexity of the tax system (except in the rare case of the elimination of derogations) since this complexity result more from legal rules than from applied tax rates (structure). Regarding tax competition, the low taxation on capital (reputed to be mobile) seems difficult to be maintained because of social and/or financial pressures (output of this tax).

[25] A big market, an industrial base and quality public services.

Klemm (2009) proposes an evaluation of the impact of the principal types of tax incentives on investment by confronting economic theory with empirical work. Tax incentives have an impact on the location of foreign direct investments (FDI) and, in a less clear way, on their volume. The tax competition of States concerns here especially the reduction of tax rates. But perverse effects are produced, for example, when foreign investments replace local investments, or when the incentives lead to fictitious financial schemes (like the change of proprietor). It thus appears that the effect on economic growth is uncertain. In addition to marginal rates, it is the effective tax rate that must be taken into account[26] (including the impact of tax incentives). Tax credit for research has an important effect. Nonetheless, it is not sure that this effect exceeds the financial cost of this tax expenditure. A direct public expense by the budget (subsidy) thus remains a more pertinent solution. The influence of tax-free zones on employment and investment seems limited. The general tax incentives for investment, notably used in developing countries, do not seem efficient even if the available studies are not numerous. This provisional result would in particular be explained by the absence of prerequisites of the environment (like the quality of institutions etc.). Another study in CFA Franc Zone (Saharan Africa) finds (Van Parys, Sebastian, 2010) no robust positive correlation between tax incentives and investments, but shows that the environment is important, namely: the complexity of the tax system, and the legal protection of foreign investors.

A study of the real investments in Germany of multinationals (Overesch, 2009) gives an interesting result: the high level of taxation on the profits of enterprises is not an obstacle for the foreign direct investments of multinationals, to the extent that they carry out transfers of profits to countries with low taxation rates. When the environment is good for the economic attractivity of enterprises, tax rate reduction policies implemented by other countries do not represent an obstacle. Finally, international institutions also have a role to play.

c. *The insufficiencies of soft law: the case of the OECD*

We will evoke here the preponderant case of the OECD, without treating other international organizations, like the IMF, the World Bank etc., that intervene notably by the issuing of studies, reports and recommendations.

Without going back to the influence of the OECD on tax policies (cf. chapters 5 and 6), we should recall that its activity takes several forms which, for the essential, depend on an informal power (soft power). Like

[26] Cf. Devereux, Griffith, 2003.

other international organizations, the OECD widely diffuses its ideas by means of reports and communications etc. One of its important actions consists, after a State has brought the matter before the OECD, in examining the tax practices harmful to economic competition.[27] This aims at preferential regimes, like for example unjustified taxes on certain imports are foreseen. The basis of its control is part of the legal principles coming from the dogma of competition: national derogatory practices must not distort economic competition by creating unjustified discriminations towards certain products or certain enterprises.

The OECD also establishes a list of non-cooperative territories, which targets tax havens. Nevertheless, it does not manage to impose an efficient regulation of offshore places (cf. chapter 10) which follows the systemic logic of financial capitalism. The search for financial profits leads to the multiplication of complex investment products to the detriment of economic logic and social goals. From this point onwards the center of world activities merges with the big stock exchanges among which the City occupies the first rank. The G20 summit of April 2009 allowed the OECD to progress in its struggle against tax havens through the media coverage generated by this political meeting. And yet, the method used, that of the list, proves to be not very efficient in the absence of strong principles of a supranational character.

Finally, it must be emphasized that the action of the OECD in the field of international tax conventions is not a panacea. The diffusion of its convention model has permitted the introduction of a certain number of common notions, such as the stable establishment and the procedure of the amicable settlement of disputes. But it has not succeeded in the complete unification and simplification of the law in this field because most of the conventions are of a bilateral nature which implies negotiations from State to State. There are in this way about 2500 conventions in the world to regulate the questions of double taxation. There again the difficulties of cooperation between national administrations in combating global evasion show that this instrument is insufficient. Each country can choose the specific content of its conventions and depart from the OECD model.

The national sovereignty of States constitutes an obstacle for the (tax) soft law of the OECD. That said, the problem is more profound than the simple improvement of this international power to influence. Let us remember that the OECD in its report of 2000 requested a "global fiscal cooperation", which is actually a wise recommendation. Even then

27 The tax aspects in the WTO's litigation are submitted to the Dispute Settlement Body (DSB). The texts are dispersed in the absence of a general agreement relative to the conduct of tax policies by member states. Some of the stipulations of GATT serve as reference.

it is necessary that principles considered pertinent from the point of view of social justice set the base for an international order. The freedom to trade is not harmful by nature, but requires to be inserted in a social logic. The challenge is really to avoid deviances due to the absence of a public regulation of the economy with reference to its social sense, as Durkheim tried to show. Within the context of neo-liberal globalization, the question of the justification of profits and of their sharing is vital. From this point of view, the liberation of capital within the framework of the competition of tax systems is an aberration of neo-liberalism which accentuates inequalities.

d. *The neo-liberal growth of inequalities*

Beyond the fact of the increase of the number of rich people in the world, it is interesting to know the impact of globalization on inequalities. The inequalities in the world appear both between the income classes of one individual country (internal inequalities) and between different countries (international inequalities). Internal inequalities of income are generally measured by the Gini index[28], or by the difference between the average incomes of the 10% (1st decile) or 20% richest people (quintile) and the 10% or 20% poorest people. Certain studies concentrate on the very high incomes (Piketty, 2001; Atkinson, Piketty, 2006; Saez, Veall, 2005). Redistribution by social transfers and taxes (cf. chapter 11) rectifies, more or less, gross income inequalities: the inequalities of disposable incomes (incomes after social and tax redistribution) are the sign of the social tax State. Difficulties exist to compare the evolution of international inequalities.[29] Nevertheless, if the methodological debate is not closed, the obtained results demonstrate the disastrous impact of financial globalization on the growth of inequalities. This statement is all the more serious because, contrary to the "new" theories of the growth of public spending, the demand for redistribution is not activated by the increase of inequalities. It depends in fact on the strength of the interventionist democracy.

Concerning internal inequalities, a study (OECD, 2008) of the 30 OECD countries observes that the inequalities of incomes have deepened since the 1980s. This phenomenon is characterized by an aggravation of wage disparities and a degradation of the distribution of

[28] Or sometimes by the Theil index. These two statistical indexes measure the inequality of a distribution of incomes and vary from 0 to 1 (or from 0 to 100 in certain presentations): 0 indicates that the distribution is uniform (complete equality), 1 that the inequality is the biggest.

[29] Availability of data in the long run, weighting or not with the number of inhabitants, utilization of GDP *per capita* calculated with the current exchange rate or according to the purchasing power parity etc.

incomes of capital (and of independent workers) to the detriment of the majority. The number of poor has risen and the inequalities in wealth are even bigger than the inequalities in incomes. These results are confirmed by the study of Förster and Pellizzari (2000, p. 21) of 21 OECD countries. In the 1990s, the poorest 30% (of working-age population) dispose only of 9.3% of gross incomes (before redistribution), the 40% of the middle class of 35.3%, while the richest 30% appropriate 55.4% of the total. Compared to the 1980s, the inequalities in gross incomes between the rich and the poor have increased in all the countries (except for Ireland): the poorest 30% have thus lost 1.7% in the sharing of incomes, the 40% of the "middle class" have lost 0.6%, while the richest 30% have gained 2.3%.

It must also be emphasized that the incomes of the most privileged have increased. The neo-liberal model of development exacerbates inequalities, as is shown in the case of Anglo-Saxon countries (Atkinson, Piketty, 2010). In the United States, where the situation of inequalities is particularly serious, the high (declared) incomes of the richest, namely of 1% of the population, have progressed strongly between 1975 and 1998 returning to levels close to those of the pre-war period[30] ones (Piketty, Saez, 2003). The difference between the salaries of the worst paid 10% and the best paid 10% has gone from 3.5 to 4.5 times between 1980 and 2005 (Atkinson, 2008, p. 5). In Canada, the progress of high incomes (the richest 1%) in the neo-liberal period is equally dramatic: it is largely explained like in the United States by the rise in salaries (Saez, Veall, 2005). In Western Europe, the growth of inequalities seems to have been more restrained.[31] In Norway, between the 1980s and the 1990s, the inequalities of salaries remain stable but the inequalities of incomes (including incomes other than salaries) before redistribution increase (Kenworthy, McCall, 2008, p. 43). But everywhere it is obvious that the remunerations of the financial executives and of those occupying leadership positions have reached unjustified levels. The neo-liberal conception of globalization has served as an ideological pretext for the abuses of the economic elite.

30 This contradicts Kuznets's theory (1955) which says that in the first stage of development of the capitalist economy the inequalities are big due to high incomes but that they decrease naturally afterwards (because of the market).

31 Nevertheless, we must remember that these studies are often based on income tax returns. But the possibilities to avoid tax have increased with globalization as is illustrated by the case of tax havens (chapter 10). As a consequence, when the increase of declared high incomes is obvious, the level of real incomes is even higher. But we must also look at the possibilities of officially escaping tax through tax expenditures which can encourage better public tax takings: we can consider that the increase of tax expenditures leads to an improvement of the level of tax returns of the richest because their taxes have been reduced. In this way the declared high incomes in France have progressed strongly since 1998 (Landais, 2007).

The study of Jaumotte and others (2008) emphasizes the harmful role of the neo-liberal financial globalization which has encouraged short-term profits and soaring remunerations. It covers 51 countries, of which 20 are developed economies and 31 developing economies. In the last two decades, there was a rise in incomes in (almost) all the countries, accentuating inequalities however. The globalization of trade (economies) has progressed, albeit less strongly than financial globalization. Since 1980 the ratio of imports and exports has gone from 36% to 55% of global GDP. The ratio of capital movements has gone from 58% in 1990 to 131% in 2004. Economic globalization (measured in the study by the rate of imports/exports and by customs tariffs) is positively correlated with the reduction of inequalities, while financial globalization (measured by the weight of foreign direct investments) increases inequalities. This result is particularly interesting because it provides empirical proof that it is not the intensification (liberation) of world trade that is harmful, but surely financial globalization. It is thus calculated that the rise of exports by 1 point (in % of GDP) reduces inequalities by 3.4% (Gini index). The reduction of customs tariffs by 1 point reduces the Gini index by 1.7%. The rise of foreign direct financial investments by 1 point increases the inequalities in incomes by 2.7%. As financial capitalism has become more intense and has priority over the economic logic of commercial exchanges, inequalities have exploded.[32]

Concerning inequalities between countries[33], globalization has accentuated the differences: thus in 1960 the GDP *per capita* of the 20 richest countries were 17 times higher than that of the 20 poorest countries and in 1996 it was 37 times higher (Giraud, 2002, p. 4). One should treat China separately, where economic development, which its high growth rates (thus of the GDP), has permitted a reduction of absolute poverty. Taking account of the demographic weight of China, such amelioration has a strong impact on world inequality (but internal inequalities of the Chinese giant have increased). This observation also concerns India

[32] The technical discussion also brings to light certain specific factors, notably the role of technical progress (like the ICT /Information and Communication Technologies/) which puts unqualified work at a disadvantage. It seems that the improvement of educational levels (measured by the average number of years of schooling of the population) reduces inequalities, by making the integration into qualified and better paid jobs easier. These clarifications do not modify the lesson on the deviance of the neo-liberal globalization: by substituting for the virtues of soft commerce dear to Montesquieu (cf. chapter 4), the priority given to financial profits and to the remunerations of executives and shareholders has reinforced social inequalities.

[33] In a very long-term perspective, Firebaugh (2000, p. 324) note that in 1820 the difference between the average income per capita in Western Europe and in Africa was 3 times. At the end of the 1990s it is about 14. The difference between the richest and the poorest countries is about 30.

where the significant growth of incomes has enabled millions of people to come out of poverty.

It is interesting to measure inequalities by large geographic regions[34] as Mann and Riley (2006) proposes it by using the Gini index over the period 1950-2000 (China is excluded from the study). Latin American countries have experienced the strongest inequality over this period. South Asia (Bangladesh, India, Indonesia, Malaysia and Thailand) comes second, but with substantial differences according to the countries. East Asia (Hong Kong, Japan, South Korea and Taiwan) has fewer inequalities. In developing countries the situation varies according to the cases. The study confirms that continental European countries have the lowest level of inequalities, which must be linked to fiscal and social redistribution resulting from compromises made in these democracies.

e. *The counterweight of democracy*

The "new" theories of public growth affirm that inequalities explain the growth of public budgets for the following reason: the increase of inequalities brings about a demand for redistribution that the governments take into account. This aspect is important because the demand for redistribution would in this way compensate the inequalities in gross incomes by reducing the differences between disposable incomes (after taxes and social transfers). A kind of natural mechanism would in this way rectify the growth of the inequalities coming from the financial globalization. But in reality, among the various possible causes of the redistribution, it is the theory of democracy that provides the best explanation for the long-term tendencies of the social public action in favour of the reduction of inequalities.

Just like tax policy as a whole, the causes for the redistribution are difficult to determine and to interpret.[35] Nevertheless, some tendencies

---

[34] Even though certain countries belonging to the same region sometimes evolve in opposite directions: in this way, in Latin America, the inequalities receded in Brazil from 1976 to 1996, but increased in Mexico from 1984 to 1994 (Giraud, 2002, p. 6).

[35] Lowery's pioneer study (1987) is on the impact of State taxes and local taxes in 46 American States. It evaluates 6 variables: economic factors, the presence of high personal incomes, the competition of political parties and their ideology, the action of pressure groups (considered at an aggregate level), the age of the tax legislation. Among these variables, it is especially the influence of the past (notably the date of adoption of the income tax) which has a positive effect on redistribution, and, to a smaller extent, the degree of industrialization (measured by the number of enterprises) as well as the competition between the parties. Another study (Berch, 1995) covering 5 American States (including the local authorities) by comparing data of 1991 with regard to 1985 confirms the importance of the historical weight of the tax structure, while at the same time insisting on other factors: economic growth favours redistribution but the influence (strength) of economic interest groups in comparison with groups representing labour is associated with the regressivity of taxation. The

are clearly established. Redistribution does not occur there where it is the most necessary that is to say during the periods or in the countries with big inequalities. It depends on the degree of political democratization and on the sense of social justice that leads to the creation of socio-fiscal compromises (cf. chapter 11).

In economics, the theory of redistribution (Meltzer, Richard, 1981) refers to the standard model of the median voter (prompted by self-interest in the sense of utilitarian rationality used in the rational choice theory) to maintain that the bigger the inequalities, the more generous is the redistribution.[36] In fact, according to this theory, which relates to the growth of public budgets, big inequalities tend to be more visible for public opinion, which would justify the following causal chain: public opinion demands a supplementary redistribution in case of an increase in inequalities (1st proposition); the government can only satisfy this demand (2nd proposition); the government increases the social programmes (3rd proposition). But this theory which is often taken up is however invalidated empirically.

This is the sense of the already mentioned remarkable Lindert's historical study (Lindert, 2004) which examines the evolution of social spending since the 18th century. It shows that the public spending in favour of the poor are at their lowest in the periods and countries where poverty and inequalities are at their highest. Historically, it is the reinforcement of democracy that has favoured the increase of social spending. Aidt and Jensen (2009, p. 379) confirm the impact of democracy on public budgets in a study of 10 Western European countries from 1860 to 1938. The extension of voting rights is correlated with the increase of public expenditure and of taxation. A country passing from a system of restricted voting to universal suffrage experiences an increase in public expenses and taxes of 8% and 2% of GDP, respectively. In this way, Tocqueville's model of the growth of public expenses in democratic regimes finds confirmation in the available studies. The intensity of electoral competition sometimes also affects the budget, as illustrated by a study (Hecock, 2006) of 29 Mexican States from 1999 to 2004 which indicates that this factor plays a role in educational expenses. Ross (2004) questions the relation between taxation and democracy on the basis of data coming from 113 countries from 1971 to 1997. He shows

---

partisan variable does not play a big role according to Berch's study. But another study (Morgan, 1994) conducted in 1991 on the American States gives other results: the historical factor plays a role rather in the sense of the regressivity of the tax system (except for 6 States); the economic growth (surplus of resources) is indifferent; the presence of a middle class is correlated to the regressivity of the tax system.

36 The median voter is a person situated at a level dividing the population in two equal parts in terms of income. The more unequal the society, the bigger is the distance between the median income and the average income.

that democracy (measured by the type of regime and by civil and political rights) does not develop with the objective of limiting the increase of State taxes as presented by the Leviathan model of Brennan and Buchanan. It is a matter of better controlling the use of public money, and not of opposing taxes: it is therefore the relation of taxes to public services, and not the opposition to (the increase of) taxation, which is correlated with democracy.

To complement this historical perspective, it should be noted that the second proposition (the satisfaction of people's demands) implies that the demands of the public opinion are followed by results and if so, that they lead to programmes consistent with people's expectations. But the institutions, as we have seen, do not respond to, or distort, demands (cf. chapter 6). In addition, the theory of the median voter is not applicable in less- or non-democratic countries where the ruling elites block, even suppress, people's demands.

Comparative studies confirm these results. Lübker's study (2007) covers 26 countries including developed countries, among which the United States, and countries in transition to the market economy: no correlation is finded between the level of the real inequalities (as measured by the Gini index) and the demand for redistribution. This therefore invalidates one of the basic propositions of the theory of the median voter. Contrary to the economic (utilitarian) approach, the socio-political approach is validated because it appears that the sentiment of justice has a certain influence. At the same level of inequalities (the Gini index), the number of people evaluating these inequalities as too important is higher in the countries in transition (+12%) than in the other countries with a market economy (Lübker, 2007, p. 137) and it is less high in the United States (-23%). There is thus no correlation between the evaluation and the reality of inequalities.

De Mello and Tiongson (2006), on the basis of a study of social spending (social redistribution) in 56 countries from 1970 to 1998, conclude that countries with low income *per capita* and significant inequalities (according to the Gini index) are not much inclined to redistribute wealth, even if the relation between inequalities and redistribution is not linear. According to the study of Kenworthy and McCall (2008), which compares separately 4 essential social programmes[37] of 8 rich countries between the 1980s and the 1990s, an aggravation of inequalities does not necessarily result in an increase of social programmes or in a change of public opinion.

[37] Namely, health insurance, pensions, unemployment benefits, social assistance, and not the global level of social redistribution measured for example by the volume of social transfers in % of GDP or by the comparison between before- and after-redistribution incomes (disposable income).

The economic approach to equity encounters limits that must be sought here in the absence of the realism of the hypotheses of the rational choice theory of the median voter. The (general) theory of democratic choices, completed by the socio-political approach to perceived inequalities, is the only theory allowing one to explain the puzzle of public action in favour of the struggle against inequalities. It is compatible with the (particular) resource power theory which insists on the importance of the social movement.[38] In this way, as we have seen (cf. chapter 7), the neo-liberal ideology of the constraints of globalised markets, constitutes a form of alienation from democratic choices to the benefit of the decisions from the ruling elite and technocracy. One should now turn towards the institutional Europe that intends to influence economic globalization[39], but struggles to ensure the coherence of tax policies.

3. The Insufficiencies of the European Response

Despite the not insignificant outcome, Europe currently seems incapable of progressing towards a tax harmonization likely to contribute to a political project based on a global functional approach that is guaranteed by Community law.

a. The blockage of the European construction

It must be recalled that the European construction is founded on the instauration of a common market, in view of consolidating peace established after the Second World War. It was a matter of eliminating customs duties (and equivalent taxes) within the European Union, by fixing a common external tariff. This programme has been carried out because Europe has become a space without internal frontiers with the completion of the internal market finalized by the Single European Act of 1986. Apart from this classic way, European Community law aims at the harmonization of indirect taxes (article 93 of the EC treaty). The VAT and excise duties (tobacco, spirits etc.) have in this way been the subject of a real Community tax policy by means of the legal instrument

---

38 Mahler (2008) shows that electoral participation influences redistribution (especially social). Now as the rich participate more in the polls than the poor, they have more influence on political choices. In this way this author intends to reconcile (by modifying it) the theory of the median voter (who as a result is closer to the average income and demands less redistribution) with the resource power theory. Its results confirm especially the validity of the democratic theory of political choices.

39 The Lisbon strategy adopted in March 2000 by the European Council aimed (for 2010) to make Europe the most competitive and most dynamic knowledge-based economy in the world. It was completed by the objectives of the Council of Gothenburg (June 2001) concerning environment and sustainable development.

of directives.[40] Even though the differences in tax rates according to the States remain significant, the success of tax Europe in this domain is undeniable: the VAT basis is harmonized; a common intracommunity VAT mechanism is applied to the trade of goods between tax subjects and the integration of new Member States into this mechanism is quite well brought into effect.

These successes must not conceal the current failure of tax Europe which does not succeed in adopting a socially legitimate common programme. There is little progress in the convergence of tax policies and structures in Europe (Leroy, 1995). Tax disparities resulting from history, national arrangements and strategies of tax competition between States remain important. The number of directives (which constitute the royal road for reform) is low and their field of application is often limited. The harmonization of taxes through Community law concerns only indirect taxes. Even in this field, apart from the noticeable persistence of tax rate differences, it must be pointed out that the transitional regime applicable to intracommunity VAT (taxation in the country of destination) has been maintained in spite of its inconveniences. The harmonization of excise duties has a relatively limited scope. As for direct taxes[41], one must mention two 1990 directives which aim at the "parent-subsidiary" regime and the merger of enterprises. But these texts remain in the background with regard to the harmonization of the taxation of enterprises: for example, the draft directive presented by the Commission already in 1975 regarding company taxes and withholding tax on dividends has never come to something. There also exists a directive on savings of 3 June 2003 (coming into force in 2005), but its scope is limited. In fact, it excludes the dividends of shares, does not concern companies and accepts a beneficial withholding tax system for several countries.[42] Concerning the direct taxes, the Community results thus remains disappointing, in spite of the contribution of the Court of Justice of the European Communities (CJEC: cf. box 25).

---

[40] Directives bind every Member State to which they are addressed as to the results to be attained while at the same time leaving to national authorities the competence as to the form and the means (art. 249-3).

[41] For direct taxation, article 94 (which has a general scope and not specifically of a tax nature) permits a rapprochement of national rights by means of directives.

[42] Austria, Belgium, Luxembourg and some other territories or countries (Andorra, Switzerland etc.).

Box 25: The construction of tax Europe by the CJEC

In the field of direct taxes, the jurisprudential construction of tax Europe (Maitrot de la Motte, in Leroy, 2006) is definitely affirmed by the Schumaker decision of 14 February 1995. This founding decision puts an end to the previous hesitations by asserting that if direct taxation falls within the competence of Member States, it is nevertheless the case that the latter must exercise it in compliance with Community law. As confirmed by further decisions, the Court bases itself on the freedoms of movement provided by the Treaty to affirm the primacy of Community law over national tax legislation, namely: the freedom of movement of persons, goods and services, and capital (and the means of payment). The Court also bases itself on the freedom of establishment. Nevertheless, it admits, in certain cases, breaches of the principle in freedom of movement, notably for reasons of public order, public safety and public health or for an "imperious reason of general interest". According to the Court's jurisprudence, this last notion (the imperious reason etc.) corresponds to three cases: the safeguard of the coherence of a Member State's tax system[43], the exclusion of purely artificial financial schemes in view of obtaining a tax advantage (a kind of abuse of a liberty), the efficiency of tax control. Here the Court verifies the proportionality of the justification invoked for the breach, which reduces the scope of possible derogations. In particular, the justification by the loss of tax receipts for the Member State has not been admitted.[44] Likewise, the use of international bilateral conventions cannot be an obstacle to the primacy of freedom of movement established by Community law. In this way the CJEC's contribution to tax Europe is significant; but it is not a complete remedy for Europe's failure, or for its refoundation on bases which subsume market logic in the principles of a social contract on fair taxation.

In an enlarged Europe, an essential obstacle to tax public action is constituted by the rule of unanimity. This decision-making procedure confers a veto right to each Member State, which explains the difficulties for the revival of the Community's tax policy. The negotiation of new directives has become very delicate in the context of an enlarged Europe, especially since tax harmonization is not a priority for several States (including for certain old members of the EU at 15). Henceforth, national tax sovereignty is a factor of social regression which Member States refuse to question again. Thus the European Council of Nice has maintained the rule of unanimity. Here the neo-liberal argumentation on

[43] But the court decision Wielockx of 11 August 1995 greatly restricts the practical relevance of this justification which is excluded from the moment that a bilateral tax convention exists between the countries involved in the dispute.

[44] Decision ICI of 16 July 1998 and decision Saint Gobain of 21 September 1999.

the benefits of tax competition is not acceptable. As we have seen, tax dumping, which still remains limited by the necessity to finance the Welfare State, does not aim at society as a whole, but benefits multinational enterprises while at the same time results in a loss of revenue for public budgets. The claim for a reduction of the taxation of enterprises (mobile factors) is made to the detriment of labour. The freedom of capital exudes a tax optimization which gains autonomy and ends by opposing itself against the economic logic of productive investments for society. By accepting the dogma of financial capitalism, Europe has shown incapable of struggling against tax havens which flourish within Europe or at its doors.

Some efforts have certainly been made to ban harmful tax competition. Tax assistance of EU Member States is in this way submitted to the Community law on financial State assistance.[45] Tax expenditures which distort competition in favour of certain enterprises or certain productions are thus prohibited. But some derogations, which must be the object of an authorization by the European Commission, are provided for. Under certain conditions, aids of a social nature granted to consumers, aids in favour of regional development, aids for investment etc. are lawful. Tax advantages granted to enterprises installed in deprived urban areas are thus validated. The list of tax expenditures in certain countries shows (cf. chapter 11) that Community action remains limited in this field. The reason for it is simple: tax competition, which applies the market conception to the public action of Member States, is considered as lawful in its essence; only its excesses are controlled.

We must also mention the "tax package" adopted at the end of 1997 to reduce tax competition. This set of measures comprises the "Code of Conduct" that came into force in 1998 and the two directives of 3 June 2003 relative to taxation on savings and to taxation on interest and royalties between enterprises of different States. The Code of Conduct concerns the rules of direct taxation which have, or could have, impact on the localization of economic activities. Even if it permitted the announcement of a list of 66 measures to be eliminated, it is legally non-binding.[46] Moreover, the demands for prolongation beyond the expiry date of 2005 of the mechanisms involved were accepted by the Council. In this way the pragmatic approach of the tax package tries, more or less successfully, to cure Europe's failure. The outcome remains meagre. In particular, the fixing of the corporate tax rate does not depend on the Code of Conduct, but on the exclusive competence of the Member

[45] Articles 87 to 89 of the EU Treaty.

[46] The report drawn up in November 1999 by a special group representing the States was submitted to the Council of economy and finance ministers of the Member States (Ecofin) that drew up the lists.

States which have committed themselves to a competitive policy of reducing company taxes, sometimes, as we have seen, in a radical way (flat tax). More fundamentally, we must emphasize that in the absence of reform on the conception of the market given concrete form in Community law, the action of tax Europe can only remain limited in its effects.

b. The functional deficiencies of tax Europe

Community policy does not fulfill the major tax functions instituted by the historic construction of nation-states. The financial function is not directly ensured for lack of a European tax directly levied in the Member States.

The economic function is not neglected, but it comes from a conception which is not adapted to the functioning of the market in the absence of a real social Europe and because of the difficulties of political Europe (cf. below). As we have seen, it was firstly a question of favouring the activities of multinational enterprises by ensuring the respect for the major freedoms of movement of capitals, goods, persons and services, as well as the freedom of establishment. It is secondly a question of avoiding abuses of the incentive measures of the Member States, but without questioning the legitimacy of tax competition aiming to attract capital and enterprises. Economic freedom and (barely regulated) competition serve in this way as founding principles for the economic function of Community tax policy, while the use of spending does not succeed in counterbalancing negative market effects. Unlike the historic construction of national Welfare States, no social contract has been proposed in order to find compensation to the tax privileges enjoyed by actors in the economic and especially financial markets.

Regional policy, financed by the structural funds, does not play this role, despite its contributions. In this case as well, the absence of harmonization of economic policies and of the legitimation of a social political project encourages a negative form of regulation based on the financial bargaining between States (Leroy, 2004). Much more, the new objective "Regional competitiveness and employment" established for 2007-2013 initiates a significant change of direction in the regional development conception, even though it represents only 16% of structural funds (Leroy, 2009). This objective covers a wide range of actions: while at the same time maintaining the priority traditionally given to fighting unemployment and by giving a place to the environment, it from now on puts forward the support to innovation, the spirit of enterprise and diverse measures coming under competitiveness. The legitimacy of economic development by means of poles or sectors of excellence is confirmed. It is really a question of reinforcing the attractiveness of competitive territories by (eventually) bringing to an end the solidary conception of a balanced territorial development.[47] Most certainly, the model of territorial planning and development by means of solidarity with backward regions is always present by the intermediary of the objective of "convergence" which is financially important. But this objective concerns only the poorest regions. For the others, reinforcing competitiveness implies a "liberal" conception of regional development[48]: specialization of initial and professional education in the most competitive sectors, mobility of the labour force towards dynamic zones, support for research in high-tech industry, polarization of activies etc. The valorization of competitiveness thus completes the acceptance of tax competition and of the superiority of economic freedoms. Together with the notions of governance and performance, they supply the arsenal of legal-administrative principles in order to implement a conception of Europe more and more impregnated with the neo-liberal ideology of the globalized market.

The social function of redistribution and of taking into account the challenges of society is absent from the tax policy followed by Europe.

The political function, in the sense of tax democracy, remains badly thought out. Only the processes of decision-making bargaining between Member States receive sustained attention. Here the procedure of unanimous decision-making renders improbable the possibility of a harmonization of national tax systems in the context of a Europe with 27 Member States (and which foresees further enlargement). As illustrated by the emblematic case of the Code of Conduct, the Commission's meritorious efforts to circumvent the decision-making obstacle can only lead to a (slow) exceptional coordination of Member States. The tax package method, which enables the extension of negotiations on several challenges presented to society, accentuates the logic of political bargaining, applied notably in the regional policy financed by the European structural funds (Leroy, 2004). The coherence and transparency of choices suffer from the compromises between the particular interests of the States which are represented by the elites in power. Democratic consent is flouted because of this pragmatism which poorly conceals the absence of a shared political project and the search of founding principles, not for the market, but for the European citizens. The debate between the

47 This conception was particularly represented by France over the period from 1945 to the years 2000, but this country also tends to abandon especially, because a policy of competitive poles is implemented.

48 Cf. for example, the Commission's annual report (2006) which includes an invitation to open up the telecommunications sectors to competition and which strongly recommends market virtues: Commission of the European Communities, *Annual report on growth and employment*, 2006.

partisans of harmonization by means of the bottom, in other words the market, and the partisans of harmonization by means of the top, in other words Community law (and therefore the reinforcement of European institutions) is from now on in favour of the first ones. Here the impregnation with the neo-liberal ideology of market efficiency is reinforced by the veto right ensuing from the procedure of unanimous decision-making which benefits the status quo. The political choice between the three forms of Community public action of integration, harmonization or coordination, on the basis of social principles to be defined, is skillfully avoided. The reference to the market which leads to the adoption of economic freedom and competition as political principles does not succeed in conforming itself to the model of liberal democracy. In fact, the predominant place given to the sovereignty of Member States is coupled with democratic deficit which implicates the absence of the political legitimacy of present-day Europe.

Regarding the legal interpretation of tax sovereignty, Europe's enlargement has mechanically increased the number of veto rights. The economic and social opportunity offered by the arrival of new States comes up against the institutional obstacle of unanimity.[49] It is vain to believe that the Commission's soft power, used by means of informal law measures such as the Code of Conduct, various official reports[50], interpretative documents, the communications etc. could ensure a re-launching of tax Europe. If other objectives, such as stabilizing Member States' tax revenues or fighting unemployment[51], have informally been proposed, the reality remains well below these attempts.

With respect to the democratic deficit, Europe today seems incapable of defining a global political project susceptible to convince citizens: this is proved by the French and Dutch refusal to support the constitutional project and the Irish "no" to the Lisbon treaty which was supposed to replace the constitutional project (but Ireland approved this treaty afterwards). The temptation is to get round the (non) consent of the nations by pursuing the implementation of sectoral compromises between sovereign states. This strategy seems doomed to failure. The lack of coordination of the responses to the current crisis is a dramatic illustration of the difficulties of this solution. The opportunity to re-

49 Contrary as well to certain opinions, the risk is bigger for the new Member States than for the old members which dispose of several economic capacities, for example in the food and agriculture sector where they can impose themselves on certain "small" markets of the new members.

50 An example is the Commission's White Book "Growth, Competitivity, Employment" of 1993 which envisaged a restructuring of national systems of tax revenue in order to stimulate employment and growth, with the idea of balancing again the part of revenues from labour as compared to financial revenues.

51 Cf. the Verona Memorandum. Monti Report of 1996 submitted to the Ecofin Council.

launch the Community construction on social foundations approved by European citizens has been ruined there as well. In tax matters, as is shown by this whole book, sovereignty must come from the people in order to constitute social progress. Taxes are not a mere economic phenomenon because it puts into play the relationship of politics with society. The pernicious results of tax competition as regards the reinforcement of privileges for the business world create a situation of tension. So in this period of the crisis of financial capitalism, social policies, left in most of the cases to the responsibility of Member States, are not able to restrain everywhere the discontent of the people.

The territorial and ecological function is hardly more advanced. The sovereignty of the States results in the territorial taboo of Community tax law: public action in this field is limited mainly to controlling the justification of advantages (aids) for certain zones. Environmental taxation has however been the subject of initiatives on the part of Community authorities. For example in 1992 the Commission submitted to the Council an action programme about the creation of an ecotax on carbon dioxide and on energy, but it was not approved. The debate continues in the world context of the objectives of the Kyoto Conference of 1997 and of subsequent initiatives. The EU Council of Gothenburg (June 2001) acknowledged as objectives the protection of the environment and the achievement of a sustainable development based on competitivity, social inclusion linked to employment, risk prevention linked to the environment. For the time being, it is especially within the framework of the directive of 31 October 1992, regarding excise duties on mineral oils, that the Commission has taken action: energy products (coal, natural gas, electricity, petrol, kerosene etc.) have since then been considered as mineral oils. Minimum tax rates are foreseen for petrol in order to limit pollution. Eco-fuels are also encouraged. But many aspects of the environment policy remain the exclusive competence of the Member States.

Conclusion

The iron law of globalization must be relativized compared to the complexity of an evolution whose outcome remains questionable. The heart of the problem resides especially in the diffusion of the neo-liberal ideology which conceals the possibility for democratic choices in favour of notably the struggle against inequalities. Within the context of globalization, the political choices of public action aim at taxpayers but tend to exclude citizens. The socio-tax contract drawn within the framework of the post-war interventionist State is again put into question. As Durkheim has indeed seen, the economy tends to lose its social functionality with the extension of (financial) capitalism. In tax matters it is moreover not the absence of public regulation which is involved, but the loss of the social meaning of the regulatory State's action.

Europe represents a nodal solution to the defunctionalisation of the social contract on public action in order to transcend national sovereignties. So its functional deficiencies, having become evident in tax matters, are no longer acceptable in the presence of the expansion (and of the crises) of financial capitalism. It is time to break the deadlock created by the institutional sources of competitive veto points linked to the number of decision-makers and by the democratic delegitimization of its future. By showing that the approval of public action by citizens constitutes the best way to socially legitimate change, the sociology of interventionist democracy indicates the method to be followed and expresses itself on its content. This way implies reinforcing the powers of the European parliament and reconsidering the great functions of a Community tax policy on the basis of its socio-political objectives. The current crisis brought up to date the harmful effects of the neo-liberal deviance which has led to the globalization of financial markets. Along with a Europe of peace, redefining the goals of the political economy involves financing an solidary social Europe.

CONCLUSION

The Social Contract of Interventionist Democracy

This work has used a number of sources from different disciplines in order to move forward with the construction of a social science of public finance, reviving the ambition of its founders. In this way, the relation between taxation, the State and society which defines the general subject of fiscal sociology has served as the main thread. The approach of fiscal phenomena in the form of social and political questioning encourages us to leave aside technical treatments that reduce the importance of the matter too much. It brings together studies normally confined to specific analyses in specialized disciplines. It compares studies, which are normally dissociated in the literature, on fiscal policy, taxpayers, public finance etc. This effort of meta-knowledge enables us to advance on the way of constructing a socio-political theory of fiscal public activity on empirical grounds, theory that assembles the levels of results. In view of the lack of international political regulation, the State keeps its place in the theory of interventionist democracy. The challenge consists in overstepping the limits of formalism and procedural justice when renewing the democratic social contract.

1. The Importance of the State

In developed countries, the public finance system is still largely focused on the tax system of the State. The interventionist State is thus at the center of interrelations with the economy and society which necessarily take into account fiscal policy related to public expenditure, and, more and more, related to loans. The splitting up of national financial systems under the impact of policies of decentralization or of associations of States, like the European Union, does not therefore mark the end of fiscal State. This observation is illustrated by the areas in which the taxation and public expenditure intervene, by socio-fiscal resilience in the presence of economic globalization, by the blocking of fiscal Europe because of the rule of unanimity, by the weakness of the international public order.

The sociological interpretation of the evolution of the fiscal State sheds indispensable light on the matter. It reveals the four general moments of its general history related to the birth of the modern State in the Middle Ages, to the 19th century State of classical liberalism, to the post-war Keynesian Welfare State and to the neo-liberal questioning since the 1970s. Without taking up again the variety of the social, economic and political transformations of the financial systems, this chronological classification of ideal-types facilitates the development of the model of the interventionist democracy.

Since its birth the fiscal State has asserted itself in presence of the tension between the obligation to the monarch and the consent to public interest. The liberal theory of the 19th century intended to limit State intervention, even though parliamentary democracy asserted itself in France on the basis of budgetary law, without solving the social question correctly. Since the end of the 19th century, a socio-financial democratic contract has been initiated. It leads to the Welfare State which establishes a link between the extension of social rights and mass taxation. Of course, the Keynesian Welfare State which blossomed after the Second World War takes shape by reaching different socio-fiscal compromises according to their social context and their democratic scope. Nonetheless, as a model, though rarely approached in historical reality, it constituted a normative horizon to the problem of the political constitution of the society. These arrangements thus ensured a certain socio-political functionalization of the interventionist fiscal State in the economic context of the "Glorious Thirty" years. A broad consensus was reached with regard to the method of introducing a socially just fiscal contract, even though the people did not directly express their opinion on the suitability of the agreements made.

Since the 1970s the diffusion of the neo-liberal ideology of the constraints of the global market has undermined the foundations of the interventionist State. The political regulation of the compromises between the market and society is delegitimized by the axiological defunctionalization of the social contract related to its stratification and classification by public finance. The resilience of past arrangements and of public action to compensate for the detrimental social effects of economic globalization should not lead to underestimating the impact of this ideological process. The failings of the regulation of the economy by the fiscal State entail a degradation of the normativity of business and, at the end, a delegitimization of taxes. Fiscal policy certainly preserves certain coherent grounds, but it renounces the macro-regulation of the market more and more, preferring micro-interventions scattered around in the tight configurations of specific challenges. By piling up specialized ways of taxation, it weakens the impact of the contribution-tax on policies of general interest through a technical categorization of society. The particularist instrumentalization of different sectors abases and puts into doubt the social value of tax law. The occultation of the reality of political choices in the case of a public action marked by the ideology of the constraints of the market alienates the enlightened consent of the people, while at the same time providing relatively large institutional access to socio-economic groups in order to obtain advantages from the authority. The use of discreet taxation practices has also been resorted to, notably by the increase of the importance of VAT in all countries.

Tax avoidance, legally encouraged by tax competition between States, has become commonplace. That often leads to tax evasion. Banks and multinationals currently adopt optimization strategies which use tax havens, legal and accounting schemes, advantageous re-invoicing etc. By becoming the reference norm, the minimization of taxes is a part of the quest for sterile profits by business leaders and shareholders. It widens the inequalities even more, by transferring the tax burden to the mass of taxpayers. Tax expenditure, seemingly aiming at important social targets, in reality benefits mostly the wealthiest people. They affect the socio-political functionality of the State by misappropriating revenue and by interfering with the general meaning of normativity. With the axiological de-functionalization of the fiscal State, administrative regulation becomes the only barrier to the de-normalization of public action whose role as a political source of legitimacy weakens. The delimitation of economic deviance loses the social reference found in the law of the interventionist State and finally falls back on the simple formal obligation to the government. We understand why it is so important for the new public management, which is favourable to the business world, to transform administrative regulation into a more cooperative method. In the legal field, the struggle, involving other participants too, concerns the dialectic of the procedure to alter the balance between the rights of taxpayers (sociologically the most favoured) and the powers of the administration.

It is therefore important to continue to consider interventionist democracy through the political category of the State. From this point of view, the reflexive perspectives opened up by the defenders of cosmopolitanism (Beck, 2002, 2006) seem distant, to say the least. It is not certain that the grand ideas of political modernization through the creation of the European fiscal State are outdated. As at the time of industrial capitalism, the challenge remains the relationship of social issues to the economy, even though the ramming attacks of the neoliberal ideology have shaken the building. The debate has a pointedly cultural tone as it involves the idealistic conception of the global society, but its field continues to be the social State. The individual does not find himself alone facing the globalized market. He is perceived in the social classification of the fiscal State which touches him in his occupation, his family, his income, his health, his consumption, his civil status, his education, his pension, his place of residence etc. This classification multiplies the rankings, and often the criteria, in a fragmented instrumentation of the public policies of taxes and expenditure. It does not reach the phase of individualization of public action which some sociologists describe, even though, at the level of taxpayers, it is approached by a reappraised sociology of the individual tax decision. Citizens' rationality in the face of taxes is not confined to a utilitarian self-interest based on the (dominant) standard theory of rational choice. The objective link to taxation produces cognitive effects which do not correspond to the economic calculations of an egoist mind. Political values may maintain the figure of the contribution-tax of citizens to the interventionist democracy.

2. The Democratic Theory of Political Choices

The corpus of multidisciplinary data of fiscal sociology gives rise to a theory of fiscal public action, which is both analytical and normative. The democratic theory of political choices (DTPC) refers to the level and contents of public action interventions. It explores the democratic character and the quality of the choices of taxation for the purposes of financing public services. It draws lessons from the political formation of the fiscal State in Europe at the basis of Western democracy. One must put an end to the neo-liberal setting of the crisis of the interventionist State initiated in the 1970s. One must also denounce the abusive rhetoric of the necessities of globalization, which has taken up the form of the financial globalization and of its avatars, consisting of competitiveness and governance. The democratization of choices related to the intervention of the fiscal State appears to be a solution of social justice for the crises of the socio-political regulation of the economy. The DTPC thus opposes the theory of public choices which constitutes the main source of influence of neo-liberalism and of proponents of putting public action under the tutelage[1] of the market.

As schematized by Figure 4, the DTPC puts the sovereignty of the people at the centre in order to determine both the institutions and the general conception at the basis of the problem formulation which leads to public action in a given context. It inverts the causal biases of the fiscal public action (cf. chapter 7) by radicalizing civic democracy in order to leave behind the ideology of global market constraints. While recognizing the role of institutions to clarify the social conceptions of problems (debate, experimentation of policies, projects), their role does not consist in shaping public decisions. It consists in translating the will

[1] Which neo-liberal ideologists call "regulation" by the market in order to manipulate better the feeling of constraint by public opinion.

of the people into public action programmes. The power of the State is to guarantee the application of principles, decided on democratically, concerning choices on taxation and public services, if need be through coercion.

The scientific and political validity of the DTPC lies in the empirical rejection of the deterministic theories of budget constraints. The target is set on the neo-liberal anti-tax ideology. Tocqueville's law on the increase of expenditure in democracies, which Wagner would reformulate by attaching it to capitalism, finds validation here in the more restraint context of the DTPC. Historically the democratization of political choices has led to the increase of public expenditure because of the importance of social policies. It used expenditure and/or taxes to justify the redistribution of income. It has taken the form of an extension of suffrage, but also comprises various means of political expression of the *vox populi.*[2]

Figure 4: Public fiscal action according to the DTPC

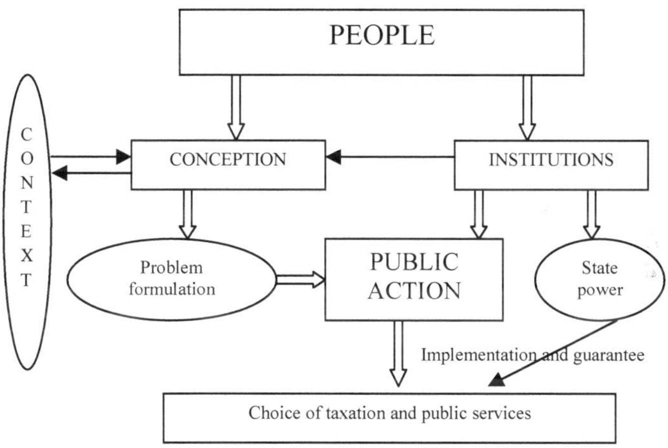

The empirical studies of fiscal sociology contradict neo-liberal clichés which call forth utilitarian economic ideas. It thus appears that the tax crisis is not an inexorable constraint which drives one to cut public expenditure, notably social expenditure. Likewise, the efficiency of the globalized market does not impel one to reduce taxes, in particular on capital, nor does it dismantle Welfare policies. There is no systematic observation of the retrenchment of the Welfare State for the purposes of satisfying the neo-liberal diktat. On the contrary, as we have seen, under

2 Social movements, the press, public debates, Internet campaigns etc.

certain circumstances the State demonstrates resilience. Socio-fiscal pacts do exist, like the one characterizing the Nordic model where the objective is to ensure a high social protection in exchange for moderate corporate taxation and an important contribution of all the taxpayers. Taxpayers do not always have an aversion for taxes, even if they do not have an economic interest in paying them. They are capable of altruism and they reason according to not only their own interest, but also their political values and their own information experienced (cognitive rationality). The excessive levels of taxes do not necessarily have a detrimental effect on economic growth and do not inexorably encourage fraudulent acts (evasion). Taxpayers are not always unrealistic in their demands for less tax and more expenditure, or in underestimating the importance of their taxes in comparison with the real cost of public services and of redistribution. More precisely, they consider other means of financing (loans, reallocation of expenditure, savings etc.).

The history of the French Revolution and of tax revolts in the world reminds us that the current situation of anomic disorganization, which is distinctive due to the participation of the State[3], is unstable. The 2008 summer crisis has clearly shown the need for a political regulation of economic globalization, while unveiling certain privileges of the nobility of financial capitalism. Protest by the people will not always be contained by democratic alienation, market injunction and hyper-classification, especially when the moment has come to accentuate tax burden in order to reimburse expenditure on support programmes of the neo-liberal economy. By going back to a Schumpeterian view of the crisis, the issue of the fiscal State brings into play, not its intrinsic viability, but the socio-political conditions of the globalized financial capitalism.

For the time being, we must insist on the point that the old socio-fiscal arrangements of the interventionist democracy have not completely been invalidated. The content of ideas, by influencing the interventionist conception and institutions, is of primary importance in order to inverse the tendency. From this angle, the reception of the neo-liberal ideology, which has legitimized the deficiencies of financial capitalism, consists in transforming the axiological idea of the economic competitiveness of the market into conceptual and legal norms of public action. The transformation is rarely pure as it is shaped in a different manner by the other basic factors of fiscal policy comprising institutions, partisan divisions, debates by experts and reactions by lobbyists. But, in the absence of a contrary social ideal, its material hegemony is logical. The DTPC is therefore an urgent alternative response to the neo-liberal

3 And not due to the simple abstention of the regulatory State as in Durkheim's analysis.

movement. It has the advantage of providing a political outlet to the people's expression of social discontent. By reinforcing the civic spirit of the contribution-tax, it valorizes the political function of interventionist public action on the base of a social contract.

3. Guidelines for a Just Social Contract

The evils of democracy are the subject of a renewal of reflection in literature: the importance of abstentions, the rise of populism, the generalization of consumerism, the role of the media, elitism, "expertocracy" etc. The conclusion appears to be obvious: representative democracy is ill and the remedies seem ineffective. More than that, the universality of the Western model is questioned by the counter-reference of China, which associates liberal growth on the market with non-democratic institutions, and by the American vision of the law of warfare applied in Iraq. Human rights and State sovereignty are subjects of a renewed questioning by using categories of ideas and action like terrorism, the right of interference etc. This picture casts a gloom over the perspective of a radicalization of democracy. The DTPC also encounters the objections to the idea of a social contract under the sovereignty of the people of Rousseau (1762)[4] and to the concept of communicational action of Habermas (1987, 1997). Even the experience of participation, which has certain limits when referring to the real influence of citizens, nourishes this pessimistic view.

In the field of socio-fiscal public action, which is a component of both the modern State and democracy, our research nevertheless shows that the democratization of political choices is both possible and positive. The DTPC offers a good way of removing the obstacles to the weakening of real democracy: in fact, it supposes that the (well-informed) consent of the people systematically be sought, which has rarely been experimented.[5] But it must be clarified that in social conditions taxpayers must be considered as real decision-makers. They are not put under a veil of ignorance.[6] Democratizing political choices

4 Rousseau's specific model of the tax State (cf. chapter 4) is historically better dated as it remains marked by the mistrust towards the taxation (to the benefit of the revenue of domains), even though he emphasizes the correction of social inequalities by taxes.

5 Just like antique democracy denied the classification as citizen to many people, representative democracy has limits because of the de-politicization of citizens.

6 Sociological realism refers to the empirical pole of fiscal sociology. Politically speaking (democracy of the people), the DTPC does not retain the idea of a veil of ignorance of Rawls, even though it admits that this theoretical-methodological position allows us to reflect on a criterion of justice likely to enrich the conception of public action.

conditions the achievement of a just social contract. The first requirement is to bring transparency to public finance, in the context of a political choice concerning the level, structure and functions of the fiscal system, taking into account comparative data. The target of this social contract for public action is the contribution-tax paid by citizens, capable of altruism, who accept the legitimacy of the functions of the interventionist fiscal State. There are several ways of organizing the system of relations between State, taxes and public services. The socio-fiscal contract concerns the distribution of the tax burden between social groups, as well as the level of social transfers. It implies seeking a socially pertinent compromise between low-income classes and rich classes. It must also consider the position and general functions of the fiscal State[7] for society and the market.

Another difficulty crops up, since the DTPC seems to reify the necessity for a democratic Welfare State in its historical synthesis, which resulted in raising taxes. We have in fact seen that the DTPC has lead to expenditure based on general interest, notably in the social field, where it has limited the deficiencies of industrial capitalism in the 19th century. It has created the post-war Welfare State. At present, it compensates (partially) for the inegalitarian defects of financial globalization. If it bolsters the legitimacy of the fiscal State, – the consented choice always enjoying more respect –, it thus seems to justify the need for a continuous increase of expenditure. This is an expression of the tendency law of Tocqueville that links democratization to the increase of public expenditure.

We must admit that this interpretation is not politically aberrant, such is the ideological deformation of the concept of crisis. Yet it does not match scientific logic nor the ethical perspective of the DTPC. In fact, this ethic is based on the idea that radical democracy is the best way to achieve a just social contract: until now this contract led to a certain level of social expenditure, but it does not imply this historical form whose universality has not been established. The tendency of the State to grow, described by Tocquevile (and later on by Wagner), finds its scientific validation in the specification provided by the subject of the DTPC: it is the social contract related to the socio-political regulation by public action which is at stake, and not directly the size of the State which is only one of the possible fields of democratic agreement (consent).

From this point of view, the synthesis of social interventionist democracy brought about in the national Welfare State was pertinent as an ideal for rebuilding social connections (solidarity) after the disaster of

---

7 In the absence of a legitimate association of tax States.

the two World Wars. At this moment, the promises of the European construction and of new international institutions (UN, UNESCO etc.) did not prohibit a more socially oriented perspective for the creation of a world order based on the pacification of relations and on a more equitable and more sustainable distribution of resources. The failure of this perspective, of course partially due to certain constitutive flaws[8] of international regulation, has created a normative vacuum in the social functionality of the economy. With the complicity or blindness of States, it prepared the ground for anomic globalization, even though the process is more complex.[9] After 1989, Europe managed to relaunch the peace-building project by integrating countries coming out of USSR dismemberment. But it did not succeed in confirming its role of international regulator with respect to global peace and with regard to the social functionality of neo-liberal capitalism. Caught in the toils of national sovereignty, it is incapable of taking up as its own the lessons of the ethical model of the social democracy of the Welfare State.

In Western democracies, the political arrangement of the relations between society and the economy has adopted different specifications with long-lasting effects, even though the social advantages have been widely questioned. Its content is therefore not frozen at a high level of expenditure and taxes.[10] The real challenge consists in redefining a contract on interventions by means of socially just public action. For developing countries, the difficulty lies in building up a viable and legitimate fiscal public action. In these countries, the creation of a genuine tax State is a means of reducing poverty by financing public services of education, health care and social security. It is also a means of casting off external tutelage. The democratization of political regimes may involve taxes that require the consent of taxpayers, while the market (like in the case of China) or economic rent (like in the case of the petroleum countries) does not require it. The solution of institutional imitation (mimetism), whether imposed or sought after by national elites, just like its negative replica wanted by anti-Westernism, are

8 Such as the myth of market perfection, the weight of the winners, the cold war, the conflicts of decolonization etc.

9 A reflection is also necessary to create an international public order, less dependent on the military strength of the United States. Such a public order must focus on the social regulation of the world economy taking into consideration the rights of the poorest countries etc.

10 The social contract derived from the DTPC differentiates from this point of view from Brennan's and Buchanan's economic theory of the fiscal Leviathan which criticizes, by generalizing it, the particular historical compromise of the Welfare State that maximizes its income. Besides, the contract defended here, while it strives for the consent to taxes like in the fiscal Leviathan theory, does not politically accept the false trail of the veil of ignorance, although it does not reject it as a theoretical and methodological metaphor, among other possibilities.

impasses. The way of political acculturation must maintain the universal principles of a social contract, while specifying it in the configuration of social solidarity, proper to each country. The conception of the socio-political functionality is not interpreted in the same way in the context of the informal economy, of religious values, of family migration etc.

Social science takes part in the search for a societal contract since its mission is to propose criteria of social justice and ethical principles for positive law. This conclusion may only propose a few guidelines, arising from fiscal sociology. The first guideline is directly derived from the DTPC. It implies paying attention to the status of rights and liberties which is never a definite or absolute attainment. More specifically, it refers to encouraging the expression of the *vox populi* in its different contexts – in the context of elections, as well as in the context of protest and refusal. Introduced by Montesquieu, the classical method of the institutional balance of powers (but which must be controlled by the people in a Rousseauist sense) demands in several cases the reinforcement of parliamentary power. The capacity of the parties to propose alternative projects about society is also concerned. In fact, partisan divisions must nourish public policies in order to confer relevance to elections for representatives and allow democratic accountability. Outside the electoral context, it is advisable to stick to the role of criticism and to that of mistrust by the people as a form of "counter-democracy" in the sense of Pierre Rosanvallon (2006). The strength of social movements in creating a counter-culture going beyond corporate challenges appears to be important. The elitist sociology of Pareto (and others), despite its methodological and ideological limits in thinking about the interventionist State, also offers an indispensible (negative) standardization: the extent of participation in public decision-making remains an important criterion reviving the debates on pluralism, corporatism, expertise etc. These observations, along with others which cannot be stated here, suppose spreading practical systems of democratic participation.[11] In fact, despite being imperfect, they promote real democracy, even though it may be doomed to remain an ideal to strive for.

But radical democracy, if it is well-prepared and organized, cannot be ordained. It cannot be imposed, which would fall under the accusation of denying being the sovereignty of the people. The debate is ancient, but we noticed that it has a particular resonance in the modern-day context where this ideal is refused by individuals, groups and nations. It is difficult to go beyond this argument, justifying the criticism of the ethic of Habermas, about procedural democracy and the rule of

---

[11] Civic associations, participatory budgeting, referendums, consultations, citizen juries, Internet websites, public debates etc.

law. Other criteria for the social contract which is a component of the DTPC are therefore necessary.

The second guidelines consists in encouraging the judgment of citizens. It requires real thinking. Education favours the preparation of citizens, provided that it is open-minded about knowledge on human beings, society and the world. In a more general sense, public action must encourage the possibility for individuals to make choices. It must develop what Amartya Sen (1991, 1992, 1999) calls "capability", which includes promoting democracy, freedom, but also social action in aid of the most destitute people (health care, education etc.). The model of the sovereignty of the people, in its radical version of democratization, requires escaping from the tyranny of the majority, to go back to the ideas of Tocqueville. Of course, in current practice, the people are rarely consulted systematically, which already invalidates those who hold democratization in contempt. For decisions subject to approval, managing governance most often circumvents electoral sanction by resorting[12] to the ideology of constraints and to more technocratic solutions etc. Whatever the case may be, the Tocquevillian obstacle remains serious for the DTPC. The capacity of citizens to state their choices, while it conditions democracy, is not sufficient for achieving a social contract of general interest. In the vein of Adam Smith's moral philosophy, public opinion must be able to place itself in the position of the impartial spectator, or at least the equitable spectator in the sense of Raymond Boudon (2001). But putting self-interests at a distance meets yet another objection, not much explored from this angle, namely that of the just positioning of the problem of public action.

This last question calls for an approach, both epistemological and political, which justifies a new criterion of justice. The study of the fiscal State, which forms a "total" phenomenon (in the meaning of Marcel Mauss), has shown the necessity to bring together several levels of analysis (articulation) within the framework of the general questioning on achieving a democratic social contract. The historical, systemic, comparative etc. analyses and the specific disciplinary materials acquire their normative meaning within the problem area of the civic legitimacy of the fiscal State. Economic and financial globalization justifies the urgent need for an epistemo-political work on the contextualization of the problem. We have thus shed light on the role of context as a variable of transition between the elemental factors of fiscal policy and the ideological biases of public action. At another level, the crisis of 2008 has dramatically popularized the effects of the system studied here from

12 At the European level, the democratic deficit which refers to the absence of social legitimacy in Europe is, more or less, denied, even when refusal prevail in consultations.

the point of view of public finance. In the same way, the role of socio-economic groups as a variable of transition between taxation and the people has been clarified. The groups express the power not so much of society or of the economy as of the State: the occultation of elitist choices by the ideology of market constraints has been complemented by the use of derogations as policy instruments. We have also seen that the criticism of utilitarian rationality is situated in the very field of rational methodological individualism by validating the possibility of a figure of a (civic) contribution-tax. This methodological position is then joined together with the denunciation of neo-liberal ideological clichés: it presents the relation to deviation as a de-normalization of the economy by social matters. The scientific hybridization of fiscal sociology therefore leads to the normative dimension of public action etc.

As a result, in order to reach a universal meaning, the socio-fiscal contract must problematize the social microcosm of individuals in a political equation that binds together the major financial, economic, social, political, territorial and environmental functions of public intervention. Tax hyper-classification, the increasing technicist use of policy instruments and the reduction of ideology by constraints are to be expelled, by the widening and bringing together of the levels of analysis, as choices of public action. There must be a debate on the link between revenue and public services, the place of the market and of social action, the environmental impact etc. When the economic scale of revenues is not socially justified anymore and when economic activity creates risks for the ecosystem, a political regulation is necessary. The fiscal State cannot be circumvented, even when ideally the international level is better adapted.

Against relativism, the epistemological-political criterion is opposed to the particularization of reasons and criteria of justice according to domains, social categories, countries, cultures etc. It accepts in return, as the essence of democratic realism, that political choices may vary from one society to another, or from one context to another. In the era of globalization and ecological risk, it insists on the need to render political choices explicit as far as their impact on the most destitute people is concerned, in line with Rawls's (1987; 1995) criterion of social justice, and on the sustainable economic-social development. Action is difficult here because the temptation of causal biases of the ruling elite is coupled with the cognitive biases socially generated by the concrete microcosm of individuals. Social science plays a role (certainly difficult as it also nourishes this game), by uncovering the clichés of political ideology. It shows that the alienation of citizens is neither natural nor fatal: the rational altruism of taxpayers is the basis of the contribution-tax for policies of general interest. Such general interest makes it then possible to have action with social objectives, even though the terms and conditions of the choices may vary. Above all, the new social contract must focus on income redistribution in order to deal with the affliction of income inequalities coming from the globalization of financial capitalism: to break the castes and the dynasties of privileged people, taxation of financial speculation, of inheritance, of wealth with regard to the citizens' contribution. The contract must also concern environmental protection and reestablish the relation of taxation to public services and social rights.[13] In the present-day context, the political regulation of the global economy has to be reformulated democratically according to a compromise able to constitute society.

As meta-knowledge of the (intermediate) variables of transition between the levels of reality, social science may help in defining the ethical indicators of society. The ethical-political de-specialization of problem positioning (configuration) dissolves the mirages of the management performance of neo-liberal economies. It places a universal critical counterpoint both to the community values of particular social microcosms, and to the ideological hegemony of economic consumerism. The ethical equation of the DTPC thus resolves into the social functionality of the contract of public action. Without being replaced by it, this theory contributes in setting the political choices of interventionist democracy concerning its general function for society.

---

13 Eco-taxes, valorization of the environmental impact on the balance sheet of enterprises etc. For the social public finance, the contract must concern retirement, health care, family etc.

Bibliography

AARON, H. J., and J. SLEMROD. 2003. *The Crisis in Tax Administration*. Washington: Brookings Institution Press.

ACKERT, L. F., A. B. GILLETTE, J. MARTINEZ-VASQUEZ, and M. RIDER. 2007. "Voting on Tax Policy Design. A Test of the Selfish versus Social Preferences Hypotheses." *Public Finance Review* 35 (2): 263-284.

AHMAD, E., and G. BROSIO (ed.). 2006. *Handbook of Fiscal Federalism*. Northampton: Edward Elgar Publishing.

AHMED, E., and V. BRAITHWAITE. 2005. "Understanding Small Business Taxpayers." *International Small Business Journal* 35 (5): 539-568.

AIDT, T. S., and P. S. JENSEN. 2009. "Tax Structure, Size of Government, and the Extension of the Voting Franchise in Western Europe." *International Tax Public and Finance* 16: 362-394.

ALARCON GARCIA, G., A. MARTINEZ SERRANO, and E. QUINONES VIDAL. 2007. "La conciencia fiscal en España." *Diritto E Pratica Tributaria Internazionale* 4 (2): 491-507.

ALBERT, M. 1991. *Capitalisme contre capitalisme*. Paris: Le Seuil.

ALLAIS, M. 1989. *L'impôt sur le capital*. Paris: Hermann.

ALLINGHAM, M. G., and A. SANDMO. 1972. "Income Tax Evasion: A Theoretical Analysis." *Journal of Public Economics* 1 (3-4): 323-338.

ALM, J., and J. L. GOMEZ. 2008. "Social Capital and Tax Morale in Spain." *Economic Analysis and Policy* 38 (1): 73-87.

ALM, J., J. MARTINEZ-VAZQUEZ, and A. TORGLER. 2005. "Russian Attitudes toward Paying Taxes, Before, During, and After the Transition." *International Studies Program, Working Paper*: Georgia State University.

ALM, J., G. H. McCLELLAND, and W. D. SCHULZE. 1999. "Changing the Social Norm of Tax Compliance by Voting." *International Review of Social Sciences* 52 (2): 141-171.

ALM, J., and B. TORGLER. 2006. "Culture Differences and Tax Morale in the United States and in Europe." *Journal of Economic Psychology* 27 (2): 224-246.

ALM, J. *et al.* 2010. "Taxpayers Information Assistance and Tax Compliance Behavior." *Journal of Economic Psychology* 31 (4): 577-586.

ALT, J. E., and D. DREHER LASSEN. 2006. "Transparency, Political Polarization, and Political Budget Cycles in OECD Countries." *American Journal of Political Science* 50 (3): 530-550.

AMABLE, B. 2003. *The Diversity of Modern Capitalism*. Oxford: Oxford University Press.

ANDRE, J. B. 2008. "L'altruisme, une question de réputation." *Sciences Humaines* 9: 34.

ANNETT, A. 2001. "Social Fractionalization, Political Instability, and the Size of Government." *IMF Staff Papers* 48 (3): 561-592.

APPEL, H. 2006. "International Imperatives and Tax Reforms, Lessons from Postcommunist Europe." *Comparative Politics* 39 (1): 43-62.

ARDANT, G. 1965, *Théorie sociologique de l'impôt*. Paris: SEVPEN.

– 1971 (T1). 1972 (T2). *Histoire de l'impôt*. Paris: Fayard.

ASHBY, J. S., P. WEBLEY, and S. H. ALEXANDER. 2009. "The role of Occupational Taxpaying Cultures in Taxpaying Behaviour." *Journal of Economic Psychology* 30 (2): 216-227.

ATKINSON, A. B. 2008. *The Changing Distribution of Earnings in OECD*. Oxford: Oxford University Press.

ATKINSON, A. B., and T. PIKETTY (ed.). 2007. *Top Incomes over the Twentieth Century*. Oxford: Oxford University Press.

BACKHAUS, J. G. 2002. "Fiscal Sociology: What for?" *The American Journal of Economics and Sociology* 61 (1): 55-77.

– 2004. "Joseph A. Schumpeter's Contributions in the Area of Fiscal Sociology: A First Approximation." *Journal of Evolutionary Economics* 14: 143-151.

BAGULEY, P. 1995. "Protest, Poverty and Power: A Case Study of the Anti-Poll Tax Movement." *Sociological Review* 43 (4): 693-719.

BAJADA. C., and F. SCHNEIDER. 2005. *Size, Causes and Consequences of Underground Economy, An International Perspective*. Aldershot: Ashgate.

BARANGER, D. 2004. "La tradition du contrôle budgétaire en Grande-Bretagne." *Revue française de finances publiques* 86: 75-86.

BAUMAN, Z. 2000. *Liquid Modernity*. Cambridge: Polity Press.

BAY, A-H, and A. W. PEDERSEN. 2006. "The Limits of Social Solidarity." *Acta Sociologica* 49 (4): 419-436.

BAYOUMI, T., and F. M. GONCALVES. 2007. "Government for the People: On the Determinants of the Size of U.S. Government." *IMF Working Paper*: 07/289.

BECK, U. 2002. *Pouvoir et contre-pouvoir à l'heure de la mondialisation*. Paris: Flammarion.

– 2006. *Qu'est-ce que le cosmopolitisme*. Paris: Aubier.

BECK, P. A., H. G. RAINEY, and C. TRAUT. 1990. "Disadvantages, Disaffection, and Race as Divergent Bases for Citizen Fiscal Policy Preferences." *Journal of Politics* 52 (1): 71-93.

BECKER, G. S. 1968. "Crime and Punishment: An Economic Approach." *The Journal of Political Economy* 76 (2): 169-217.

BECKER, H. S. 1963. *Outsiders*. New York: The Free Press of Glencoe.

BECKER, U. 2007. "Open Systemness and Contested Reference Frames and Change. A Reformulation of the Varieties of Capitalism Theory." *Socio Economic Review* 5 (2): 1745-1761.

BEEDLE, P., and P. TAYLOR-GOOBY. 1983. "Ambivalence and Altruism: Public Opinion about Taxation and Welfare." *Policy and Politics* 11 (1): 15-39.

BERAMENDI, P., and D. RUEDA. 2007. "Social Democracy Constrained: Indirect Taxation in Industrialized Democracies." *British Journal of Political Science* 37 (4): 619-641.

BERCE, Y.-M. 1980. *Révoltes et révolutions dans l'Europe moderne (XVIe-XVIIIe siècle)*. Paris: PUF.

– 1991. *Croquants et nu-pieds. Les soulèvements paysans en France du XVIe au XIXe siècle*. Paris: Gallimard.

BERCH, N. 1995. "Explaining Changes in Tax Incidence in the States." *Political Research Quarterly* 48 (3): 629-641.

BERGMAN, M. 2002. "Who pays for Social Policy? A Study on Taxes and Trust." *Journal of Social Policy* 31 (2): 289-305.

BERLIANT, M., and P. ROTHSTEIN. 2003. "Possibility, Impossibility, and History in the Origins of the Marriage Tax." *National Tax Law* 56 (2): 303-317.

BEVIR, M., and R. A. RHODES. 2003. *Interpreting British Governance*. London: Routledge.

– 2004. "Interpreting British Governance." *British Journal of Politics and International Relations* 6 (2): 130-136.

BIZIOU, M. 2003. *Adam Smith et l'origine du libéralisme*. Paris: PUF.

BLOCK, F., and P. EVANS. 2005. "The State and the Economy." in Smelser and Swedberg, 2005: 505-521.

BLOUNT, S. 2000. "Public Opinion and Tax Aversion in Australian." *Journal of Sociology* 36 (3): 275-290.

BOCCACIO, M., and V. De BONIS. 2003. "Political Sociological Theories in the Italian Tradition of Public Finance." *Pensiero Economico Italiano* 11 (1): 75-97.

BODIN, J. 1986 (1576). *Les six livres de la République*. Paris: Fayard.

BOGGERI, M. L., and J. W. SUNDELSON. 1938. "Italian Theories of Fiscal Science." *Political Science Quarterly* 53 (2): 249-267.

BONNEY, R. (ed.). 1996. *Systèmes économiques et finances publiques*. Paris: PUF.

– 1999. *The Rise of the Fiscal State in Europe, 1200 1815*. New York: Oxford University Press.

BORGATTA, G. 2007 (1920). "The Scientific Study of Fiscal Phenomena." in McLure, 2007: 203-248.

BORNHORST, F., S. GUPTA, and J. THORNTON. 2008. "Natural Resource Endowments, Governance, and the Domestic Revenue Effort: Evidence from a Panel of Countries." *IMF Working Paper*: 08/170.

BOSSUET, J. B. 1967 (written in the 17th century). *Politique tirée des propres paroles de l'Écriture sainte*. Genève: Droz.

BOUDON, R. 1986. *L'idéologie*. Paris: Fayard.

– 1989. "La théorie de l'action sociale de Parsons: la conserver, mais la dépasser." *Sociologie et Sociétés* 21 (1): 55-67.

– 1998. "Le phénomène idéologique: en marge d'une lecture de Pareto." in *Études sur les sociologues classiques*. Paris: PUF.

– 1999. *Le sens des valeurs*. Paris: PUF.

– 2001. "*Vox populi, vox Dei*? Le spectateur impartial et la théorie des opinions." in Boudon, Demeuleneare, et Viale (dir.). *L'explication des normes sociales*. Paris: PUF: 93-127.

– 2003. "Beyond Rational Choice Theory." *Annual Review of Sociology* 29 (1): 1-21.

BOUVIER, J., et H. GERMAIN-MARTIN. 1969. *Finances et financiers de l'Ancien Régime*. Paris: PUF.

BOWLES, S. 2006. "Groups Competition, Reproductive Leveling, and the Evolution of Human Altruism." *Science* 314: 1569-1572.

BOYER, R. 2004. *Une théorie du capitalisme est-elle possible?* Paris: Odile Jacob.

BRAITHWAITE, V. (ed.). 2003. *Taxing Democracy, Understanding Tax Avoidance and Evasion*. Aldershot: Ashgate.

– 2007. "Responsive Regulation and Taxation: Introduction." *Law and Society* 29 (1): 3-10.

BRAUDEL, F. 1949. *La Méditerranée*. Paris: Armand Colin.

– 1979. *Civilisation matérielle, Économie et Capitalisme*. Paris: Armand Colin.

BRENNAN, G., and J. M. BUCHANAN. 1977. "Towards a Tax Constitution for Leviathan." *Journal of Public Economics* 8 (8): 155-273.

– 1980. *The Power to Tax: Analytical Foundations of a Fiscal Constitution*. New York: Cambridge Unversity Press.

BRODSKY, D. M., and E. THOMPSON. 1993. "Ethos, Public Choice and Referendum Voting." *Social Science Quarterly* 74 (2): 286-299.

BROOKS, C., and J. MANZA. 2006. "Why Do Welfare States Persist?" *The Journal of Politics* 68 (4): 816-827.

BROWN, D. S., and W. HUNTER. 1999. "Democracy and Social Spending in Latin America." *American Political Science Review* 93 (4): 779-790.

BUCHANAN, J. M. 1950. "Federalism and Fiscal Equity." *American Economic Review*: 583-599.

– 1960. "La Scienza delle Finanze: The Italian Tradition of Fiscal Studies." in Buchanan J. M. (ed.). *Fiscal Theory and Political Economy*. Chapel Hill: University of North Carolina: 24-74.

– 1979. "The Potential for Taxpayer Revolt in American Democracy." *Social Science Quarterly* 59 (4): 691-696.

BUCHANAN, J. M., and G. A. TULLOCK. 1962. *The Calculus of Consent. Logical Foundations of Constitutional Democracy*. Ann Arbor: University of Michigan Press.

BURG, D. F. 2004. *A World History of Tax Rebellions*. London: Routledge.

BURMAN, L. E. 2003. "Is the Tax Expenditure Concept Still Relevant." *National Tax Journal* 56 (3): 613-627.

BURNAM, L. E., E. TODER, and C. GEISSLER. 2008. "How Big Are Total Individual Income Tax Expenditure, and Who Benefits from Them?." *Discussion Paper* 31: The Urban Institute, Washington.

BURTON, H. A., S. S. KARLINSKY, and C. BLANTHORNE. 2005. "Perception of a White-Collar Crime: Tax Evasion." *The ATA Journal of Legal Tax Research* 3 (1): 35-48.

BUSEMEYER, M. R. 2009. "From Myth to Reality: Globalization and Public Spending in OECD Countries Revisited." *European Journal of Political Research* 48: 455-482.

BUTTON, J. W. 1992. "A sign of Generational Conflict. The Impact of Florida's Aging Voters on Local School and Tax Referenda." *Social Science Quarterly* 73 (4): 786-797.

CAMPBELL, J. L. 1993. "The State and Fiscal Sociology." *Annual Review of Sociology* 19: 163-185.

– 2002. "Ideas, Politics, and Public Policy." *Annual review of Sociology* 28: 21-38.

CANTILLON, B., V. De MAESSCHALCK, S. ROTTIERS, and G. VERBIST. 2006. "Social Redistribution in Federalised Belgium." *West European Politics* 29 (5): 1034-1056.

CAPRON, M. (dir.). 2005. *Les normes comptables, internationales, instruments du capitalisme financier*. Paris: La Découverte.

CAROLL, J. S. 1987. "Compliance with the Law: A Decision-making Approach to Taxpaying." *Law and Human Behavior* 11: 319-335.

CARON, J.-C. 2002. *L'été rouge*. Paris: Aubier.

CARONE, G., J. H. SCHMIDT and G. NICODEME. 2007. "Tax revenues in the European Union." European Economy, Economics Paper, 280: Brussels.

CASTLES, F. G. 2009. "What Welfare States Do: A Disaggregated Expenditure Approach." *Journal of Social Policy* 38 (2): 45-62.

CENTENO, M. A. 1997. "Blood and Debt: War and Taxation in Nineteenth-Century Latin America." *American Journal of Sociology* 102 (6): 1565-1605.

CHAUNU, P. 1977. "L'État." in *Histoire économique et sociale de la France*. Paris: PUF: 15-228.

CHAUSSINAND-NOGARET, G. 1993. *Gens de finance au XVIIIe siècle*. Paris: Complexe.

CHEFF. 2002. *L'impôt au Moyen Âge* (3 vols.). Paris: CHEFF.

– 2005. *L'impôt des campagnes*. Paris: CHEFF.

– 2005. *L'impôt dans les villes de l'Occident méditerranée (XIIIe-XVe siècle)*. Paris: CHEFF.

CHEIBUB, J. A. 2006. "Presidentialism, Electoral identifiability, and Budget Balances in Democratic Systems." *American Political Science Review* 100 (3): 353-368.

CITRIN, J. 1979. "Do People Want Something for Nothing: Public Opinion on Taxes and Government Spending." *National Tax Journal* 32: 113-129.

CLAMAGERAN, J.-J. 1867. *Histoire de l'impôt en France*. Paris: Guillaumin.

CLARAMUNT, C. O., and S. C. ARROYO. 2000. "The Role of the Resources of the Power Hypothesis in Explaining the Spanish Welfare State between 1975-1995." *European Journal of Political Research* 38 (2): 261-284.

CLOTFELTER, C. T. 1983. "Tax Evasion and Tax Rates: An Analysis of Individual Returns." *Review of Economics and Statistics* 65: 363-373.

CNRS. 1987. *Genèse de l'État moderne*. Paris: CNRS.

COBHAM, A. 2008. "Tax Evasion, Tax Avoidance and Development Finance." Queen Elizabeth House, *Working Paper*: 129.

COHEN, M. D., J. G. MARCH, and J. P. OLSEN. 1972. "A Garbage Can Model of Organizational Choice." *Administrative Science Quarterly* 17 (1): 1-25.

CONSEIL D'ANALYSE ECONOMIQUE. 2005. *Croissance équitable et concurrence fiscale*. Paris: CAE.

CONSEIL DES IMPÔTS. 2003. *La fiscalité dérogatoire*. Paris: 21e Rapport.

COURANT, P. N., E. M. GRAMLICH, and D. L. RUBINFELD. 1980. "Why Voters Support Tax Limitation Amendments: The Michigan Case." *National Tax Journal* 1: 1-20.

COWART, A., T. HANSEN, and K. E. BROFOSS. 1975. "Budgetary Strategies and Success at Multiple Decisions Levels in the Norvegian Urban Setting." *American Political Science Review* 69: 543-558.

COWELL, F. A. 1985. "The Economic Analysis of Tax Evasion." *Bulletin of Economic Research* 37 (3): 164-193.

COX, J., and D. LOWERY. 1990. "The Impact of the Tax Revolt Era State Fiscal Caps." *Social Science Quarterly* 71 (3): 492-509.

CREPAZ, M. M.-L., and A. W. MOSER. 2004. "The Impact of Collective and Competitive Veto Points on Public Expenditures in the Global Age." *Comparative Political Studies* 37 (3): 259-285.

CROZIER, M. 1963. *Le phénomène bureaucratique*. Paris: Le Seuil.

– 1987. *État modeste, État moderne*. Paris: Fayard.

CRUSH, J. 1985. "Colonial Coercion and the Swazi Tax Revolt of 1903-1907." *Political Geography Quarterly* 4 (3): 179-190.

CULLIS, J., P. JONES, and A. LEWIS. 2006. "Tax Framing, Instrumentality and Individual Differences: Are there two Different Cultures?" *Journal of Economic Psychology* 27 (2): 304-326.

CUMMINGS, R. G., J. MARTINEZ-VASQUEZ, M. McKEE, and B. TORGLER. 2004. "Tax Morale Affects Tax Compliance: Evidence from

Surveys and an Artefactual Field Experiment." *Journal of Economic Behavior and Organization* 70 (3): 447-457.

CUSACK, R., and P. BERAMENDI. 2006. "Taxing Work." *European Journal of Political Research* 45 (1): 43-73.

CUSACK, T. R. 1999. "Partisan Politics an Fiscal Policy." *Comparative Political Studies* 32 (4): 464-486.

DAHL, R. 1961. *Who Governs? Democracy and Power in an American City*. New Haven: Yale University Press.

DAUNTON, M. 2001. *Trusting Leviathan: The Politics of Taxation in Britain, 1799-1914*. New York: Cambridge University Press.

DEAN, H. 2007. "The Ethics of Welfare-to-work". *Policy and Politics* 35(4): 573-589.

DELORME, R., et C. ANDRE. 1983. *L'État et l'économie. Un essai d'explication de l'évolution des dépenses publiques en France (1870-1980)*. Paris: Seuil.

DE MELLO, L., and E. TIONGSON. 2006. "Income Inequality and Redistributive Government Spending." *Public Finance Review* 34 (3): 282-305.

DEVEREUX, M. P. 2006. "Developments in the Taxation of Corporate Profit in the OECD since 1965." *Working Paper*.

DEVEREUX, M. P., and R. GRIFFITH. 2003. "Evaluating Tax Policy for Location Decisions." *International Tax and Public Finance* 10: 107-126.

DEVINE, J. A. 1983. "Fiscal Policy and Class Income Inequality: The Distributional Consequences of Governmental Revenues and Expenditures in the United States, 1949-1976." *American Sociological Review* 48: 606-622.

DHALMI, S., and A. AL-NOWAIHI. 2007. "Why Do People Pay Taxes? Prospect Theory versus Expected Utility Theory." *Journal of Economic Behavior and Organization* 64: 171-192.

DINGELDEY, I. 2007. "Between Workfare and Enablement. The Different Paths to Transformation of the Welfare State." *European Journal of Political Research* 46 (6): 823-851.

DOGAN, M., et R. PAHRE. 1991. *L'innovation dans les sciences sociales*. Paris: PUF.

DORNSTEIN, M. 1976. "Compliance with Legal and Bureaucratic Rules: The Case of Self-Employed Taxpayers in Israel." *Human Relations* 29 (11). 1019-1034.

DOWNS, A. 1957. *An Economic Theory of Democracy*. New York, Harper.

– 1960. "Why the Government Budget Is too Small in a Democracy." *World Politics*, 12: 541-563.

DREHER, A. 2006. "The Influence of Globalization on Taxes and Social Policy: An Empirical Analysis for OECD Countries." *European Journal of Political Economy* 22 (1): 179-201.

DRURY, A. C., J. KRIECKHAUS, and M. LUSZTIG. 2006. "Corruption, Democracy, and Economic Growth." *International Political Science Review* 27 (2): 121-136.

DUBERGE, J. 1961. *La psychologie sociale de l'impôt dans la France d'aujourd'hui*. Paris: PUF.

– 1990. *Les Français face à l'impôt*. Paris: LGDJ.

DURKHEIM, E. 1984. *The Division of Labor in Society*. Besingstoke: Palgrave Macmillan. (1893. *De la division du travail social*).

– 1977 (1895). *Les règles de la méthode sociologique*. Paris: PUF.

– *Suicide*. 2002. London and New York: Routledge. (1897). *Le Suicide*).

– 2001. *The Elementary Forms of Religious Life*. Oxford New York: Oxford University Press. (1912. *Les formes élémentaires de la vie religieuse*).

EBNER, A. 2006. "Institutions, Entrepreneurship, and the Rationale of Government: An Outline of the Schumpeterian Theory of the State." *Journal of Economic and Organization Behavior* 59: 497-515.

EDGELL, S., and V. DUKE. 1982. "Reactions to the Public Expenditure Cuts: Occupational Class and Party Realignment." *Sociology* 16 (3): 431-439.

EISENSTEIN, L. 1961. *The Ideologies of Taxation*. New York: Ronald Press.

ELIAS, N. 1969. *Die höfische Gesellschaft*. Darmstadt und Neuwied: Luchterhand. (1974. *La société de cour*. Paris: Flammarion).

ESPING-ANDERSEN, G. 1990. *The Three Worlds of Welfare Capitalism*. New Jersey: Princeton University Press.

ETZIONI, A. 1986. "Tax Evasion and Perception of Tax Fairness: A Research Note." *The Journal of Applied Behavoiral Science* 22 (2): 177-185.

– 1998. *The Moral Dimension: Toward a New Economics*. New York: Free Press.

EVANS, M. R., and J. KELLEY. 2002. "*Moral Feelings about Tax Cheating and Welfare Fraud in 29 Nations.*" in Evans et Kelley, 2002. *Australian Economy and Society: Religion, Morality and Public Policy in International Perspective 1984-2002*. Sydney: Federation Press.

FALCH, T., and J. RATTSO. 1997. "Political Economic Determinants of School Spending in Federal States: Theory and Time-series Evidence." *European Journal of Political Economy* 13: 299-314.

FASIANI, M. 2007 (1949). "Pareto's Contributions to the Science of Public Finance." in McLure, 2007: 266-305.

FAULK, D. 2002. "Do State Economic Development Incentives Create Jobs? An Analysis of State Employment Tax Credits." *National Tax Journal* 55 (2): 263-280.

FAVIER, J. 1978. *Philippe le Bel*. Paris: Fayard.

FAYOL, H. Administration industrielle et générale. Paris: Dunod, 1962.

FELD, L. P., FREY B. S. 2002. "Trust Breeds Trust: How Taxpayers are Treated." *Economics of Governance* 3: 87-99.

FELD, L. P., and J. R. TYRAN. 2002. "Tax Evasion and Voting: An Experimental Analysis." *International Social Sciences Review* 55 (2): 197-222.

FELDMAN, S., and M. R. STEENBERGEN. 2001. "The Humanitarian Foundation of Public Support for Social Welfare." *American Journal of Political Science* 45 (3): 658-677.

FENNO, R. 1973. *Congressmen in Committee*. Boston: Little Brown.

FIREBAUGH, G. 2000. "The Trend in Between-Nation Income Inequality." *Annual Review of Sociology* 26: 323-339.

FISMAN, R., and J. SVENSSON. 2007. "Are Corruption and Taxation really Harmful to Growth? Firm Level Evidence." *Journal of Development Economics* 83 (1): 63-75.

FORGEOT, G., et C. STARZEC. 2003. "L'impact redistributif des impôts indirects en France." *Economie publique* 13: 3-43.

FORSE, M., et M. PARODI. 2002. "L'horizon du spectateur équitable. Un modèle pour comprendre l'opinion." *L'Année sociologique* 52 (1): 15-82.

– 2004. *La priorité du juste. Éléments pour une sociologie des choix moraux*. Paris: PUF.

FOSTER, M. F., and M. PELLIZZARI. 2000. "Trends and Driving Factors in Income Inequality and Poverty in OECD Area." *OECD Occasional Paper 3* WD.

FOUCAULT, M, et A. FRANCOIS. 2005. "La politique influence-t-elle les décisions publiques locales? Analyse empirique des budgets communaux de 1977 à 2001." *Politiques et Management Public* 23 (3): 79-100.

FURNHAM, A. 1983. "The Protestant Work Ethic, Human Values and Attitudes towards Taxation." *Journal of Economic Psychology* 3 (2): 113-128.

– 1984. "Determinants of Attitudes toward Taxation in Britain." *Human Relations* 37 (7): 535-546.

GAMBARO, L., J. MEYER-SPASCHE, and A. RAHMAN. 2007. "Does Aid Decrease Tax Revenue in Developing Countries." *London School of Economic and Political Science*.

GARMAN, C., D. HAGGARD, and E. WILLIS. 2001. "Fiscal Decentralization, A Political Theory with Latin American Cases." *World Politics* 53 (2): 205-236.

GARRET, G. 1998. *Partisan Politics in the Global Economy*. Cambridge: Cambridge University Press.

GARRET, G., and D. MITCHELL. 2001. "Globalization, Government Spending and Taxation in the OECD." *European Journal of Political Research* 39 (2): 145-177.

GASTELLU, J.-M., J.-Y MOISSERON, et G. POURCET. 1999. *Fiscalité, Développement et Mondialisation*. Paris: Maisonneuve et Larose: 85-106.

GENET, J.-P. 1990. (ed.). *L'État moderne. Genèse Bilans et perspectives*. Paris: CNRS.

GENET, J.-P, et B VINCENT (ed.). 1986. *État et Église dans la genèse de l'État moderne*. Madrid: Bibliothèque de la Casa de Velasquez.

GERRING, J., P. BOND, W. T. BARNST, and C. MORENO. 2005. "Democracy and Economic Growth: A Historical Perpective." *World Politics* 57 (4): 323-364.

GERSHON, R. 2004. "Teaching Federal Income Taxation Using Socioeconomics." *San Diego Law Review* 41: 201-209.

GËRXHANI, K. 2007. "Did You Pay Your Taxes? How (Not) to Conduct Tax Evasion Surveys in Transition Countries." *Social Indicators Research* 80 (3): 555-581.

GIDDENS, A. 1990. *The Consequences of Modernity*. Cambridge: Polity Press.

– 1991. *Modernity and Self Identity*. Cambridge: Polity Press.

GILL, J., and J. A. THURBER. 1999. "Congressional Tightwads and Spendthrifts: Measuring Fiscal Behavior in the Changing House of Representatives." *Political Research Quarterly* 52 (2): 387-402.

GILLEY, B. 2006. "The Meaning and Measure of State Legitimacy: Results for 72 Countries." *European Journal of Political Research* 45 (3): 499-525.

GIRAUD, P-N. 2002. "Mondialisation et dynamique des inégalités." *Risques*.

GODBOUT, L. 2006. *L'intervention gouvernementale par la politique fiscale. Le rôle des dépenses fiscales: Canada, États-Unis, France*. Paris: Economica.

GOLD, S. D. 1995. *The Fiscal Crisis of the States*. Washington: Georgetown University Press.

GOLDSCHEID, R. 1917. *Staatssozialismus oder Staatskapitalismus*, Leipzig: Brüder Suschitzky.

– 1967. "Sociological Approach to Problems of Public Finance." in Musgrave and Peacock, 1967: 202-213.

GRASMICK, H. G., R. J. BURSK, and J. K. COCHRAN. 1991. "Render unto Caesar what is Caesar's: Religiosity and Taxpayers' Inclinations to Cheat." *The Sociological Quarterly* 32 (2): 251-266.

GRASMICK, H. G., and W. J. SCOTT. 1982. "Tax Evasion and Social Control." *Journal of Economic Psychology* 3: 213-230.

GRIZIOTTI, B. 2007. "At the School of Vilfredo Pareto and Maffeo Pantaleoni." in McLure, 2007: 259-265.

GUPTA, S., B. CLEMENTS, A. PIVOVARSKI, and E. R. TIONGSON. 2003. "Foreign Aid and Revenue Response: Does the Composition of Aid Matter?" *IMF Working Paper*: 03/176.

HA, E. 2008. "Globalization, Veto Players, and Welfare Spending." *Comparative Political Studies* 41 (6): 783-813.

HABERMAS, J. 1978. *Raison et légitimité, problèmes de légitimation dans le capitalisme avancé*. Paris: Payot.

– 1987. *Théorie de l'agir communicationnel*. Paris: Fayard.

– 1997. *Droit et démocratie*. Paris: Gallimard.

HADENIUS, A. 1985. "Citizens Strike a Balance: Discontent With Taxes, Content With Spending." *Jounal of Public Policy* 5 (3): 349-363.

HALIM, N. 2008. "Testing Alternative Theories of Bureaucratic Corruption in Less Developed Countries." *Social Science Quarterly* 89 (1): 236-257.

HALL, P., and D. SOSKICE (eds.). 2001. *Varieties of Capitalism: The Institutional Foundations of Comparative Advantage*. Oxford: Oxford University Press.

HALL, P. A., and C. R. TAYLOR. 1996. "Political Science and the Three New Institutionalisms." *Political Studies* 44 (5): 936-957.

HANOUSEK, J., and F. L. PALDA. 2003. "Quality of Government Services in the Civic Duty to Pay Taxes in Czech and Slovak Republics, and Other Countries." *International Review Social Sciences* 57 (2): 237-252.

HANSEN, J. M. 1998. "Individuals, Institutions, and Public Preferences over Public Finance." *American Political Science Review* 92 (3): 513-531.

HANSSON, A. 2008. "Integration and the Structure of Public Spending." *Comparative Political Studies* 41 (7): 1001-1027.

HART, A. 2010. "Death of the Partisan Globalization and Taxation in South America, 1990-2006". *Comparative Political Studies* 43 (3): 304-328.

HASSELDINE, J., and P. A. HITE. 2003. "Framing, Gender and Tax Compliance." *Journal of Economic Psychology* 24: 517-533.

HAYES, M. T. 2007. "Policy Characteristics, Patterns of Politics, and the Minimum Wage: Toward a Typology of Redistributive Policies." *Policy Studies Journal* 35 (3): 465-480.

HEADEY, B., R. E. GOODIN, R. MUFFELS, and H. J. DIRVEN. 2000. "Is there a Trade-off Between Economic Efficiency and a Generous Welfare State? A Comparison of Best Cases of The Three Worlds of Welfare Capitalism." *Social Indicators Research* 50 (2): 115-157.

HECOCK, R. D. 2006. "Electoral Competition, Globalization, and Subnational Education Spending in Mexico, 1999-2004." *American Journal of Political Science* 50 (4): 950-961.

HEIDER, F. 1944. "Social Perception and Phenomenal Causality." *Psychological Review* 51: 358-384.

HEINRICH, J., R. BOYD, S. BOWLES, C. CAMERER. 2001. "In Search of Homo Economicus: Behavioral Experiments in 15 Small-Scale Societies." *The American Economic Review* 91 (2): 73-78.

HEINRICH, J., R. McELREATH, A. BARR, and J. ESMINGER. 2006. "Costly Punishment across Human Societies." *Science* 312, 23: 1767-1770.

HERVIEU, H. 1879. *Recherche sur les premiers États Généraux et les assemblées représentatives pendant la première moitié du XIVe siècle*. Paris: Thorin.

HITE, P. A. 1987. "An Application of Attribution Theory in Taxpayer Noncompliance Research." *Public Finance* 42: 105-118.

HOFFMANN, S. 1956. *Le mouvement Poujade*. Paris: PUF.

HOLTBLATT, J., and J. McCUBBIN. 2003. "Issues Affecting Low-Income Filers." in Aaron and Slemrod, 2003: 148-181.

HOMANS, G. C. 1958. "Social Behavior as Exchange." *American Journal of Sociology* 62: 697-706.

HUBER, E., and J. D. STEPHENS. 2005 "Welfare States and the Economy." in Smelser and Swedberg, 2005: 552-569.

HUBER, E., T. MUSTILLO, and J. D. STEPHENS. 2008. "Politics and Social Spending in Latin America." *The Journal of Politics*, 70 (2): 37-45.

HUDSON, J., G. J. HAWANG, and S. HÜHNER. 2008. "Between Ideas, Institutions and Interests: Analysing Third Way Welfare Reform Programmes in Germany and the United Kingdom." *Journal of Social Policy* 37 (2): 207-230.

IBRAHIM, M. M. 1994. "Party Politics and Spending Decisions in Local Authorities" *International Journal of Public Sector Management* 7 (5): 67-71.

IMAN, P. A., and D. F. JACOBS. 2007. "Effect of Corruption on Tax Revenues in the Middle East." *IMF Working Paper*: 07/270.

IVERSEN, T., and J. D. STEPHENS. 2008. "Partisan Politics, The Welfare State, and Three Worlds of Human Capital Formation." *Comparative Political Studies* 41 (4): 600-637.

JACOBS, A. M. 2009. "How Do Ideas Matter? Mental Models and Attention in German Pension Politics." *Comparative Political Studies* 42 (2): 252-279.

JACOBS, D. 1987. "Business Resources and Taxation: A Cross-Sectionnal Examination of the Relationship between Economic Organization and Public Policy." *The Sociological Quarterly* 28 (4): 437-454.

JACOBY, W. G. 2000. "Issue Framing and Public Opinion on Government Spending." *American Journal of Political Science* 44 (4): 750-767.

JAMET, J. F., and F. LIRZIN. 2009. "L'Europe à l'épreuve de la récession." Fondation Robert Schuman. *Questions d'Europe* 130.

JAUMOTTE, F., S. LALL, and C. PAPAGEORGIOU. 2008. "Rising Income Inequality: Technology, or Trade and Financial Globalization." *IMF Working Paper*: 08/185.

JERIT, J., and J. BARABAS. 2006. "Banktupt Rhetoric. How Misleading Information Affects Knowledge about Social Security." *Public Opinion Quarterly* (70) 3: 278-303.

JINNO, N., and A. DEWITT. 1998. "Japan's Taxing Bureaucrats: Fiscal Sociology and the Property-Tax Revolt." *Social Science Japan Journal* 1 (2): 233-246.

JOB J., A. STOUT, and R. SMITH. 2007; "Culture Change in Three Taxation Administrations: From Command-and-Control to Responsive Regulation." *Law and Policy* 29 (1): 84-101.

JOHNSON, C. M., and K. J. MEIER. 1990. "The Wages of Sin: Taxing America's Legal Vices." *Western Political Quartely* 43 (3): 577-595.

JONAKIN, J., and M. STEPHENS. 1999. "The Impact of Adjustment and Stabilization Spending in Central America." *North American Journal of Economics and Finance* 10 (1): 293-308.

JONES, C. O. 1970. *An Introduction to the Study of Public Policy*. Belmont: Duxbury Press.

JONES, E. A, and K. E. DAVIES. 1965. "From Acts to Dispositions: The Attributions Process in Person Perception." in L. Berkowitz. *Advances in Experimental Social Psychology*. New York: Academic Press.

JONES, B. D., *et al*. 2009. "A General Empirical Law of Public Budgets: A Comparative Analysis." *American Journal of Political Science* 53 (4): 855-873.

JOYCE, T. 2008. "An Overview of Select Federal Tax Administrative Procedures: Navigating the Audit and Appeals Process." in Leroy, 2008: 121-130.

KAHNEMAN, D., and A. TVERSKY. 1972. "Subjective Probability: A Judgment of Representativeness." *Cognitive Psychology* 3: 430-454.

– 1973. "Availability: A Heuristic for Judging Frequency and Probability." *Cognitive Psychology* 5: 207-232.

KALDOR, N. 1963. "Will Underdeveloped Countries Learn to Tax?" *Foreign Affairs* 41: 410-419.

KANTER, A. 1972. "Congress and the Defense Budget: 1960-1970." *American Political Science Review* 66: 129-143.

KANTOR, P., and S. DAVID. 1983. "The Political Economy of Change in Urban Budgetary Politics." *British Journal of Political Science* 13 (3): 251-274.

KAPLAN, S. E., P. M. RECKERS, and K. D. REYNOLDS. 1986. "An Application of Attribution and Equity Theories to Tax Evasion Behavior." *Journal of Economic Psychology* 7: 441-466.

KASTLUNGER *et al*. 2010. "Sex Difference in Tax Compliance: Differentiating between Demographic Sex, Gender-Role Orientation, and Prenatal Masculinization (2D:4D)." *Journal of Economic Psychology* 31 (4): 479-497.

KEEN, M., Y. KIM, and R. VARSANO R. 2008. "The Flat Tax: Principles and Experience." *International Tax and Public Finance* 15: 712-751.

KEENAN, A., and P. N. DEAN. 1980. "Moral Evaluations of Tax Evasions." *Social Policy and Administration* 14 (3): 209-220.

KELLEY, H. H. 1967. "Attribution Theory in Social Psychology." in D. Levine. *Nebraska Symposium on Motivation*. Lincoln: University of Nebraska Press: 192-238.

KEMP, S. 2002. *Public Goods and Private Wants*. Cheltenham: Edward Elgar.

KENWORTHY, L., and L. McCALL. 2008. "Inequality, Public Opinion and Redistribution." *Socio-Economic Review* 6 (1): 35-68.

KHEMANI, S. 2007. "Does Delegation of Fiscal Policy to an Independent Agency Make a Difference? Evidence from Intergovernmental Transfers in India." *Journal of Development Economics* 82 (2): 464-484.

KING, D. S., and T. R. GURR. 1988. "The State and Fiscal Crisis in Advanced Democracies." *International Journal of Urban and Regional Research* 12 (1): 87-106.

KIRCHLER, E. 2007. *The Economic Psychology of Tax Behaviour*. New York: Cambridge University Press.

KIRCHLER, E., B. MACIEJOVSKY, and F. SCHNEIDER. 2003. "Everyday Representations of Tax Avoidance, Tax Evasion, and Tax Flight: Do Legal Differences Matter." *Journal of Economic Psychology* 24 (4): 535-553.

KIRCHLER, E., A. NIEMIROWSKI, and A. WEARING. 2006. "Shared Subjective Views, Intent to Cooperate and Tax Compliance: Similarities between Australian Taxpayers and Tax Officers." *Journal of Economic Psychology* 27 (4): 502-517.

KITE, C. 2002. "The Globalized, Generous Welfare State: Possibility or Oxymoron." *European Journal of Political Research* 41 (3): 307-343.

KLEMM, A. 2009. "Causes, Benefits, and Risks of Business Tax Incentives." *IMF Working Paper*: 09/21.

KOREN, S., and A. STIASSNY. 1998. "Tax and Spend, or Spend and Tax." *Journal of Policy Modeling* 20 (2): 163-191.

KORPI, W., and J. PALME. 1998. "The Paradox of Redistribution and the Strategy of Equality: Welfare State Institutions, Inequality and Poverty in the Western Countries." *American Sociological Review* 63 (5): 661-687.

– 2003. "New Politics and Class Politics in the Context of Austerity and Globalization: Welfare State Regress in 18 Countries, 1975-1995." *American Political Science Review* 97 (3): 425-446.

KUZNETS, S. 1955. "Economic Growth and Income Inequality." *American Economic Review* 45 (1): 1-28.

LACHMANN, R. 2009. "Greed and Contingency: State Fiscal Crises and Imperial Failure in Early Modern Europe". *American Journal of Sociology* 115(1): 39-73.

LAMBERT, A., et D. MIGAUD. 2005. *La mise en œuvre de la loi organique relative aux lois de finances*. Rapport au gouvernement.

LANDAIS, C. 2007. "Les hauts revenus en France (1998-2006): une explosion des inégalités?" École d'économie de Paris.

LAUFENBURGER, H. 1956. *Théorie économique et psychologique des finances publiques*. Paris: Sirey.

LAURY, S. K., and L. A. TAYLOR. 2008. "Altruism Spillovers: Are Behavior in Context-free Experiments Predictive of Altruism toward a Naturally Occuring Public Good." *Journal of Economic Behavior and Organization* 65: 9-29.

LAUZON, L. P., and M. HASBANI. 2008. "Les banques canadiennes et l'évasion fiscale dans les paradis fiscaux." *Working Paper*: Chaire d'études socio-économiques de l'UQAM.

LE DUFF, R., and G. ORANGE. "Essai de typologie du maire-entrepreneur des grandes villes françaises." in R. Le Duff et J.-J Rigal. 1997 (dir.). *Premières Rencontres Ville-Management*. Université de Pau et des Pays de l'Adour: 35-69.

LELOUP, L. T. 1978. "The Myth of Incrementalism: Analytical Choices in Budgetary Theory." *Policy* 10: 491-509.

LEROY, M. 1992. "L'individu et l'impôt. Contribution à une sociologie cognitive de l'impôt." *L'Année sociologique* 42: 319-343.

– 1993. *Le contrôle fiscal, Une approche cognitive de la décision administrative*. Paris: L'Harmattan.

– 1994. "L'organisation du contrôle fiscal. Une forme originale de bureaucratie." *Revue française de science politique* 44 (5): 811-835.

– 1995. "Quelle convergence pour les politiques fiscales en Europe?" *Revue du Marché commun et de l'Union européenne* 393: 669-684.

– 1996. "L'impôt sur le revenu entre idéologie et justice fiscale. Perspective de sociologie fiscale." *Politiques et Management Public* 14 (4): 41-71.

– 1997. "Fiscalité et patrimoine culturel. Des incitations contrôlées." *Droit fiscal* 31: 1016-1022.

– 1999. "La négociation de l'action publique conventionnelle dans le contrat de plan État-Région." *Revue française de science politique* 49 (4): 571-597.

– 2000. *La logique financière de l'action publique conventionnelle dans le contrat de plan État-Région*. Paris: L'Harmattan.

– 2001. "Le cadre financier de l'action publique régionale." in B. Jouve *et al.* *La région laboratoire politique*. Paris: La Découverte.

– 2002. *Sociologie de l'impôt*. Paris: PUF.

– 2003. "Pourquoi la sociologie fiscale ne bénéficie-t-elle pas d'une reconnaissance institutionnelle en France." *L'Année Sociologique* 53 (1): 247-274.

– 2003 (ed.). *Fiscalité et évitement de l'impôt*. Paris: L'Harmattan.

– 2003. "Sociologie du contribuable et évitement de l'impôt." *European Journal of Sociology (Archives européennes de sociologie)* 44 (2): 213-244.

– 2004. "Quelle évaluation de la politique structurelle régionale pour l'élargissement de l'Europe?" *Revue du marché commun et de l'Union européenne* 427: 215-225.

– 2005 (ed.). *Regards croisés sur le système fiscal: Allemagne, France, Italie, Russie*. Paris: L'Harmattan.

– 2006 (ed.). *Mondialisation et fiscalité. La globalisation fiscale*. Paris: L'Harmattan.

– 2006. "Compte rendu de l'ouvrage de Thomas Piketty: les hauts revenus en France au XXe siècle." *L'Année sociologique* 56 (1): 231-235.

– 2007. *Sociologie des finances publiques*. Paris: La Découverte.

– 2007. "L'approche sociologique du contrôle fiscal." *Revue Tunisienne de Fiscalité* 7: 21-43.

– 2008. "Tax Sociology: Sociopolitical Issues for a Dialogue with Economists." *Socio-logos* 3: 1-28.

– 2008 (ed.). *L'administration de l'impôt en France et dans le monde*. Paris: L'Harmattan.

– 2008. "Sociologie du contentieux fiscal." *Revue Tunisienne de Fiscalité* 9: 27-50.

– 2008. "La modernisation de la bureaucratie fiscale." *Gestion et Management Publics* 3: 1-18.

– 2009. "Sociologie de la fiscalité de la famille." *Gestion et Finances Publiques* 6: 485-491.

– 2010. "Tocqueville Pioneer of Fiscal Sociology." *European Journal of Sociology* (*Archives européennes de sociologie*) 51 (2): 195-239. htpp://journals.cambridge.org

LEROY, M., et A. TISSERAND. 2003. *Sedan, ses deniers, ses archives du XVI*[e] *au XIX*[e] *siècle*. Langres: Editions Dominique Guéniot.

LEROY-BEAULIEU, P. 1906. *Traité de la science des finances*. Paris: Guillaumin et Félix Alcan.

LEWIS, A. 1979. "An Empirical Assessment of Tax Mentality." *Public Finance* 2: 245-257.

– 1982. "The Social Psychology of Taxation." *British Journal of Social Psychology* 21: 151-158.

– 1982. *The Psychology of Taxation*. Oxford: Martin Robertson.

LEWIS, A., and D. JACKSON. 1985. "Voting Preferences and Attitude to Public Expenditure." *Political Studies* 33: 457-466.

LIEBERMAN, E. 2002. "Taxation Data as Indicators of State-Society Relations: Possibilities and Pitfalls in Cross-national Research Studies." *Studies in Comparative International Development* 36 (4): 89-115.

LINDBLOM, C. E. 1959. "The Science of Muddling Through." *Public Administration Review* 19: 79-88.

LINDERT, P. H. 2004. *Growing Public. Social Spending and Economic Growth Since the Eighteenth Century*. Cambridge: Cambridge University Press.

LINDSAY, P. H., and D. A. NORMAN. 1980. *Human Information Processing*. New York: Academic Press.

LOWERY, D. 1987. "The Distribution of Tax Burdens in the American States: The Determination of Fiscal Incidence." *The Western Political Quarterly* 40: 137-158.

LOWERY, D., and L. SIGELMAN. 1981. "Understanding the Tax Revolt: Eight Explanations." *American Political Science Review* 75: 963-974.

LOWRY, R. C., and M. POTOSKI. 2004. "Organized Interests and the Politics of Federal Discretionary Grants." *The Journal of Politics* 66 (2): 513-533.

LOZZA, E., S. CARRERA, and C. BOSIO. 2010. "Perceptions and Outcomes of a Fiscal Bonus: Framing Effects on Evaluations and Usage Intentions." *Journal of Economic Psychology* 31 (3): 400-404.

LÜBKER, M. 2007. "Inequality and the Demand for Redistribution: Are the Assumptions of the New Growth Theory Valid?" *Socio-Economic Review* 5: 117-148.

LYNCH, J., and M. MYRSKYLÄ. 2009. "Always the Third Rail? Pension Income and Policy Preferences in European Democracies." *Comparative Political Studies* 42 (8): 1068-1097.

MACIEJVOSKY, B., E. KIRCHLER, and H. SCHARZENBERGER. 2006. "Misperception of Chance and Loss Repair: On the Dynamics of Tax Compliance." *Journal of Economic Psychology* 28 (6): 678-691.

MAHLER, V. A. 2008. "Electoral Turnout and Income Redistribution by the State: A Cross-national Analysis of the Developed Democracies." *European Journal of Political Research* 47 (2): 161-183.

MAHLER, V. A., and D. K. JESUIT. 2006. "Fiscal Redistribution in the Developed Countries: New Insights from the Luxembourg Income Study." *Socio-Economic Review* 4 (3): 483-511.

MAHON, R., and S. McBRIDE. 2009. "Standardizing and Disseminating Knowledge: The Role of the OECD in Global Governance." *European Political Science Review* 1 (1): 83-101.

MANN, F. K. 1943. "The Sociology of Taxation." *Review of Politics* 5: 225-235.

– 1947. "The Fiscal Component of Revolution: An Essay in Fiscal Sociology." *The Review of Politics* 9 (3): 331-349.

– 1949. "Re-Orientation through Fiscal Theory;" *Kyklos* 3 (2): 116-129.

MANN, M., and D. RILEY. 2006. "Explaining Macro-regional Trends in Global Income Inequalities." *Socio-Economic Review* 5: 81-115.

MARCH, J. G., and J. P. OLSEN. 1984. "The New Institutionalism Organisational: Factors in Political Life." *American Political Science Review* 78: 734-749.

– 1989. *Rediscovering Institutions. The Organisational Basis of Politics*. New York: Free Press.

MARCUSE, H. 1964. *One-Dimensional Man*. Boston: Beacon Press.

MARSHALL, T. H. 1950. *Citizen and Social Class*. Cambridge: Cambridge University Press.

MARTIN, F. A., J. G. LOPEZ, and M. L. LOBO. 2000. *Sociedad impuestos y gasto publico, La perspectiva del contribuyente*. Madrid: Centro de investigaciones sociologicas.

MARTINEZ, M. D. 1997. "Don't Tax You, Don't Tax Me, Tax the Fella behind the Tree: Partisan and Turnout Effects on Tax Policy." *Social Science Quarterly* 78 (4): 895-906.

MATHIAS, P., and P. O'BRIEN. 1976. "Taxation in Britain and France, 1715-1810. A Comparison of the Social and Economic Incidence of Taxes Collected for the Central Governments." *Journal of European Economic History* 5 (3): 601-655.

MAUREL, C. 2006. "Comparaison des collectivités départementales à partir de leur latitude budgétaire." *Gestion et Management Public*.

MAUSS, M. 1950 (1923). "Essai sur le don. Forme et raison de l'échange dans les sociétés archaïques." in Mauss. *Sociologie et anthropologie*. Paris: PUF.

McBARNET, D. 1991. "Whiter than White Collar Crime: Tax, Fraud Insurance and the Management of Stigma." *The British Journal of Sociology* 42 (3): 323-344.

McCAFFERY, E., and J., BARON. 2004. "Framing and Taxation: Evaluating of Tax Policies Involving Household Composition." *Journal of Economic Psychology* 25: 679-705.

Mc LURE, M. 2005. "Equilibrium and Italian Fiscal Sociology: A Reflection on the Pareto-Griziotti and Pareto-Sensini Letters on Fiscal Theory." *European Journal of the History of Economic Thought* 12 (4): 609-633.

– 2006. "The Fiscal Sociology of Gino Borgatta: Pareto, Extra-economic Redistribution and Economic Growth." *Cambridge Journal of Economics* 30: 521-539.

– 2007. (ed.) *The Paretian School and Italian Fiscal Sociology*. New York: Palgrave Macmillan.

McMANUS, J., and N. WARREN. 2006. "The Case of Measuring Tax Gap." *Ejournal of Tax Research* 4 (1): 61-79.

McNUTT, P. A. 2002 *The Economics of Public Choice*. Cheltenham: Edward Elgar Publishing.

MELTZER, A. H., and S. F. RICHARD. 1981. "A Rational Theory of the Size of Government." *Journal of Political Economy* 89: 914-927.

MERTON, R. K. 1949. *Social Theory and Social Structure*. New York: Free Press.

MIDTBO, T. 1999. "The Impact of Parties, Economic Growth, and Public Sector Expansion: A Comparison of Long-term Dynamics in the Scandinavian and Anglo-American Democracies." *European Journal of Political Research* 35 (2): 199-223.

MILLER, C. 1996. "Demographics and Spending for Public Education. A Test of Interest Group Influence." *Economics of Education Review* 15 (2): 175-185.

MILLER, J. 2007. "Wherefore the Liberal State? Post-Soviet Democratic Blues and Lessons from Fiscal Sociology." *East European Politics and Societies* 21 (3): 294-315.

MITTONE, L. 2006. "Dynamic Behaviour in Tax Evasion: An Experimental Approach." *The Journal of Socio-Economics* 36: 813-835.

MOISERON, J.-Y. 1999. "Pression, structure fiscale et niveau de développement." in Gastellu *et al.*, 1999: 85-106.

MONTESQUIEU, Charles-Louis de Secondat. 1964 (1750). *L'Esprit des lois.* Œuvres complètes. Paris: Seuil.

MOORE, M. 2004. "Revenues, State Formation, and the Quality of Governance in Developing Countries." *International Political Science Review* 25 (3): 297-319.

MORELAND, W. 1975. "A Nonincremental Perspective on Budgetary Policy Actions", in R. Ripley, and G. Franklin. *Policy Making in the Federal Executive Branch*. New York: Free Press.

MORGAN, D. R. 1994. "The Equity in the American States: A Multivariate Analysis." *Social Science Quarterly* 75 (3): 510-523.

MORGAN, K. J., and M. PRASAD. 2009. "The Origins of Tax Systems: A French-American Comparison." *The American Journal of Sociology* 114 (5): 1350-1394.

MUELLER, E. 1963. "Public Attitudes Toward Fiscal Programs." *The Quarterly Journal of Economics* 77: 210-235.

MURPHY, K. 2004. "The Role of Trust in Nuturing Compliance: A Study of Accused Tax Avoiders." *Law and Human Behavior* 28 (2): 187-209.

MURPHY, R. 2009. "The Direct Tax Cost of Tax Havens to the UK." *Tax Justice Network* www.taxjustice.net.

MURRAY, R. A. 2007 (1915). "The Science of Public Finance, Fiscal Law and the Notion of State." in McLure, 2007: 179-184.

– 1920. *Leçons d'économie politique*. Paris: Payot.

MUSGRAVE, R. A. 1959. *The Theory of Public Finance*. New York: Mac Graw Hill.

– 1979. "The Tax Revolt: Causes and Cure." *Social Science Quarterly* 59 (4): 697-703.

– 1992. "Schumpeter's Crisis of the Tax State: An Essay in Fiscal Sociology." *Journal of Evolutionary Economics* 2 (2): 89-113.

MUSGRAVE, R. A., and A. T. PEACOCK. 1967. *Classics in The Theory of Public Finance*. New York: St Martin's Press.

NATCHEZ, P. B., and I. C. BUPP. 1973. "Policy and Priority in the Budgetary Process." *American Political Science Review* 67: 951-963.

NDIKUMANA, L., and J. BOYCE. 2008. "New Estimates of Capital Flight from Sub-Saharan Countries: Linkages with External Borrowing and Policy Options." PERI University of Massachussets Amberst *Working Paper*: 166.

NICHOLSON-CROTTY, S., N. A. THEOBALD, and B. D. WOOD. 2006. "Fiscal Federalism and Budgetary Tradeoffs in the American States." *Political Science Quarterly* 59 (2): 313-321.

NISBET, R. A. 1966. *The Sociological Tradition* New York: Basik Books.

NISBETT, R., and L. ROSS. 1980. *Human Inference*. Prentice-Hall: Englewood Cliffs.

NISKANEN, W. 1971. *Bureaucracy and Representative Government*. Chicago: Aldine Atherton.

NORREGAARD, J., and T. S. KHAN. 2007. "Tax Policy: Recent Trends and Coming Challenges." *IMF Working Paper*: 07/274.

OATES, W. E. 1972. *Fiscal Federalism*. New York: Harcourt Barce Jovanovich.

O'CONNOR, J. 1973. *The Fiscal Crisis of the State*. New York: St Martin's Press.

OECD. 2007. *Performance Budgeting in OECD countries*

– 2008. *Revenue Statistics*.

– 2008. *Growing Unequal? Income Distribution and Poverty in OECD Countries*.

OLSON, M. 1966. *The Logic of Collective Action*. Cambridge: Harvard University Press.

OVERESCH, M. 2009. "The Effects of Multinationals' Profits Shifting on Real Investments." *National Tax Journal* 62 (1): 5-19.

PAGE, E. C., M. GOLDSMITH, and P. KOUSGAARD. 1990. "Time, Parties and Bugetary Change: Fiscal Decisions in English Cities, 1974-1988." *British Journal of Political Science* 20 (1): 43-61.

PAMPEL, F. C. 1994. "Population Aging, Class Context, and Age Inequality in Public Spending." *American Journal of Sociology* 100 (1): 153-195.

PANTALEONI, M. 1967. "Contribution to the Theory of the Distribution of Public Expenditure." in Musgrave and Peacock, 1967: 16-27.

PARETO, V. 1964. *Cours d'économie politique*. Genève: Droz.

– 1965. *Écrits sur la courbe de la répartition de la richesse*. Genève: Droz.

– 1983. *The Mind and Society: A Treatise on General Society*, Nex York: Dover (1916. *Trattato di sociologia generale*).

PARKER, D., and K. HARTLEY. 2003. "Transaction Costs, Relational Contracting and Public Private Partnership: a Case Study of UK defence." *Journal of Purchasing and Supply Management* 9 (3): 97-103.

PARSONS, T. 1977. *Social Systems and the Evolution of Action Theory*. New York: Free Press.

PATON, D., D. S. SIEGEL, and L. V. WILLIAMS. 2004. "Taxation and the Demand for Gambling: New Evidence from the United Kingdom." *National Tax Journal* 57 (4): 847-864.

PEACOCK, A. T., and J. WISEMAN. 1967. *The Growth of Public Expenditure in the United Kingdom*. London: Allen and Unwin.

PELLEGRINI, L., and R. GERLAGH. 2008. "Causes of Corruption: A Survey of Cros-country Analyses and Extended Results." *Economics of Governance* 9: 245-263.

PEUKERT, H. 2006. "Justi's Moral Economics and his System of Taxation." *Journal of Economic Behavior and Organization* 59: 478-496.

PFEIFER, M. 2009. "Public Opinion on State Responsibility for Minimum Income Protection." *Acta Sociologica* 52 (2): 117-134.

PIERSON, P. 1994. *Dismantling the Welfare State? Reagan, Thatcher and the Politics of Retrenchment*. Cambridge: Cambridge University Press.

PIKETTY, T. 2001. *Les hauts revenus en France au XXe siècle. Inégalités et redistribution 1901-1998*. Paris: Grasset.

PIKETTY, T., and E. SAEZ. 2003. "Income Inequality in the United States, 1913-1998." *Quarterly Journal of Economics* 118 (1): 1-39.

POMMEREHNE, W. W., and H. WECK-HANNEMANN. 1996. "Tax Rates, Tax Administration and Income Tax Evasion in Switzerland." *Public Choice* 88 (1-2): 161-170.

PORCHNEV, B. 1963. *Les soulèvements populaires en France de 1623 à 1648*. Paris: SEVPEN.

POTOSKI, M., and J. TALBERT. 2000. "The Dimensional Structure of Policy Outputs: Distributive Policy and Roll Call Voting." *Political Research Quarterly* 53 (4): 695-710.

PRIMO, D. M., and J. M. SNYDER. 2010. "Party Strength, the Personal Vote, and Government Spending". *American Journal of Political Science* 54 (2): 354-370.

RAWLS, J. 1987. *Théorie de la justice*. Paris: Seuil.

– 1995. *Libéralisme politique*. Paris: PUF/Quadrige.

RAYNAUD, P. L. 1947, 1948. "La psychologie du contribuable devant l'impôt." *Revue de science et de législation financières*.

RECKERS, P. M., D. L. SANDERS, and S. J. ROARK. 1994. "The Influence of Ethical Attitudes on Taxpayer Compliance." *National Tax Journal* 37 (4): 825-836.

REED, W. R. 2006. "Tax Burden and the Mismeasurement of State Tax Policy." *Public Finance Review* 34 (4): 404-426.

REINHART, C. M., and K. S. ROGOFF. 2010. "Growth in a Time of Debt". *American Economic Review* 100 (2): 573-578.

RIAHI-BELKAOUI, A. 2004. "Relationship between Tax Compliance Internationally and selected Determinants of Tax Morale." *Journal on International Accounting, Auditing and Taxation* 13: 135-143.

RICHARDSSON, G. 2006. "Determinants of Tax Evasion: A Cross-Country Investigation." *Journal of International Accounting, Auditing and Taxation* 15: 150-169.

RICHTER, B. K, K. SAMPHANTHARK, and J. F. TIMMONS. 2010. "Lobbying and Taxes". *American Journal of Political Science* 53 (4): 893-909.

RIGAUDIERE, A. 2003. *Penser et construire l'État dans la France du Moyen Âge (XIIIe-XVe siècle)*. Paris: CHEFF.

ROBBINS, J. W. 2010. "Party System Institutionalization and Government Spending." *Comparative Politics* 42 (2): 229-248.

ROBERTS, M. L., P. A. HITE, and C. F. BRADLEY. 1994. "Understanding Attitudes toward Progressive Taxation." *Public Opinion Quarterly* 58: 165-190.

RODDEN, J. 2002. "The Dilemma of Fiscal Federalism: Grants and Fiscal Performance around the World." *American Journal of Political Science* 46 (3): 670-687.

ROSANVALLON, P. 1981. *La crise de l'État-providence*. Paris: Seuil.

– 2006. *La contre-démocratie, La politique à l'âge de la défiance*. Paris: Seuil.

ROSE, R., and P. L. DAVIES. 1994. *Inheritance in Public Choice without Choice in Britain*. New Haven: Yale University Press.

ROSS, M. L. 2004. "Does Taxation Lead to Representation." *British Journal of Political Science* 34: 229-249.

ROTHSTEIN, B., and E. M. USLANER. 2005. "All for All: Equality, Corruption, and Social Trust." *World Politics* 58 (1): 41-72.

ROUSSEAU, J.-J. 1959 (1755). *Discours sur l'économie politique*. Œuvres complètes. Paris: Gallimard.

– 1996 (1762). *Le contrat social*. Paris: Le livre de poche.

RUDOLPH, T. J., 2009. "Political Trust, Ideology, and Public Support for Tax Cuts." *Public Opinion Quarterly*, 73 (1), p. 144-158.

RUDRA, N. 2002. "Globalization and the Decline of the Welfare State in Less-Developed Countries." *International Organization* 56 (2): 411-445.

– 2007. "Welfare States in Developing Countries: Unique or Universal?" *Journal of Politics* 69 (2): 378-396.

RYU, J., C. J. BOWLING, C. L. CHO, and D. S. WRIGHT. 2007. "Effects of Administrators' Aspirations, Political Principal's Priorities, and Interest Groups Influence on State Agency Budget Requests." *Public Budgeting and Finance* 27 (3): 22-49.

SAEZ, E., and M. R. VEALL. 2005. "The Evolution of High Incomes in Northern America: Lessons from Canadian Evidence." *American Economic Review* 95 (3): 831-849.

SAHA, D., and J. von WEIZSÄCKER. 2009. "Estimating the Size of the European Stimulus Package for 2009." *Bruegel Policy Brief*: 2008/12.

SAKURAI, Y. 2002. "Comparing Cross-cultural Regulatory Styles and Processes in Dealing with Transfer Pricing." *International Journal of Law* 30: 173-199.

SCHARPF, F. 2000. "The Viability of Advanced Welfare States in International Economy: Vulnerabilities and Options." *Journal of European Public Policy* 7 (2): 190-228.

SCHICK, A. 2008. "Getting Performance Budgeting to Perform." *Working Paper*.

SCHMITTER, P. 1974. "Still the Century of Corporatism?" *Review of Politics* 36: 85-103.

SCHMÖLDERS, G. 1932. *Steuermoral und Steuerbelastung*. Berlin: Heymann.

– 1970. *Finanz-und Steuerpsychologie*. Hamburg: Rowohlt Taschenbuch Verlag GmbH. (1973. *Psychologie des finances et de l'impôt*. Paris: PUF).

SCHNEIDER, F. 2008. "The Shadow Economy in Germany: A Blessing or a Curse for The Official Economy." *Economic Analysis and Policy* 38 (1): 89-111.

SCHNEIDER, F., and D. ENSTE. 2000. "Shadow Economies Around the World: Size, Causes, and Consequences." *IMF Working Paper*: 00/26.

SCHOKKAERT, E. 1987. "Preferences and Demands for Local Public Spending." *Journal of Public Economics* 34 (2): 175-188.

SCHOLZ, J. T., and N. PINNEY. 1995. "Duty, Fear, and Tax Compliance: The Heuristic Basis of Citizenship Behavior." *American Journal of Political Science* 39 (2): 490-512.

SCHRÖDER, M. 2009. "Integrating Welfare and Production Typologies: How Refinements of the Varieties of Capitalism Approach Call for a Combination of Welfare Typologies." *Journal of Social Policy* 38 (1): 19-43.

SCHUMPETER, J. 1918. "Die Krise des Steuersstaats." *Zeitfragen aus dem Gebiete der Soziologie* 4, Graz und Leipzig. (1954. "The Crisis of the Tax State." In T. Peacock (ed.), *International Economic Paper* 4 Macmillan: 5-38. Translated by Stolper and Musgrave).

SEN, A. 1991. *On Ethics and Economics*. Oxford: Blackwell Publishers.

– 1992. *Inequality Reexamined*. Oxford: Oxford University Press.

– 1999. *Development as Freedom*. Oxford: Oxford University Press.

SENAT. 2008. *Rapport sur les prélèvements obligatoires et leur évolution*. Paris.

SENSINI, G. 2007 (1929). "Outline of Theorical Public Finance." in McLure, 2007: 249-258.

SHROPSHIRE, P. 2009. "The Multi-Billion Dollar US International Tax Gap." *Memorandum for Commissioner Shuman*: 2009-IE-R001.

SIMON, H. A. 1982. *Models of Bounded Rationality*. Cambridge: The MIT Press.

SINE, A. 2003. *L'ordre budgétaire*. Thèse ENS Cachan.

SLEMROD, J. 2001. "Trust in Public Finance." Paper for the conference *Public Finance and Public Policy in the New Milennium*.

SMELSER, N. J., and R. SWEDBERD (ed.). 2005. *The Handbook of Economic Sociology*. New York: Russel Sage Foundation and Princeton University Press.

SMITH, A. 2002 (1759). *The Theory of Moral Sentiments*. Cambridge: Cambridge University Press.

– 1979 (1776). *An Inquiry into the Nature and Causes of the Wealth of Nations*. Oxford: Clarendon Press.

SPICER, M. W., and R. E. HERO. 1985. "Tax Evasion and Heuristics." *Journal of Public Economics* 26: 263-267.

SPICER, M. W., and S. B. LUNDSTEDT. 1976. "Understanding Tax Evasion." *Public Finance* 31 (2): 295-305.

SPICER, M. W., and J. E. THOMAS. 1982. "Audit Probabilities and The Tax Evasion Decision: An Experimental Approach." *Journal of Economic Psychology* 2: 241-245.

STEENSLAND, B. 2006. "Cultural Categories and the American Welfare State: The Case of Guaranteed Income Policy." *American Journal of Sociology* 111 (5): 1273-1326.

STEINMO, S. 1993. *Taxation and Democracy: Swedish, British and American Approaches to Financing the Modern State*. New Haven and London: Yale University Press.

– 2002. "Globalization and Taxation. Challenges to the Swedish Welfare State." *Comparative Political Studies* 35 (7): 839-862.

– 2003. "The Evolution of Policy Ideas: Tax Policy in the 20th Century." *British Journal of Politics and International Relations* 5 (2): 206-236.

STIGLER, G. 1972. "Economic Competition and Political Competition." *Public Choice* 13: 91-106.

STIGLITZ, J. E. 2002. *Globalization and Its Discontents*. New York: Norton.

– 2006. *Making Globalization Work*. New York: Norton.

STREECK, W. 2007. "Endgame?, The Fiscal Crisis of the German State." *Max Planck Institute Discussion Paper*.

SVALLFORS, S. 1995. "The End of Class Politics? Structural Cleavages and Attitudes to Swedish Welfare Policies." *Acta Sociologica* 38 (1): 53-74.

SWANK, D. 2006. "Tax Policy in an Era of Internationalization: Explaining the Spread of Neoliberalism." *International Organization* 60 (4): 847-882.

SWANK, D., and S. STEINMO. 2002. "The New Political Economy of Taxation in Advanced Capitalist Democracies." *American Journal of Political Science* 46 (3): 642-653.

TANZI, V. 1995. *Taxation in Integrating World*. Washington: The Brookings Institution.

TANZI, V., and H. H. ZEE. 2000. "Tax Policy for Emerging Markets: Developing Countries." *IMF, Working Paper*: 00/35.

TARDE, G. 1979 (1895). *Les lois de l'imitation*. Paris: PUF.

TAYLOR, F. W. 1990. "Direction des ateliers." in F. Vatin. *Organisation du travail et économie des entreprises*. Paris: Les éditions d'organisation: 27-138.

TAYLOR-GOOBY, P., H. DEAN, M. MUNRO, and G. PARKER. 1999. "Risk and the Welfare State." *British Journal of Sociology* 50 (2): 177-194.

THAMES, F. C., and M. S. EDWARDS. 2006. "Differentiating Mixed-Member Electoral Systems." *Comparative Political Studies* 39 (7): 905-927.

THEVENON, O. 2008. "Les politiques familiales des pays développés: des modèles contrastés." *Population et Sociétés* 448: 1-4.

TIEBOUT, C. 1956. "A Pure Theory of Local Expenditure." *Journal of Political Economy* 64 (5): 416-424.

TILLINGHAST, D. R. 2003. "Issues of International Tax Enforcement." in Aaron and Slemrod, 2003: 38-67.

TILLY, C. 1986. *La France conteste de 1600 à nos jours*. Paris: Fayard.

TIMMONS, J. F. 2005. "The Fiscal Contract, States, Taxes, and Public Services." *World Politics* 57 (4): 530-567.

TOCQUEVILLE, A. de. 2004. *Democracy in America*. New York: Library of America. (1835. *De la démocratie en Amérique*).

– 1998. *The Old Regime and the Revolution*. Chicago: Chicago University Press. (1856. *L'Ancien Régime et la Révolution*).

TORGLER, B. 2003. "To Evade or Not To Evade: That Is the Question." *Journal of Socio-Economics* 32: 283-302.

– 2004. "Cross-Culture of Tax Morale and Tax Compliance: Evidence from Costa Rica and Switzerland." *International Journal of Comparative Sociology* 45 (1-2): 17-43.

2006. “The Importance of Faith: Tax Morale and Religiosity.” *Journal of Economic Behavior and Organization* 61 (1): 81-109.

TORGLER, B., I. C. DEMIR, A. MACINTYRE, and M. SCHAFFNER. 2008. “Causes and Consequences of Tax Morale: An Empirical Investigation.” *Economic Analysis and Policy* 38 (2): 313-339.

TORGLER, B., and F. SCHNEIDER. 2007. “What Shapes Attitudes Toward Paying Taxes? Evidence from Multicultural European Countries.” *Social Science Quarterly* 88 (2): 443-470.

– “The Impact of Tax Morale and Institutional Quality.” *Journal of Economic Psychology* 30 (2): 228-245.

TOYE, J. 2000. “Fiscal Crisis and Fiscal Reform in Developing Countries.” *Cambrige Journal of Economics* 24: 21-44.

TSEBELIS, G. 1995. “Decision Making in Political Systems: Veto Players in Presidentialism, Parliamentarism, Multicameralism and Multipartyism.” *British Journal of Political Science* 25: 228-235.

– 1999. “Veto Players and Law Production in Parliamentary Democracies: An Empirical Analysis.” *American Political Science Review* 93: 591-608.

TUCCI, M. 2007. *La politique et son double, Éléments pour une critique de l’économie politique d’aujourd’hui*. Université de Nice: Thèse de doctorat de philosophie.

TULLOCK, G. 2006 (1976). *The Vote Motive*. London: The Institute of Economic Affairs.

VAN PARYS, S., and J. SEBASTIAN. 2010. “The Effectiveness of Tax Incentives in Attracting Investment: Panel Data Evidence from the CFA Franc Zone.” *International Tax and Public Finance* 17 (4): 400-429.

VERBOON, P., and M. Van DIJKE. 2007. “A Self-interest Analysis of Justice and Tax Compliance.” *Journal of Economic Psychology* 28 (6): 704-727.

VIS, B. 2007. “States of Welfare or States of Workfare? Welfare State Restructuring in 16 Capitalist Democracies, 1985-2002.” *Policy and Politics* (35) 1: 105-122.

VOGEL, J. 1974. “Taxation and Public Opinion in Sweden: An Interpretation of Recent Survey Data.” *National Tax Journal* 27 (4): 499-513.

VUITRY, M. A. 1883. *Le régime financier de la France avant la Révolution de 1789*. Paris: Félix Alcan.

VULETIN, G. 2008. “Measuring the Informal Economy in Latin America and the Caribbean.” *IMF Working Paper*: 08/102.

WACQUET, J.-C. 1990. *Le Grand-duché de Toscane sous les derniers Médicis*. Rome: École Française de Rome.

WAGNER, A. 1913. *Traité de la science des finances, Histoire de l’impôt depuis l’Antiquité jusqu’à nos jours*. Paris: Giard et Brière.

– 1967. “Three Extracts on Public Finance.” in Musgrave and Peacock, 1967: 1-15.

WALLSCHUTZKY, G. 1984. “Possible Causes of Tax Evasion.” *Journal of Economic Psychology* 5 (4): 371-384.

WARNERYD, K.-E., and B. WALERUD. 1982. "Taxes and Economic Behavior: Some Interview Data on Tax Evasion in Sweden." *Journal of Economic Psychology* 2: 187-211.

WATRIN, C., and R. ULLMANN. 2008. "Comparing Direct and Indirect Taxation: The Influence of Framing on Tax Compliance." *European Journal of Comparative Economics* 1.

WEBBER, C., and A. WILDAVSKY. 1986. *A History of Taxation and Expenditure in the Western World*. New York: Simon and Shuster.

WEBER, M. 1971. *Economie et société*. Paris: Plon.

WEBLEY, P., H. ROBBEN, H. ELFFERS, and D. HESSING. 1991. *Tax Evasion, An Experimental Approach*. Cambridge: Cambridge University Press.

WEINER, B. 1979. "A Theory of Motivation for some Classroom Experiences." *Journal of Education Psychology* 1979 71: 3-25.

WELCH, S. 1985. "The 'More for Less' Paradox: Public Attitudes on Taxing and Spending." *Public Opinion Quarterly* 49: 310-316.

WELCH, M. R., *et al.* 2005. "But Everybody Does It: The Effects of Perceptions, Moral Pressures, and Informal Sanctions on Tax Cheating." *Sociological Spectrum* 25 (1): 21-52.

WENZEL, M. 2004. "An Analysis of Norm Process in Tax." *Journal of Economic Psychology* 25 (2): 213-228.

WILDAVSKY, A. 1964. *The Politics of the Budgetary Process*. Boston: Little Brown.

– 1975. *Budgeting: A Comparative Theory of Budgetary Processes*. Boston: Little Brown.

– 1985. "A Cultural Theory of Expenditure Growth and (Un)balanced Budgets." *Journal of Public Economics* 28: 349-357.

WINTER, S., and P. E. MOURITZEN. 2001. "Why People Want Something for Nothing: The Role of Asymmetrical Illusions." *European Journal of Political Research* 39 (1): 109-143.

WITT, P.-C. (ed.). 1987. *Wealth and Taxation in Central Europe*. New York: St Martin's Press.

YITZHAKI, S. 1974. "A Note on Income Tax Evasion: a Theoretical Analysis." *Journal of Public Economics* 3: 201-202.

ZEE, H. H. 1996. "Empirics of Crosscountry Tax Revenues Comparisons." *World Development* 24 (10): 1659-1671.

ZOLLER, E. 2004. "Les pouvoirs budgétaires du Congrès des États-Unis. *Revue française de finances publiques*." 86: 267-308.

"Public Action"

The series "Public Action" studies the State and how it works from a variety of perspectives. It focuses on public policy analysis (environment, health, employment culture etc.) as well as the institutional and organisational study of public administrations. The mutations that characterise nowadays public action (deregulation, externalisation, contractualisation and networking) are at the heart of these preoccupations.

Consequently, the series "Public Action" also places further emphasis on the relationship the State maintains with its environment, – not only the political apparatus and, of course, civil society, but also with broader social changes such as individualism and globalisation.

Multidisciplinary work is an essential characteristic of contemporary research in the field. Given the essential need for such approaches to the topic, this series encourages economic, historical, judicial, politological, sociological and philosophical perspectives.

Series Editors :

Jean-Louis GENARD, Professor at the Université Libre de Bruxelles

Steve JACOB, Professor at the Université Laval

Series Titles

No.7 – Marc LEROY, *Taxation, the State and Society. The Fiscal Sociology of Interventionist Democracy*, 2011, 400 p.

N° 6 – Guy LEBEER & Jacques MORIAU (dir.), *(Se) gouverner. Entre souci de soi et action publique*, 2010, 211 p.

N° 5 – Fabrizio CANTELLI, Marta ROCA I ESCODA, Joan STAVO-DEBAUGE et Luca PATTARONI (dir.), *Sensibilités pragmatiques. Enquêter sur l'action publique*, 2009, 444 p.

N° 4 – Frédéric DOBRUSZKES, *Libéralisation et desserte des territoires : le cas du transport aérien européen*, 2008, 287 p.

No.3 – Isabelle DE LOVINFOSSE, *How and Why Do Policies Change? A Comparison of Renewable Electricity Policies in Belgium, Denmark, Germany, the Netherlands and the UK*, 2008, 317 p.

N° 2 – Fabrizio CANTELLI, *L'État à tâtons. Pragmatique de l'action publique face au sida*, 2007, 268 p.

N° 1 – Steve JACOB, Frédéric VARONE et Jean-Louis GENARD (dir.), *L'évaluation des politiques au niveau régional*, 2007, 218 p.